Mobility and Migration

EAST ANGLIAN FOUNDERS O

AMHERST

Mobility and Migration

NEW ENGLAND, 1629–1640

Roger Thompson

The University of Massachusetts Press

For Pamela

Contents

CONTENTS

Maps and Tables

MAPS

TABLES

Preface

On 1 April 1688, according to the diarist Samuel Sewall, John Beale of
Hingham, Massachusetts, "a good man of an hundred year old was
found dead in his yard." He had been born in or around the Armada
Year of Queen Elizabeth's reign at Hingham in Norfolk, one of the
counties in the region of East Anglia. His family, leatherworkers for
generations, had lived in or near the little market town 14 miles southwest of Norwich since the middle of the fifteenth century. John too had
kept close to home. Having trained locally as a shoemaker, he had
married in 1616 Frances Ripley from the neighboring market town of
Wymondham five miles away. After her death, his second wife, in 1630,
was Nazareth Turner, a widow. She was a member of an equally well-
established Hingham clan, the Hobarts. When John was approaching
50, he, Nazareth, eight children, and two servants left old Hingham. In
a large party of 125 neighbors led by their vicar, the Reverend Robert
Peck, they traveled 45 miles south to the Suffolk port of Ipswich,
boarded the *Diligent*, and sailed to Massachusetts. Among the contingent was John's first wife's kinsman William Ripley, a weaver, and
his family. In the New World Beale and his family settled alongside 20
Hobart in-laws at "New Hingham" on the south shore of Massachusetts Bay. There he served as town selectman and deputy to the General
Court in Boston. He saw his son Nathaniel follow in his footsteps as a
town representative. After Nazareth's death, he married for a third time
in 1659. Mary, the new Goodwife Beale, was the widow of John's
lifelong neighbor in England and America, Nicholas Jacobs. Having
outlived her for seven years and having seen his three daughters and six
sons married (one to a Hobart, one to a Ripley, and one to a Lincoln), he
finally succumbed to old age. The first half of his life had been spent in
one place in England, the second similarly settled in his Massachusetts

home. The upheaval of migration—a quite literal midlife crisis—had rocked an otherwise stable and well-rooted life.[1]

Historians have often assumed that John Beale's parochial and settled life was typical of the 14,000 to 20,000 founders of New England. Their impressions have been based on the life stories of a few individuals or from small samples of better-documented emigrants. This study presents a systematic investigation of the personal and lineal roots of more than 2,000 people who sailed to New England from England's five eastern counties of Lincolnshire, Norfolk, Suffolk, Essex, and Cambridgeshire—a region here designated Greater East Anglia, to be described in Chapter 2—as part of the Great Migration of the 1630s. This is the largest documented investigation of regional origins ever attempted.

By analyzing a mass of local records and family histories. I have been able to uncover both the personal and ancestral experiences of three-quarters of the early eastern counties emigrants. I have followed them across the Atlantic and investigated their lives in the New World, especially whether they moved about frequently and if so, how often and how far. The central question of this study is whether this was, as for John Beale, a solitary uprooting from a stable and predictable world of familiar neighborhoods or simply a longer move among many relocations.

Reconstructing the life and ancestral histories of the emigrants depends on the happenstance of documentary survival and the pinpointing of individuals. For every John Beale, about whom information is reasonably plentiful, there crops up a name like "Brice," mentioned in one of Winthrop's predeparture letters. His biography has been painfully and only partially recovered as "Brice," "Brease," and "Bruise" after extended search.[2] With such a large contingent, my own research in local records on two continents could not hope in one lifetime to uncover all the details of emigrants' backgrounds. I have therefore also relied on the findings of generations of genealogists researching over a period of a century and a half. Emigrants who failed to perpetuate their lines in the New World have received scant attention in comparison with progenitors of enduring families. In general, problems of identification increase as the hunt descends the social scale, as it crosses the gender line, and as the quarry's name becomes commoner. My information on the English backgrounds of menservants is by far the patchiest, except for the maids. It proved much easier to follow the ancestral lines and personal career of the Norwich locksmith William Ludkin than to disentangle Browns or Fullers or Smiths.[3]

Two recurrent nightmares for family historians are elision and duplication. If an emigrant father and son have the same forenames, for instance, it can prove almost impossible to distinguish them. Two men with the same names from nearby parishes can all too easily blur into one.[4] Skilled genealogists have spent years separating the four William Hammonds, the four Thomas Lincolns, and the five John Clarkes.[5] Donald Lines Jacobus eventually and reluctantly came to the conclusion that there must have been two sets of emigrant brothers called John and William Guttridge.[6] Trying to identify the emigrant Samuel Morse among several candidates has used up thousands of hours of research.[7] In such cases there are always dangers of creating extra persons because the known facts do not seem to fit one person's life. Too often researchers have to cope with missing or ill-kept parish registers, shipping lists, and New England church records, or with stolen sheets from archival collections.[8]

At the heart of the problem, however, is the "snapshot" nature of almost all surviving vital evidence. John Beale was only recorded for posterity when he was married, buried, held office, paid taxes, received, bought, or sold land, or appeared in court. The fact that before 1638 all such events in his life occurred in Hingham, Norfolk, and all after in Hingham, Massachusetts, plus his absence from other parish or town records, leads us to infer his residential stability. It is impossible to *prove* that Beale or any of his fellow emigrants actually stayed still or moved about only as officially recorded. I have tried to offset this absence of proof both by using extreme caution in identification and in tracing ancestral lines and by weighting the scales against assumptions of residential longevity.[9] The founding generation has been divided into socioeconomic and gender groups. This detailed analysis of the Greater East Anglian contingent in the Old and New worlds along with their crucial transit between the two occupies the core of the book, Parts II and III.

Behind these evidential challenges loom two much larger questions. Over the last 40 years, historians have disagreed sharply over the extent that people moved around England and New England before industrialization and urbanization. Since geographical mobility is seen as a crucial motor of change, this discussion is often located within the all-encompassing debate about "modernization," about when, where, how, and why the attitudes and values of people burst out of the supportive but constricting chrysalis of "traditionalism."

Though models derived from modernization theory have been rightly criticized as value-laden, anachronistic, or ideologically driven, historians are not thereby excused from the evaluation of agents of change. The past *is* a foreign country, and finding out about the journey from there to here must be our central challenge.

Second, since the 1920s, scholars have differed about motivations for emigration. Were settlers "pulled" by the hope of eventual enrichment or of founding a purified society? Were they "pushed" by intolerance, persecution, or despair at home? Was New England seen as a haven of escape or an opportunity to exploit? Could these divergent aims and responses be reconciled? In the last decade discussion has focused on whether New Englanders sought to replicate "English Ways," preserving traditional culture and society, or whether they embraced change and innovation. Should we emphasize New *England* or *New* England?

There can be no final answer to these vexing questions because we do not know with any precision why the vast majority of people went. My central concern here is with the geographical stability or mobility of families before and after migration rather than with motivation. Nonetheless, these new findings add important pointers to migrants' likely motives. If most were like the Beales, wrenched out of settled, circumscribed lives, their reasons for going are likely to have been far different than if the majority were transient drifters for whom New England was a last resort in an itinerant existence. In researching the residential and ancestral histories of the various social, occupational, and gender groups of emigrants I have therefore also sought to discover whether they were likely to regard their move to the New World in an innovative or preservative light. This context of the study, along with a brief description of Greater East Anglia, is outlined in Part I. The Conclusion seeks to weigh the evidence presented on these interpretative scales.

A project such as mine, conducted over many years on two continents, owes an enormous debt to individuals and institutions. It is a source of inspiration that while universities are perverted by business values and management goals the unofficial community of scholars maintains its high standards of generosity and kindliness. With great gratitude, I thank the following: David Grayson Allen, Bob Anderson, Bob Ashton, John Ashworth, Marc Bowman, Ann Cook, John Corey, Richard Crockatt, David Dearborn, Steve Fender, David Hall, Jim Holderness, Stephen Innes, Barbara MacAllan, Vic Morgan, Norman Pettit, Dixon Smith, Hassell Smith, Guy Strutt, Frank Thistlethwaite, Kit Thompson, and Norman Tyack. I likewise thank the staffs of the following institutions: Boston Athenaeum, Cambridge University Library, Essex

Record Office, Massachusetts Historical Society, New England Historic Genealogical Society, Norfolk and Norwich Record Office, Norwich Central Library, Research Grant and Study Leave Committees, and Library staff of the University of East Anglia, the University of Michigan, and West Suffolk County Record Office.

P A R T   I

The Context

꙰

Mobility, Migration,
and Change

THE HUNDREDS of men, women, and children who left England's eastern counties of Essex, Suffolk, Norfolk, Lincolnshire, and Cambridgeshire for New England during the 1630s were migrants. They had moved at least once in their lives. All shared the extraordinary experience of a transatlantic voyage and of confronting a wilderness literally howling with the baying of wolves at night. Most knew they would never return. We apply to these people the words "mobility" and "migration," words that underlie an interpretation of the "character" of Americans: an individualistic, restless, questing people, breaking free from hierarchies and institutions, in love with the new.[1] These distinctive qualities have commonly been projected backward to the colonial pioneers,[2] but for the founding generation of New Englanders things may well have been different. In this book, I reexamine the social history of a contingent of founders, concentrating on the roles of mobility and migration in that wider social history. I investigate the importance of localism and neighborhood stability, of family culture, of spatial and mental horizons among different socioeconomic groups, and the strength, survival, or shipwreck of migrant folkways.

The basis of this study is an investigation of the life histories of these first-generation migrants, specifically the likely impact on those lives of the decision for America. It could have been a traumatic uprooting, or it could have been "nothing remarkable . . . an extension outward and an expansion in scale of domestic mobility in the lands of the immigrants' origins."[3] The voyage might have exacerbated the confusion and displacement of leaving home. It may, however, have been that, "for some, the worst part of the journey was the road journey across England; their troubles ceased when they embarked. The Atlantic had ceased to be a barrier and had already become a highway."[4] The new arrivals on the New England shore might have been shaken into restless dynamism; yet they might have resumed settledness there. To probe these alternative possibilities, I have focused my research on four topics: (1) the migrants' own experience of mobility before emigration; (2) the depth or shallowness of migrants' ancestral roots; (3) the organization of migration; (4) the migrants' movements in New England.

Much of what I have found has been presented in the form of tables. This is inevitable, given the numbers studied. I have fleshed out these bare statistical bones with biographies of representative individuals and examples of different trends among different classes and occupations.

In this chapter, I explore two topics that form the background to the Great Migration: theories of geographical mobility and its recent historiography. The theoretical section covers different types of spatial mobility and the factors, both personal and societal, that affect them. It touches on the sources of the individual's sense of locality and horizon. These ideas are briefly related to changes in attitudes and values. The historiography section reports on the state of the art in early modern English and colonial mobility, migration, and local history studies, findings about transatlantic travel, and resulting models of colonization.

Geographical mobility is a major factor—some would say *the* major factor—in the "deep changes" that have affected people in the Western world over the last three or four centuries.[5] The migration to New England was a small but significant part of a much larger out-movement of Britons during the seventeenth century; between a third and a half million of them migrated to Ireland, North America, the Caribbean, Asia, and Africa.[6] Some historians trace this massive diaspora to changes in mentality already taking place in England, a new, venturesome, exploratory, exploitive outthrust. Moreover, once begun, the very acts of migration and colonization can themselves induce further attitudinal shifts. New challenges elicit new responses. "Migration is both a cause and an ingredient of social change," it is claimed.[7] Such alleged causes and effects have not gone unchallenged. Colonization could have been a safety valve, a stabilizer. New England settlers may have been seeking refuge *from* change.[8] This context to the debate about mobility makes it a central question in both English and colonial history of the seventeenth century.

Many people treasure a nostalgic myth of traditional society as almost static; they imagine "a picture of a stable village England where the rude forefathers of the hamlet slept, where time stood still and generations of Hodges ploughed the patriarchal furrows." Such legendary ancestors were folk who, to paraphrase Pope, on the self-same spot, are born, take nurture, propagate, and rot. A completely static society, however, is a dead society.[9] Every marriage required one of the parties to move his or her home. Residential domestic service meant moving households, as did apprenticeship or seasonal occupations. Cultures are therefore evaluated along a spectrum from geographic stability to geographic mobility.

Spatial mobility, as distinct from the connected topic of social mobility, is a concept full of nuances. Moving one's home, or residential mobility, can involve many varieties of experience. There is, for instance, more than a quantitative difference between short- and long-range moving. Going to live and work in the next parish will have far less impact on the mover than transatlantic migration. Frequency of movement also matters. The woman who moves once when she marries and then settles down to raise a family will have quite a different lifestyle and outlook than the female member of a gang of rogues and vagabonds roaming in search of work, charity, or loot all over southern England. Starting point and destination can make a huge difference to the experience of moving one's home. The effect of arrival in the vast conurbation of London could be very different on a Norwich man, already versed in large-town life, than on a countryman. Village to village, village to town, village to city, town to city, these moves and their obverses would all vary in kind.

Age, family formation, and socioeconomic status can all be expected to affect mobility. Much mobility is nowadays related to age. Adolescence and young adulthood can often be a time of moving about, for training, for work, for higher education, or for adventure. Married life and raising children are usually equated with "settling down." Class structure could well produce different types of residential mobility. Sons of clergymen or gentlemen would be more likely to go to university or inns of court than sons of laborers. The poor might have to be more mobile in their battle for survival than those more comfortably placed.[10]

All these different kinds of residential mobility might arise from a combination of causes. The state of the economy had a powerful effect on mobility. At the family level, the poor would customarily "export" older offspring to wealthier households in need of extra labor. Workers in areas suffering from economic decline would be forced to migrate to more dynamic regions. The large underclass of landless laborers would have to move about in times of dearth to find work or charity. In times of economic expansion, on the other hand, aspiring migrants might move to local towns or provincial centers or even to London in order to better themselves.[11] Different kinds of husbandry could influence mobility. In the later sixteenth and seventeenth centuries farmers with insecure tenures and landless laborers tended to be displaced from arable regions by economic recession, enclosure, and labor-saving changes in farming methods and preferences. The wood-pasture regions with labor-intensive dairying and woodworking or textile by-employment absorbed some of this overplus. The effects of near doubling of the English population and the resultant inflation and long-term squeeze on the land available for farming for the century after 1540 percolated right up the social scale. There came a point when even the most compassionate landlord had to raise his income from his land or face his own ruin. Similarly, decline in traditional textile manufactures, like Suffolk broadcloths, would have a ripple effect from humble spinners and weavers to clothiers and shippers. Long downturns like these pushed out more recruits to the ranks of the subsistence migrants.[12] When proponents of colonization sought to influence government and the ruling local elites, they stressed the benefits to the national economy and to reasserting law, order, and settledness.[13]

As well as the economy, there are examples among the life histories of the Greater East Anglian emigrants of religious and political reasons for people moving their homes. Several puritan ministers were forced on the run or into exile by Anglican persecution. Nonconformist laymen were also harried into uprooting by punitive church courts. Such was the hunger for spiritual instruction and consolation that some puritan laymen moved to live near their favorite preachers or soul doctors. The increasingly arbitrary money-raising methods of the personal government of King Charles I were given as a reason by ship-money collectors for migration.[14] A sense that reformed religion was on the point of extinction in Europe in face of the grand conspiracy of Antichrist was voiced by leading colonists and intending emigrants.[15]

So far, we have discussed residential mobility, moving one's home either temporarily or permanently. There are other kinds of mobility, however: occupational, recreational, and attitudinal.

Certain callings would be much more peripatetic than others and would require travel over territories of different area. As we shall see, arable farmers are likely to be less occupationally mobile than dairymen or stock raisers; the clothier will have to move around in his job farther and oftener than the weaver, the fuller, or the calenderer. Some crafts, like weaving, or smithing, are much more static than others, carpenters, masons, or mariners, for instance. Occupational mobility often increases up the social scale. The country gentleman may have to travel greater distances from his home—to the quarter sessions or assizes, for instance, or to London on legal business—than his social subordinates. Clergymen gave sermons in other parishes as visiting preachers and lecturers and attended diocesan or group meetings.[16] At the other end of the scale, the living-in farm worker or dairymaid might have only rare opportunities to cross the parish boundary.

One of these opportunities might be a Michaelmas trip to the local market town to arrange a year's hiring or to visit the local fair. These outings were also social activities, chances to meet friends, relatives, and sweethearts from other farms or parishes and to gawk at exotic strangers from "away," peddlers, traders, mountebanks, actors, or acrobats. Other excursions from the village might be for those three family events publicly recorded in the parish registers: baptisms, marriages, and burials. Again, social position would affect the range of these recreational jaunts. On visits to kin, for instance, gentry or clergy would be far more likely to cross county boundaries than yeomen or artisans. The embryonic social season in London during the winter months was a recreation only for the wealthy. Though puritans would bridle at the idea of religion as recreation—except in the literal sense—they were notorious for "gadding to sermons," sometimes as far as 20 miles. Traditional holidays, like the twelve days of Christmas or Shrove Tuesday, disgusting to puritans, were nonetheless opportunities for the less precise to visit another village or the local town.

There is a kind of "mobility" that does not need physical movement. It is a mobility of the mind, a breadth of horizon, an ability to transcend face-to-face relationships and personally observed experience. This attitudinal mobility depends on several factors. Anthropologists and sociologists place literacy high on the list. Being able to read provides potential for an opening of the mind to a range of new stimuli, to views that differ from each other or from those of local dogmatists, to enrichment of the imagination, to the vicarious experience of others' lives. The Suffolk diarist, the Reverend John Rous of rustic Santon Downham, rarely ventured beyond the sleepy town of Brandon, but through reading ballads, broadsides, "corantos," and royal proclamations bought from chapmen he kept up to date with national news and debates. How literacy was used would depend on education and religious persuasion. A petty or elementary school training would hardly prepare the mind for a critical reading of a John Cotton treatise. Puritanism encouraged literacy and a range of spiritual and biblical reading, but the sophistication of response and understanding would reflect social experience and schooled intelligence.[17] Where one lived had an effect on horizons too. An innkeeper on a well-traveled highway or a craftsman with a shop on a busy market square would see more, hear more news, and meet more people than the husbandman in a remote hamlet or the rural weaver. Attendance at markets could inform as well as enrich even the illiterate. Between 1623 and 1634 in the north Essex borough of Colchester, a government informer described how a leading subversive, Thomas Cotton, received a newsletter from "a peevish intelligencer in London." This "he redd out each market day, about whom the zealants throng as people use where Ballads are sung."[18]

All these types of mobility will affect an individual's sense of locality. People living out their lives in the parish of their birth, with infrequent visits to the nearest market town a few miles away, would have a far more cramped sense of locality than the Cambridge-educated gentleman or clergyman, who equated "my country" with his county. The country clothier regularly journeying to buy raw materials, distribute them to spinners and weavers, collect cloths, take them to finishers and then to the carter or buyer, might well have a wider sense of locality than a yeoman, though an educated, highly literate yeoman could offset his remoteness and more sedentary life with reading, contemplation, and correspondence.[19] He might be active too in the land market. Every man, woman, and child had a different sense of the local, depending on life experience. For all, the most intense feelings would be reserved for the home parish. The word "familiar" with its dual connotations embodies this sense of the intimately known. For many, a sense of a known neighborhood would depend on foot travel, the ironically named "shanks' mare" of the unprivileged, limiting range to a radius of 5 to 10 miles, a distance that could be walked both ways in a day. Regular access to a horse expanded one's local range, but the state of roads, especially in wintertime, would restrict travel.[20] Though all types of mobility affect the individual's range and sense of locality, it is reasonable to assume that the strength of a sense of place depends on residential stability or mobility. Someone deeply rooted in one parish, with generations of ancestors buried in the churchyard, relatives among many long-familiar neighbors, and an accepted place in the social order, is more likely to have a deep sense of loyalty and belonging to that

8

neighborhood than the person who perches there briefly before rest-lessly moving on, or being moved on.

Whether the mover and the moved are more open to change than the stable stay-at-homes is a mooter point. Homebodies can be receptive to change, given sufficient incentives.[21] Highly mobile societies can be deeply conservative: hunter-gatherers, pastoralists, even peasants in-volved in seasonal migrations. From the time of the Roman poet Horace, doubt has clouded the cliché "Travel broadens the mind." It can, as Mark Twain enjoyed recounting, merely confirm parochial prejudice and blinkered "innocence."

We have considered mobility from the point of view of the mover, but it is a two-way process. When someone moves away, the dynamics of the household and the community they have left are also affected. Easing of pressure on space and scarce resources may provide safety valves, a return to stability for those who remain. On the other hand, departures could induce in those left behind a sense of discontent, desolated loss, or envious restlessness. Relatives or former neighbors living away open up broader horizons or reveal outside opportunities to the less venture-some. Kinfolk in nearby towns can help to integrate these centers into their hinterlands through regular communication. Even London can become less awesome through contacts with friends there. Excessive mobility or unsettledness of population often produces widespread social problems: crime, vice, feuding, disorder, poverty. These in turn prompt elite alarm, social criticism, and demands for change.[22]

Most theorists of mobility agree that generally it is an important, even necessary, factor in altering attitudes and values. There is far less concurrence as to whether spatial mobility is *the* sufficient cause of such "deep change."[23] This broad question will be a theme of our analysis of different socioeconomic groups of emigrants.

The theoretical possibilities embodied in the concept of geographical mobility have excited a wide range of historical research in the sixteenth and seventeenth centuries in both Britain and America over the last 30 years. I have reviewed elsewhere this large and impressive body of work.[24] Here, to delineate the context in which my research has been conducted, some major findings and some unresolved disagreements need to be mentioned.

Those scholars who have compared series of listings of population are generally agreed that in seventeenth-century England the model of a residentially static society is no longer tenable. Over quite short periods of time, significant numbers of surnames have disappeared from subsequent lists.[25] Though some of these later omissions resulted from high mortality rates, leavers and new arrivals call for explanation. What comparisons of listings cannot tell us is the distance traveled by these migrants. Answers to this puzzle from court records, parish registers, probate materials, and family reconstitution confirm that most mobility in early modern England was, except for the desperate poor, short-range and age-specific. The great majority of moves were made by young people; they were usually under 20 miles, often under 10. The major exception to this predominant local rule was migration to London. One out of every eight Englishmen and women in the early seventeenth century had the experience of living in the capital.[26]

Historical geography has come up with some valuable lessons about the comparative magnetic fields of various sorts of places. Villages exert a feeble pull in terms of distance and intensity compared with local ports or market towns. These, in turn, have less attractive power than county towns or provincial centers like Lincoln, Cambridge, or Norwich. The whole of the British Isles forms the field for that most powerful magnet of all, the bustling, burgeoning conurbation of London, drawing immigrants toward the southeast corner of England.[27] Yet even the alleged instability of London life may have been exaggerated. Each ward, each parish, had a solid core of well-established families providing a sense of community.[28] This ballast of settled households reflected the situation across the whole country. The strong community control and maintenance of moral standards in early modern England would have been impossible without it.[29]

Though Englishmen were not the circumscribed, sedentary folk of myth, then, many people had experienced considerable residential stability. The large number of small trading towns within 10 or so miles of each other suggests that most people's sense of locality would be quite limited. If the Greater East Anglian contingent left "Worlds in Motion" habituated to change, they would have been unusual. Assessing their personal and lineal settledness or mobility will be our first task.

Even if the emigrants were typical Englishmen in this regard, however, they might have been jolted out of a sense of stability before their arrival in the New World. Scholars have recently focused attention on the effects of the transtlantic voyage itself. Using mainly diary and confessional sources, they claim that the hazardous and terrifying encounter with the ocean and the vast distances traveled turned the experience into a rite of passage, profoundly changing perceptions and attitudes. Shedding all but essentials for the voyage initiated the pared-down simplifications of New World existence. On board, emigrants began the process of becoming New Englanders by their encounter with the watery wilderness. Shared dangers forged a new seaborne *communitas*. The survivors of storms, scurvy, seasickness, and stomach ailments who disembarked at Salem or Boston were different people from those who embarked at Yarmouth, Ipswich, or London. This view is at sharp variance with the belief that going to America was simply an extension of English betterment migration. The impact of the voyage would depend on people's mental preparedness and could be much more powerful if they traveled as isolated individuals. Demonstration of the rite-of-passage thesis would require new arrivals to exhibit radically new traits and attitudes.[30]

When we come to review mobility studies for colonial New England, broad agreement is harder to come by. Some town studies have found little residential mobility for three or four generations in these "peaceable kingdoms" or "christian utopian closed corporate communities." The older generation used its control of family capital through inheritance to keep children within reach and conserved part of their town land for forthcoming generations. Elders retained power and respect until dotage. The high moral tone of New England communities would bear out this sense of continuity and communal stability.[31] Other researchers, however, have found that generational or economic or religious divisions within towns led to dissatisfied groups moving elsewhere. Hunger for particular types of land also played its part in dispersal.[32] Recent local studies emphasize the variety of New England town cultures and the importance of investment and entrepreneurship. Though some towns clung to subsistence agriculture, others were quickly drawn in to colonial or Atlantic markets, to fishing, fur trading, mining, ironworks, timber production, provisioning, and market gardening. Some towns rapidly divided land into individual farmsteads. In others, land was frequently traded as a commodity, and tenancy was not uncommon. Where such "improvements" were pioneered, patron–client relationships also grew. These developments induced greater occupational mobility, as they expanded individuals' horizons.[33] Socioeconomic stratification also affected mobility. Residentially, better-endowed families were less prone to move on than those less endowed. Occupationally, though, magistrates, ministers, and merchants were more frequent travelers to sessions, the General Court, sermons, synods, ports, or markets than many farmers or craftsmen.

Subsistence migration in search of sustenance was virtually unknown until the last quarter of the seventeenth century. There was, however, a persistent remigration to England, starting with 80 members of the 1630 *Arbella* fleet and rising in the 1640s.[34]

The conflicting findings in New England local and mobility studies have encouraged two models of early colonial mentality. The "Turnerian Frontier" model depicts the typical pioneer as mobile, individualistic, experimental, adaptable, and innovative. Even if this type was self-selected from venturesome, risk-taking Englishmen, the frontier environment heightened these characteristics.[35] The "Both Englands" model, to use David Grayson Allen's felicitous phrase, derives from Herbert Baxter Adams's "germ" theory and Edward Eggleston's *Transit of Civilization* against which Frederick Jackson Turner and his followers rebelled. It sees the immigrants as unwilling refugees from persecution, absolutism, and economic depression, who sought to conserve as much as possible of the best of the culture of the old country in a terrifying new world. Indeed, preservation of local traditions threatened by English innovations may well have been their main motive for abandoning ancestral homes. Rather than breaking free of old constraints to become "This new man, the American," the first New Englanders could hardly move for all their cultural baggage. Like the raj in India, they became "more English than the English."[36] On the resolution of this major clash of interpretations hangs the basic relationship between New England colonization and continuity and change.[37]

Setting the recent scholarship in an adversary stance does some violence to its subtlety. The work we have been describing occupies points along a spectrum between "inheritance" or "tradition" or "persistence" at one extreme and "experience" or "design" or "environment" at the other. Though a few deterministic commentators perch at one end or the other,[38] most scholars concede that cultural antecedents and New World conditions both played some part in the settlement process. Some changes are undeniable. The relative abundance of land— "enough to satisfy the aspirations of a duke"—and shortage of labor reversed British trends; the intensive gave way to the extensive. Simplification was inevitable. So was some erosion of tradition in a land empty of the physical and material props of ancient folk culture. On the other hand, Joyce Appleby is right that no one now contends that "America was born free rich and modern" or that "newly minted America gave currency to every passing innovation." No serious local study would neglect the English background of settlers and the perpetuation of English ways in New England. Town meetings, gathered churches, colonial constitutions, legal precedents and procedures, settlement patterns, agrarian techniques, and a host of other responses to a new world have been traced to English regional models. Of course, as some have observed, preservationist intentions may produce unexpected changes—as Suffolk emigrant John Winthrop would have ruefully agreed on his deathbed. Conservative rhetoric may disguise radical ends. Continuity depended to some extent on luck, on the single decade-long surge of emigration abruptly halted in 1640, the comparative austerity of the New England environment, the lack of an agricultural staple, the absence of external threats, and the relative homogeneity of the population. Despite this tendency to mix elements of continuity and change and to emphasize colonial society's "variety, its fluidity and its conflicting tendencies," there remain broad disagreements about the precise input of inheritance and experience to New England colonization.[39]

The new evidence presented here feeds into this debate. Findings about individuals' prior movements, their ancestral roots, their migration experiences, and their New England mobility will not settle these complex arguments. There are too many other variables for that. They will, however, provide important indicators of the likely leanings toward innovation or preservation of the Greater East Anglian founders of New England.

2

Greater East Anglians

FROM 1629 to 1640 between 14,000 and 21,000 people emigrated from England to the New England colonies. Leading elements in this movement were settlers from the five eastern counties between the estuaries of the Humber and the Thames: Lincolnshire, Norfolk, Suffolk, Cambridgeshire, and Essex (see Fig. 1).[1] I have called this collection of counties Greater East Anglia. During the English Civil War, Parliament acknowledged their sense of regionalism by combining them in the Eastern Association. Their armed forces formed the core of the New Model Army, which defeated Charles I at Marston Moor (1644) and Naseby (1645). At their center are the two counties of Norfolk and Suffolk, East Anglia proper, which also form the episcopal diocese of Norwich. It is not unusual to link Essex to them as part of the semi-circular land mass between the Thames Estuary and the Wash. Essex was part of the diocese of London, but the Stour Valley, which marked the county boundary with Suffolk, had major textile centers on each bank, and roads and coasting routes to London helped pull the three counties together. For the rural peasantry and small-town craftsmen and traders, the concept of a region was altogether beyond their horizons. Even lesser gentry were often limited in geographical scope to the idea of the county community, "my country," as they called it. Their wealthier and more sophisticated cousins and betters did transcend county lines. They often married across them, like John Winthrop from Suffolk and Essex's Margaret Tyndal, or Winthrop's neighbor Brampton Gurdon, whose wife, Muriel, came from Norfolk. They also held land across county borders, as did Winthrop's first father-in-law or John Haynes, later governor of both Massachusetts and Connecticut, who lived in Essex but had property in Norfolk. At the magnatial level, the sense of region was strongest. It is here that Lincolnshire, north of the Wash, was linked to Greater East Anglia. The earl of Warwick, lord

14

lieutenant of Essex, and the earl of Lincoln, his kinsman by marriage, were close political and religious allies at court and in the House of Lords. With greater gentlemen, like Sir Thomas Barrington, premier baronet of Essex, and Sir Nathaniel Barnardiston of Suffolk and Sir Thomas Wodehouse of Norfolk, enjoying the discreet encouragement of the bishop of Lincoln, they led a powerful opposition to what they saw as the extension of royal and episcopal prerogatives and the undermining of county rights and liberties.[2] Lincolnshire had important economic connections with East Anglia, sending fine wool for the textile industry and fattened beef for consumption. The shallow Wash with its twin towns of Boston and King's Lynn and busy coasting trade pulled Lincolnshire and Norfolk together. Several leading Lincolnshire emigrants had regional ties. William Coddington's wife came from Suffolk and Herbert Pelham's from Essex, where he eventually settled. Simon Bradstreet grew up in Horbling, Lincolnshire, but the family came from Norfolk and kinsman Humphrey Bradstreet emigrated from Suffolk. John Winthrop and Isaac Johnson of Sempringham, Lincolnshire, son-in-law of the earl of Lincoln, collaborated closely in organizing the *Arbella* fleet in 1630. Winthrop's letters in the 1620s and 1630s are peppered with references to and letters from all five eastern counties.[3]

Leading clergy likewise shared a sense of region. A letter to Margaret Winthrop in Groton, Suffolk, forewarned of a visit from the Reverend John Cotton of Boston, Lincolnshire. The Reverend Samuel Whiting, from a mercantile family in Boston, mingled with East Anglians at Emmanuel College, Cambridge, and then served as domestic chaplain and curate in north Norfolk before becoming rector of Skirbeck by Boston. A branch of his wife's family lived in Norfolk. Sir Nathaniel Barnardiston held the advowson of a Lincolnshire parish. In the New World, Lincolnshire men settled with other East Anglians in towns like Boston and Ipswich and shared as religious dissidents in founding Rhode Island and New Hampshire. Cambridgeshire, the only inland county and part of the diocese of Ely, has been added because Cambridge University formed the intellectual and theological focus of the region. Almost all the graduates in our contingent were Cambridge men; initial discussions about New England and the signing of the Agreement to emigrate had taken place there. By 1640 the regional contribution to New England's foundation was acknowledged by the naming of five towns after important Greater East Anglian centers: Lynn, Boston, Cambridge, Ipswich, and Dedham.[4]

The region supported a considerable range of economic activities,

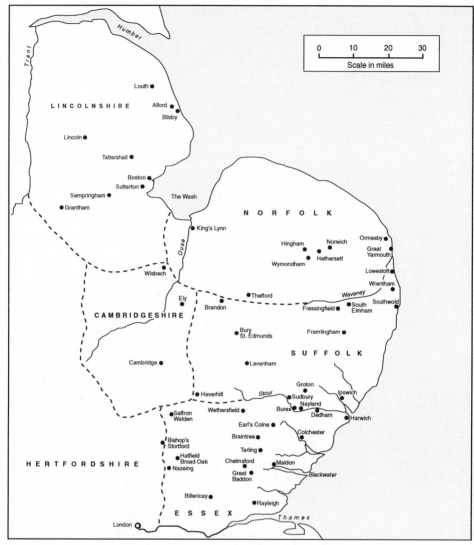

Figure 1. Greater East Anglia

16

which help to make it reasonably representative of southern England, from which the vast bulk of early emigrants came. At its southern end, Essex and parts of Suffolk produced cereals, meat, and dairy products for the ever-growing London market. A central sweep of these counties and of south Norfolk—the wood-pasture region—was largely enclosed, with independent farmers virtually emancipated from medieval manorial conventions. The lighter soils of north and east Norfolk, east and west Suffolk and east Cambridgeshire were devoted to sheep–cereal husbandry with a considerable amount of open-field farming. There were still many areas of marsh and fenland: southeast Essex; parts of the Suffolk, Norfolk, and Lincolnshire coasts; and a great swathe running from central Lincolnshire down to northwest Norfolk and north Cambridgeshire. Cattle were fattened on these coastal marshlands and parts of the fens during the drier months. In eastern Lincolnshire these vast watery flatlands were interrupted by the rise of the Wolds, uplands producing fine wools.[5]

Greater East Anglia was internationally renowned as a cloth-producing area. Though spinning and weaving were cottage industries throughout the region, there were two important centers of manufacture: the Stour Valley, known since the Middle Ages for its heavy broadcloths, especially its Suffolk whites and blues and its more recent Bocking and Colchester bays and says, and the provincial capital of Norwich, headquarters of the Norfolk worsted weaving and home of lighter "stuffs," increasingly popular in southern Europe and the Mediterranean countries. Norwich was still the second city of the kingdom, with a population of around 20,000. To the west, Lincoln, another cathedral city, and Cambridge were smaller cultural centers. In a lower tier were leading market towns like Bury St. Edmunds, Colchester, Chelmsford, or Sudbury and ports like Boston, King's Lynn, Great Yarmouth, and Ipswich. Above the hundreds of villages like Fressingfield or Nazeing, or dispersed hamlets like Winthrop's Groton, were dozens of market towns like Braintree, Framlingham, or Alford. It was unusual for the distance between such markets to exceed 10 miles. Around the great market of Norwich, the market towns on the roads that radiate out from the city form a rough circle between nine and sixteen miles from the center.[6]

The eastern counties were among the most advanced economically and educationally in England. The region's population was comparatively densely settled, between a quarter and a third of Norfolk and Suffolk people living in towns. Fifty thousand residents of the Stour

Valley were said to be employed in the textile industry. Much farming was commercially oriented, with London as an ever-growing consumer, but Norwich and other towns also bought in meat and grain. Population pressures and lucrative markets led to a very active trade in land and escalating prices, especially in Essex and Suffolk. In some favored districts rents quadrupled between 1600 and 1620. Winthrop echoed a repeated chorus of the 1620s when he declared that "our land is over-burdened with people." A preacher caught the mood in a wedding sermon: "The choice of many about wives is like that in use about bargains and farms. The questions are mostly What is it worth besides the rent? What house upon it, how near the market, the mill, the sand?"[7]

The effect of such demand was to squeeze out middling or small farmers, especially on the "champion" farmland in the west of the region. In the wood pasture, by-employments like the fashioning of staves for barrels in Hingham, brush making and the turning of wooden spoons in nearby Wymondham, or linen weaving in the wetlands of the Waveney Valley between Norfolk and Suffolk cushioned the pressure, but the growing population was vulnerable to food shortages. Burgeoning population and proximity to London also acted as a challenge. Greater East Anglia would be the pioneer of the eighteenth-century agricultural revolution, and some pathfinders were already experimenting with drainage, floating of meadows, new rotations, and mixed husbandry, which would dramatically increase yields and annual output.[8]

Educationally the region was blessed with impressive school provision. There were famous grammar schools like Martin Holbeach's Felsted in Essex, where Oliver Cromwell sent his sons to study, and Bury St. Edmunds whose alumni included the famous puritan master of St. Catherine's Hall, Cambridge, Richard Sibbes, would-be colonist Sir Simonds D'Ewes, and John Winthrop, Jr. Not only did other county towns support secondary schools, like Ipswich whose master had been the father of emigrant Emmanuel Downing, but many smaller market towns, Raynham, Earl's Colne, Lavenham, Aylsham, North Walsham, Braintree, Dedham, Alford, or Boston, had resident schoolmasters or were recipients of educational philanthropy. Between 1480 and 1660 the enormous sum of £40,000 had been given to education in Norfolk alone. By our period the county had 27 endowed schools, and except for two remote areas, no one lived more than nine miles from an endowed school. In Suffolk, which benefited more from infusions of philanthropy from London, the male literacy rate was second only to the capital's in the whole kingdom.[9]

Greater East Anglia furnished many centers of obstinate opposition to the ecclesiastical pretensions and innovations of the Laudians and the political authority of the crown during the 1630s. A local official observed "Great numbers of his majesty's subjects . . . ill-affected and discontented as well with civil as ecclesiastical government." The region's puritan tradition went back to fifteenth-century support for Lollardry. The Lollard Pit outside the city walls of Norwich was one of several places of martyrdom. Zealous Protestants throughout the region likewise suffered for their faith during the Catholic revival under Queen Mary (1553–58). During Elizabeth's reign, more than half of the puritan ministers in England came from Essex, Suffolk, and Norfolk. After 1600, "the brains and energy of the puritan party" were to be found in Essex and Lincolnshire, and Essex and Suffolk were two counties where "puritan gentlemen concentrated in any numbers." Henry Jessey, a friend and correspondent of John Winthrop, praised Essex and Suffolk in 1624 as the home of "famous preachers and many precious Christians." In 1640, the see of Norwich was described as "the Diocese in which there are as many strict professors of religion as any in England." Braintree, Dedham, Ipswich, Yarmouth, Norwich, and Boston were the most famous of many regional centers of godly activity.

Several Cambridge colleges, like Emmanuel, St. Catherine's Hall, Sidney Sussex, and Christ's, were notorious for their nonconformity and the puritan graduates they produced, from the earl of Warwick down to country vicars like Nathaniel Ward. Frequent interchanges with the Netherlands, to which some ministers like Thomas Hooker and Hugh Peter were forced to flee, reinforced awareness of the "Calvinist International" and its vulnerability to resurgent Catholicism. Outrage at "Laudian innovations" like bowing at the name of Jesus, reinstatement and railing of altars, close supervision of lectureships, suppression of conventicles, and the 1633 reissue of the antisabbatarian Book of Sports, combined with the silencing of puritan preachers and prosecution of the godly, led to agitation in Ipswich, Yarmouth, Wymondham, Colchester, and Boston. The dioceses of Lincoln, Norwich, and London were the most subversive in the Church of England.[10]

East Anglian opposition to the crown was likewise renowned. Not only were magnates like the earls of Warwick and Lincoln and wealthy country gentlemen like Sir Francis Barrington, Sir William Masham,

Sir Simonds D'Ewes, Sir Christopher and Sir John Wray, and Sir Nathaniel Barnardiston bitterly hostile to Charles I's policies and financial expedients, but men of the middling sort also stood on constitutional principle. Clothing workers, especially, were "trained up as nurseries of sedition and rebellion." Antagonism to benevolences, forced loans, and ship money was notable in areas that would produce companies of emigrants, like Boston, Great Yarmouth, the Stour Valley, and western Essex. The commitment that empowered the russet coats of the Eastern Association Army in the 1640s was not a nine-day wonder.[11]

Though the homes of the Greater East Anglian contingent were scattered throughout the region, there were certain areas of concentration. In Lincolnshire, the Wolds, and Boston and its hinterland were major catchment areas. In Norfolk, the southern half of the county, and especially Norwich with its satellite villages, the coastal area around Great Yarmouth and the south-central wood pasture provided the bulk of the migrants. The wood pasture of High Suffolk and Essex continued the trend through the central swathe of East Anglia. There were also important sources for New Englanders on the northeast Suffolk coast and around Bury and Ipswich. An area feeding much early emigration was the Stour Valley of south Suffolk and north Essex, especially such famous wool towns as Sudbury, Lavenham, Nayland, Stoke, Bures, Dedham, and the Colne Valley of north Essex. Two other areas of Essex deserve mention: the district around the county town of Chelmsford— the base of Thomas Hooker and William Pynchon—and a sweep of villages on the western border of Hertfordshire, from John Eliot's Nazeing through Hatfield Broad Oak to Saffron Walden. These catchment areas have provided analysts of motivation with suggestive but often contradictory ammunition.

Although the geographical mobility of the migrants and their forefathers rather than motivation to "voyage beyond the seas" is the major topic of this study, it is nonetheless relevant to point out that Greater East Anglia in 1630 was enduring "probably the most terrible years through which the country has ever passed." The cloth industry had been disrupted by government interference, changing fashion, foreign competition, and international war. The Suffolk broadcloth industry was in terminal decline, pirates infested the North Sea, and England's inglorious involvement in the Thirty Years' War raised taxes and levies as European hostilities played havoc with exports. Nature added calamities. Heavy rains had reduced harvests between 1621 and 1623. The parish register of Woodham Walter, Essex, for 1622 reads: "there was no one marryed—it was a deare yeare." In February of that year the churchwardens and overseers of the poor of Winthrop's neighborhood of Groton, Boxford, and Edwardstone were presented because "the aged and impotent are not relieved in such comfort and sufficient manner as their necessities require, and that other sort of poor which are of able bodyes to work are in great distress and many of them likely to perish."

Robert Whitehead, of the emigrant minister Thomas Weld's parish of Terling, also in Essex, justified the theft of a sheep in the starving winter of 1623 with his "beinge a verie poore man and having a wiefe and seven smale children and being very hungery." In 1623, a Lincolnshire land-owner reported: "Dog flesh is a dainty dish, and found upon search in many houses. . . . And the other day one stole a sheep which for mere hunger tore a leg out and did eat it raw." There was a fearsome plague epidemic in 1625–26. The coups de grace were provided by the harvests of 1628, 1629, and 1630. The first year was meager; the next two disastrous. Clothiers trying to cope with "lack of vent"—2,500 unsold bays at Bocking, for instance, 3,000 at nearby Dedham (both large sources of emigrants)—were confronted with the prospect of starving workers. A petition of 200 weavers in Braintree and Bocking in 1629 spoke of 30,000 people facing beggary. In Witham, near Colchester, spinners and weavers were dying of malnutrition in 1630 and 1631. In December 1630 specific quantities of corn were ordered to be marketed there each week and in Colchester, Coggeshall, and Maldon, Essex. In Nayland on the Stour "want of corn is so great that most of the inhabitants are ready to perish." In 1629 a woman and three men were hanged for "breaking house openly in the daytime and taking only some corn and the woman saying 'Come, my brave lads of Maldon, I will be your leader and we will not starve.'" Mobs rioted in Colchester, seizing a grain wagon, about the same time. Things were similar in both Suffolk and Norfolk: "Times are so exceeding hard." At Yarmouth a merchant trying to export buckwheat (normally poultry food) found poor people "laying violent hands on the boatmen." The sheriff of Norfolk reported in March 1631 that corn prices had doubled since October 1628 and were "deemed excessive," especially by worsted weavers and stocking knitters, who were always hovering near the subsistence line. Robert Ryece in neighboring Suffolk observed "the greatest number of poor where the clothiers do dwell or have dwelt." Sudbury spinners were having to sell vital tools of their trade in order to eat. Improvements after 1632 were undone by plague from 1636 to 1638 and another bad

Table 1. Greater East Anglian Emigration by County and Year

County	1630	1631	1632	1633	1634	1635	1636	1637	1638	1639	1640	Total
Essex	143	30	84	41	63	161	22	49	45	25	12	675
Suffolk	181	15	13	22	140	118	60	80	82	43	36	790
Norfolk	12	1	5	33	5	54	17	213	158	5	10	513
Lincoln	38	0	5	16	49	3	6	3	10	2	0	132
Cambridge	1	0	2	0	2	11	11	0	0	0	1	28
Total	375	46	109	112	259	347	116	345	295	75	59	2,138

harvest in 1637. Hingham had only one good harvest in the whole decade, and the parish register records more burials than births. A serious two-year depression returned to the Essex textile industry in 1636. A wool comber in Bocking voiced the prevalent sense of desperation. He needed work "that I may take no unlawful course." Throughout the 1620s and 1630s country gentlemen and justices of the peace whose own incomes were suffering because of unpaid rents or loans expressed fears of riots by "our tumultuous vulgar."[12]

The economic depression from 1620 to 1640 revealed how exposed many people's lives were. The safety margins, even in a comparatively prosperous region like Greater East Anglia, were paper thin. Little wonder that John Winthrop wrote of "the land weary of its inhabitants." The depression psychology of the region pervaded the whole of society. Such cycles of calamities were never mere mischance to minds obsessed with providences. It must have seemed that the God who had so favored the English nation in Queen Elizabeth's reign had changed his merciful smile into a vengeful frown. There might have seemed almost too many reasons to escape these eastern counties for the 2,138 emigrants.[13]

Emigration from Greater East Anglia to New England during the 1630s came in three surges: 1630, 1634–35, and 1637–38 (see Table 1). The first surge came with the *Arbella* fleet of 11 ships. Of the 695 identified passengers, 375 came from the eastern counties, the great majority, 324, from Essex and south Suffolk. The second, far larger and more sustained wave helped the Massachusetts population of about 2,000 in early 1634 double by a year later. Between 1635 and 1640, 2,000 to 3,000 immigrants were arriving each year. Between one-third and one-quarter of those identified came from the five counties, but the ingredients subtly changed. The southern regional domination of Essex and south Suffolk gave way to north Suffolk and Norfolk in 1637 and 1638. This changing emphasis has been associated with the expansion of Laud's ecclesiastical jurisdiction from Essex during his 1628–33 tenure as bishop of London to the whole region when he ascended to the primacy. The replacement of the negligent Bishop Corbett in Norwich by the zealous antipuritan Matthew Wren in 1636 exacerbated the northward trend. However, a host of other factors like the reissue of the Book of Sports in 1633, the violent government reprisals against Prynne, Burton, and Bastwick in 1636, the seesawing of the economy, and political blows like ship-money levies and the death of Gustavus Adolphus have all been cited as causes. The falling off of numbers in

Table 2. Adult Male Ages at Emigration (total, 705; 591 = 84%)

Age Group	Age	Known	Estimated	Total	%
1	15–20	44	69	113	19
2	21–25	66	20	86	15
3	26–30	74	36	110	19
4	31–35	47	24	71	12
5	36–40	65	22	87	15
6	41–45	37	11	48	8
7	46–50	29	9	38	6
8	51–55	22	2	24	4
9	56–60	10	1	11	2
10	61–65	2	0	2	
11	66–70	1	0	1	
		397	194	591	100

Note: Ages have been estimated from such data as date of marriage, entrance to university or apprenticeship, birth order, or first wife's age. Where dates of birth have subsequently been discovered, estimates have proved accurate within two or three years.

1639 and 1640 must have resulted from the king's increasing difficulties with the Scots. The translation of Wren to Ely may also have contributed to the reduction.[14]

Apart from its size, between one-tenth and one-sixth of the entire Great Migration, the contingent studied here has the added merit of covering the whole of the 1630s. Recent investigations have often concentrated on the period after 1635 when more detailed shipping lists are available.[15] However, it has proved possible to uncover a good deal about the earliest pioneers, thus illuminating the critical, cliff-hanging stage of plantation. Greater East Anglia was heavily represented in these first years when so many enduring patterns of settlement were established.

The eastern counties contingent in the Great Migration comprised 443 married men (including a few widowers with children and husbands without their wives) and 427 married women. There were 262

Table 3. Comparative Age Structures of Emigrant Groups

	Thompson		Anderson		Leung	
Under 20	1,036	(48%)	200	(48%)	667	(48%)
15–20	113	19%	51	19%	230	19%
21–30	196	34	102	39	529	44
31–40	158	27	71	27	289	23
41–50	86	14	29	11	118	10
51–60	35	6	10	4	31	3
	588	100%	263	100%	1,197	99%

Sources: Anderson, *New England's Generation*, 222, Table 1; Leung, "New England's Call," 149, Table 5-1. The 15–20 group in both these tables has been calculated by dividing 11–20 age groups in half. The ages of 1,634 of Leung's contingent are known.

unmarried men and 83 unmarried women. Children under 15 totaled 923. Of these, 10 are listed as servants. The ages of the males over 15 are recorded in 397 cases and can be estimated from other data in a further 194. The five-year groupings set out in Table 2 show that the great majority were under 40 years old, with the late teens and the late twenties most numerous.

In years of heavy emigration, the percentage of singles was between 10 and 16, but in 1631 it rose to 31 percent, and in the last three years ran at 23 percent, 25 percent, and 47 percent. The early peak is explained by the number of servants accompanying Margaret Winthrop's party. The high in 1640 may be distorted by the 15 percent known to have been in New England "by 1640."

Comparison with recent analyses of emigrant age structure is set out in Table 3. Anderson's percentages are derived from 412 emigrants whose ages are recorded in seven shipping lists compiled between 1635 and 1638. Five sailings were from the Channel ports of Sandwich (2), Southampton (2), and Weymouth, and two are from the East Anglian port of Yarmouth. Leung's 1,872 emigrants who sailed for New England from 1620 to 1640 are mainly culled from Banks, *Topographical Dictionary*.[16] The identical proportions in all three groups for those under 20 and those aged from 15 to 20 are striking. The adult Greater East Anglians, however, are weighted toward age, with one-fifth over 40

Table 4. Status or Occupation of
Male Emigrants

Gentlemen	36	8%
Clergy	37	8
Mercantile	54	12
Professional	21	5
Entrepreneurial	10	2
Artisans	151	34
Farmers		18
Yeomen	44	
Husbandmen	37	
Servants	55*	12
Total	445	99%

*Ten "servants" were under 15 years old.

and nearly a half over 30. This contrast is partly explained by the absence of women from my list, but it also highlights the number of well-established families that left the region.

The status or occupational complexion of the adult male group of 705 on which more detailed personal analysis will be based is more difficult to discover. Only 445 callings have been recovered, as set out in Table 4.

There is considerable variation from the English norms here. Apart from the disproportionate representation of gentlemen and clergy in the emigrant sample, the percentage of artisans is way above the English average. Some of this overplus is accounted for by specialist recruits like shipwrights or housewrights. The shortage of farmers would almost certainly be corrected if we knew the occupations of the undesignated 270 adult and adolescent males. Many of them were probably husbandmen or farm laborers. This could bring up the total of agricultural workers to around 350, much closer to the ratio in the old country. Compared to the English average of 17 percent of the population in service, the 55 males, 32 females, and 11 unnamed but specifically designated as "servants" is an extremely meager number, only about 5 percent of the total. A considerable number of emigrants under 20 or without designation may have been servants, often "servants in husbandry" or young farm laborers.[17]

Socially, the Greater East Anglian group has important similarities in composition to other groups of immigrants to New England that have been analyzed. It springs from the broad "middling sort" of England.[18] No members of the aristocracy or leading county families settled permanently in the puritan colonies. Nor were the lower class of landless day laborers or the underclass of rogues and vagabonds heavily represented in the surviving lists. Only a handful of young men were classed as "indentured servants," the group most numerous in the settling of colonies like Virginia, Maryland, and, later on, Pennsylvania.[19] The very high percentage of artisans is likewise mirrored by the findings of Cressy, Anderson, Leung, and Breen and Foster. Cressy's 1635–38 list, which includes London embarkations for New England and is thus more representative of national emigration patterns than Anderson's, has 47 percent artisans compared to my 34 percent, and 22 percent farmers compared to my 18 percent. However, lay and spiritual leaders are far more evident in the Greater East Anglian group, the clergy comprising half of the 76 emigrant ministers of the 1630s. Many gentlemen sailed (and returned) in the first years of settlement. Many fewer from the eastern counties were classified as servants or laborers, 12 percent as compared with 25 percent.[20] The identifiable Greater East Anglian contingent was thus a rung or two up the social ladder compared with a cross-section of later 1630s emigrants. Very few emigrants from the eastern counties to New England brought with them reputations for rootlessness and lawlessness. New England was not to be a rubbish bin for England's trash.

With a somewhat older and slightly higher-class contingent than the full range of known emigrants, it is hardly surprising that the Greater East Anglians played such a crucial leadership role in the first decade. These differences mark distinctions between the first surge and the later two and between our emigrants and people from London, the southern counties, and the West Country. The composition of this essentially middling-order group from one region otherwise holds few surprises. Nonetheless, it substitutes systematic analysis for what have often been loose assumptions. It is now time to look more closely at the personal and ancestral backgrounds of 934 men and women, over three-quarters of all those over 15, about whom details survive.

PART II

Personal and Ancestral

Backgrounds

PART II investigates the personal histories of 934 adult men and women emigrants. Their names, with individual and ancestral details, are presented in lists. Sources of information on each individual may be found at the back of the book (Table Source Notes). The contingent has been divided into socioeconomic and gender groups. Each group is further sorted into age bands. The specific focus is on the extent to which these people had moved in their own lifetimes. We inquire whether certain groups were more geographically dynamic than others and what effects such movement might have on them. Prevalent personal stability would make uprooting traumatic both for individual families and for the contingent as a whole. However, if influential groups were already emancipated from settledness, they might mediate and mitigate the challenge of change for their followers and fellow travelers.

Information about each socioeconomic group is presented in two similar formats in the next four chapters (Tables 5–25). First come the listings of names (as in Table 5). The first column in these tables gives the individual's age group (AG) as set out in Table 2, with 15–20-year-olds in group 1, 21–25-year-olds in group 2, and so on up to group 10, the 61–65-year-olds. The ages of people in group 11 are not known. "Age" refers to age at emigration. DOB and DOE stand for date of birth and date of emigration. BP, FR, AH, and WP stand for birthplace, family roots, adult home, and workplace. The letters S, E, C, N, and L in columns 6, 7, and 8 are abbreviations for the five counties: Suffolk, Essex, Cambridgeshire, Norfolk, and Lincolnshire. The date and letters or No and N1, in the FR column, refer to the earliest record of the family and the dependability of the source, A, B, and C indicating reasonable certainty, probability, and possibility, respectively. No and N1 signify either that the individual himself had made the move to the adult home (No) or that the move was made by the previous generation (N1). (This will be fully explained in Chapter 7.) Numbers in parentheses in the FR column show the distance in miles from an individual's family roots to his or her adult home when their place of birth is missing from the record. Thus, in the case of James Downing in Table 5, his adult homes, first in Dublin and then in London, were 325 and 65 miles respectively from the family's ancestral home in Beccles, Suffolk. The use of the word "area" in this column means that the family is recorded in parishes near its root parish. The last two columns, "Distances," refer to the distance in miles from the individual's birthplace to ancestral birthplaces and how far he or she has moved from place of birth to adult residence. The only variation from the standard presentation is for the clergy (Tables 7 and 8), whose mobility is more complex and is explained in the text.

The second table for each group (as in Table 6) summarizes the age structure and distances moved from both ancestral vicinity and birthplace to the adult home from which emigration took place. The first set of mileages are those distances between emigrants' birthplaces and their ancestral roots. The second set represent the number of miles from where emigrants were born to where they were living when they decided to go to New England. Thus, in Table 6, for example, there are five gentlemen in age group 5, aged 36 to 40. Two were born within 4 miles of where their ancestors had lived, one within 9, and one within 14. The fifth's birthplace and ancestral roots are unknown (UK). Three of the five remained close to their childhood homes in adult life, one moved over 20 miles away, and one person's movements are unknown.

3

The Better Sort:
Gentlemen and Clergy

IN A society obsessed with status or degree, the God-given leaders of the emigration process of plantation in the New World would be the two groups who had governed and guided communities in the old—gentlemen and clergy. To puritans they were conventionally bearers of the "sword" and the "word" of the Lord. We will consider their role in organizing the Great Migration in Chapter 8. Here we ask whether their experiences prior to sailing would precondition them toward continuity or change in the "desert land" they were planting.[1]

Gentlemen

Under great regional magnates like the earls of Lincoln and Warwick, the gentry were the lay leaders of the county communities. (See Tables 5 and 6.) They served on the commission of the peace as justices and administrators. They oversaw their neighborhoods as lords of the manor and patrons of the living. They were expected to "bear the port of a gentleman," which entailed the obligations of "good neighbourhood and hospitality" to clients, tenants, and the "lesser sort." Their incomes came from rents, but many also invested in commercial or industrial ventures. A significant number even put money into colonization. Marriage alliances were a potential source of enrichment. Professional by-employment, particularly in the law, could supplement rental income eroded by inflation.[2]

The title of "gentleman" in fact covered a wide social range. At the top were wealthy county magnates like Sir Thomas Barrington, premier baronet of Essex, or Sir Nathaniel Barnardiston, an equivalent power in Suffolk. At the bottom were parish or minor or "mere" gentry whose

Table 5. Gentlemen Emigrants

AG	Name	Age	DOB	DOE	BP	FR		AH	Distances	
									BP:FR	BP:AH
7	Sam APPLETON	48	1586	c1634	Lit. Waldingf'd, S	Lit. Waldingf'd S	1433A	Lit. Waldingf'd S	0	0
2	Thos BRADBURY	c23	1611	c1634	Wicken Bonant, E	Wicken Bonant area E	1546A	Wicken Bonant E	4	0
1	Benj BRAND*	20	1610	1630	Edwardstone, S	Boxford S	1563A	Edwardstone S	2	0
2	Geo COOKE*	25	1610	1635	Gt.Yeldham, E	N.Essex	1560A	Gt.Yeldham E	5	0
3	Jos COOKE	27	1608	1635	Gt.Yeldham, E	N.Essex	1560A	Gt.Yeldham E	5	0
4	John COOLIDGE	32	1604	1636	Cottenham, C	Cottenham C	1588A	Cottenham C	0	0
11	Edw COPE			c1640	Bury, S			Bury S		0
4	John CROWE	c34	c1600	1634		Tibenham N	1505C (4)	Carleton Rode N		
11	Yelverton CROWE					Tibenham N	1505C (4)	Carleton Rode N		
1	Jas DOWNING*†	c20	c1610	1630		Beccles S (325/65)		Dublin/London		
8	Emm DOWNING*†	53	1585	1638	Ipswich, S	Beccles S	No	Dublin/London	32	325/65
11	Hen GOSNOLD			1630	Bury, S	Boxford area S	N1	Bury S	16	0
1	Edm GURDON*	c19	c1616	1635	Assington, S	Ass'ton/Dedham E	c1440A	Assington S	0/8	0
11	Bram GURDON*†			1630	Assington, S	Ass'ton/Dedham E	c1440A	Assington S	0/8	0
2	Rog HARLAKENDEN	23	1612	1635	Earl's Colne, E	Earl's Colne E/Kent	1602A	Earl's Colne E	0/60	0
6	John HAYNES†	c45	c1588	1633		?Colchester	1508C (4)	Copford E		0
2	Chris HELME	c24	c1615	c1639	Lutton, L	Lutton L	1551A	Lutton L	0	
5	John HUMPHREY*	38	1596	1634	Chaldon, Dorset		No	Sempringham L Connections		170

	Name									
3	Isaac JOHNSON†	29	1601	1630	Stamford, L		No	Sempringham L		14
3	Hen JOSSELYN	28	1606	1634	Roxwell, E	Roxwell E	1507A	Roxwell E	0	0
7	Abr MELLOWS	c50	c1583	1633	?Cambridge C	Coningsby L	1582A	Boston L	42	48
5	John MOODY	40	1593	1633	Moulton, S	Moulton area	1560A	Moulton S	4	0
7	Rob PARKE	50	1580	1630	Poslingford, S	Gestingthorpe E	1327A	Bures E	7	12
5	Herb PELHAM*†	38	1600	1638	Hastings, Sussex	Warbleton, Sussex	N1	Swineshead L/Bures E	14	150/77
1	John PELHAM*	20	1615	1635	Hastings, Sussex	Warbleton, Sussex	N1	Swineshead L	14	150
3	Wm PELHAM	c28	c1602	1630	Hastings, Sussex	Warbleton, Sussex	N1	Swineshead L/Bures E	14	150/77
11	Josi PLAISTOW*			1630			No	Ramsden Grays E	0–6	
5	John PLUMBE	39	1594	1633	Gt.Yeldham, E	Gt.Yeldham E area	1553A	Gt.Yeldham E	3	0
5	Wm PYNCHON*†	c40	c1590	1630	Springfield, E	Writtle E	1465A	Springfield E	0	0
11	Rob SAMPSON*			1630	Kersey, S	Kersey S	1456B	Kersey S	0	0
3	John SAMS*	c28	c1612	1640	Maldon, E	Maldon E	1540A	Maldon E		0
3	John THORNDIKE	29	1603	c1632	Lit.Carleton, L	Lit.Carleton L	1538A	Lit.Carleton L	0	0
2	Hen VANE*†	23	1612	1635	Debden, E	Kent	No	London	65	30
2	Wm WENTWORTH†	21	1616	1637	Alford, L	Grimsby L area	N1	Alford L	30	0
6	John WINTHROP†	42	1588	1630	Edwardstone, S	Lav'ham S/Groton S	1530A	Gt.Stambridge E/Groton S	6/1	30/1
2	John WINTHROP Jr.†	25	1606	1631	Groton S	Lav'ham S/Groton S	1530A	Groton/London	6/0	0/50
2	Hen WINTHROP	22	1608	1630	Groton S	Lav'ham S/Groton S	1530A	Groton/London	6/0	0/50

*Returned to England.
†Eldest sons.

33

Table 6. Age, Roots, and Mobility of Gentlemen Emigrants

AG	Age	No.	Distance, BP:FR (miles)						Distance, BP:AH (miles)					
			0–4	5–9	10–14	15–19	20+	UK	0–4	5–9	10–14	15–19	20+	UK
1	16–20	4	2		1			1	2				1	1
2	21–25	8	3	3			2		5				3	
3	26–30	6	3	1	1			1	4		1		1	1
4	31–35	2			1			1	1					1
5	36–40	5	2	1	1			1	3				1	1
6	41–45	2		1				1					1	
7	46–50	2	1	1					1		1			
8	51–55	1					1						1	
9	56–60	0												
10	61–65	0												
11	UK	6	2			1		3	4					2
	Total	36	13	7	4	1	3	8	20	0	2	0	8	6

pedigrees and pretensions alone separated them from wealthy yeoman farmers. They would themselves run the farming of their estates rather than leasing farms to tenants. Their younger sons might well have to go into trade, and the heir would be lucky if he avoided having to sell to a newly rich London merchant ascending the social ladder. Such a mere gentleman was no doubt in Sir Thomas Overbury's mind when he composed his "character" of a country squire. "His travel is seldom farther than the next market town, and his inquisition is about the price of corn. . . . Nothing under a subpoena will draw him to London, and when he is there, he sticks fast upon every object, casts his eye upon gazing, and becomes the prey of every cutpurse. . . . But this is not his element. He must home again, being like the dor that ends his flight in a dunghill." We are irresistibly reminded of Shakespeare's comic creations, Justices Silence and Shallow, who vegetated in self-satisfied rusticity.[3]

We explore here the horizons, the influence, and the personal experience of change of the 36 gentlemen who emigrated from Greater East Anglia. Their personal and family backgrounds, especially their rootedness or restlessness, will indicate the likely impact of emigration.

The best-documented among this historically visible group is the leader and inspiration of settlement, John Winthrop. The Winthrop family had been settled in southern Suffolk since the Middle Ages. His great-grandfather Adam lived in the wool town of Lavenham and sired a son, Adam II, born in 1498. As a young man, this Adam moved to the national headquarters of the cloth industry, London. In 1526 he became a freeman of both the Clothworkers Company and the City. Enriched by the booming cloth trade, elected master of the Clothworkers Company in 1551, Adam II followed the pattern of so many successful London merchants, and in 1554 he bought himself a country estate. The place he chose was Groton, a mere six miles southeast of his birthplace, back among the web of relatives, friends, and business associates he had left three decades before. Much former monastic land had come on the market, and after 1540 there was "a rapid turnover of land in the area."[4] His grandson, our John, was born at Edwardstone, which merges into Groton, in 1588. His mother, Ann (Brown), was the daughter of an Edwardstone clothier. Her family also owned land at Prittlewell in southeast Essex. John was probably sent off to grammar school at Bury St. Edmunds, 16 miles to the northwest. He then proceeded to Trinity College, Cambridge, of which his father, Adam III, was auditor. Adam III was a younger son who had been trained as a lawyer before unexpectedly taking over the lordship of the manor of Groton. Like many gentlemen's sons at Cambridge, John did not take a degree; much more unconventional was his marriage at the tender age of 17. His bride was Mary Forth, an heiress from Great Stambridge in southeast Essex, 30 miles south of Groton. Mary's father had been born in Hadleigh, four miles east of Groton, and her cousins still lived there. Her brother had been a friend of John's at Trinity. The young couple divided their time between Groton and Great Stambridge.[5] A major attraction at Great Stambridge was the rector, Ezekiel Culverwell, one of the outstanding puritan apologists of his generation. In 1613, at the age of 25, John was entered at Gray's Inn, one of the London "law schools." Although most law students were unmarried and fresh from university, Winthrop typically needed a background in the law to manage estates and help run local government. His first wife died in 1615, and his next two came, respectively, from Groton itself and from Great Maplestead, 10 miles southwest. John was appointed a justice of the peace for Suffolk in 1617 and took over the active running of the family estate the next year, when he was 30. In 1623 he debated whether to follow his uncle and emigrate to Ireland. In 1627 Winthrop was appointed one of the attorneys of the Court of Wards in London and had to spend the four law terms of three to seven weeks there. The rest of the year he was in Groton. In the summer of 1629 he traveled first to the earl of Lincoln's seat at Sempringham in Lincolnshire to discuss New England settlement, and then to Cambridge in late August, where he signed the Agreement to emigrate. The seven remaining months of his life in England were a frenzy of planning and preparation with his time divided between London and Groton.

In some ways, the life Winthrop had led before he emigrated seems extraordinarily modern: the adolescent moving from place to place, the young adult moving away from his parental home, the specialist vocational training, the commuting marriage between 1627 and 1630, redundancy in 1629, the thought and then the act of emigration and the fresh start. He was even on his third marriage when he left. Yet, unlike the modern professional, Winthrop was first squireen, then squire, of Groton. There was always that residential center to his life, with its associations and familiar faces and places. Winthrop's letters both in England and in Massachusetts are full of references to Suffolk neighbors, kinsmen, and former servants. Through his parents, his ancestors, his wives, and his sisters he was related to many of the gentle and clothier families of the Stour Valley.[6] The Groton–Lavenham–Sudbury neighborhood was very much "home," as it had been for his family for more than a century and a half. It was on such strong pulls that Robert Ryece sought to play in his letter of 12 August 1629 seeking to deter his cousin from emigrating: "All your kynsfolkes and moste understandinge friendes wyll more reioyce at your stayeng at home. . . . how harde wyll it bee for one browghte up amonge bookes and learned men to lyve in a barbarous place where is no learnynge and lesse cyvillytie."[7] Whatever private agonies of decision Winthrop endured have been lost to us. One of the few personal reasons that he gave was his fear that his estate, once it had been shared with his three eldest sons, would anyway have to be sold; "he cannot live in the same place and callinge with that which remaines, his charge being still as great as before, when his meanes was double."[8] Threatened loss of the ancestral base made the prospect of emigration credible.

Winthrop had lived in five different places before he emigrated at the age of 42 in 1630. His mobility had three distinct causes. In his youth he was sent to two local cultural centers for education. He moved in his young adulthood because of marriage alliances and religious needs. Having inherited Groton in his mid-thirties, he became a part-time resident in London to help pay for his growing family and responsibilities.

An important part of being a gentleman (and a professional) was a wider geographical network of kin and acquaintance. The Winthrop correspondence before and after departure shows his relationship with such leading regional families as the D'Eweses, Barringtons, Springs, Cranes, Mildmays, Barnardistons, and Riches, as well as more local worthies like Robert Ryece, Brampton Gurdon, or Richard Harlakenden. As a justice of the peace, Winthrop worked at quarter or petty sessions with his fellow magistrates, most of whom were the heads of the gentry families of the county. His kinship involved London businessmen like Thomas Fones or professionals like Emmanuel Downing. Horizons were further widened by a branch of the family joining in the great transplantation to Munster in the south of Ireland during the 1590s and by his sister Lucy Downing moving to Dublin during the 1620s.[9]

Lucy's husband, Emmanuel Downing, who was Winthrop's fellow attorney at the Court of Wards, seems to confirm the pattern of the mobile gentleman-professional with wide horizons.[10] His family had lived for generations in Beccles on the border of Suffolk and Norfolk until his father, a Cambridge graduate, became the master of the grammar school at Ipswich (1589–1610), 33 miles to the south. Emmanuel went up to Cambridge in 1602, then attended the Inner Temple for legal training. His first wife was the daughter of an English official in Ireland.[11] After marrying Lucy Winthrop in 1622, he lived in Dublin and then in 1626 moved to London, where his brother Nathaniel was in trade and where three of his sisters had married merchants.[12] Emmanuel planned to emigrate in 1632, but Lucy, who bore three children in the early 1630s, feared the voyage, wilderness hardship, and poverty. Following offspring and servants who were sent ahead, the Downings finally immigrated to Salem in 1638. Emmanuel visited Britain in 1642, 1644, and 1652 and died there in 1660. His Harvard-educated son, Sir George, made a great career for himself in England and Scotland as a civil servant and politician.[13]

Emmanuel Downing appears thoroughly mobile, an urbanized professional. His perspective is national. His letters to his brother-in-law and nephew discuss crises in Parliament, the war in Europe, the broad geographical features of New England, investment and land sales on the London property market. Yet his family retained its East Anglian connections. Emmanuel's brother Joseph became rector of St. Stephen's, Ipswich. Joseph wrote to his "cousin" John Winthrop in 1634, mentioning other cousins in New England.[14] Lucy visited Maplestead, Ipswich, and Groton during the 1630s. When they came to choose a name for their home in Salem, they called it "Groton."

The largest adult gentle contingent was provided by the three Pelham brothers and a sister who immigrated to Massachusetts during the 1630s.[15] The family originated in East Anglia but had lived in Sussex during the sixteenth century. Enriched by the sale of timber to fuel iron smelting on the Sussex Weald, they had intermarried with the family of Lord De La Warr of Virginia fame. However, the emigrants' father, a distant relative of the earl of Lincoln, also owned land near Boston, Lincolnshire, and was buried there in 1624. He may have been drawn there by the national reputation of the Reverend John Cotton or by the pressure of an important cadet branch of the family at Brockelsby, Lincolnshire. William Pelham was temporarily marooned on the Isle of Wight in 1630 with Henry Winthrop when the wind suddenly shifted and the *Arbella* fleet got underway.[16] He settled in Cambridge, where he was joined in 1635 by his siblings John and Penelope. Herbert Pelham (1600–73) the eldest son, had married into a leading Essex family. His first wife was Jemima Waldegrave of Ferrers Court, Bures, a textile town on the banks of the Stour and the source of several migrant families. He immigrated to Cambridge, Massachusetts, in 1638, was a member of the colonial elite, but returned to Bures in 1647 with his third wife. She was Elizabeth, widow of a cadet of another north Essex gentle family, Roger Harlakenden. Pelham's sister Penelope married the magistrate Richard Bellingham from Lincolnshire, under circumstances that scandalized Winthrop, and remained in New England.[17]

In the brick church at Writtle, just outside Chelmsford, the county town of Essex, is a magnificent memorial to Sir Edward and Dorothy, Lady Pynchon. Sir Edward had died in 1627. His wife, a Weston, came from the next village of Roxwell, whence Henry Josselyn, son of Sir Thomas, immigrated to Maine as an agent of Sir Ferdinando Gorges, and his brother John went on two voyages to New England, which he described in a rather acid account finally published in 1674. Sir Edward's nephew, William Pynchon, was the son of John Pynchon of Springfield, adjacent to Writtle, and his mother, born Frances Brett, came from Terling, close by. The wife of the lord of the manor of Springfield was Alice, Lady Mildmay, John Winthrop's sister. William Pynchon was 40 when he sailed in the *Arbella* fleet. In mid-Atlantic, he was rowed across to the flagship to dine with the governor. His wife, Anna (Andrew), was a gentlewoman from Twywell, Northamptonshire, 64 miles northwest of Chelmsford. Her family had previously lived for generations in Warwickshire. How she and William met is something of a mystery. Pynchon is known to have had business contacts in London, 30 miles to the southwest. In 1621 he was in partnership with a city mercer, Thomas Brock, when they won £202 in damages against Thomas Elliott of Roxwell. Chelmsford was the grain market for the area providing London. William and Anna may have been introduced there, though another possibility is that there was a Springfield–Chelmsford family called Andrew, which may have been a branch of the Northampton clan. Pynchon had invested in the Massachusetts Bay Company, signed the Cambridge Agreement in 1629, and was treasurer of the fledgling colony.[18]

Higher education, long-distance marriages with concomitant acquisitions of land, professional duties, and the spiritual attraction of certain puritan ministers were the main contributors to the mobility of these gentlemen emigrants. Their eventual return to England may suggest that the pull of home remained strong, as does the long-delayed, reluctant emigration of Lucy Downing and Herbert Pelham.

Several members of the younger generation of gentlemen had lived quite mobile and even adventurous lives. Emmanuel Downing's eldest son, James, preceded him to Massachusetts in 1630. He had grown up partly in Dublin, partly in London.[19] The younger Winthrops had also been around. John Jr., after grammar school at Bury St. Edmunds, had been sent to Trinity College, Dublin, in 1622 at the age of 16 and then to the Inner Temple in London. In 1627 he took part in the military expedition to the Ile de Ré, a disastrous attempt to relieve the French Protestants besieged in La Rochelle. The following April he debated joining the pioneering voyage to Salem but instead went eastward to the Mediterranean and the Levant, visiting Leghorn, Zante, Constantinople, and Venice before returning overland to London, where he arrived in August 1629.[20] His younger brother Henry had meanwhile tried his hand none too successfully at planting in Barbados between 1627 and 1629.[21] The young Harry Vane, antinomian governor of Massachusetts in 1636–37, was the radical son of the comptroller of Charles I's household. He had been educated at Westminster School and Magdalen College, Oxford, before traveling in Europe and serving the English ambassador to Vienna in 1631.[22] Isaac Johnson, baptized at Stamford in western Lincolnshire, was the only other gentleman to attend university. This wealthy grandson of a bishop of Lincoln and an archdeacon of Leicester (the founder of both Uppingham and Oakham Schools in his native Rutland) went up to Emmanuel in 1617. He married the earl of Lincoln's sister in 1623 and settled at Sempringham.[23]

As Tables 5 and 6 show, however, these mobile gentlemen were hardly typical. Most upper-class voyagers came from much more stable backgrounds. They appear to have lived comparatively sedentary lives before embarking. Sometimes they had kinsfolk who lived at some distance, often maternal relatives. Thus Samuel Appleton's mother came from Wells Court in Kent;[24] the Gurdon brothers' maternal grandparents were Sedleys from Morley in Norfolk,[25] and Roger Harlakenden's mother had been raised at Stansted Mountfitchet, 22 miles west of Earl's Colne, the daughter of a wealthy clerk in Chancery.[26] Thomas Bradbury[27] was the great-nephew of Archbishop Whitgift, and Henry Gosnold[28] of Bury St. Edmunds was probably related to Bartholomew Gosnold, who had moved to the town after his marriage, before he perished in the founding of Virginia. John Moody,[29] son of George, a gentleman "famous for his housekeeping," was baptized at Moulton, near Newmarket, but spent some time in Bury where his wife had been born and where his brother Samuel was a leading citizen. John Haynes,[30] who bought Copford Hall near Colchester about 1620, had a brother living on other family lands at Much Hadham, 30 miles west, and a first wife from Hingham, Norfolk. Most of these ties were within the Greater East Anglia region. Other gentlemen married closer to home. As we shall see, a considerable number of those who emigrated were interrelated. Such links would expand horizons, but although visits would have been paid and repaid, these gentlemen seem to have led residentially stable and predictable lives.[31] Many of these emigrants came from the parish as opposed to the county gentry. Their families had usually been settled in their seats for generations and had intermarried with neighboring landowners. They are far more typical of upper-class planters than the cosmopolitan professionals or fringe members of the aristocracy.[32]

Winthrop, Downing, Pynchon, and Pelham were also unusual in being older than most gentle emigrants. Most of those whose ages are known were under 30. There was a slight peaking of men in their late thirties, like Herbert Pelham and John Humphrey, but young unattached or recently married men were more typical. Several youthful emigrants seem to have been under the tutelage of emigrant patriarchs. The Gurdons, William Pelham, Benjamin Brand, and Robert Sampson were near neighbors of John Winthrop. The *Winthrop Family Papers* imply that John and Margaret were keeping an eye on these sprigs. Similarly, Charles Fiennes seems to have traveled with Isaac Johnson. Other young gentlemen were the sons or siblings of older leaders, like John Jr. and Henry Winthrop, John Pelham, and James Downing. Younger sons are less predominant than among gentle emigrants to other colonies.[33]

Though the age balance tended toward the young, the older gentlemen emigrants were the men who organized and led settlement and expansion: Winthrop, Pynchon, Humphrey, Pelham, and Haynes.[34] One or two young men assumed public responsibilities: John Winthrop, Jr., as a founder of Ipswich, Saybrook, and New London; the Cooke brothers as representatives at the General Court; and Henry Vane as one-term antinomian governor of Massachusetts. They were exceptional, however. Some older men were far less influential in government than anticipated. Samuel Appleton was a deputy at the General Court for one year only. John Humphrey returned to England after seven years, a disillusioned and much poorer man. Emmanuel Downing served as deputy, judge of the county court, and recorder of deeds. These were very modest challenges for a man of his talent and experience.

Another striking feature of these gentle emigrants from the eastern counties is the number that went back to their roots. Thirteen of the 36 returned permanently to England. This suggests that even after the trauma of emigrating, the pull of home continued to exert its influence on these men. They had the means to gratify it. Transplantation for most of them was not an extension of prior restlessness but rather a yanking out of very deep roots.

As a group, the 36 Greater East Anglian gentlemen do not appear to have wielded the administrative influence we might have expected. Too many were too young, or too impermanent, or too unassertive. Of course, the two Winthrops, Haynes, and Pynchon were important shapers of policy and attitudes. They were the only members of our group to be regularly elected to governorships or assistantships. Of these, the elder Winthrop, despite his seemingly modern life of mobility before emigrating, was, once in New England, profoundly conservative. His most dearly held convictions and intentions were overwhelmingly traditional: authority, hierarchy, uniformity, community, cooperation, and providence were his watchwords. In Boston, he had advocated the rationing of land against those who agitated for large and rapid allocations. Though he had been granted over 2,000 acres by 1640 (his wife a further 3,000) and had received more than £1,000 for his service as governor, his duties led to his dying nearly bankrupt. Before migrating to Connecticut, Haynes had shown his ultraconservatism by criticizing Winthrop for leniency![35]

Cases have been made for the younger Winthrop and Pynchon as influences for change, as examples of what used to be called "bourgeois gentry." Winthrop was a restless mover in the New World and a famous projector. By 1657, he had lived in Boston, Salem, Ipswich, Saybrook, New London, New Haven, and Hartford. He was elected a Fellow of the Royal Society, experimented with technological innovation, owned a telescope, collected a huge library containing many modern works, and followed the latest practice as a doctor. He opposed persecution and acted the conciliator rather than the crusader. He indulged in widespread and large-scale land speculation. A biographer epitomizes him as "All things to all men, a highly receptive person, open to new ideas, adaptable to new situations." Though he has been depicted as a forerunner of Benjamin Franklin, he retained many reactionary traits. His explanation for libels against Massachusetts in England was that "the divell stirs up his instruments where he is so mightily opposed." He firmly rejected all ideas about dismantling hierarchy and could still turn to providence and prayer to explain or allay secular crises. Much of his "scientific" research and many of his books were on the subject of alchemy. His involvement in the promotion of the early iron industry reveals him as more concerned about community self-sufficiency than international profit making. Winthrop's period of wide-ranging influence only began in the 1650s, a decade often associated with the accession to power of the second generation in New England.[36]

William Pynchon emerges from his account books as a hard-driving fur trader and frontier developer. He was, nonetheless, forced to leave the colony because he refused to recant published religious opinions deemed heretical by the Massachusetts authorities. Theological studies absorbed the rest of his life after his return to England. Despite being attuned to the embryonic transatlantic market, he was at the same time a fervent believer in witchcraft. Unlike the younger Winthrop, there is no evidence of widespread travel before he embarked for America. However, Pynchon did have commercial contacts in London. As early as 1633, he and the younger Winthrop worked together in a consortium with Emmanuel Downing and his brother-in-law Francis Kirby in London to export beaver skins and import dry goods to the colony. Though Connecticut accused Pynchon in 1639 of trying to monopolize the Indian trade "and so to rack the country at his pleasure," he indignantly refuted the charge and claimed to be the colony's defender against Indian racketeering. By the time he withdrew to England in 1652, he had invested heavily in the central Connecticut Valley, and Springfield was a "company town" under his patronage. His son John, often a commercial partner of the younger Winthrop, would build on his father's fur monopoly and landed investment to become the political and economic power broker of western Massachusetts.[37]

One of the three towns John Winthrop, Jr., founded was Ipswich, in 1633, to which several Greater East Anglian entrepreneurs and gentlemen were attracted, including Samuel Appleton, Brampton Gurdon, and John Thorndike. The town developed into a major trading center second only to Boston in wealth. Raising cattle for market, it had "many hundred quarters of meat to spare yearly and feed at the latter end of summer the town of Boston." Ipswich soon had a committee for furthering trade and an endowed grammar school. Samuel Appleton ran the town's malthouse, and Winthrop encouraged the setting up of an iron bloomery. Its land was quickly allocated and as quickly bought and sold, reflecting the active land market back in Suffolk and Essex. Town government in Ipswich was oligarchic, reminiscent of the East Anglian closed vestries or of boroughs like its Suffolk namesake. East Anglian gentlemen also dominated Boston and Salem, the other two major Massachusetts trading centers.[38]

Though most gentlemen emigrants had horizons that might be countywide or even transcend county boundaries, they had not usually led mobile lives before emigrating. Bernard Bailyn has argued that, like the elder Winthrop or Haynes, such transplanted landowners exerted a conservative influence on the fledgling New England colonies. They opposed such reforms as the codification of the laws and liberties, the constraining of magisterial discretion, and the uncontrolled actions of market forces. They reproduced hierarchical land divisions and status values in the places where they settled and kept their inferiors in order.[39] Certainly a majority of them had lived comparatively sedentary lives back home, and some of them bore the stamp of "backwoods gentry" long before they encountered the backwoods of New England.

Yet, as the example of Ipswich suggests, the gentlemen emigrants cannot be that easily categorized. A few, like the younger Winthrop, William Pynchon, and the founders of Ipswich, were "developmental" and "entrepreneurial," perhaps reflecting broader horizons deriving from prior overseas experience or contact with London. Though the senior Winthrop and Haynes come across as more conservative, seeking a cleansed traditional society, attitudes were not clear-cut. Entrepreneurs could be deeply religious; utopians were concerned to improve material life. Though some historians have claimed that the elder Winthrop's communitarian vision had vanished by the 1640s, there is considerable evidence to suggest that gentlemen and other leaders of colonial life did not seriously start seeking "profits in the wilderness" until the 1650s, as the younger emigrants or second generation assumed control.[40]

Clergy

The other leaders of Greater East Anglian migration were those "faithful shepherds," the clergy. Indeed, some scholars have argued that their power of persuasion was wider and deeper than that of the gentry.[41] Their vocation had undergone a major reform during the last two generations. The old "dumb dogs," nonpreaching, ill-educated, and often woefully underpaid parson-farmers whose morals and behavior reflected rather than uplifted their parishioners', were being replaced by university graduates.[42] In the case of the puritan clergy, reformation of manners and spiritual conversion were two major objectives of their frequent sermons and lectures, their catechizing, and their moral wardship. Their leaders, men like John Cotton, Thomas Hooker, or John

44

Rogers, undoubtedly exerted influence far beyond the bounds of their own parishes to a regional or national level. According to a Laudian official, Rogers of Dedham, north Essex, a major emigrant center, "hath troubled the country these thirty years, and did poison all these parts for ten miles round about that place." Sir Thomas Barrington sent his sons across Essex to Braintree, another emigrant town, to board with the Reverend Samuel Collins, "whose name God hath made precious among the saints." Placed outside the social hierarchy by their learning and their cloth, they could on occasion correct and upbraid the gentry and even the nobility. Thus Ezekiel Rogers felt he had the right and duty to warn the formidable Joan Lady Barrington to be more discriminating about the company she kept.[43] There is no question that the clergy had enormous influence over the godly. Here we investigate the extent of their residential and occupational mobility, the breadth of their horizons, and whether they were likely to exercise their authority in the direction of continuity or change. (See Tables 7 and 8.)

The new clerical vocation demanded considerable occupational mobility from those who felt and answered God's call. Typically, a clergyman could expect to live in at least four places during his life span: his childhood home, his university college, his curacy (or college fellowship or domestic chaplaincy or schoolmastership), and his benefice as a vicar or rector. Since there were only two universities in England, undergraduates might have to travel relatively long distances for their higher education. Life at university (all but two East Anglian emigrants went to Cambridge) could introduce clever young men to the wider world of patronage and to a national rather than a local range of career opportunities.

Table 7, listing the 37 emigrant clergy, and Table 8, analyzing their mobility, show that there are indeed examples of long-range movement among the clergy. Fifteen moved between 40 and 100 miles from their homes to clerical posts, and 11 traveled over 100 miles from well outside the region of the eastern counties. Five came over 100 miles to attend Cambridge, and 19 traveled between 40 and 99 miles. Fifteen had moved twice since graduating, three three times, and one four times. This did not include exile to the Netherlands (as endured by Hooker, Peter, and Weld) before immigration to New England.

Several of the clergy who did move long distances from their home towns to their benefices were the leading voices of their generations: Ward, Wilson, Hooker, and Cotton among the older emigrants, and Shepard, Knowles, and Peter among the younger.[44] They were a cut

Table 7. Clerical Emigrants

AG	Name	Age	DOB	DOE	BP	Dist. to Univ. (from BP)	FR	College, BA	Cure†	Dist. from BP
4	John ALLEN	c40	c1597	1637				Christ's '17	Wrentham S; c; Saxlingham N, v, c '24	
2	Thos ALLEN*	30	1608	1638	Norwich N	66	Norwich	Caius '28	Norwich, v	0
2	Fran BRIGHT*	26	1603	1629	London	57		New, Ox. '25	Rayleigh E, c '25	25
3	Edm BROWN	32	1606	1638	Lavenham S	29		Emm '28	Gt.Bromley E, dc; Sudbury S, c	17,6
3	Geo BURDETT	33	1602	1635	Saffron Walden E	290		Trin, Dub. '23	Yarmouth N, l '25–'32; Norwich, l '32–'35	77,68
3	Jonathan BURR	34	1605	1639	Redgrave S	38		Corpus '23	Horringer S, c; Rickinghall S, v '27	17,2
2	Thos CARTER	25	1610	1635	Hinderclay S	38	Hinderclay area	St. John's '30		
6	John COTTON	48	1585	1633	Derby	116		Trin '02	Cambridge, f; Boston L, v '12	116,60
6	Tim DALTON	48	1588	1636				St. John's '13	Woolverstone S, v '16	
2	Nat EATON*	28	1609	1637	Gt.Budworth, Ches	160		Trin '30	Salcott/Gt.Wigborough E, c, s	170
2	John ELIOT	27	1604	1631	Widford, Herts	26	Bishop's Stortford (5)	Jesus '23	Lit.Baddow E, s	23
4	John FISKE	36	1601	1637	St.Jas.S.Elmham S	53	Laxfield (6)	Peterhse '29	St.Jas.S.Elmham S, s	0
3	Pet HOBART	31	1604	1635	Hingham N	44	Hingham area (3)	Mag '26	Southwold S, s; Haverhill S, c	34,41

No.	Name	Age			Place	No.		College	Church	No.
6	Thos HOOKER	47	1586	1633	Marshfield, Leics	70		Emm '08	Cambridge, f, '09–'18; Esher, Surrey, v '20; Chelmsford E, l '25; Lit.Baddow E, s, '29; Neths '31	70,100, 90,93, (180)
4	Thos JAMES	37	1595	1632	Boston L	55		Emm '14	Boston L, s 1619	0
2	Thos JENNER*	30	1605	1635	Fordham E	33	Fordham	Christ's mat. '24		
4	Hans KNOLLYS*	40	1598	1638	Cawkwell L	106		St.Cath Hall '29	Humberston L, v '31–'34	16
3	John KNOWLES*	33	1606	1639	?Sutton L	56		Mag '23	Cambridge, f '27; Col-ch'r E, l '35	56,85
2	Wm LEVERITCH	30	1603	1633	Drawlington, Warws	96		Emm '26	Gt.Livermere S, v '31	100
2	John NORTON	29	1606	1635	Bps.Stortford, Herts	23	Bps.Stortf'd area (7)	Peterhse '24	Bps.Stortf'd, c, s '24; Hi.Laver E, dc	0,9
8	Rob PECK*	58	1580	1638	Beccles S	68	Beccles	Mag '99	Hingham N, v '05	26
4	Hugh PETER*	36	1599	1635	Fowey, Corn-wall	280	Antwerp (315)	Trin '18	Laindon E, c '23; Lon-don, l, Neths '29	250,240, 230(310)
9	John PHILLIPS*	56	1582	1638				Emm '04	Wrentham S, v '09	
4	Geo PHILLIPS	37	1593	1630	S.Raynham N	54		Caius '14	Boxted E, c '15	55
6	Ezek ROGERS	48	1590	1638	Wethersfield E	24	Dedham E (22)	Christ's '04	Hatfield B.Oak E, dc; Rowley, Yks, v '21	14,140
4	Nat ROGERS	38	1598	1636	Haverhill S	16	Dedham E (25)	Emm '18	Bocking E, c '19; As-sington S, v '30	20,8
2	Thos SHEPARD	30	1605	1635	Towcester, N'ha'nts			Emm '23	Earl's Colne E, l; But-tercrambe, Yks, dc; Heddon, N'umbl'd, l	75,125, 200
5	Sam SKELTON	45	1584	1629	Coningsby L	65		Clare Hall '11	Sempringham L, c, v '15, dc '20	18

Table 7. *Continued*

AG	Name	Age	DOB	DOE	BP	Dist. to Univ. (from BP)	FR	College, BA	Cure†	Dist. from BP
3	John WARD	33	1606	1639	Haverhill S	16	Haverhill	Emm '26	Hadleigh E, v '33	35
8	Nat WARD*	56	1578	1634	Haverhill S	16	Haverhill	Emm '00	Ebbing, Germany, dc '20; Stondon Massey E, v '24	(350),28
4	Thos WATERHOUSE*	c39	c1600	1639	London	34		Emm '35	Coddenham S, c, v	65
4	Thos WELD*	37	1595	1632	Sudbury S	26	Sudbury area (3)	Trin '13	Haverhill S, c '19; Terling E, v '24	13,18
4	John WHEELWRIGHT	38	1598	1636	Saleby L	82		Sidney Sx '14	Belleau L, c; Bilsby L, v '23	3,2
4	Sam WHITING	39	1597	1636	Boston L	55	Kirton L (2)	Emm '17	Stiffkey N, dc '21; Lynn N, c '24; Skirbeck L, v '25	32,24,1
2	Rog WILLIAMS	27	1603	1630	London	54	St. Albans, Herts (15)	Pemb '27	Hi.Laver E, dc '29	23
5	John WILSON	42	1588	1630	Windsor, Berks	55		King's '09	Cambridge, f; Sudbury S, l '20	60,65
4	John YOUNGS	39	1598	1637	Carlton S	66	Yarmouth N (30)	Emm '20	Covehithe S, v	13

Notes: All colleges are Cambridge unless otherwise noted. Numbers in parentheses in FR column are distances from birthplace; numbers in parentheses in last column refer to overseas exiles.
*Returned to England.
†c = curate, dc = domestic chaplain, f = fellow, l = lecturer, s = schoolmaster, v = vicar or rector. Numbers are dates of appointment.

Table 8. Clergy: All Professional Moves

AG	Age	No.	Distance, BP:Cures (miles)											Total Moves
			0–4	5–9	10–14	15–19	20–39	40–59	60–79	80–99	100+	200+	UK	
1	21–25													
2	26–30	10	2	1			3		1		2	2	2	13
3	31–35	6	1	1		2	2	2	2	1				11
4	36–40	12	5	1	2	2	3	1	1			3	2	20
5	41–45	2				1			2					3
6	46–50	4			1				2	2	3		1	9
7	51–55													
8	56–60	3					2					1	1	4
9	61–65													
Totals		37	8	3	3	5	10	3	8	3	5	6	6	60

Note: 13 moved once, 15 moved twice, 3 thrice, 1 four times, and 4 unknown, a total of 56 known moves.

above the run-of-the-mill parish clergy. Their reputations and ambitions no doubt gave them a wider appeal and outlook. One or two others were clerical rolling stones. George Burdett[45] was a man of unsteady theological and sexual reputation, and Nathaniel Eaton[46] turned out to be a sadist and an alcoholic during his brief, inglorious term as the first head of Harvard. William Leveritch was restlessly mobile in the New World, moving some eight times, always to fringe settlements, during his 44-year sojourn.[47]

Yet many ordained emigrants did start their transatlantic journeys from places quite close to where they grew up. One out of three was ministering less than 20 miles from his childhood home and one-half within 40 miles. Roger Williams and John Norton were successively chaplains to the Masham family at Otes, High Laver, in northwest Essex. Both came from the adjacent county of Hertfordshire (as did many other emigrants). Norton was a Bishop's Stortford man, and Williams came from a St. Albans merchant and clerical family.[48] John Eliot, the Apostle to the Indians, was also raised in the Essex–Hertfordshire borderlands. Though he had spent some time in eastern Essex at Little Baddow, near Chelmsford, he evidently emigrated from his home village of Nazeing.[49] Thomas Allen, who became minister of Charlestown in 1639, had fled as a "notable and dangerous refractory" from his parish of St. Edmund in Norwich. Norwich was the city of his birth and of his ancestors.[50] John Phillip of Wrentham near the north Suffolk coast came from a family long settled in the neighboring South Elmham parish of St. James.[51] Mrs. Hutchinson's ally and probable kinsman, John Wheelwright, emigrated from the Lincolnshire parish of Bilsby near Alford. He had been born at Saleby, two miles away, and his first wife was the daughter of his predecessor at Bilsby.[52] The forebears of Samuel Whiting had been merchants and councilmen of the Lincolnshire port of Boston. He served briefly as chaplain to the linked north Norfolk families of Bacon and Townshend, then as curate of Boston's sister port of King's Lynn before returning in 1625 as rector of Skirbeck, which is nowadays an integral part of his birthplace.[53] Nathaniel Rogers, vicar of the Gurdon village of Assington, was a scion of a famous clerical family, the son of the Reverend John Rogers, the mighty thunderer of Dedham, the former Gurdon residence eight miles to the east. The Rogers family had been associated with Dedham since 1383. Other examples can be seen in Table 7. Eighteen of the 37 clerical emigrants had held office in the county of their birth. Had there not been a serious shortage of openings, more might have done so.[54]

Why were so many clergy so "parochial"? Where benefices depended on lay patronage, many studious young men would have been well known to local patrons before they went up to Cambridge. Alternatively, a local sponsor might recommend them as "sound in religion" to one of the great regional patrons like the earl of Warwick.[55] Cambridge might be less of a national clearinghouse than it later became. Most Norfolk men went to one college, Caius.[56] The recent foundation of Emmanuel was also well attended by East Anglian puritans, including lay patrons like Warwick, Sir Thomas Pelham, two sons of Brampton Gurdon, and one of Sir William Spring, financier of emigration. Its graduates regularly returned to puritan benefices in their home neighborhoods.[57] During the 1630s, St. Catherine's Hall also became fashionable with puritan laymen like Barnardiston, Masham, and D'Ewes; much credit for this must go to the 1639 emigrant, the Reverend John Knowles, a brilliant and magnetic tutor there until 1635. Trinity was probably the only Cambridge college attended by eventual emigrants that had a wider recruitment area. It was the college of the adopted East Anglian from Cornwall, Hugh Peter. However, even there, Thomas Weld, the early victim and later tormentor of Archbishop Laud and founder-minister of Roxbury, Massachusetts, went out from Great Court, Trinity, in the same direction from which he had come: to Haverhill, Suffolk, 12 miles west of his birthplace, Sudbury, then on to Terling, Essex, 17 miles to the south.[58]

Although many clergy who went to New England had strong ties to the eastern counties, their horizons might well be countywide or farther afield. Within their counties they are known to have traveled frequently. Winthrop's father records having heard 36 different preachers at the tiny wool town of Boxford in the single year of 1620. The 1634 will of Gilbert Seaman of Mendlesham in northern Suffolk (a kinsman of the 1630 emigrant) listed 15 puritan clergymen as beneficiaries. They had all been to Mendlesham to preach and were due again, "according to their courses." Such combination lectures as well as regular official gatherings of clergy and secret conventicles of puritan ministers all added to their breadth of outlook.[59]

Though Robert Peck, John Phillip, Timothy Dalton, and John Cotton had all been in their cures for two decades at least, most clerical emigrants were younger men. Nearly one-third were in the 26–30 years age band. This was the time in the life cycle when people were often bringing a period of mobility to an end and starting to settle down. We may think of Roger Williams, John Norton, John Eliot, or Nathaniel Eaton as typical: either just married or just about to be, still domestic chaplains, teachers, and/or curates, a career chosen but barely launched. The other prominent age group was the 36–40-year-olds, men like Weld of Roxbury, Massachusetts, Wheelwright of Boston, Massachusetts, Youngs of Southold, Long Island, or Nathaniel Rogers of Ipswich, Massachusetts, who came from established callings. They had begun making reputations as the leaders of the puritan agitation for cleansing church and society and for resisting Arminian innovations. Nine of these 12 left in the second half of the 1630s, when persecution became systematic and pervasive.[60] These two age groups mirror the leading overall male emigrant figures, bearing in mind that it was unusual to become ordained before one's mid-twenties.

A final clerical characteristic deserves notice. Like the gentry—the lay rulers with whom they shared authority in New England—an unusually high proportion returned to England. Eleven of the 37 emigrants and four young men who were subsequently ordained ended their days in England. Some like Robert Peck and John Phillip were elderly men long established in English parishes. Once Laudian persecution was halted in the early 1640s, they abandoned the wilderness. Nathaniel Ward was 68 when he returned to London in 1646, partly because of ill health and partly to see his *Simple Cobler of Agawam* through the press. Others returned on colony business but stayed. Such were Hugh Peter, so influential in Civil War England, and Thomas Weld.[61] What is significant about these countermigrants is that they often took up posts back in England close to the parishes they had left. In 1651 Thomas Allen returned to Norwich, where 13 years earlier his parishioners had been "addicted to his views." Young William Ames, after graduating from Harvard in 1645, lived out his life as teacher of the congregation in his mother's hometown of Wrentham, Suffolk.[62] Ward's new cure was at Shenfield, Essex, only four miles from his old one at Stondon Massey. John Sams of the Maldon landowning family ministered at Kelvedon and Coggeshall, both within an hour's ride of home.[63] Richard Jennings had just graduated from St. Catherine's College, Cambridge, when he left England in 1636. Nine years later he was inducted at Grundisburgh, five miles from his Ipswich birthplace.[64] Thomas Waterhouse spent only three years in New England. By the mid-1640s he was ministering to the parishioners of Ash Bocking, the neighbor to Coddenham, which he had left in 1639.[65] Immigration to the New World did not upset the persistent localism of these men.

More than any other occupational group, except for the small subgroup of gentlemen-professionals, the clergy had been displaced from ancient roots and personal surroundings. They had other characteristics that might make them open to change: university education, social position based on achievement, belief in a culture of hard work, family discipline, and individual conscience, calling and conversion. A significant number came from bourgeois-mercantile backgrounds.[66] A clergyman, John White of Dorchester, had initiated puritan settlement in Massachusetts in 1624 and had been a dynamic force behind the formation of the Massachusetts Bay Company and the decision to emigrate in 1629. John Wilson made hazardous return journeys to recruit further settlers during the 1630s. Six divines from East Anglia were in the first wave of emigration between 1628 and 1632. Hugh Peter and Nathaniel Ward were both active boosters of commerce and industry in New England.[67] Thomas Hooker, Roger Williams, and John Wheelwright helped found new colonies. John Youngs, Edmund Brown, and John Fiske led new settlements in the wilderness.[68] The very act of emigration made all the clergy rebels against the established order in England.

Some ministers continued this spirit of opposition in early Massachusetts. George Phillips led Watertown's protest against taxation without representation in 1631. John Eliot spoke out three years later against the magistrates treating with the Pequot Indians without "the consent of the people." Nathaniel Ward, Ezekiel Rogers, Peter Hobart, and Thomas Hooker were all outspoken critics of unchecked magisterial power.[69]

The most profound change they wrought was in the new church they created in America. Evidence survives that Cotton, Hooker, Norton, Shepard, Ezekiel and Nathaniel Rogers, George Phillips, Peter, Peck, and Eliot had all ministered to gathered churches of the godly before they had left England. Others probably had also. The intense sabbatarianism of New England was likewise imported from their English practice, which had been outraged by the 1633 reissue of the Book of Sports. Without that gratuitous provocation, according to Hugh Peter, "many had staid." New England's rejection of surplices, ceremonies, altars, icons, episcopal courts, and episcopal hierarchies were all foreshadowed in England. They were all nonetheless revolutionary as a new orthodoxy in the New World. The effect of puritan reimposition of discipline, industry, improvement, and single-mindedness was a powerful intensification of energy.[70]

Paradoxically, though, revolutionary ideologies can be not only reactive but also reactionary. Caroline puritanism has been seen as a response to a sense of rising evil, disorder, change, and authoritarianism, and there are powerful reasons for considering the clergy as a group a strongly conservative influence. Clergy who appeared politically radical were often defending local interests against the center. Those divines who questioned authority were usually in the minority. Most preferred "to uphold the honor and power of the magistrates" rather than encourage the liberty of the people and their deputies. They advocated a bond of love between rulers and ruled rather than the obligations of accountability. They were vehement supporters of hierarchical order, "a speaking aristocracy in the face of a silent majority." John Cotton typified their viewpoint with his famous question, "If all would be governors, who should be governed?" Cotton likewise spoke for many of his clerical brethren when he criticized usury and advocated the medieval principle of the just price. He assumed inherent antagonism between material and spiritual values. "There will ever be difference between the world and the church" was the reiterated message of all preachers. It justified the colonial policy of tying "power to piety in place of worldly standards."[71]

The clerical training in Ramistic logic at Cambridge perpetuated the ancient system of deductive reasoning from general to particular rather than the inductive experimental approach championed by Francis Bacon. Much of the clergy's considerable learning was directed toward deeper understanding of Scripture and to the interpretation of daily events and historical process in terms of divine providence. They "exhibited no special concern over the extension of the mind for the solution of problems of earthly existence." Rather than developing a self-conscious profession, most emigrant clergy whose reasons are known described their choice of career as answering God's insistent call.[72] Finally, most of them left England because they were either subject to church disciplinary procedures or under imminent threat. Cotton, Hooker, Peter, and Ward had all been approached by the Massachusetts Bay Company in 1629, but all declined at the time. Hooker, Weld, and Peter preferred exile in the Netherlands, and Cotton initially planned to join them.[73] Some younger men, like Williams, Fiske, and Norton, could not get cures because of their conscientious objections to Laudian innovations. Samuel Rogers, a young Essex divine, friend and kinsman of emigrants, considered leaving England but wavered in face of family opposition and fears about "future accommodations." Once he found a chaplaincy, New England quickly receded from his mind. He stayed, along with the vast majority of the puritan clergy. Of those who left, most did not make a positive choice to emigrate, to lead "an errand into the wilderness" for the "Calvinist International." They did not jump; they were pushed.[74]

Clergy and gentlemen led the Great Migration. Though their status and education gave them broader horizons, many of them had previously kept close to ancient seats and places of birth. A minority of each group, older, more widely oriented gentlemen with London connections and regionally recognized divines, often former Cambridge dons, were most active. These gentlemen were largely responsible for launching colonization; the ministers, reluctant refugees, led the second and third waves as Laudian persecution intensified. Though they claimed to be only cleansers and purifiers of corrupted English ways, they helped create in both church and state a reoriented society. We defer judgment on the extent of New England change until the contribution of other groups can be evaluated.

4

The Enterprising Sort:
Mercantile, Professional,
and Entrepreneurial Emigrants

F OR AT least a century and a half, historians have debated the relationship between puritanism and capitalism. In some cases, puritanism has
been seen as a prerequisite if not a cause of the rise of capitalism; others
have depicted the puritans as essentially otherworldly. In recent years,
the most thoughtful contributions have been those which sought to
reconcile extremes and to demonstrate that apparent opposites were less
mutually exclusive than they had been made to seem.

The classic model of New England history, as Jack Greene has recently reminded us, is the declension model. This stands in contrast
to his developmental model, which characterized colonial aims and
achievements to the south of puritan settlement. The sources of decline
from utopian origins were seen by contemporaries as manifold, but one
common target was "the enterprising sort of people," those engaged in
commerce, manufacturing, and the professions.[1]

The founders of the Massachusetts Bay Company were dominated by
a group of London merchants, lawyers, and manufacturers under the
governorship of Matthew Craddock. Without their financial support,
the *Arbella* fleet would never have sailed.[2] Once settled, several emigrants from the eastern counties quickly began trading with the Indians, with England, or with needy new arrivals. The classic declension
model depicts such settlers as ideologically at odds with the high-
minded traditionalism of community leaders like Winthrop or Cotton.
A tragic example cited as symbolic of this conflict is that of the Reverend John Wilson's brother-in-law, Robert Keayne, a Boston merchant
punished for profiteering in time of shortage. In 1639, the values of the

puritans condemned the values of the Yankees; sooner or later, it is claimed, they would succumb to them.[3]

Mercantile Emigrants

Of the 85 emigrants classified as "the enterprising sort of people," the 54 engaged in trade are listed in Table 9. Of these, 31 called themselves "merchants" or "traders," 12 were connected full- or part-time with merchant shipping, 14 were involved with the retail or wholesale trades, and three were innkeepers before they emigrated.[4] They had lived mostly in market towns or ports. Seven either traded in or had close connections with London,[5] and five came from Norwich.[6] Life in commercial centers could be expected to open people's eyes to the possibilities of progress.[7]

However, when we examine the factor with which we are particularly concerned, mobility, the mercantile group looks decidedly stable. The great majority were born in or within 10 miles of the market towns in which they did their business. In some cases merchants who moved longer distances did so for noncommercial reasons. Both William Coddington and Thomas Willett moved their homes in the old country for religious reasons.[8] Thomas Coytmore and William Vassall were sons of wealthy London merchants. They had their countinghouses and wharves in the shadow of the Tower of London but owned rural estates in the Essex countryside, 30 miles down the Thames Estuary.[9] The English movements of two ship captains, Edmund Thompson and John Cullick, are clouded in mystery.[10] Removing these anomalies from the tables would make all but two of the merchants operate within a 15-mile radius of where they were born, or a morning's easy ride. Although it has been difficult to trace the family roots of some merchants, 57 percent of those traceable (24 out of 41) grew up in or very near where their families had been settled for at least two generations before their own, 74 percent (31 out of 41) under 10 miles.[11] The fact that 9 out of 54 sets of family roots cannot be traced and that five more were relative newcomers may indicate geographical mobility, but lost records may be to blame.

It would be a mistake to conclude that men engaged in commerce tended to lead static lives. Some traders like Edmund Onge, a shopkeeper in Lavenham's market square, or Alexander Knight, the Chelmsford innkeeper, would stay put by the very nature of their jobs. So would Norwich grocers like Simon Huntington, John Baker, and

Table 9. Mercantile Emigrants

AG	Name	Age	DOB	DOE	Trade	BP	FR		Trade Location	Distances BP:FR	BP:WP
3	John ALLEN	30	1605	1635	Merchant/shipowner	Haverhill S	Mildenhall S area	No		18	
4	Wm ANDREWS	c34	1600	c1634	Shipmaster	Bramford S		No	Ipswich S		3
2	Edm ANGIER	24	1612	1636	Woolen draper	Dedham E	Colchester E area	1518B	Dedham E	7	0
5	John BAKER	36/9	1598	1637/40	Grocer	Norwich N	Norwich N	1566A	Norwich N	0	0
3	Wm BROWN†	26	1609	1635	Fishmonger	?Brandon S	?Thetford N	1593B		5	
7	Clem CHAPLIN*†‡	48	1587	1635	Chandler/clerk	Semer S		No	Bury S		14
5	Eph CHILD†‡	37	1593	1630	Merchant	Bury St.E. S	W of Bury S	1462C	Bury S	2/5	0
3	Wm COCKRAM*	26	1609	1635	Mercer/mariner	E.Bergholt S		No	Southwold S		40
3	Wm CODDINGTON†‡	29	1601	1630	Merchant	Grantham L	Grantham L	No	Gr'm/Boston L	0	26
4	John COGGESHALL†	31	1601	1632	Mercer	Halstead E	Hundon S	1337A	Castle Hedingham E	9	4
11	Sam COLE			1630	Tavernkeeper	Navestock E	Brentwood E	1529B	Brentwood E	4	4
3	Thos COYTMORE*	26	1611	1637	Merchant/shipowner	Prittlewell E		No	Wapping, London		30
3	John CROMWELL	c30	c1600	1630	Trader	Woodbridge S		No	Woodbridge S		0
11	John CULLICK†			by1639	Ship captain	Upminster E	Felsted E	No	Felsted E		35

Ref	Name	Age			Occupation	Origin 1	Origin 2	Code	NE place		
3	Nich DAVISON	28	1611	1639	Trader/sea captain	Norwich N	Norwich N	N1	Norwich N	0	0
6	Giles FIRMIN	c42	c1590	1632	Apothecary	Sudbury S	Glemsford S area	1441B	Sudbury S	5	0
11	Wm FOSTER	61	1575	1634	Shipmaster	Suffolk	Ipswich S	1474B	Lavenham S	4	0
10	Wm HAMMOND	23	1607	1636	Trader	Lavenham S	Lawshall S	1440A	Maldon E	6	6
2	Rob HARDING†			1630	Mariner/ merchant	Boreham E	Witham E	1557A			
3	Val HILL†‡	26	1610	1636	Merchant	Croft L	Authorpe L	No	Alford L	14	10
5	Jos HILLS†‡	36	1602	1638	Woolen draper	Gt. Burstead E	Ingatestone E	No	Maldon E	3	13
8	Atherton HOUGH†	c52	c1580	1633	Merchant	Coningsby L	Coningsby L	No	Boston L	0	15
7	Sim HUNTINGTON	50	1583	1633	Grocer	Norwich N	Blyth-borough S area	N1	Norwich N	20	0
2	Nich KNAPP	25	c1605	1630	?Vendor of medicines	Bures S	Bures S	1521A	Bures S	0	0
4	Alex KNIGHT	c35	c1600	1635	Innkeeper	Chelmsford E	Chelmsford E	1666A	Chelmsford E	0	0
4	Rich LEEDS†	32	1665	1637	Navigator	Yarmouth N	Yarmouth N	1579A	Yarmouth N	0	0
7	Jos LOOMIS	c48	c1590	1638	Woolen draper	Braintree E	Braintree E	1567A	Braintree E	0	0
5	John MILLS†	c38	c1592	1630	Merchant/ innkeeper	Cockfield S	Lavenham S area	1521B	Lavenham S	4	4
5	Jos MYGATT†‡	37	1596	1633	Merchant/Indian trader	Roxwell E		No	Chelmsford E		4
8	John NEWGATE*	53	1580	1633	Merchant/ haberdasher	Hornings-heath S	Hornings-heath S area	1530A	Bury S	2	3

59

Table 9. *Continued*

AG	Name	Age	DOB	DOE	Trade	BP	FR		Trade Location	Distances	
										BP: FR	BP: WP
4	Edm ONGE	c34	c1596	1630	Shopkeeper	Lavenham S	Sudbury/Lav'ham S	1506A	Lavenham S	4	0
6	Rob PAYNE†‡	44	1595	1639	Merchant	Naughton S	Lawshall S	1533A	Hadleigh S	4	5
7	Thos RUCKE*†	c47	1591	by1638	Draper	Maldon E		N1	Maldon E		0
3	John SALES	c28	c1602	1630	Merchant	Lavenham S		No	Lavenham S	0	0
3	Rich SCOTT	29	1605	1634	Merchant/clothier	Glemsford S	Glemsford S	1498A	Glemsford S	0	0
4	Rich SHERMAN	c34	c1600	1634	Merchant	Dedham E	Dedham/Colch E	1590A	Dedham E	0/6	0
2	Ralph SMITH†	c23	c1610	1633	Trader	Hingham N	Hingham N area	1462C	Hingham N	4	0
5	Nat SPARHAWK†‡	40	1598	1638	Merchant/innkeeper	Dedham E	Dedham E	c1591A	Dedham E	0	0
6	Sam SYMONDS†	c42	c1595	1637	Merchant	Gt. Yeldham E			Earl's Colne E	0	8
3	John TAYLOR*	c30	c1600	1630	Trader/fur trader	Haverhill S	Haverhill S	1500A	Haverhill S	0	0

60

11	Edm THOMPSON*			1637	Ship captain	Holkham N	Gt. Yarmouth N	No	Gt. Yarmouth N	46	46
3	John THROCK-MORTON	29	1601	1630	Grocer/scrivener	Norwich N	S.Elmham S area	N1	Norwich N	20	0
6	Wm VASSALL*	43	1592	1635	Merchant	Prittlewell E	Caen, Fr.	c1595A	Ratcliffe, Lond	150	28
2	Jonathan WADE†	c25	c1607	1632	Merchant	Denver N		N1			
2	Fran WAIN-WRIGHT	c20	c1617	1637	Merchant	Halstead E		No	Chelmsford E	0	16
5	Jos WELD†	c36	1599	c1635	Merchant (dry goods)	Sudbury S	Sudbury S	1561A	Sudbury S	0	0
6	John WHIPPLE†‡	42	1596	c1638	Merchant	Bocking E	Bocking E	c1570A	Bocking E	0	0
7	Matt WHIPPLE‡	48	c1590	c1638	Merchant	Bocking E	Bocking E	c1570A	Bocking E	0	0
6	Wm WHITING†	41	c1595	c1636	Merchant	Boxford S	Boxford S	1567A	Boxford S	0	0
2	John WHITTING-HAM†	22	1616	1638	Merchant	Sutterton L	Sutterton L	1543A	Boston L	0	8
3	Sam WILBORE	39	c1594	1633	Woolen draper	Sible Heding-ham E	Braintree E	1548A	Braintree E	7	7
2	Thos WILLETT†	21	1611	1632	Trader	Norwich N	Norwich N	N1	Leiden, Neths.	0	125
4	Jos YOUNGS	36	c1607	1638	Ship captain	Southwold S	Gt. Yarmouth N	1554A	Southwold S	20	0

*Returned to England.
†Elected lay officer.
‡Elected church officer.

61

Table 10. Age, Roots, and Mobility of Mercantile Emigrants

AG	Age	No.	Distance, BP:FR (miles)						Distance, BP:WP (miles)					
			0–4	5–9	10–14	15–19	20+	UK	0–4	5–9	10–14	15–19	20+	UK
2	21–25	8	4	2				2	3	2			1	1
3	26–30	13	3	1	1	1	3	4	7		1	1	3	2
4	31–35	7	3	2			1	1	7				1	
5	36–40	8	6	1				1	6	1	1			
6	41–45	6	3	1			1	1	3	2			1	
7	46–50	5	2				1	2	4		1			
8	51–55	2	1			1			1			1		
9	56–60													
10	61–65	1	1						1					
11	UK	4	1				1	2	1				2	1
	Total	54	24	7	1	2	7	13	33	5	3	2	7	4

John Throckmorton, or Giles Firmin, the Sudbury apothecary. But we can assume that his competitor—and possible supplier—Nicholas Knapp of nearby Bures, traveled frequently around the Stour Valley, much like a hawker or chapman, to vend his medicines.[12] Many merchants also moved about to neighboring market towns, as well as the many local and great regional fairs, like the Stourbridge Fair held annually near Cambridge. They had contacts too in the ports and the institutional centers like Bury, Norwich, Lincoln, or Chelmsford.[13] This vocational movement needs to be distinguished from residential mobility, because the traders were circulating around a fixed base, not relocating themselves in new homes.

Much of this movement would be small-scale, however. The fact that market towns were "scattered up and down the countryside at intervals of very few miles [reflected] the intense localism of society and the absence of mechanical transport." Many towns in the region had populations of only 900–1,200, and their customers lived within a radius of five or six miles. The society of the typical market town from which most traders emigrated "was as deeply rooted and inbred as that of the peasant villages of its hinterland." The enormous number of annual fairs—69 in Suffolk alone—and the fact that their dates often clashed likewise argue for small-scale commercial horizons. A quarter of all buyers and sellers (including gentlemen and other wealthy customers) at fairs in the eastern counties came from within a 10-mile radius, and just over half from less than 30.[14]

Even mariners and seagoing merchants often traded on a quite restricted scale. The trade of the North Sea ports was mostly coastal. A few transatlantic voyages embarked at Yarmouth or Ipswich, and, given favorable conditions, trade with the Low Countries could be brisk. Occasionally, sea captains who later settled in New England, like William Andrews, Thomas Coytmore, or Joseph Youngs, had previously engaged in transatlantic trade. For most port merchants and mariners, however, London or Newcastle or intermediate outports were much more usual destinations.[15] Following the mobility of seafaring families over generations confirms that this comparatively easy form of transport seems to have led to their moving from port to port, or spreading different branches up and down the coast. Inshore waters served as a busy highway, turning the East Anglian coastal strip into an extended neighborhood. Captain Edmund Thompson, born in Holkham, on the north Norfolk coast but dying in Great Yarmouth 46 miles around to the east, was not all that unusual among the seafarers. The Youngs family of

Southwold had kinsmen in Yarmouth. Thomas Moore, who married Alice Youngs, had namesakes in the ports of Yarmouth, Aldburgh, Dunwich, and the coastal hamlet of South Cove.[16]

In a few trading families who emigrated, especially from larger centers like Norwich, betterment mobility had taken place over previous generations. The Throckmortons had moved the 20 miles from northeast Suffolk to the regional capital during Queen Elizabeth's reign.[17] The Tidds, who also left from Norwich, were a Wells family on the north Norfolk coast during the fifteenth and sixteenth centuries.[18] The West Suffolk county town of Bury St. Edmunds promised upward mobility for John Newgate,[19] haberdasher, and Clement Chaplin, chandler.[20] Between 1337 and 1553, the Coggeshall ancestors had inched their way from Hundon the nine miles southeast to the cloth town of Halstead in north Essex, where the emigrant John was baptized in 1601.[21] The Mills, Paine, Weld, and Whittingham families had all previously migrated short distances to market or industrial towns in the classic betterment pattern.[22]

John Newgate's father was probably one of those longer-range migrants, described by E. A. Wrigley, who traveled to London from rural parts. The Suffolk land was still in the family, however, when John made his will before a return voyage to England in 1638. The Coytmores had similarly moved from Ipswich to London in the latter half of the sixteenth century,[23] and Valentine Hill's brother John and William Hutchinson's brother Richard had traveled from Lincolnshire to try their luck as young merchants in the capital.[24] Only two other trading families had indulged in long-range migration of this order: the Wilbores, who had come south from Yorkshire around the year 1500 as cloth merchants and settled in the Colchester area, and the Vassalls, who came to England as Huguenot refugees during Elizabeth's reign.[25]

Table 10 shows that once again the 26–30-year-olds predominated, though their juniors, having completed apprenticeships, were more heavily represented than among the clergy, who in their early twenties would still await cures. The other well-represented group was the 36–40 age band, already established traders, with some capital and a range of business contacts. Of the 35 whose backgrounds are sufficiently known, 28 came from families already established in trade and/or married into such families.[26] For them, commerce was not a new departure but rather a case of following in a tradition. Their wives usually came from the same town, a sign of limited social horizons.[27] Several traders were interrelated before emigration; in their cases, the decision to leave

64

might have been taken by an extended family rather than individually.[28] Eight did not stay permanently in New England.

The terms "trader" and "merchant" have the same kind of catch-all quality as our modern "businessman," who may be anything from the proprietor of a corner store to the chairman of a multinational corporation. A few were influential figures in England. Vassall, Wade,[29] Coddington, and Joseph Hills[30] had invested in the Massachusetts Bay Company; Paine,[31] Coytmore, Symonds,[32] and Valentine Hill[33] had considerable available capital. Most of our group, however, were in a smaller way of business, as their small-town origins suggest. Men like Mills, Knight, Loomis, or Matthew Whipple left only modest estates.[34] The oldest trader, William Hammond of Lavenham, had gone bankrupt in 1632, a casualty of the depression affecting the textile industry for much of the 1620s and 1630s. This gave some hint of color to official jibes about the insolvent escaping their creditors under cover of religious zeal for the New Zion in America.[35]

This predominance of small traders gives the overall impression of spatial stability among the mercantile group. They moved bases much less than the clergy. Traveling around their districts to nearby fairs and neighboring markets or hearing news from customers in their shops or inns would extend their horizons beyond the parochial level; it would hardly reduce their sense of belonging to a tightly knit small-town world.

Some Greater East Anglian merchants found emigration an enriching experience. Eleven of the 54 are known to have made considerable fortunes out of fur trading, fish exports, Virginian and West Indian voyages, money-lending agencies for London merchants, land speculation, and general import–export ventures. They pioneered settlements on the Maine coast, lumbered in the forests, and made voyages to Spain and the Wine Islands.[36] Valentine Hill, for instance, who arrived in Boston in 1636 at the age of 26, initially acted as an agent for his London-based brother. In 1641 he became a partner in the development of Boston Town Dock—sharing in a total investment of over £800. Along with John Winthrop, he put capital into the Mill Dam which, like the mill at Woodbridge, Suffolk, harnessed tidal power to drive two grist mills. During the 1640s Hill made a fortune trading in wheat from the North Shore, collecting cargoes of fish and timber along the Maine coast for shipment to England, importing sugar, indigo, and tobacco, selling shiploads of English goods, lending money, and dealing in Boston town lots and real estate along the coast. He was involved in the

Indian trade and in the project to break into the Delaware Valley fur trade. Those who see a meetinghouse-versus-countinghouse conflict of values make much of the fact that when the elder Winthrop's mansion had been lost because of the governor's debts it was Valentine Hill who mortgaged it to fellow merchant Richard Hutchinson in 1650.[37] Seven other East Anglian entrepreneurs who became wealthy were, like Hill, under 30 when they arrived. The merchants and others of the enterprising sort responsible for turning Ipswich into the second-wealthiest port in Massachusetts were in their forties, however. They often brought considerable capital with them, like Robert Payne, the richest townsman, and his brother William from Hadleigh, a Suffolk market town, who left £4,329 in 1660. Robert, Simon Bradstreet, and the Whipple brothers from the textile center of Bocking, Essex, were members of a committee of the town for furthering trade. William Foster, Giles Firmin, and Alexander Knight were all mature men from the East Anglian boroughs of Ipswich, Sudbury, and Chelmsford; Samuel Symonds from north Essex became Ipswich's representative at the General Court in 1638, an assistant for 30 years, deputy governor, and owned 1,700 acres and a personal fortune when he died in 1678. Ipswich's entrepreneurs not only developed the town as a major center of commerce and food grower for the market but were also active in land deals. Apart from Ipswich, the majority of merchants operated from the other New England ports favored by Greater East Anglians: Boston, Salem, and Charlestown.[38]

Nine of the merchants from the eastern counties became leaders of opposition groups seeking to subvert the orthodoxy of Massachusetts. Seven were core supporters of Anne Hutchinson, whose proto-Quakerism seemed, to some historians, to free adherents from man-made restrictions. Two of these religious exiles, Samuel Wilbore and John Porter, a farmer, became cofounders in the late 1650s of the Pettaquamscut Company, a land speculating syndicate, and two others, Philip Sherman, kinsman of Richard, and John Coggeshall, invested in the Misquamicut Purchase. Both of these ventures were in Rhode Island, as were the large acquisitions of land by another antinomian, William Coddington.[39] William Vassall was a fellow campaigner in 1646 with Dr. Robert Child to liberalize a franchise limited to adult male church members. Both Child and Roger Williams, scion of a merchant family, advocated toleration during the post-1640 New England depression as a means of stimulating the economy. Traits such as these have persuaded some historians that these early merchants were agents of

change, individualistic, libertarian, venturesome. They claim that trying to be both a pious puritan and a successful merchant imposed
"insupportable pressures."[40]

Other interpreters of early New England have doubted the validity of
such a crude "puritan versus Yankee" dichotomy. Most of the fur
traders, it is asserted, were pillars of their congregations.[41] The greatest
of them all, William Pynchon, gave up his profitable business because
of a theological dispute.[42] Almost all the mercantile group were church
members. Baker and Rucke left England after presentment to ecclesiastical courts. Ten, including successful entrepreneurs like Valentine
Hill, Joseph Hills, and William Whiting, held elected church appoint-
ments, and 23 were elected by their fellow citizens to town and colony
offices. Seven were chosen to be innkeepers by the Massachusetts authorities. Licensees had to be pillars of social and religious rectitude in
those early days.[43] The sons of four merchants became ministers; six
other traders had close clerical connections.[44] Roger Williams engaged
in the fur trade of Narragansett Bay; Clement Chaplin became a minister after his return to England. The Pettaquamscut partners donated
300 acres to maintain a minister. Winthrop described William Coddington as "a godly man of good estate," and the great landowner
insisted that he had left England, like the fleeing "Lot out of Sodom,"
after listening to Cotton's sermons. John Mills, among other merchants,
opened his will with a long religious preamble.[45]

The reconciliation of godly and commercial ambitions is confirmed by
confessions recorded by the Reverend Thomas Shepard at Cambridge,
Massachusetts. William Andrews, master of the ship *Diligent*, which
carried John Beale to New England, related the following "Temp-
tation" while he was still in East Anglia: "I built a new ship and my
mind was much upon it even on the Sabbath. And I desired [God] to
deliver me from this [temptation] whatever he did with me. But that
ship was split and all drowned but a few, four of my men myself naked
upon the main topsail in very cold weather and on morning some on the
shore came in a boat. And glad I was I lost my ship and so lost my sin."
Similarly, Nathaniel Sparhawke, a Cambridge, Massachusetts, innkeeper sprung from an Essex clothier family, recorded how, in his
"coming to deal in the world," his covetous "carking cares" were
corrected by a divine who reminded him of Proverbs: "There is that
scattereth and yet increaseth; and there is that withholdeth more than is
meet, but it tended to poverty." The Christian requirement was clear:
"The liberal [generous] soul shall be made fat; and he that watereth shall

be watered himself." Even so, Sparhawke continued "to let out my heart too eagerly" after profit, until "the Lord let me see that I looked to men too much . . . my own heart reaching after things of this world." Such revelations, and the taking to heart of the parable of the laborers in the vineyard, tempered the innkeeper's commercial ambitions. Nonetheless, both Andrews and Sparhawke remained active in trade after admission to church membership.[46]

What many recent studies emphasize is that "puritan versus Yankee" is a false dichotomy. Puritans were not antagonistic to wealth or prosperity or profit or financial inequality per se. They were passionate advocates of hard work—diligence in one's calling—of "improvement" or developing the wilderness and their own towns, and of such virtues as frugality, delayed gratification, temperance, order, and foresight. Wealth, calling, and worldly success were providential—"it hath pleased God so to dispose that our town chiefly consists of trade," as Boston petitioners put it in 1648. Those so blessed shared the view of Abraham Toppan, from the Norfolk port of Yarmouth, that "the Lord had merely lent him the 'good things of the world' for his 'Care and Management during my pilgrimage in this present life.'" This sense of stewardship required the fortunate to be generous both to their neighbors and to the public at large. Puritan philanthropy was legendary. There was little in Calvinist culture antagonistic to business. The major area of potential conflict concerned the sin of covetousness, the greed for more than a "competency," the distraction of the soul "taken up with the income of a large profit and purses filled with coin," the source of the deceit, false dealing, and hypocrisy that Michael Wigglesworth depicted in "God's Controversy with New England" in 1662. Provided the love of money was restrained, puritanism and enterprise were not mutually incompatible. It was perfectly normal that market day should also be lecture day. It had been so in Dedham, Ipswich, or Colchester before the emigrants had left East Anglia.[47]

For most of the Greater East Anglian mercantile group, small-scale operators in old and New England, poverty rather than affluence was the main danger. They would be grateful for the golden mean of a competency, and "Nothing sorts better with piety than competency," in the words of John White. "A man that hath competency may not pray for more enlargement," preached John Wilson, once of Sudbury, Suffolk, and now of Boston, Massachusetts, both thriving trade centers. Yet God-given prosperity could enhance godliness and communal stability. Given the power and watchfulness of local opinion, traders would exercise restraint and respect community values. This is all the more likely since most of them came from such well-rooted lives in Stuart market towns, which were "embedded in traditional ways of life of exceptional strength and obstinacy."[48]

Professionals and Entrepreneurs

The small town was customarily the home of the groups of professional men and manufacturers who emigrated from the eastern counties. From among the professionals came several distinguished leaders of New England society (see Table 11). Bellingham, Bradstreet, Dudley, and John Leverett, who emigrated with his family as an adolescent, are all celebrated by a memorial in St. Botolph's Church, Boston, as Lincolnshire men who became governors of Massachusetts. Dudley's daughter Anne married Simon Bradstreet and became the first major poetess of the English language in the New World.[49] Dr. John Clarke was one of the founders of the Baptist church in America and a determined, ingenious defender of the rights of Rhode Island at the courts of both Cromwell and Charles II. He was later elected deputy governor.[50] John Sandford, another antinomian, became president of Rhode Island.[51] Philemon Portmont exercised considerable influence at a less exalted level as first master of the Boston Latin School.[52]

Nowadays, we might expect all professionals to step naturally into leadership roles. We should beware of anachronistic perceptions, however. Doctors in the seventeenth century were not regarded with the respect or envy they currently elicit. Given their frequent inability to save or prolong life, this popular skepticism was hardly surprising.[53] Surgeons were often more akin to artisans. Indeed, John Dane, Jr., started adult life as a tailor but called himself a surgeon in his will.[54] Drs. Pratt, Gager (who soon died), and Palsgrave all emigrated in 1630 as employees of the Massachusetts Bay Company. None of the East Anglian medical men had any university training. They had probably picked up their lethal expertise from country quacks and sawbones.

The stewards were land agents for large estate owners. Thomas Dudley and Simon Bradstreet worked consecutively for the earl of Lincoln, John Masters for Sir Francis Barrington and Sir Richard Saltonstall, and John Sandford looked after John Winthrop's Suffolk business interests. Bradstreet was the only university graduate among the group. Proximity to aristocrats and county magnates would have given these stewards a sense of social confidence and placed them on the

Table 11. Professional Emigrants

AG	Name	Age	DOB	DOE	Profession	BP	FR		WP	Distances	
										BP:FR	BP:WP
8	Sim AYRES	54	1588	1637	Surgeon	Lavenham S	Lavenham S	1443B	Bury St.E. S	0	10
6	Rich BELLINGHAM	42	1592	1634	Lawyer	?Gainsborough L		No	Boston L	0	35
2	Rich BRACKETT	19	1611	1630	Schoolmaster	Sudbury S	Sudbury S	1540A	Sudbury S	0	0
3	Sim BRADSTREET	27	1603	1630	Steward	Horbling L	Gislingham S	N1	Tattershall/Sempring-ham L	70	2
4	John BRIDGE	c32	c1600	1632	Schoolmaster	Braintree E	Felsted E	1548A	Rayne E	6	2
10	Lion CHUTE			1630	Schoolmaster		Steeple E (20)	No	Dedham E		2
3	John CLARKE	28	1609	1637	Doctor	Westhorpe S	Ashfield S	1440A		3	
3	Wm DINELY	c27	c1607	c1634	Surgeon		Louth L	1561C			
9	Thos DUDLEY	56	1574	1630	Steward	Northampton-shire	Northampton-shire	No	Tattershall/Semp'ham L	0	38
10	Thos FOSTER			1634	Soldier	Ipswich S	Ipswich S	1474B	Ipswich S	0	0

6	Wm GAGER	c45	c1585	1630	Doctor	Lit. Waldingfield S	Lit. Waldf'd S	1522B	Lit. Waldf'd/ Groton S	0	3
7	Thos LEVERETT	c49	c1584	1633	Lawyer	Boston L	Grantham L	1506C	Boston L	26	0
9	John MASTERS	c56	c1574	1630	Steward		Herts/Essex border (5/22)	1530B	Hatf'd B.Oak/ Ockendon E		
6	Rich PALSGRAVE	c45	c1585	1630	Doctor	Barnham Broom N	Thruxton N	1516A	Wymondham N	4	4
5	Philem PORTMONT	39	1595	1634	Schoolmaster	Grimsby L	Grimsby L	1585B	Grimsby L	0	0
5	Mich POWELL	c34	c1605	1639	?Schoolmaster	Woolverstone S	Ipswich S	1471C	Woolverstone S	4	0
5	Abr PRATT	c40	c1590	1630	Surgeon	Wood Ditton C	Fulbourne C	1545A		9	
2	John SANDFORD	c25	c1606	1631	Steward		Dedham/Polstead E (8/3)	1590B	Groton S		
3	Anth SOMERBY	29	1610	1639	Schoolmaster	Lit.Bytham L	Greetham L	1538A	Lit.Bytham L	6	0
3	Art TYNDAL	c30	c1600	1630	Lawyer	Gt.Maplestead E	Gt.Maplestead E	1530A	?London	0	?45
10	John WARD	?	?	c1640	Doctor	Stratford St.Mary S	Stratford St.Mary S	1591B	Stratford St.Mary S	0	0

Table 12. Entrepreneurial Emigrants

AG	Name	Age	DOB	DOE	Profession	BP	FR		WP	Distances	
										BP:FR	BP:WP
5	Rob COE	38	1596	1634	Clothier	Thorpe Morieux S	Gestingthorpe E	N1	Boxford S	11	9
3	Thos FITCH	26	1612	1638	Clothier	Bocking E	Bocking E	1559A	Bocking E	0	0
7	Wm HUTCHINSON	48	1586	1634	Clothier	Alford L	Lincoln	N1	Alford L	30	0
8	Mich METCALFE	51	1586	1637	Clothier	Tatterford N	Yorks (Appersett)	N1	Norwich N	165	25
2	Thos PARISH	22	1613	1635	Clothier	Nayland S	Nayland S	1583A	Nayland S	0	0
3	Edm SHERMAN	c30	c1602	1632	Clothier	Dedham E	Dedham/Colch. E	1590A	Dedham E	0/6	0
5	Sim STACEY	c40	c1595	c1635	Clothier	Bocking E		No	Bocking E		0
3	John STANSBY	c26	c1610	1636	Clothier/ farmer		Lavenham area	1552A			
6	Mart UNDERWOOD	41	1596	1637	Clothier	?St.Jas.S.Elmham S	St.Jas.S.Elmham S	1490B	St.Jas.S.Elmham S	0	0
5	And WARNER	37	1594	1631	Maltster	Hatfield B.Oak E	Gt.Waltham E	1360A	Hatfield B.Oak E	10	0

Table 13. Age, Roots, and Mobility of Professionals and Entrepreneurs

AG	Age	No.	Distance, BP:FR (miles)						Distance, BP:WP (miles)					
			0–4	5–9	10–14	15–19	20+	UK	0–4	5–9	10–14	15–19	20+	UK
2	21–25	3	2					1	2					1
3	26–30	8	3	2			1	2	4					4
4	31–35	2	1	1					2					
5	36–40	5	1	1	2			1	3	1				1
6	41–45	4	3					1	3				1	
7	46–50	2					2		2					
8	51–55	2	1				1						1	
9	56–60	2	1					1			1		1	1
10	UK	3	2					1	2					1
Total		31	14	4	2	0	4	7	18	1	1	0	3	8

73

edges of the gentry class. The responsibility delegated to them was also excellent training for administering colonial affairs.[55]

In an education-conscious plantation, schoolmasters like John Bridge, immortalized by his nineteenth-century statue on Cambridge Common near Harvard, were welcomed as valuable assets. Though none of the early East Anglian schoolmasters had degrees, Philemon Portmont must have been exposed to some English grammar school classics to become first master of the Boston Latin School in 1635. The rest probably taught at a more elementary level. Michael Powell, whose exquisite Italian hand accorded him office as Dedham's recorder and additional income as a scrivener, moved to Boston in 1647. He became elder and a popular and "gifted" lay preacher in the North End, but, when the North Church was gathered, he was forbidden ordination because of his lack of education. The first graduate schoolmaster from East Anglia was Elijah Corlett, who brought skills developed in Framlingham, Suffolk, and Halstead, Essex, to Cambridge, Massachusetts, in the early 1640s.[56]

New England puritans shared contemporary hostility to lawyers as "caterpillers of the commonwealth."[57] This may explain why only three emigrated, and one, Arthur Tyndal, Winthrop's brother-in-law, returned to England almost immediately. Of the two Lincolnshire Bostonians, Thomas Leverett came from a long-established county family and was an alderman of the borough. Apart from representing the corporation in a case in London, he appears to have operated at a local level as a typical country-town attorney. Richard Bellingham had rather wider experience. As well as serving as recorder, or borough magistrate, he was elected a member of Parliament in 1628 and was a patentee of the Massachusetts Bay Company in 1629. His citation before the Court of High Commission in 1633 no doubt hastened his flight to the New World in the following year. His legal expertise proved valuable in 1648 when he was the principal compiler of the *Lawes and Liberties* of Massachusetts.[58]

Table 11 reveals that in England most of these mainly humble professionals had worked on a local scale within familiar neighborhoods long settled by their ancestors. One exception, Simon Bradstreet, was the son of a clergyman, who had moved north from Suffolk for ecclesiastical preferment. His professional predecessor, Thomas Dudley, came from that most footloose of callings, the military. His move from Northamptonshire to Lincolnshire derived from the early patronage of Lord Saye and Sele, a kinsman and political ally of the earls of Lincoln.[59] Though

Dudley quickly became a leading figure in Massachusetts, along with Bellingham and Leverett, most professionals did not have the standing or vision for such responsibilities. Their viewpoint was essentially artisanal, small-town, and localist.

The nine entrepreneurs described on emigration documents as clothiers (Table 12) might have been expected to become leaders of progress in the New World. The textile industry was still the major manufacturing sector of the English economy, and the East Anglian weaving areas of the Stour Valley and Norwich–East Norfolk had seen innovations like the new draperies drive the old broadcloths into retreat. New markets had been pioneered for the lighter cloths, and new wools and linen fibers were developed.[60]

Our expectations might be further whetted by the names of some of the clothier emigrants. Coe, Fitch, Hutchinson, and Sherman were long-established textile families,[61] as were some of the emigrants not designated clothiers but whose families were involved in managing the complex cloth-making industry.[62] Fitch, Hutchinson, Sherman, and Stacey were relatively wealthy men.[63] Some rose to positions of responsibility in New England. Fitch became deputy governor of Connecticut. Coe, who is hard to distinguish from his son of the same name, moved at least four times in the New World, eventually serving as a judge and sheriff on Long Island. Simon Stacey, who was a kinsman of Fitch, was a leading townsman of Ipswich, Massachusetts, and Andrew Warner, the maltster, was deacon of a Hartford, Connecticut, church from 1639 to 1659.[64]

The clothiers were in the upper echelons of a profession that covered a wide range of activities and incomes. They acted as middlemen, coordinating the various handicraft processes from wool purchase, combing, and spinning through weaving to the finishing and sale of the cloths. Like Winthrops and Appletons, members of these families had achieved gentry status and sent their sons to university and inns of court. Thomas Fitch's father, who died in 1632, had a fine clothier's house on Bradford Street, Bocking, and left over £1,000 in personal property as well as extensive lands. The Fitch family had owned Lyons Hall in Bocking between 1582 and 1618.[65]

Michael Metcalfe, on the other hand, was a Norwich dornick weaver who, as an independent master, employed in his workshop in St. Edmunds parish a group of journeymen working at his looms. Later, parliamentary propaganda against Matthew Wren, Laudian bishop of Norwich, claimed that Metcalfe put more than a hundred people to work, but this would include spinners, finishers, and considerable exaggeration. Martin Underwood was similarly a manufacturing clothier; his textiles probably included linen and linen-wool union cloths, as he worked in the hemp-growing Waveney Valley. He probably put some work out to local dairy farmers who were part-time clothworkers. Though Underwood might have to travel up to 10 miles coordinating production in the sparsely settled South Elmham district, other clothiers would be more occupationally static in manufacturing towns like Norwich, Bocking, or Dedham.[66]

Table 12 confirms the impression that these entrepreneurs were usually long established in their neighborhoods and had not experienced personal upheaval before emigration. The one exception is Michael Metcalfe. Like Simon Bradstreet among the professionals, Metcalfe was the son of a clergyman, who had moved from his birthplace of Appersett in Wensleydale, Yorkshire, for ecclesiastical preferment in west Norfolk. Michael went from the remote vicarage near Fakenham to learn his trade as a dornick weaver at the capital of the new draperies, Norwich. Otherwise, as Table 13 for both professionals and entrepreneurs demonstrates, the whole group was remarkably settled and stable before they left. The few short-distance moves were to establish practices or businesses at a local center like Bury, Norwich, Ipswich, Sudbury, or Boston. Robert Coe set up operations in the cloth town of Boxford, Suffolk, after growing up in the rustic hamlet of Thorpe Morieux. Dr. Richard Palsgrave similarly chose the market town of Wymondham, Norfolk, as the center of his practice rather than the nearby hamlet of Barnham Broom where his father was vicar. Neither group had to look far for their marriage partners. As well as Bradstreet, Fitch, Stacey, Leverett, Powell, Hutchinson, Portmont, Metcalfe, and Coe are all known to have married local brides. Simon Stacey was related to Fitches, Lords, and Whipples, with whom he settled in Ipswich.

This East Anglian background of manufacturing, port, and trading towns did not negate profound religious convictions. Stansby and Metcalfe, in trouble with the church courts, were quite specific in their accounts that religious innovations and pollutions, rather than economic conditions, drove them out. Stansby's confession at a Cambridge, Massachusetts, church cites Satan's tempting of Christ in the wilderness with worldly wealth and power, and God's comparing the claims of those who say "I am rich, and increased with goods and have need of nothing" with their actual spiritual poverty and wretchedness.[67]

Sherman, Hutchinson, Leverett, Bellingham, and Underwood were closely involved with emigrating religious leaders.[68] Stacey and Hutchinson soon became church deacons, Leverett and Powell elders, and Fitch's younger brother took the minister's, not the manufacturer's, cloth. Dudley was an early critic of Winthrop's leniency. His daughter's deep piety shines through her poetry.

On the economic front, it is true that the East Anglian textile industry was undergoing serious depression in the early 1630s, but it has been argued that New England was unlikely to restore fortunes in the short run with a rejuvenated cloth industry.[69] Some older leaders, like Dudley and Leverett, became absorbed in colony, town, and church affairs and seem to have had little time for economic initiatives. Parish, Sherman, and Stansby returned to England in the 1640s. Metcalfe never made much impact in the New World. He served as a Dedham selectman only once and became the town schoolmaster in his seventies. Coe lived in frontier settlements; Underwood's impression was similarly light. Others, however, did apply their professional and entrepreneurial skills to colonial development. William Hutchinson and his younger brother Edward joined Leverett and merchants Coggeshall and Newgate in 1636 in the syndicate of 14 to build a dock, wharfage, and crane in Boston. Bellingham, Bradstreet, and Stacey were involved in the early development of the commercial town of Ipswich, and Fitch helped open up the Connecticut Valley at Hartford and then in 1652 invested heavily in the founding of Norwalk on Long Island Sound. Bellingham bought up Samuel Maverick's farm on the North Shore and leased it to a tenant. He was described as "very greedy for more money," and when he died his estate included three farms rented out.[70]

Simon Bradstreet was more representative of the younger generation. He made considerable profit on the frontier land market, selling part of a land grant to the breakaway town of Hadley for £200 in 1659. He became a shareholder in the Atherton Company of land speculators in 1660 and when he died owned 1,556 acres, mainly leased out, in five different towns. His contemporary, Edward Hutchinson, acquired five properties and lands in three colonies during his lifetime. John Leverett, 16 years old when he arrived in Boston with his father and the Reverend John Cotton, was importing cloth from England by 1650. In the early 1670s, in association with John Pynchon and William Payne (born in Naughton, Suffolk), he tried to break into the lucrative fur trade of the upper Hudson Valley, only to be frustrated by King Philip's War. As a land speculator, he acquired nearly 10,000 acres in Maine, as well as a thousand acres on the Merrimack. He owned saw and grist mills and lent capital to settlers. Bradstreet, Leverett, and Pynchon all served in high office for many years, and some of their realty was awarded for onerous public service. The greatest entrepreneurs were born to these immigrants in New England—Joseph Dudley (born 1647) and James Fitch (born 1649), Thomas's nephew. Dudley acquired vast holdings in Nipmuck country, and "Black James," "the Great Land Pirate," laid claim to most of northeastern Connecticut.[71]

These developers were men of the future. The values and attitudes of the mature first-generation professionals and entrepreneurs were generally more restrained and infused with godliness. Their Greater East Anglian training and skills were often invaluable to the fledgling colonies, but, like the merchants, they balanced "diligence in their callings" with obligations to church and state.

5

🕸

The Industrious Sort:
Artisans and Farmers

IN 1584, a Suffolk vicar sought to persuade Queen Elizabeth of the merits of colonization. Among 23 reasons, he included the following: "If England cry out and affirm, that there is so many in all trades that one cannot live for another, as in all places they do, America offreth the remedy." The ecological disasters that struck Greater East Anglia in the 1620s and 1630s were simply deeper crevasses traversing a downhill glacier that was bearing the less fortunate among the industrious sort of people, small and middling farmers or master craftsmen, into a nether world of tenancy, landlessness, and wage labor. This slow slide into proletarianization had begun in the early sixteenth century as population increase began to put pressure on resources. It was clearly observable when Richard Hakluyt wrote his "Discourse of Western Planting." From a sparse society of comparatively equal peasants emerged "a few market-oriented large farmers and many cottars and labourers working for them. . . . Ratepayers became almstakers, a line more easily crossed financially than emotionally." Some craftsmen, who should previously have expected to set up shops as small masters, now found themselves forced to work for others as employees. Some, ground down by the pressure on land and jobs, became rolling stones, forced to move in search of subsistence.[1]

There can be no denying this trend, which lasted from the sixteenth to the nineteenth century. However, it affected different people in different regions at different times in different ways and was slowed or hastened by a host of other factors. Moreover, a significant proportion of the population managed to buck the trend and better themselves. By a combination of luck, judgment, and hard work they became those larger farmers or employing manufacturers who could exploit the new conditions.

The great majority of adult male emigrants from the eastern counties were either artisans or people in farming. Here we investigate their life experiences prior to embarkation and especially whether they had moved to improve their prospects or been forced on the road to survive.

Artisans

The experience that the large contingent of 151 emigrant artisans (Table 14) had all shared was apprenticeship, having learned their trade from a master while living in his household. Two myths cling to the apprentice. He is depicted as a Dick Whittington figure, walking to some distant city with his few possessions hanging in a bundle from a stick to seek a master and eventual fame and fortune. The second myth has him wooing and marrying his master's daughter, a useful boost up the ladder to success. The most sensational contemporary example of upward mobility thus begun was that of Lionel Cranfield, who eventually became James I's lord treasurer and earl of Middlesex. In both cases, mobility, geographic and social, is the key motif. In Whittington's experience the one led to the other, the classic betterment pattern.[2]

In theory, our emigrant artisans should have fit this model of mobility and aspiration. The craftsman was not tied to land in the same way as the gentleman, yeoman, or husbandman. His skills and his tools could release him from the binding tendrils of family roots. As with other occupational groups, the great majority of artisan emigrants were 40 and below, 111 out of 151. Old age, complacency, dulled ambition, or hearthbound indolence *should* not have tied them down. If betterment migration proves common among this group, then their emigration could merely have extended ambition and horizons to embrace wider opportunities.

Some emigrant artisans did fit this liberated pattern. Abraham Toppan, or Tappan, sailed in the *Mary Ann* in 1637 with his Yarmouth-born wife and two young children and his mother-in-law, Elizabeth Goodale. There are no signs of the Toppan family in earlier East Anglian records, until his apprenticeship to the Great Yarmouth cooper Richard Elwyn and his freemanship of the borough in 1627 on completion of his training at the age of 21. Genealogical research explains this lack of local background. Toppan has been traced to a family living in the Yorkshire Dales. His baptism is recorded in the parish register of Calbridge, Coverham, 180 miles northwest of Yarmouth. This upland upbringing may account for his abandoning coopering in Newbury, Massachusetts, and becoming a sheep raiser. His Yarmouth experience may have encouraged his trading ventures to Barbados and Virginia. How or why he came nearly 200 miles to learn his trade is not known, but he fits the myth of artisan mobility to a T.[3]

So too does Toppan's shipmate on the *Mary Ann*, Thomas Jones. He was a recently qualified master butcher who came from the village of Elsing, 12 miles west of Norwich. His name was also quite new to the area. His native land was Wales, and he was a particularly far-ranging member of that great exodus eastward from the principality which so exercised xenophobe satirists in the sixteenth and seventeenth centuries.[4]

Even more dramatic migrations lay behind the Leager and Pingry names. Both families had fled as refugees from Europe's religious wars in the sixteenth century. The tailor Jacob Leager, baptized at Hadleigh, Suffolk, in 1603, was the grandson of Jacob Legare, described as "alien" in the town records of 1568. The family had intermarried with Suffolk clans. The Pingry brothers, Aaron the husbandman and Moses the saltmaker, have been traced to Auren de Pingrée of Tours, France (1538–1602), their grandfather. As Huguenots they belonged to the burgeoning foreign population of the textile center of Colchester from which they emigrated about 1640 to Ipswich, Massachusetts.[5]

Another emigrant craftsman with a foreign-sounding name, the tanner George Keyser, represents an allegedly common form of internal migration. Baptized in 1610 at the grazing and butchering center of Leighton Buzzard, Bedfordshire, he had moved, by the time he immigrated to Lynn, Massachusetts, in 1639, to West Ham, Essex, a village four miles east of London. He had traveled 37 miles to learn or practice his trade, but the family may have been fairly recent arrivals at his birthplace.[6]

Emigrant family surnames sometimes reveal earlier migratory habits. The fuller Thomas Philbrick of Bures St. Mary in the cloth-making region of the Stour Valley derived his name from Felbrigg near Sheringham in north Norfolk. Unlike Jones of Elsing, however, the Philbricks had been in the Stour Valley since at least the early 1400s. A William Fybregge lived in the cloth town of Dedham in 1408; a tenement called Fibrigg is recorded there 25 years later. Similarly, Earl's Colne, three miles from Bures, has many of the family in its fifteenth-century manorial rolls, and a house in the High Street is called Filbrecks.[7]

Apart from London, the great regional magnet was, as we have seen, Norwich. Ambitious tradesmen would be drawn to it as the seat of over 20,000 people and a marketing and manufacturing center. Thus Francis

Table 14. Emigrant Artisans

AG	Name	Age	DOB	DOE	Trade	BP	FR		WP	Distances	
										BP: FR	BP: WP
11	Ferd ADAMS			1636/37	Shoemaker	Ipswich S	SW of Ipswich S	1447B	Ipswich S	7	0
5	Walt ALLEN	c38	1601	by 1639	Hatter	Bury S	Bury S	1394B	Bury S	0	0
11	John AMYE			1636	Ship carpenter		Coggeshall E (6)	1540A	Bocking E		
3	Jas BABCOCK	c28	1612	by 1640	Blacksmith			No			
6	Geo BACON	43	1592	1635	Mason	Hessett S	Hessett S	1444A	Hessett S	0	0
2	Thos BARBER	21	1614	1635	Carpenter			No	Stamford L		
1	Jas BARKER	20	1618	1638	Tailor	Stradishall S	Clare S	1463C	Stradishall S	5	0
4	Thos BARNES	35	1602	1637	Weaver	Hingham N	Shipdham N	1531B	Hingham N	5	0
8	Geo BARRELL	c54	c1583	1637	Cooper	St.Mich.S. Elmham S	St.Mich.S. Elmham S	N1	St.Mich.S. Elmham S	0	0
7	John BEALE	45	1593	1638	Shoemaker	Hingham N	Lit.Ellingham N	1473A	Hingham N	2	0
1	John BIGELOW	c20	1617	by 1637	Blacksmith	Wrentham S	Wrentham S	1597A	Wrentham S	0	0
11	John BIRDE			by 1637	Basketmaker	Hatfield B.Oak E	Herts/E border	1559B	Hatfield B.Oak E	4	0
3	Thos BLODGETT	30	1605	1635	Glover	Stowmarket S	Haughley S	1560A	Stowmarket S	4	0
3	Jas BOOSEY	c28	c1606	c1634	Wheelwright	Colchester E	Chelmsford E	No	Colchester E	22	0
11	Thos BRICE			1630	Ship carpenter	Edwardstone S	Kersey S	1592A	Edwardstone S	5	0

	Name										
3	John BROWNE	27	1608	1635	Tailor	Gt/Lit.Baddow E	Chelmsford E	1559A	Gt/Lit.Baddow E, Essex	3	o
11	Wm BUCKLAND	c29	c1610	1630	Carpenter	Bury S		No	Bury S	5	o
3	Thos BUMSTEAD	c27	c1603	c1639	Pewterer/brazier		Rattlesden S	1501B			o
3	Jehu BURR	28	1609	1630	Carpenter	Roxwell E	Beauchamp Roding E	1484C	Roxwell E	4	o
3	John BURROWS	50	1587	1637	Cooper	Yarmouth N	Norwich N	N1	Yarmouth N	20	o
7	Nich BUSBY	32	1603	1637	Worsted weaver	Norwich N		No	Norwich N		o
4	Thos BUTTOLPH	c38	c1600	1635	Leatherwork/glover	Lit.Baddow E	Danbury E	1550A	Lit.Baddow E	2	o
11	Thos CAKEBREAD			1630	Miller	Hatfield B.Oak E	Lit.Hadham, Herts	1555A	Hatfield B.Oak E	6	o
5	Hen CHAMBERLAIN	c33	c1597	1638	Shoemaker	Hingham N	Attleborough N	1591B	Hingham N	5	o
4	Wm CHASE	20	1610	1630	Carpenter		Colchester area E	1540A			
1	Rich CHURCH	c22	c1610	1630	Carpenter	Polstead S	Polstead S	1575A	Polstead S	o	o
2	Nich CLARKE	41	1589	1632	Carpenter	Nazeing E		No			o
11	Rich CLOUGH			1630	Tailor			No			o
6	Edw CONVERSE	41	1589	1630	Miller	Navestock E	Stapleford Abbots E	1488A	Shenfield E	4	4
2	Wm DADY	25	1605	1630	Butcher	Wanstead E	Hornchurch E	1576A	Wanstead E	10	o
7	Philem DALTON	45	1590	1635	Linen weaver			No	Wolverstone S	o	o
	John DANE Sr.	c50	c1586	c1636	Tailor	Bps.Stortford, Herts	Bps.Stortford, 1502A Herts		Bps.Stortford		o

Table 14. *Continued*

									Distances	
AG	Name	Age	DOB	DOE	Trade	BP	FR	WP	BP: FR	BP: WP
2	John DANE Jr.	23	1613	1636	Tailor	Lit. Berkhamp-st'd, Herts	Bps. Stortford, Herts 1502A	Hatfield B.Oak E	14	10
5	Philem DICKERSON	c39	c1598	1637	Tanner	Beccles S	Theberton S 1554A	Wrentham S	15	6
6	Sam DIX	43	1594	1637	Joiner	Norwich N	Norwich N N1	Norwich N	0	0
2	Wm DIXON	25	c1605	1630	Cooper	Groton S	Groton S 1585A	Groton S	0	0
	Sam EDDY	22	1608	1630	Tailor	Cranbrook, Kent	Bristol No	Boxted E	150	53
4	Hen FARWELL	c35	c1602	c1637	Tailor	Boston L		Boston L		
	Benj FELTON	c31	c1604	1635	Turner	Gt. Yarmouth N	Gt. Yarmouth N 1558A	Gt. Yarmouth N	0	0
4	Fran FILLINGHAM	32	1605	1637	Cordwainer	Halesworth S	Brampton S 1504C	Brampton S	4	4
2	Gab FISH	c21	c1617	c1638	Fisherman	Sutton L	SE Lincs coast N1	Boston L	12	15
8	Josh FISHER	55	1585	1640	Blacksmith	Syleham S	Wingfield S 1523A	Fressingfield S	2	4
1	Josh FISHER Jr.	16	1621	1637	Blacksmith	Syleham S	Wingfield S 1523A	Fressingfield S	2	0
8	Step FOSDICK	52	1583	1635	Carpenter	Wenham S	NW Wood-bridge S No (1504A)	Wenham S	c15	0
4	Edm FROST	c33	c1602	1635	Weaver	Rattlesden S	Cent.S 1404B	Ratt'sden area S	10	0
1	Thos FULLER	c20	c1618	1638	Weaver	Norwich N	Norwich N 1479B	Norwich N	0	0

3	John GAGE	27	1603	1630	Carpenter	Kersey S	Boxford/Polstead S	1540A	Polstead S	4	4
11	Herm GARRETT			1638	Blacksmith	Wickham Mkt. area S	Wickham Mkt. area	1539B	Wickham Mkt. S	3	5
11	Rich GARRETT	c30	c1600	1630	Shoemaker	W.Hanningfield E	Margaretting E	1549B	Chelmsford E	2	5
11	Hen GARROLD/ETT			1638	Tanner		Linstead S	1530B	Wangford 100 S		
3	Wm GAULT	29	1608	1637	Cordwainer	Yarmouth N	Mundesley N	1466C	Yarmouth N	22	0
4	John GEDNEY	c34	c1603	1637	Weaver	Norwich N	Norwich N	1436C	Norwich N	0	0
1	Pet GEORGE	c20	1620	by 1640	Oatmeal maker	Barnardiston S	Haverhill S	1475B	Hundon/Ba'ston S	5	2
8	Edw GILMAN	c51	c1587	1638	Sawyer	Caston N	Caston N	1585A	Hingham N	0	6
3	Sam GREENFIELD	27	1610	1637	Weaver	Norwich N	Norwich N	c1571A	Norwich N	0	0
7	Edm GREENLEAF	c48	c1586	by 1634	Dyer/hosier	Ipswich S	Ipswich S	1409A	Ipswich S	0	0
3	Rich GRIDLEY	c29	c1601	1630	Mason		Haverhill S (17m)	No	Groton S		
1	Hum GRIGGS	c20	1620	c1640	Wool comber	Cavendish S	Cavendish S	1446A	Cavendish S	0	0
2	John GUTTRIDGE	c22	c1615	1637	Tailor	Hessett S	Felsham S	1423A	Rattlesden S	4	4
8	Rich HAFFIELD	54	1581	1635	Currier			No	Sudbury S		
3	Abr HARDING	c26	1619	c1635	Glover	Boreham E	Chelmsford area E	1585A	Boreham E	5	0
3	Thos HART	29	1606	1635	Tanner	Gt./Lit.Baddow E	Hatfield Peverel/Maldon E	1541B	Baddow E	0	4/6

Table 14. Continued

AG	Name	Age	DOB	DOE	Trade	BP	FR	WP	Distances	
									BP: FR	BP: WP
11	Jos HAYWARD			1637	Dornick weaver	Norwich N	Norwich N 1596A	Norwich N	0	0
11	Luke HEARD			by 1635	Weaver	Assington S	Boxford S 1560B	Assington S	3	0
11	Thos HETT			1632	Cooper	Folkingham L	No	Folkingham L	0	0
3	Edm HOBART	29	1604	1633	Weaver	Hingham N	Hingham area 1532A N	Hingham N	3	0
2	Just HOLDEN	23	1611	1634	Carpenter	Lindsey S	Boxford area S 1470A	Lindsey S	4	0
2	Rich HOLDEN	25	1609	1634	Glazier	Lindsey S	Boxford area S 1470A	Lindsey S	4	0
3	John HOOD	c26	c1612	1638	Weaver	Halstead E	Halstead/ 1541B Braintree E	Halstead E	7/0	0
1	Dan HOVEY	19	1618	1637	Glover	Waltham Ab-bey E	Ware/Ches-hunt Herts 1581A	Waltham Ab-bey E	7/2	0
11	Jerem HOWCHEN			c1639	Tanner	Rickinghall S	Rickinghall S 1497B	Harleston N	0	15
4	Jas HOWE	31	1604	1635	Weaver	Hatfield B.Oak E	Hatfield B.Oak E 1558A	Hatfield B.Oak E	0	0
2	Thos HOWLETT	24	1606	1630	Carpenter	S.Elmham S	Southwold S 1491B	S.Elmham S	10	0
3	Fran INGALLS	c28	c1601	1629	Tanner	Skirbeck L	Skirbeck L 1555A	Skirbeck L	0	0
4	Gawdy JAMES	35	1604	1639	Cordwainer	Winfarthing N	Winfarthing 1538A N	Winfarthing N	0	0
2	Thos JONES	25	1612	1637	Butcher	Elsing N	No	Elsing N	0	0

3	Geo KEYSER	29	1610	1639	Tanner	Leighton Buzzard, Beds	Leighton Buzz., Beds	No	West Ham E	0	37
1	Edw KIDBY	c18	c1612	1630	Sawyer			No	Groton S		
3	Lew KIDBY	c27	c1603	1630	Fisherman			No	Groton S		
6	Hen KIMBALL	44	1590	1634	Wheelwright	Lawford E	Manningtree area E	1570A	Mistley E	6	3
5	Rich KIMBALL	39	1595	1634	Wheelwright	Hitcham S	Hitcham S	1452A	Hitcham S	0	0
4	Thos LAMB	c32	c1598	1630	Mason/quarryman	Stowlangtoft S	Bury area S	1473B	Stowlangtoft S	5	0
8	Fran LAWES	c51	c1586	1637	Weaver	Norwich N	Carleton Forehoe N	1465A	Norwich N	8	0
4	Jacob LEAGER	35	1603	1638	Tailor	Hadleigh S	France/Low Countries	1592A	Kersey S	100+	2
4	Thos LINCOLN	c35	1600	c1635	Miller	Swanton Morley N	Hingham/Swanton Morley N	1543A	Swanton Morley N	0/9	0
1	Thos LINCOLN	c20	c1613	1633	Weaver	Hingham N	Hingham N	1543A	Hingham N	0	0
3	Thos LINCOLN	c30	c1605	1635	Cooper	Hingham N	Hingham N	1543A	Hingham N	0	0
1	Hen LOOKER	c19	c1620	1639	Glover	Bures S	Bures S	1561A	Bures S	0	0
7	Thos LORD	50	1585	1635	Smith	Felsted E	Felsted E	1530B	Wethersf'd E	0	7
4	Wm LUDKIN	33	1604	1637	Locksmith	Norwich N	Norwich N	1590A	Norwich N	0	0
5	Eliaz LUSHER	c38	c1600	1638	Sawyer	Fressingfield E		No	Fressingf'ld E	0	0
5	Thos MARSHALL	c39	c1595	c1634	Shoemaker	Alford L	Hogsthorpe/Mumby L	1543A	Alford L	5/6	0
3	Hugh MASON	28	1606	1634	Tanner		N. Thames E (16/25)	No	Maldon E		

Table 14. *Continued*

AG	Name	Age	DOB	DOE	Trade	BP	FR	WP	Distances	
									BP: FR	BP: WP
1	John MARSTON	20	1617	1637	Carpenter	Martham N	Martham N 1514B	Ormesby N	0	3
4	Isaac MIXER	31	1603	1634	Weaver	Capel St.Mary S	S of Ipswich S 1461A	Capel St.Mary S	8	0
3	Wm MOODY	c27	c1607	1634	Saddler		?Moulton C No	Ipswich S		
11	Abr MORRILL			1632	Blacksmith	Hatfield B.Oak E	Takeley E 1605A	Hatfield B.Oak E	3	0
5	Adam MOTT	39	1596	1635	Tailor		NW S/East C 1484B	Cambridge		
6	Rob MOULTON	c44	c1585	1629	Shipwright	Ormesby N	Ormesby N c1490A	Yarmouth N	0	4/6
2	Thos MOUNT	c25	c1605	1630	Bricklayer/mason	Colchester E	Tendring 100 E 1505A	Colchester E	5	0
1	Thos MULLINER	c20	c1619	1639	Joiner	Ipswich S	N1	Ipswich S		0
5	Geo MUNNINGS	38	1596	1638	Cordwainer	Rattlesden S	Rattlesden S area 1468A	Rattlesden S	4	0
4	Wm NICKERSON	32	1605	1637	Weaver	Norwich N	Norwich N 1585A	Norwich N	0	0
5	Thos OLIVER	36	1601	1637	Calendrar	Norwich N	Norwich N c1590A	Norwich N	0	0
2	John PAGE	c21	c1614	c1635	Carpenter	Hingham N	No	Hingham N	0	0
4	Step PAINE	c34	c1604	1638	Miller	Gt.Ellingham N	Gt.Ellingham N 1427A	Gt.Ellingham N	0	0
8	Thos PAINE	51	1586	1637	Weaver	Wrentham S	Wrentham S 1486A	Wrentham S	0	0
1	Geo PALMER	c19	c1620	1639	Wine cooper	Bradwell nxt Cogs E	1595A	Coggeshall E	0	1

4	Rob PARKER	31	1603	1634	Butcher	Woolpit S	E of Bury S	1440B	Woolpit S	c5	0
8	John PARMENTER	c51	1588	c1639	Tailor	Lit. Yeldham E	Lit. Yeldham E	1566A	Bures S	0	8
2	Dan PIERCE	23	1611	1634	Blacksmith	Norwich N	Norwich N	1470B	Norwich N	0	0
7	John PIERCE	49	1588	1637	Weaver	Norwich N	Norwich N	1470B	Norwich N	0	0
3	John PEMBERTON	c27	c1605	1632	Weaver			No	Lawford E	0	0
8	Thos PHILBRICK	52	1584	1636	Fuller	Bures S	Bures S	1408A	Bures S	0	0
3	Moses PINGRY	c30	1610	c1640	Saltmaker	Colchester E	France (Tours)	N1	Colchester E	c280	0
2	John PICKERING	c25	1615	c1640	Carpenter			N1	Sudbury S		
2	Edm PITTS	24	1613	1637	Weaver	Hackford N	Hackford/Hingham N	1457A	Hingham N	3	3
2	Rob POND	c25	c1605	1630	Carpenter	Groton S	Gt. Walding-field S	1566A	Groton S	4	0
5	Thos RAWLINS	c40	c1590	1630	Carpenter		E/Herts border (6–10)	1557A	Nazeing E		
5	Rob REYNOLDS	c38	c1592	1630	Shoemaker	Boxford S	Boxford S	1456A	Boxford S	0	0
5	Wm RIPLEY	c38	c1600	1638	Weaver			No	Wymondham N		
2	Wm RIX	c22	c1618	1640	Weaver	Kenninghall N	Hingham area N	N1	Kenninghall N	10+	0
5	John ROBINSON	c40	c1596	1636	Wheelwright	Lit. Walding-field S	Groton S	1585A	Lit. Walding-f'd S	4	0
2	John ROGERS	24	1612	1636	Shoemaker	Moulsham E	Moulsham E	1550A	Moulsham E	0	0
3	John ROPER	26	1611	1637	Carpenter	Shelfanger N	S. Norfolk	1432B	New Buckenham N	5	6

Table 14. *Continued*

AG	Name	Age	DOB	DOE	Trade	BP	FR		WP	Distances	
										BP: FR	BP: WP
2	Rob ROYCE	c25	c1605	1630	Shoemaker	Exning S	Exning S	1602A	Exning S	0	0
6	John RUGGLES	44	1591	1635	Shoemaker	Nazeing E	Elsenham E	No	Nazeing E	12	0
6	Wm SALTER	c43	1592	c1635	Shoemaker	Buxhall S	Buxhall S	1472A	Buxhall S	0	0
5	Mart SANDERS	40	1595	1635	Currier	Sudbury S	Lavenham/Chelsworth S	N1	Sudbury S	6	0
4	Wm SAVILL	c33	c1605	1640	Joiner	Saffron Walden E	Stansted E	1593A	Saff. Walden E	10	0
1	John SCARLET	c17	c1623	1640	Mariner	Ipswich S	N. Suffolk coast	N1	Ipswich S	c35	0
5	Thos SCOTT	39	1595	1634	Glover	Rattlesden S	Felsham S	1475A	Rattlesden S	3	0
4	Hen SKERRY	31	1606	1637	Cordwainer	Repps c Bastwick N	Gt. Yarmouth N	1510A	Gt. Yarmouth N	7	7
2	Fran SMYTH	c25	c1605	1630	Cardmaker	Dunmow E	Dunmow E	1558A	Dunmow E	0	0
3	Thos SNOW	c26	c1610	1636	Barber	Witham E	E/Herts border	No	Chelmsford E	c18	8
6	John SUTTON	c45	c1595	1638	Carpenter			No	Attleborough N		
2	Phil TABER	c25	c1605	1630	Carpenter		Margaretting E	1545B		5	0

3	John THURSTON	30	1607	1637	Carpenter	Wrentham S	Wrentham area S	1492A	Wrentham S	5	0
6	John TIDD	c45	c1592	1637	Tailor	Norwich N	Wells N	No	Norwich N	30	0
4	Abr TOPPAN	31	1606	1637	Cooper	Calbridge, Yks	Yorkshire	No	Gt.Yarmouth N	80	190
1	Rich TRUESDALE	c20	c1613	1633	Butcher			No	Boston L		
1	Wm VENTRIS	c17	c1623	c1640	Weaver	Braintree E		No	Braintree E		0
4	Jas WALL	c35	c1596	1631	Carpenter	Braintree E	Braintree area E	1552A	Braintree E	6	0
4	Thos WARDALL	32	1602	1634	Shoemaker	Alford L	Alford L	1558A	Alford L	0	0
3	Wm WARDALL	26	1607	1633	Carpenter	Alford L	Alford L	1558A	Alford L	0	0
1	Benj WARDE	c20	c1615	c1635	Ship carpenter			No	Suffolk		
3	Law WATERS	28	1602	1630	Carpenter	Nayland S	Bildeston S	1582B	Nayland S	10	0
3	Rob WILLIAMS	28	1608	1637	Cordwainer	W.Somerton N	Gt.Yarmouth area N	1479B	Gt.Yarmouth N	8	8
5	Thos WILSON	c39	c1594	1633	Miller	Donnington L	Donnington area L	No	Bocking E		
4	Wm WILSON	c35	c1600	1635	Joiner			1553B	Donnington L	6	0
6	Rich WOODWARD	45	1589	1634	Miller			No	Suffolk		
6	Nich WYETH	c43	c1595	c1638	Mason	Framlingham S	Framsden S	1536B	Framlingham S	6	0
3	Chris YOUNG	c28	c1610	1638	Weaver	Gt.Yarmouth N	Gt.Yarmouth N	1611A	Gt.Yarmouth N	0	0

Table 15. Age, Roots, and Mobility of Emigrant Artisans

AG	Age	No.	Distance, BP:FR						Distance, BP:WP					
			0–4	5–10	11–15	16–20	20+	UK	0–4	5–10	11–15	16–20	20+	UK
1	16–20	18	9	3			1	5	14					4
2	21–25	23	11	4	1		1	6	17		1			5
3	26–30	30	13	6		2	2	7	18	5			1	6
4	31–35	23	10	10		1		2	20	1				2
5	36–40	16	6	3	1		1	4	11	1			1	3
6	41–45	11	5	2	1		1	2	9					2
7	46–50	7	5					2	5	1				1
8	51–55	9	5	1	1			2	6	2				1
9	56–60													
10	61–65													
11	UK	14	6	3				6	8	1	1			4
Total		151	70	32	4	3	6	36	108	11	2		2	28

Lawes, a weaver, who left Norwich for Salem in 1637, came from a clan concentrated in the fifteenth and sixteenth centuries in a group of villages 8 and 10 miles west of the city. A branch of the family moved into Norwich, however. One Hugh Lawes lived in a southern suburban parish in 1473, but the name is not common until the mid-sixteenth century. Francis left behind country cousins in the villages, the remnant of the family who had stayed put on the land.[8] Similarly, Robert Williams, fellow citizen and migrant with Lawes, had strong east coast connections. His namesake grandfather had been a husbandman and churchwarden at West Somerton, eight miles north of Great Yarmouth. His own wife, Elizabeth, originated from Stalham nearby. In 1625, however, Robert, aged 17, had been apprenticed to a cordwainer, John Gannett, in Norwich. The date coincided with his father's death from plague. Since Stephen Williams was also a cordwainer, he may himself have been training son Robert in the mysteries of the shoemaking craft for three years until his sudden death. Robert's wife's family had similarly moved into the city. Her father was a master mason who lived in the parish of St. George's Tombland (a puritan hotbed), conveniently close to the great stone cathedral.[9] Another Norwich textile specialist, Thomas Oliver, a calendrar or smoother of worsteds, came from a family concentrated for two centuries in the village of West Tofts near Thetford in south Norfolk. The Norwich Freemen's Rolls reveal that a branch of the clan had become permanently resident in the city by the early years of Queen Elizabeth's reign. In 1603 John Oliver, son of Thomas Oliver of Norwich, deceased, was admitted to freemanship. These two were probably our emigrant's father (or uncle) and grandfather, born about 1578 and 1548, respectively. Even if the grandfather had only arrived in Norwich as an apprentice, he would have been there since about 1562.[10]

A mason's or a calendrar's Norwich residence suggests one more reason for artisan mobility. Certain specialist crafts needed a large constituency or sustained demands for rare skills.[11] The most obvious examples are the four emigrant ships' carpenters, Benjamin Warde, Thomas Brice (or Brease), John Amye, and Robert Moulton. Little is known about the first three, but Moulton, recruited in 1629 as chief shipwright at Salem by the Massachusetts Bay Company, came from a numerous family long settled in the inland villages of Ormesby, Filby, and Martham just north of Yarmouth. Some Moultons had moved in the sixteenth century to the port, where Robert learned and practiced his craft. Shipwrights needed water.[12]

The family history of another specialist, William Ludkin, locksmith, of the parish of St. Clement's, Norwich, provides a classic example of betterment migration. Robert Lotekyn of East Harling (20 miles southwest of Norwich) left a will in 1433. The unusual family name next appears in 1560, when Henry Ludkin, a tailor, son of John of Garboldisham (the next village) became a freeman of Norwich. John Ludkin must have been born around 1500. In 1589 Christopher Ludkin died. His branch was still in the south Norfolk wood-pasture country at Garboldisham. However, another Christopher, probably a grandson of his namesake, was "of Norwich, Locksmith," by 1619, when his son William, our emigrant, was apprenticed for eight years. It seems very probable that Henry Ludkin the tailor stayed on in Norwich in Queen Elizabeth's reign and that our William (and George Ludkin, his emigrant kinsman) was his great-grandson or great-nephew. We can be sure that Ludkins had been in Norwich since about 1590 when Christopher would have begun his locksmith's training. Our emigrant spent a few years in Hingham, Massachusetts, but soon moved to more populous Boston where he opened a shop. The South Shore town could no more support such a specialized calling than a village in southwest Norfolk. He was reenacting a family tradition.[13]

Other specialists are similarly found in larger centers. Two hatters, the disreputable Walter Allen and the still-apprenticed Theodore Atkinson worked in the West Suffolk county town of Bury St. Edmunds. So did the pewterer and brazier Thomas Bumstead, though another branch of the family remained in the ancestral village of Rattlesden, eight miles to the southeast. William Moody was a specialist leather worker, a saddler. No small community would have been able to offer him enough custom to sustain him. He lived in Ipswich, the main town and port of east Suffolk. Though there were plenty of Moodys over in west Suffolk and east Cambridgeshire, where they had flourished since 1327, none is recorded among Ipswich decedents. Perhaps William himself had emigrated the 35 miles from the neighborhood of Newmarket.[14]

Some craftsmen, though permanently resident in a town or village, would by the very nature of their skills move about within a neighborhood. An obvious example would be the stone mason, who would have to move from site to site, as might the carpenter, repairing or constructing dwellings or farm buildings, or the glazier. In all, 30 of these peripatetic craftsmen emigrated from Greater East Anglia during the 1630s.

94

Finally, artisanal mobility might result from marriage. Hugh Mason was a tanner. He emigrated in the *Francis* from Ipswich in 1634 and settled in Watertown. Two years before, he had married Esther Welles, daughter of Thomas, glover, at St. Peter's Church in Maldon, Essex. This is the first record of a Mason in Maldon, though Welleses had thrived there as leatherworkers since 1404. The Mason family was concentrated in villages on the north shore of the Thames Estuary like Barking, Corringham, and Runwell. It seems probable that Hugh may be an example of the young craftsman who improved his prospects by allying with a leading artisanal family, much like the apprentices of popular legend.[15] Marriage migration might more likely affect the bride, as we shall see later. There were a number of emigrant women like Elizabeth Woodruff of Skirbeck by Boston in Lincolnshire. When she married the shoemaker Thomas Wardall, she moved 20 miles north to the market town of Alford, a modest overture to the journey to Boston, Massachusetts, in 1634.[16]

Although these factors and examples might give the impression that craftsmen were among the most mobile members of the emigrating contingent, this was not the case. A glance at Table 15 and other life histories will illustrate this. The great majority of artisans remained close to their family roots (102 out of a known 115). Even more worked within a radius of 10 miles of their birthplaces (119 out of a known 123).

The craftsman about whom most is known is the tailor John Dane, Jr. (c1613–84), who immigrated to Roxbury, then moved on to Ipswich in 1636. There, toward the end of his life, he composed his spiritual autobiography (1682). His father was also a tailor, and his mother had been a servant to Lady Denny of Bishop's Stortford on the Essex–Hertfordshire border. The Dane family had been settled for a century or more just north of the town. Although John himself had been born 14 miles to the southwest at Little Berkhamstead, the family moved back to Stortford when he was a baby. As a young man, Dane moved about within the local area. Having fallen out with his father, he was apprenticed to a Mr. Tidd in Hertford. Qualified, he admitted to considerable restlessness in his early twenties. The great landed magnates of this district were the Barrington family of Hatfield Broad Oak. They had intermarried with the Dennys. They were eager proponents of puritan colonization, and Dane might easily have gone with a friend to St. Kitts in the West Indies had it not been captured by the Spaniards. He then contemplated "journey work through all the counties of England like a pilgrim," but instead he was taken on as a butler to a younger son,

Robert Barrington, who lived at Woodrow Green near Barrington Hall. He married a local woman of yeoman stock, and his sister married James Howe, a Woodrow Green weaver. As a family man, he practiced his trade in Hatfield, where hard-pressed established tailors ganged up on the competing newcomer and several times tried to drive him out of town. His ambition to go to New England was strongly opposed by his parents, until, as a test, the Bible was opened at random and the word of God was plainly in favor of emigration. Dane's newly widowed father went too.

As a man Dane was probably exceptional. In Ipswich, Massachusetts, he prospered and eventually styled himself "surgeon." The climb from tailor to surgeon was, as we have seen, somewhat less dizzying then than now, but his probate inventory of more than £469 marked him as a man of some wealth. Nonetheless, as a young apprentice and qualified tailor in England, his ambit had been quite narrow. Although his autobiography gives a sense of restless youthful mobility, none of the places he visited or worked in was more than 12 miles from his parental home. Hatfield Broad Oak, his eventual home, was less than four miles from Bishop's Stortford, which, significantly, was also the hometown of the Reverend John Norton, who helped place John with Robert Barrington and whom the Danes followed to Ipswich, Massachusetts. Although the idea of emigration overseas was much in the air in the neighborhood, it was still an awesome step compared with adolescent moves within a familiar locality.[17]

One of Dane's fellow townsmen in Ipswich, Massachusetts, was Richard Kimball. He was 39 when he sailed with his family in the *Elizabeth* from Ipswich, Suffolk, in 1634. Kimball came from Hitcham in Suffolk, near Bury St. Edmunds. He had been born there in 1595 and looked only as far as the next village for his wife, Ursula Scott, whom he married in 1619. Kimball was a wheelwright like his father and his fellow emigrant Henry Kimball. Scotts and Kimballs owned land in several parishes in the district and were intermarried with local farming and artisanal clans. Kimball continued work as a wheelwright in the New World, though he also acquired considerable tracts of land; his estate when he died in 1675 at age 80 was valued at £737. In his following a family craft, in his stake in the land, and in his marital choice, Richard Kimball gives an impression of stability and localized horizons which typified the artisanal group.[18]

The example of John Dane or Richard Kimball could be repeated many times over. Family continuity in certain crafts is common; John

Beale, the Hingham shoemaker who emigrated in midlife in 1638, had leatherworking in his blood; the craft went back in his family to at least the middle of the sixteenth century. George Barrell, an aptly named cooper from the wood-pasture hamlet of St. Michael South Elmham, was the son of a carpenter. John Hood, who grew up in the Essex textile town of Halstead, learned the textile trade at his father's knee.[19]

Persistence close to family roots was also normal, as Table 14 shows. Often, as we shall soon discover, clans had been settled in a particular neighborhood for at least a century, three generations or more. Land was still important to these craftsmen. They grew up in a culture dominated by agriculture. They would be required to help with the annual battle for survival, the harvest. Many craftsmen also had a hand in farming. Their own holdings might be worked by themselves, by hired labor, or by kinsmen; services would be bartered. On 16 January 1630, the Reverend Nathaniel Ward wrote from Stondon Massey, Essex, to Winthrop to reserve berths for two artisans: "One of them hath put off a good farm this week and sold all." Several artisans acknowledged their dual craft–farming interests. Edward Converse, from Navestock near Brentwood in the cereal-raising area of central Essex, called himself "miller-husbandman." John Thurston, from Wrentham in northeast Suffolk, was a "husbandman carpenter." From Bures in the Stour Valley, John Parmenter was recorded as a "yeoman tailor," as was his son John. Thomas Barnes appears in a 1637 listing as "farmer and weaver." The importance of land even in an artisanal family was demonstrated in the will of the carpenter Stephen Fosdick. In 1664 he bequeathed his land in Charlestown, Massachusetts, to his son John, then his grandson Stephen, "and so to run in the generation of Fosdicks for ever."[20]

Analysis of most of the crafts practiced by the artisans who emigrated suggests why the great majority came from settled backgrounds. Most were textile, leather, wood, and metal workers. The 41 men in the cloth industry were dominated by 29 producers—24 weavers and five finishers. The seventeenth-century cloth business was a largely decentralized handicraft industry coordinated by clothier entrepreneurs, as we have seen. Apart from fulling and dyeing, the other specialized processes were performed in the homes of the individual spinners (usually women and children) and weavers, who had their own looms, often situated by the unusually large windows that still mark weavers' cottages. So there was little call for producers to be mobile; either the clothiers brought the materials to them and collected the completed work, or the small independent craftsmen bought materials and sold their products at the local market.[21] The exception to this "putting-out" or self-employment might be in Norwich, where employed weavers might work on a master's looms in a small workshop. Manufacturing remained intensely local in the city, however, with certain parishes like St. Edmunds specializing in cloth making. Like the fulling mills and dyeing vats of the clothing districts, the tanning pits of the leather industry, the sawpits for timber, and the grist mills for cereals imposed a certain stasis on their operators.

Most of the processors among the artisans came from relatively common, low-paid crafts: tailors (12), shoemakers (16), carpenters (23), coopers (6), and blacksmiths (8). Because most emigrants hailed from the thickly settled wood-pasture areas of East Anglia, where cattle raising was important, local communities would support this variety of craftsmen. There were several tailors in the small town of Hatfield Broad Oak since all clothing had to be made by hand. Carpenters would be needed not just for building work but for making and maintaining farm and industrial machinery; smiths, too, would be needed for more than their regular business of shoeing horses. Shoemakers and cordwainers could be called on to make the plethora of leather goods used on the farm and in the home. Once again, then, these processor artisans had no need to migrate from their communities in order to make a living. Significantly, 89 artisans emigrated from villages or hamlets, the most hidebound communities, as opposed to 55 known to have come from towns or cities. Less than a third came from the most mobile age group, those under 25. Even among this group, unlike Dick Whittington, most stayed put in their familiar English neighborhoods.

If the majority of artisans were so resolutely rooted, what drove them to emigrate across the Atlantic in such disproportionate numbers? "Bishops, bastards and bankrouts" were nominated by the noxious Ned Ward as the main populators of New England.[22] Although only one East Anglian artisan, Walter Allen of Bury St. Edmunds, was accused of fleeing to escape the maintenance of his two bastards,[23] there is more evidence of religious radicalism among artisan refugees. Several, like Thomas Oliver, calenderer, Ferdinando Adams, shoemaker, or Michael Metcalfe, dornick weaver and clothier, fled the wrath of the church courts.[24] There was a long record of religious nonconformity in the Mixer family, whose offspring Isaac left Capel St. Mary in southeast Suffolk for Watertown in 1634.[25] Many towns from which craftsmen emigrated were notorious wasps' nests of dissent: Braintree-Bocking,

Ipswich, Maldon, Chelmsford, Norwich, Yarmouth, Sudbury, Boston, Alford, and Bury.[26] Artisans and farmers were politically aware in the region. The crown's attempts to raise extraparliamentary subsidies in the 1620s and 1630s were resisted in west Essex and the Stour Valley. George Barrell and Henry Garrett were listed as ship-money defaulters in 1637. Perhaps they were "village Hampdens" resisting political extortion by flight.[27]

None of the artisans is known to have left to escape creditors. John Roper, carpenter of New Buckenham, was to fail repeatedly in Massachusetts before the Indians put him out of his misery at Lancaster in 1676, but at age 26, when he sailed, he was probably too young to have begun his career of insolvency.[28] Many of the weavers and other textile workers must have been motivated to some extent by economic deprivation. The depression in the industry during the 1620s and early 1630s gravely threatened their already modest livelihoods. "Lack of vent," beggary, riot, and starvation were reported from the clothing districts. John Winthrop no doubt had the plight of the neighboring Stour Valley textile workers in mind when he wrote of the undoing of "many poor families" from actions brought by "the multitudes of Attorneys in the courts" and the "multitude and lewdness of bailiffs" seizing assets, "the pitiful complaint of the orphans fatherless and many poor creditors" unable to collect what was owed them. The small farmer was similarly intolerably burdened. Winthrop graphically described the increase in the poor: "Why meet we so many wandering ghosts in the shape of men, so many spectacles of misery in all our streets, our houses full of victuals, and our entries of hunger-starved Christians? Our shops are full of rich wares and under our stalls lie our own flesh in nakedness. . . . Our people perish for want of sustenance and employment; many live miserably . . . our towns complain of the burden of poor people." This outraged lament was echoed by the city authorities in Norwich. Their welfare problems were not helped by decimating plague epidemics in 1625, 1626, and 1637–38 or by the harrying out of employers like Michael Metcalfe. Prices plummeted with recession so that "no man may look for recompense suitable to his expense of time and industry," and farming was so unprofitable that it would "soon eat up our stocks." The intense pressure on jobs was reflected by the hostile reception of John Dane by the established tailors in Hatfield Broad Oak; they wanted him out of town "because he takes up all our work and we know not how to live." Such seismic shocks as religious persecution or economic disaster were perhaps the only forces strong enough to propel these deeply embedded artisans into contemplating emigration.[29]

This picture of home-loving artisans tends to be borne out by other findings. Contemporary observers commented on the resistance of Stour Valley clothworkers to the "New Draperies," despite the declining market for the thickly woven and fulled "whites" and "blues." The adoption of lighter Walloon "stuffs" among the Norfolk weavers was slow and reluctant, even though it was only a modest extension of their long tradition of worsted weaving. Most weavers were "in a small way of business," living from week to week and working "by the piece" with intervening relaxation. The idea of modern, regular shift hours was alien to their work patterns and mindsets.[30] In general, low wages discouraged technological advances and labor-saving devices. Signing/reading literacy levels of Norfolk and Suffolk craftsmen rose from only 20 percent in 1530 to 65 percent in 1710, but most communication seems to have remained face-to-face and in the time-honored way.[31] During the English Interregnum, textile workers contributed a major element to millenarian sects like the Fifth Monarchy Men, but we may doubt whether this strain of biblical literalism represented a leap forward into enlightened rationalism.[32] Certainly most artisans shared the weavers' suspicion of technological innovation.[33] Even the greater emphasis on subsistence agriculture for craftsmen in the New World was a shift of balance for the majority rather than a radical redeployment.[34]

There is some evidence of artisans seeking to profit from their scarcity value. In 1630 there were complaints about the exorbitant rates being charged by "carpenters, joiners, bricklayers, sawyers and thatchers." A large number of Greater East Anglian artisans like Kimball and Dane were attracted to the entrepreneurial trading settlement of Ipswich, which boasted "twelve carpenters, twelve leatherworkers, coopers, butchers, bakers, wheelwrights, blacksmiths and tallow chandlers." However, Dane's stated reason for moving up from Roxbury was to follow his religious mentor John Norton. Such mixtures of motives were no doubt commonplace.[35]

Although the weavers who emigrated seem to have brought their own looms and thus to have been independent masters rather than marginal wage workers, they were not by and large agents of change in the Old or New World. For most emigrant artisans, diligence in their callings was "the price of survival," not the launch rocket for economic takeoff. Then, as now, the Dick Whittingtons and the Lionel Cranfields were the rare exceptions, not the rule.[36]

Farmers

Nowadays, if you ask people in Britain or the United States about the last harvest, most will not have the remotest idea about its success or failure. Such ignorance would have been unbelievable three centuries ago. In the England of the 1630s, and even more so in New England, every man, woman, and child would have known the answer. Most would have had a hand in gathering it in, and most would have contributed to its cultivation. In economies that stood closer to the modern Third World than to advanced "postindustrial" states, feeding mouths was a matter of constant concern and frequent uncertainty. Church services after harvest were not the mere rituals they so often are today. Either they were heartfelt sighs of relief that an unfathomable God had providentially manipulated nature in humanity's favor, or they were anguished cries of penitence and humiliation at having offended the Almighty.[37]

The 81 emigrants from the eastern counties formally listed in English documents as farmers are therefore somewhat misleading—almost every emigrant was involved in agriculture. Many of those whose callings are unknown were almost certainly on the land.

All except one of the group are listed as either yeomen or husbandmen (see Table 16). Though the meanings of these designations varied from place to place and from man to man, yeomen were conventionally more prosperous and secure than husbandmen.[38] The difference between a yeoman and a gentleman was often not so much a matter of wealth as of lifestyle or "port." The yeoman was a working farmer. He said to his men, "Let us go to the field," not "Go to the field." The adjectives most frequently used to describe yeomen are frugal, hardheaded, thrifty, careful, unostentatious, solid, money-loving, honest, prudent, and sturdy. Winthrop's friend Robert Ryece castigated them for their penny pinching, "their continuall under-living," which enabled them to "grow with the wealth of the world." Others attacked them for their "gripinge of poore men by usurious contracts and bargains." They were, according to some historians, early rural capitalists or commercial farmers, and thanks to a hyperactive land market, rising food prices, and a growing population, the century from 1550 to 1650 has been called "the Golden Age of the Yeoman." Prosperity would fall to the farmer who was not content "to keepe mony lyinge idley by him, but as soon as he had gathered together any some [sum] he eyther bought land therewith or put the same out to interest."[39] In Greater

Table 16. Farmer Emigrants

AG	Name	Age	DOB	DOE	Type	BP	FR	WP	Distances BP:FR	Distances BP:WP
6	Nathan ALDOUS	c43	c1595	1638	Y	Fressingfield S	Fressingfield S 1499A	Fressingfield S	0	0
5	Boz ALLEN	c38	c1600	1638	Y	Grimston N	Grimston area 1379B	King's Lynn N	0	6
4	Matt ALLYN	c32	c1600	1632	H	Chelmsford E	Chelmsford area 1552A	Chelmsford E	2	0
3	John ASTWOOD	26	1609	1635	H			Nazeing E		
10	Mich BACON	c61	1579	c1640	Y	Winston S	Helmingham S 1535A	Winston S	3	0
10	Wm BACON	c63	1577	c1640	Y	Winston S	Helmingham S 1535A	Winston S	3	0
4	Wm BALLARD	32	1603	1635	H		Beccles S (12) 1599C	Bradwell S		
2	Geo BARBER	c23	c1615	1638	Y	Fressingfield S	Fressingfield area 1506A	Fressingfield S	0	0
11	Fran BILLINGTON		c1610		H			Spalding L		
1	Jos BIXBY	17	1621	1638	H	Lit. Waldingfield S	Thorpe Morieux S 1459A	Lit. Waldingfield S	5	0
5	Hum BRADSTREET	40	1594	1634	Y	Ipswich S	Bentley E 1531B	Capel St. Mary S	10	6
3	Walt BRIGGS	c27	1612	c1639	Y	Bucklesham S	Bucklesham S 1504A	Bucklesham S	0	0
3	Abr BROWN	c30	c1600	1630	Y	Hawkedon S	Hawkedon S 1538A	Hawkedon S	0	0
5	Hen BULLOCK	40	1595	1635	H	St. Lawrence E	Gt. Wigboro area E 1503A	St. Lawrence E	8	0
9	Rich CARVER	60	1577	1637	H			Scratby N		
7	Fran CHICKERING	c46	c1592	1638	Y	Ringsfield S	Fressingfield S N1	Ringsfield S	15	0
7	Hen CHICKERING	50	1588	1638	Y	Ringsfield S	Fressingfield S N1	Henstead/Wrentham S	15	6/7
4	Thos CLARKE	33	1605	1638	Y	Westhorpe S	Gt. Ashfield area S 1440A	Westhorpe S	3	0
6	Thurston CLARKE	44	1590	1634	Y	Ipswich S	Ipswich S 1451B	Ipswich S	0	0
7	Benj COOPER	50	1587	1637	H	Brampton S	Walberswick/Southwold S 1451C	Brampton S	5	0

No.	Name	Age	Year	Year	Y/H	Origin	Origin area	Code	Destination		
4	Thos CURTIS	33	1598	1631	Y	Nazeing E	Nazeing E	1585A	Nazeing E	0	0
8	John CURTIS	54	1577	1631	Y	Nazeing E	Nazeing E	1585A	Nazeing E	0	0
5	Wm CURTIS	40	1592	1632	Y	Nazeing E	Nazeing E	1585A	Nazeing E	0	0
7	Matt CUSHING	49	1599	1638	Y	Hardingham N	Hingham/Harding-ham N	1357A	Hingham N	0	2
7	Theoph CUSHING	49	1584	1633	Y	Hardingham N	Hingham/Harding-ham N	1357A	Hingham N	0	2
7	John CUTLER	c47	c1590	1637	Y	Sprowston N	Norwich N	1445B	Sprowston N	2	0
3	Jas CUTLER	28	1606	1634	Y	Sprowston N	Norwich N	1445B	Sprowston N	2	0
7	Nich DANFORTH	46	1589	1635	Y	Framlingham S	Framlingham S	1512A	Framlingham S	0	0
1	Isaac DESBOROUGH	20	1615	1635	H	Eltisley C	Eltisley C	1550A	Eltisley C	0	0
4	Hen DOW	32	1605	1637	H	Runham N	Runham N	1544A	Ormesby N	0	3
3	Phil ELIOT	29	1602	1631	H	Widford E	Bps.Stortfd area, Herts	1542A	Nazeing E	6	6
2	Jacob ELIOT	25	1606	1631	H	Widford E	Bps.Stortford, Herts	1542A	Nazeing E	6	6
2	Fran ELIOT	c25	1615	c1640	H	Nazeing E	Bps.Stortford, Herts	1542A	Nazeing E	6	0
7	Anth FISHER	47	1591	1637	Y	Syleham S	Fressingfield area S	1523B	Syleham S	3	0
3	John FOLGER	28	1607	1635	Y	Diss N	Diss N	1472A	Diss N	0	0
1	Adam FOULSHAM	c18	c1621	1639	Y	Scoulton/Hing-ham N	Hingham area	1534A	Scoulton/Hing-ham N	3/0	0
2	John FOULSHAM	c24	c1614	1638	Y	Hingham N	Hingham N	1534A	Hingham N	0	0
5	Edw GOFFE	40	1594	1634	Y	Burgh Castle S		1613A	Burgh Castle S	0	0
6	Ric GOODALE	44	1594	1638	Y	Yarmouth N	Yarmouth N	1579A	Yarmouth N	0	0
4	Thos HAMMOND	33	1603	1636	Y	Lavenham S	Lawshall S	1440A	Lavenham S	4	0
11	Hen HARWOOD			1630	H	Shenfield E	Brentwood E	1573B	Shenfield E	2	0
5	Ab HOWE	c36	c1602	1638	H	Hatfield B.Oak E	Hatfield B.Oak E	1558A	Hatfield B.Oak E	0	0
5	Wm HUBBARD	40	1595	1635	H	Thorrington E	Thorrington E	1518B	Tendring 100 E	0	0

Table 16. *Continued*

AG	Name	Age	DOB	DOE	Type	BP	FR		WP	Distances BP: FR	Distances BP: WP
4	Edw INGALLS	c31	c1598	1629	Y	Skirbeck L	Skirbeck L	1555A	Skirbeck L	0	0
11	Fran JAMES			1638	Y	Hingham N	Rockland area N	1453B	Hingham N	4	0
4	Phil JAMES	c32	c1603	1635	Y	Hingham N	Rockland N	1453B	Hingham N	4	0
9	Thos JENNER Sr	c55	c1580	1635	H	Fordham E	Fordham E	1559A	Fordham E	0	0
6	Thos JOSSELYN	43	1592	1635	H	Roxwell E	Hi. Roding E	1524A	Roxwell E	3	0
11	Dan LINCOLN	c22	c1616	1638	H	Hingham N	Hingham area N	1543A	Hingham	0	0
2	Thos LINCOLN	c33	1603	c1636	H		Hingham area N (5)	1543A	Wymondham N		
4	Rob LORD				Y	Sudbury S	Groton S	1457A	Sudbury S	5	0
11	John LOVERAN			c1636	Y	Ardleigh E	Ardleigh E	1600A	Ardleigh E	0	0
6	Wm MANNING	42	1592	1634	Y	Broomfield E	Springfield E	1595A	Chelmsford E	2	3
4	Matt MARVIN	35	1600	1635	H	Gt. Bentley E	Ramsey E	1503A	Gt. Bentley E	8	0
6	Reyn MARVIN	41	1594	1635	H	Gt. Bentley E	Ramsey E	1503A	Gt. Bentley E	8	0
5	John MERRIALL	37	1599	1636	Y	Belstead S	Wherstead S	1444A	Wherstead S	2	2
4	Nat MERRIALL	35	1601	1636	Y	Belstead S	Wherstead S	1444A	Wherstead S	2	2
5	John MOULTON	38	1599	1637	H	Ormesby N	Ormesby N	c1530A	Ormesby N	0	0
3	Thos MOULTON	29	1608	1637	H	Ormesby N	Ormesby N	c1530A	Ormesby N	0	0
8	Jas OLMSTEAD	52	1580	1632	Y	Fairstead E	Gt. Waltham E	1553A	Fairstead E	5	0
8	John PAGE	54	1576	1630	Y	Boxted E	Lavenham S	1605A	Dedham E	9	3
3	John PAGE	c27	1610	c1637	Y	Boxted E	Lavenham S	1605A	Dedham E	9	3
4	Rob PAGE	33	1604	1637	H	Ormesby N	Acle N	1587A	Ormesby N	6	0

Wm PAYNE	5	37	1598	1635	H	Lavenham S	Lavenham area S	1533A	Lavenham S	0	0
Jos PECK	8	51	1587	1638	Y	Beccles S	Halesworth/S.Elmham S	No	Hingham N	8	26
Aar PINGRY	1	c20	c1620	c1640	H	Colchester E	Tours, France	N1	Colchester E	c280	0
John PORTER	3	c27	c1603	1630	H	Broomfield E	Hatfield Peverel E	1537A	Broomfield E	3	0
John PROCTER	5	c40	c1595	1635	H		Groton S	N1	Groton S		0
Sim RAY	3	29	1610	1639	Y	Cowlinge S	Hundon area S	1452A	Hundon S	4	4
John READ	6	41	1598	1639	Y	Blythborough S	Blythborough S	1540B	Blythborough S	0	0
Thos READE	2	22	1612	1634	Y	N.Benfleet E	Wickford E	1534A	Wickford E	3	3
Wm ROSCOE	6	41	1594	1635	H	Sawbridgeworth, Herts	Sawbridgeworth, Herts	No	Billericay E	0	12
Edw SAWYER	3	28	1608	1636	Y	Lincolnshire	Lincolnshire	No	Lincolnshire		
Sam SHERMAN	4	34	1601	1635	H	Dedham E	Dedham E	1590A	Dedham E	0	0
Fran SKERRY	3	29	1608	1637	H	Gt.Yarmouth N	Gt.Yarmouth N	1510B	Gt.Yarmouth N	0	0
Hen SMITH	3	30	1607	1637	H	New Buckenham N	New Buckenham N	1391C	New Buckenham N	0	0
Greg STONE	6	43	1592	1635	Y	Gt.Bromley E	Gt.Bromley E	1350A	Nayland S	0	6
John STONE Jr.	1	17	1618	1635	Y	Nayland S	Gt.Bromley E	1350A	Nayland S	6	0
Sim STONE	7	50	1585	1635	H	Gt.Bromley E	Gt.Bromley E	1350A	Boxted E	0	4
Thos TOWNSEND	6	43	1595	1638	H	Braconash N	Braconash N	1591B	Braconash N/Gedding S	0	0/31
Dan WELD	8	c54	1585	c1639	Y	Sudbury S	Sudbury S	1561A	Sudbury S	0	0
Thos WELLES	4	31	1605	1636	H	Colchester E	Colchester E	1535B	Colchester E	0	0
Rob WING	9	60	1574	1634	L	Lawford E	Dedham E	1571A	Lawford	4	0

Note: Y = yeoman; H = husbandman; L = laborer.

Table 17. Age, Roots, and Mobility of Yeomen Emigrants

AG	Age	No.	Distance, BP:FR						Distance, BP:WP					
			0–4	5–9	10–14	15–19	20+	UK	0–4	5–9	10–14	15–19	20+	UK
1	16–20	2	2						2					
2	21–25	3	3						3					
3	26–30	6	4	1				1	5					1
4	31–35	7	7	1					7					
5	36–40	5	2		1			1	3	2				
6	41–45	5	5						4	1				
7	46–50	7	5			2			6	1				
8	51–55	4	1	3					3				1	
9	56–60	0												
10	61–	2	2						2					
11	UK	2	2						2					
	Total	43	33	5	1	2		2	37	4			1	1

Table 18. Age, Roots, and Mobility of Husbandmen Emigrants

AG	Age	No.	Distance, BP:FR						Distance, BP:WP					
			0–4	5–9	10–14	15–19	20+	UK	0–4	5–9	10–14	15–19	20+	UK
1	16–20	3	1	1			1		3					
2	21–25	3		2				1	1	1				1
3	26–30	7	4	1				1	4	1				1
4	31–35	7	4	3				1	7					1
5	36–40	6	4	1				1	5					1
6	41–45	4	3	1					2		1		1	
7	46–50	2	1	1					2					
8	51–55	0												
9	56–60	3	2					1	2					1
10	61–	0												
11	UK	3	2					1	2					1
	Total	38	21	10	1		1	6	28	2	1		1	6
	Y&H Totals	81	54	15	1	2	1	8	65	6	1		2	7

East Anglia, this century saw the building or extension of so many of the substantial farmhouses and great barns that survive today. Yeomen's sons appeared in unprecedented numbers at the universities and the inns of court. New methods of farming also developed: the alternating of land under pasture and under the plow, or "lea farming," the improvement of pasture and fodder, the "floating" of grazing meadows, or the reclamation of fenland.[40] In the Essex village of Terling, a campaign of disciplining the lower orders, especially in their drinking, sexual, and work habits, was carried out in the decades before the Great Migration by yeomen who ran the parish and manorial government. Established yeomen like Nicholas Danforth from Framlingham or the Marvin brothers from Great Bentley served regularly as churchwardens, overseers of the poor, and jurymen in the manorial court. Perhaps these rural money-makers and parish administrators might provide the drive to change and improvement among the emigrants.[41]

Three factors might lend weight to yeoman influence. The first was their disproportionate numbers. Seventeenth-century English local censuses suggest that the ratio of yeomen to husbandmen was roughly one to four, but among the emigrants more farmers were designated yeomen than husbandmen. Second, the New World venture would initially live or die by the planters' ability to wrest sustenance from the land. The thriving farmers would both lead and profit from this battle for group survival. Third, yeomen continued to emigrate into their fifties, whereas most occupational groups show a marked drop in numbers after the age of 45.[42]

Why yeomen continued to emigrate after middle age is something of a mystery. It might be inferred that this marked them out as agrarian entrepreneurs with sights set on the main chance. However, the economic risks involved in immigrating to a wilderness hardly fit the prudential, cautious image of the yeomanry. Other motivators are suggested by the fact that 11 of the 13 who were over 45 years of age were brothers of emigrants[43] or that 11 came from areas of heavy migration like Fressingfield, Nazeing, Hingham, Norwich, or Dedham.[44] They therefore tended to be members of large companies of planters. Ten were identified with clerical emigrants, either by kinship links or by known religious affinity.[45] One or two of these older men had moved considerable distances during their lifetimes in England. Joseph Peck had followed his clerical brother Robert from his birthplace, Beccles on the Norfolk–Suffolk border, to Hingham, 26 miles to the northwest. There is evidence that the Bacon brothers, Michael and William, may have spent some time during the 1630s as planters in Ireland. The Chickering brothers had been born in Ringsfield, some 15 miles north of the family's roots at Fressingfield.[46] On the whole, though, these older yeomen displayed all the tenacity of their fellow farmers in clinging to familiar soil. As we shall see in Chapter 7, roots going down three or more generations were typical of the whole farmer group. Such embeddedness in their communities could be expected to "temper their individualism." Long-established farming families would think twice before flouting village traditions.[47]

What were these wealthier farmers like? A typical group of yeomen came from the neighborhood of Fressingfield in north-central Suffolk. The village sent a company of 18 people to Massachusetts in 1638. The country roundabout is still wood pasture, the clay soils ideal for dairy farming. In the seventeenth century hemp and flax were also raised; its processing into linen or wool-linen textiles provided by-employment for dairymen's families. The area had a long radical-puritan tradition, and the old feudal manorial system had decayed, allowing yeomen independence to farm commercially. By the end of the sixteenth century, lea farming had been adopted, alternating cereals and dairying. Butter by the 56-pound firkin and large Suffolk bang cheeses—"Dogs bark at them because they are too hard to bite!"—were ferried or carted to London. Aldous, Barber, and Fisher families had long been prominent in the district. They lived in substantial Suffolk farmhouses, still to be seen in the village. A house on New Street was named "Barbers." An Aldous farm stood beside one of the seven parish grazing greens. Probate inventories reveal the occupations of yeomen inhabitants. Butteries, cheese houses, dairies, cattle stalls, and pasture fields are commonly listed. In 1558 the widow Alice Barber left 25 kine (head of cattle) in her will. James Barber's inventory named individual milch cows: "Old Pearse, Pricke Horne, Red Dawe, Red Pie, Grymble, Dymble, Slutte and Pawle." John Barber, who died in 1602, left silver spoons—a sign of affluence—to his three daughters. One Aldous forebear is described as a linen weaver, and another bequeathed two looms. Stephen Aldous, who died in 1628, possessed a set of virginals.[48]

Yeomen like our emigrants often owned or leased pasture closes and arable land in several parishes, but wills in the records of the archdeaconry of Suffolk make it clear that the activities of the Aldous, Barber, and Fisher families had long been centered on Fressingfield. The exceptions to this long-lasting local settlement seem to have been the Chickering brothers. There are no Norwich or Suffolk wills for this family until that of Henry, their father, who died in 1626. He had lived as a young man at Bramfield and then moved 10 miles north to Rings-field, but he also owned considerable land in Henstead six miles to the east. Absence of wills does not rule out family residence, of course. Four miles west of Fressingfield is a village called Chickering, which may have been the origin of this unusual family name.[49]

As surviving probate inventories show, these four yeoman families were comfortably off. This affluence seems to have been sustained in New England. For instance, Francis Chickering left £309 when he died at Dedham, Massachusetts, in 1658. His elder brother Henry's estate still included land and a house in Henstead, Suffolk, valued at £200. The families were traditionally used to filling important parish offices and continued to take an active role in the town and church of Dedham, Massachusetts. Joshua Fisher, Jr., in association with his Fressingfield and Dedham neighbor Eleazer Lusher, combined land development with his craft of blacksmith and public office as a selectman and deputy. The two leaders acquired extra grants from the General Court for their town, which launched the daughter settlements of Medfield, Wren-tham, and Natick nearby, and the frontier settlement of Deerfield in the Connecticut Valley. Dedham, like Fressingfield, quickly be-came market-oriented and produced surplus grain for Boston. The two founders, both of yeoman stock, shared in their community's pros-perity. Fisher, who had arrived as a 16-year-old apprentice and had married an Aldous in 1643, was worth £1,145 when he died. Half his wealth was in land in four towns. Lusher had 15 much more modest parcels of land in four towns by 1672. However, much of their real estate was a reward for onerous service to the Commonwealth, and it is probably misleading to label them as land speculators.[50]

The Aldous, Barber, and Fisher families had large networks of kin in their English neighborhood, and they and the Chickerings were all connected by marriage. Indeed, the most striking characteristic of the yeomen emigrants is their kin-connectedness. Almost all of them trav-eled west as part of larger family groups rather than as individuals. Older, more traditional, clan loyalties seemed to activate their decision to leave the sinking ship of England.[51]

The husbandman conventionally lived closer to the subsistence line. According to Ryece, "though he ordinarily thriveth ordinarily well, yet he laboureth much, and if the frowning years should not sometimes diminish his crop, hee would never care what he offered for the hyre of hands." He was seen by one contemporary as "plain, frugal, painstak-

ing, close and unintelligible." On average worth only a fifth to a third of
the yeoman, much more likely to be illiterate, it followed that "poverty
and ignorance are the ordinary inhabitants of small farms." In contrast
to the yeoman's accumulative drives, the husbandman would be quite
content with a "competency." Writing on the eve of the Great Migration, John Earle chose to emphasize the husbandman's blinkered nar-
rowness and sluggish simplemindedness. If the century before the Civil
War had been kind to the yeomanry, part of their rise had been at the
expense of their poorer neighbors. The husbandman rarely owned land
in freehold and suffered from the gradual conversion from copyhold to
the less secure and more expensive leasehold. However, as Ryece suggests, these stoic survivors in Greater East Anglia had by and large
managed to hold out against the slide into landless laboring, which was
the bottom of the agricultural heap.[52]

In comparison with the High Suffolk dairymen, the east Norfolk
villages of Scratby, Ormesby St. Michael, and Ormesby St. Margaret
provide a contrasting group of six husbandmen emigrants and their
families.[53] In all, there were 38 members of the 1637 company, and
another 14 who were probably from leaseholding families. This highlights one major difference from the Fressingfield yeomen: the number
of servants who emigrated. Six of these were maidservants, probably
reflecting the large number of children in the company, and five were
male "servants in husbandry," or young laborers hired for the year and
living with their employers. Most of them came from families already
intermarried with the six masters' families. Why the male servants?
Partly, servants reflect the younger average age of the husbandmen.
Except for the 60-year-old Richard Carver, their average age was 33,
whereas the four Fressingfield yeomen were in their forties and fifties.
The husbandmen could not, then, call on adult or adolescent sons to
help on their farms. But servants were also necessary because the
Ormesby farmers practiced a different kind of agriculture. Their villages, just north of Great Yarmouth and just inland from the sea,
specialized in cereal growing with some dairying and stock rearing. This
mixed farming involved much greater use of arable land and was much
more labor-intensive than the dairying of High Suffolk. The emphasis
on the plow and cereal growing may help to account for the designation
"husbandman." Some or all of the rich, light loam was probably still
farmed in open fields, though the heavy-clay neighborhood was enclosed and given over to dairy farming. Whereas a family could live
comfortably on a 50-acre Suffolk dairy farm with time to spare for

cottage industries, the smaller holdings of the coastal region made subsistence less assured.[54]

The major similarity of the husbandmen with the Fressingfield yeomen was their residential rootedness. With the exception of the elderly Richard Carver, the rest of the husbandmen's clans had been in the neighborhood for generations. Thus Henry Dow's ancestors had been within six miles of Ormesby since 1393. His direct pedigree has been traced to John Dow, who died at Runham in 1544. The surname of his wife, the widow Joan Nudd, went back in manorial rolls to 1324. The brothers John and Thomas Moulton could boast an Ormesby lineage beginning about 1465, and the surname (derived from the local place-name, no doubt) was recorded on a manorial roll in 1440. Moultons had intermarried with Estow and Webster families who also emigrated. Robert Page's namesake ancestor had died at Acle, six miles southwest, in 1450. His wife, Lucy (Ward), came from a local family that had lived at Filby since at least 1490. William Palmer's forebears can be found in Great Yarmouth by 1520. Servants like the Goodwins had lines in the district going back to 1433; maidservant Mirabel Underwood's pedigree began in Yarmouth in 1430. John Moulton's wife, Anne (Green), had had ancestors on the Ormesby manorial rolls since 1325.[55]

This residential embeddedness coincides with the national picture of husbandmen generally. As a group they tended to be even more stable than the yeomanry. This is partly explained by the fact that "their limited economic opportunities and horizons meant that there was less scope for them to take risks and hence less chance of failing." Furthermore, their small holdings were less tempting to speculators, and tight-knit webs of local kinship could provide mutual protection.[56]

It is tempting to fall for the contemporary caricature of slow-moving, slow-speaking, and slow-witted Hodges and write off these small farmers as "your mouldy old leavened husbandmen who themselves and their forefathers have been accustomed to such a course of husbandry as they will practice and no other." However, the Ormesby group and probably many other East Anglian husbandmen were becoming more market-oriented by the early seventeenth century. Their decision to emigrate may have been in response to land hunger in the old country. Expansion and affluence could only occur on the free and seemingly limitless lands of New England.

Though economic opportunities probably encouraged emigration, the area around Great Yarmouth also had a reputation for religious dissent. Palmers and Goodwins had been in trouble with the church courts as absentees from Anglican services and as conventiclers in the late 1620s and the 1630s. The Yarmouth lecturer George Burdett was an outspoken critic of orthodox complacency. He fled to New England in 1635 with other townsmen after being cited before the church courts.[57]

The Ormesby group continued to cohere in New England. Most of them, after brief rests at Watertown and/or Newbury, became residents of the topographically similar country at Hampton on the New Hampshire coast. All except Palmer and Carver (who died in 1641 at Watertown) quickly assumed leadership as selectmen or representatives. John Moulton and Robert Page became wealthy men. Page's inventory was valued at £759 in 1679.[58]

However much their agrarian backgrounds might differ, these yeomen and husbandmen shared residentially stable lives (as Tables 17 and 18 demonstrate) in long-familiar and kin-knit neighborhoods before emigrating. They were bound together as much as they were bound to the land. Eagerness to innovate does not appear to have played a major part in their decision to emigrate.

Although the depression of the 1620s and 1630s made life hard for many artisans and farmers, there is little evidence that they were driven to emigrate by worries about economic survival. Dane, whose fare was assisted by Sir Thomas Barrington, "afterwards found great friendship from those that were my professed adversaries" among the tailors of Hatfield Broad Oak. Finding passage money of £50 to £80 per family would eliminate those already financially struggling. Husbandmen and middle-ranking tradesmen like shoemakers, blacksmiths, or carpenters would have little left over to start anew. Their comparative scarcity and the abundance of natural resources in the New World would, as Hakluyt predicted, offer a remedy. Religious, economic, and political discontents and expectations all jostled in different personal combinations in the minds of the industrious sort of people, the most numerous socioeconomic grouping. What most of them shared was the shock of dislocation as the price they had to pay for their remedies.

6

Dependents: Servants, Women, and Unknowns

A DEPENDENT was under the ultimate control of another because he or she could not command a competency through land or labor. In early modern England, most people were dependents: all children, almost all adolescents, most women, and the impotent aged. Thus subservience gives added meaning to the concept of freemanship, into which the ex-dependent apprentice emerged once his masterpiece was accepted. There is insufficient evidence about the emigrant children, and the aged will be discussed in Chapter 9. Here we concentrate on the servants and the adult women who emigrated from the eastern counties. To them are added the many men whose occupations are unknown.

Servants

Most servants who emigrated from Greater East Anglia in the 1630s were adolescents (see Tables 19–21). As such they were usually living in the households of their masters and mistresses, undergoing "training unalloyed by the sentiment of family." In Greater East Anglia and England generally, most adolescents were deemed servants. Service was a normal part of vocational education, even for the sprigs of the aristocracy. In a predominantly agrarian society, farm service deployed a physically strong but only partially skilled labor force where it was most needed. It transferred hungry mouths from the cottages and hovels of smallholders and laborers to the farms of the better-off husbandmen, yeomen, or gentlemen who required additional help. Apprenticeship controlled numbers entering crafts and maintained standards of production, pricing, and skill.[1]

Service had an important social and psychological function. It provided a controlled environment for the transition from childhood to adulthood. Servants were still dependents but removed from their emotionally charged parental homes. Their masters were answerable to authority for them, but they also provided board, lodging, and modest wages in kind, thus shielding them from the far more marginal existence of the day laborer. The servant might have little property (like Whittington with his small bundle), but at least he or she would not starve. The period between mid-teens and mid-twenties was also an opportunity for accumulating modest capital or money-earning skills in preparation for marriage. Service provided possibilities for young people to meet but placed a damper on sexual urges by its demand for hard work and obedience to strict discipline.[2]

The status of "servant" borne by 55 male emigrants covered a range of distinctive types. The very young so designated in shipping lists, like Henry Hayward, aged 7, or Stephen Beckett, 11, must have been as much foster children as servants. All five of the ambivalently listed *Hopewell* servants were 16 or younger.[3] Servants to artisans were usually trainees living in their masters' households for their seven-year terms. Their parents might well have had to pay fees for such skilled training. Apprenticeship was governed by the traditional formulas of contractual indentures. Craft trainees were closely controlled. They could not marry, go to pubs, divulge their masters' secrets, gamble, or even go out without permission. There are 18 youths between 14 and 21 years of age who were probably craft apprentices.[4]

The third subadult group designated servants were young agricultural workers or "servants in husbandry." Some "servants" in lists of emigrant artisan households may have been servants in husbandry responsible for helping craftsmen who also farmed. Unlike apprentices, this group were usually hired by the year. Their verbal contracts were often sealed by payment of a hiring penny and might be formally recorded at a petty sessions or statute sessions. These forerunners of the servant-hiring fairs were usually held around Michaelmas (29 September), and provided a holiday occasion for a whole neighborhood's youth. Kinship networks were useful sources of information, contacts, and often contracts in these annual redeployments of the agrarian labor force.[5]

Much migration to other colonies, like Virginia or Maryland, was by indentured servants who sold their labor in the New World for a set period in return for their passage. Some passengers in the Winthrop fleet of 1630, who were skilled craftsmen hired by the Massachusetts

Table 19. Emigrant Male Servants

AG	Name	Age	DOB	DOE	Master	Trade	BP	FR		WP	Distances	
											BP: FR	BP: WP
2	John ALBRO	14	1620	1634	Wm Freeborne				No	?Suffolk		
8	Thos ANDREW			1630					No	Essex		
2	Sam ARRES	15	1622	1637	John Baker	Grocer			No	Norwich N		
3	Theo ATKINSON	20	1612	1632	John Newgate	Haberdasher/feltmaker	Bury S	Bury S	1521B	Bury S	0	0
7	Thos BARTLETT	36	1594	1630	Wm Pelham		Essex		No	Bures S		
8	Rich BAXTER			1638	Fran James		Melton/Bawburgh N	Hingham/Melton N	1543A	Hingham N	9	9
2	Step BECKETT	11	1623	1634	Rich Pepper		Belchamp Water E	Mt.Bures E	1598A	Belchamp Water E	7	0
2	John BILL	13	1622	1635	Rich Tuttle	Shoemaker	?Nazeing E		No	St.Albans, Herts		?16
4	Hanniel BOSWORTH*	c23	c1615	1638	John Whittingham	Agriculture			No	Sutterton L		
4	Wm BROWN	c23	c1608	1631	John Winthrop		Groton S	Groton S	1570A	Groton S	0	0
8	Jas BUCK			1638	Phil James		?Barnham Broom N	Barnham Broom/Hingham N	1503B	Hingham N	0/4	?4

8	John BUCK			1638	Phil James		?Barnham Broom N	Barnham Broom/Hingham N	1503B	Hingham N	0/4	?4
5	—— BURGESS	26	1611	1637	John Gedney	Weaver	Norwich N	Fundenhall/Norwich N	N1	Norwich N	9/0	0
5	Clem COLE	30	1605	1635	Rob Keayne	?Merchant	E.Bergholt S	E.Bergholt S	1472A	E.Bergholt S	0	0
3	Thos COMBER-BATCH	16	1621	1637	Mich Metcalfe	Weaver	Norwich N	Norwich N	No	Norwich N	0	0
3	Matt COYS*	c16	c1622	1638	John Whitting-ham	Agriculture	Stamford L		N1	?Boston L		?30
2	Rich COYS*	14	1624	1638	John Whitting-ham	Agriculture	Stamford L		N1	?Boston L		?30
5	Thos DOG-GETT	30	1607	1637	Thos Oliver	Calendrar	?Norwich N	N'ch/St. Faiths N	1478B	Norwich N	0/2	0
4	Thos FLEGGE	21	1616	1637	Rich Carver	Agriculture	?Hardingham N	Shipdham area N	1500A	Scratby N	4/6	30
3	John GEDNEY	19	1618	1637	John Pierce	Weaver	?Norwich N	Norwich N	c1436C	Norwich N	?0	?0
8	Hen GIBBS			1633	Edm Hobart		?Hingham N	Tuddenham N	c1432C	Hingham N	?6	?0
2	Thos GOAD	15	1620	1635	Thos Reade	?Shoemaker			No	?Wickford E		
3	John GOADBY	16	1619	1635	John Ruggles				No	?Nazeing E		
3	Adam GOOD-WIN	20	1617	1637	John Moulton	Agriculture	Ormesby N	Ormesby/Gt.Yarmouth N	1529A	Ormesby N	0	0/4
2	Thos GREENE	15	1620	1635	John Ruggles	?Shoemaker		E/Herts border	1566B	?Nazeing E		4
3	Sam HALE	c19	c1615	1634			Gt.Maplestead E	Gt.Maplestead E	1595A	Gt.Maplestead E	0	0

Table 19. *Continued*

AG	Name	Age	DOB	DOE	Master	Trade	BP	FR		WP	Distances BP: FR	BP: WP
4	Isaac HART	22	1615	1637	Rich Carver	Agriculture	Scratby N	Ormesby N	1558A	Scratby N	2	0
2	Job HAWKINS	15	1620	1635	Rich Haffield	Currier	?Sudbury S	Lavenham S	1530A	Sudbury S	5	0
1	Hen HAYWARD	7	1627	1634	John Barnard		Maldon E	Southminster E	1610A	Maldon E	3	0
4	Wm HILL	24	1608	1632	Rich Lyman		Upminster E	Ongar E	1485A	Ongar E	12	12
8	Thos HOWES		1637		Wm Ludkin	Locksmith	Norwich N	Norwich N	1586B	Norwich N	0	0
4	Matt IRONS	c25	c1605	1630	Wm Colbron		Roxwell/Danbury E		No	Roxwell/Danbury E	0	0
2	Edw KEELE	14	1621	1635	John Ruggles	?Shoemaker			No	?Nazeing E		
8	John KILLIN		1637		Benj Cooper	Agriculture	?Wangford S	Wangford S	N1	Brampton S	0	3
2	John LAVE-RICK	15	1619	1634	Rich Kimball	Wheelwright	?Hitcham S	Felsham	1440A	Hitcham S	?5	?0
3	Sam LINCOLN	18	1619	1637	Fran Lawes	Weaver	Hingham N	Hingham N	1543A	Norwich N	0	11
8	Edw MITCHELL			1638	Phil James		?Scarning N	Scarning N	1539A	Hingham N	0	7
2	Isaac MOORE	13	1622	1635	Matt Marvin	Agriculture	?Elmstead E	W of Colchester E	1572B	Gt.Bentley E	3/5	4
8	John MOR-FIELD			1638	Phil James				No	Hingham N		

					?John Ruggles	?Shoemaker	?Roydon E	?Roydon E	1586B	?Nazeing E	0	2
1	Isaac MORRIS	9	1626	1635	?John Ruggles	?Shoemaker	?Roydon E	?Roydon E	1586B	?Nazeing E	0	2
3	Wm MOULTON	20	1617	1637	Rob Page	Agriculture	Ormesby N	Ormesby N	c1530A	Ormesby N	0	0
8	Wm PITTS			1638	Phil James		Hackford N	Hackford N	1457A	Hingham N	0	3
8	Rich RIDLEY	16	1619	1635	Mart Sanders	Currier			No	Sudbury S		
8	Rob SKOUL-DING			1638	Thos Cooper			Norwich N (13)	N1	Hingham N		
2	John SMITH	13	1622	1635	Rich Haffield	Currier	Sudbury S	Sudbury S	1578B	Sudbury S	0	0
2	Rich SMITH	14	1621	1635	Mart Sanders	Currier	Sudbury S	Sudbury S	1578B	Sudbury S	0	0
4	Wm STOREY	23	1614	1637	Sam Dix	Carpenter	?Gt.Yarmouth N	Gt.Yarmouth N	1560A	Norwich N	0	20
8	Thos SUCK-LING			1638	Fran James		Hingham N	Wicklewood N	1433C	Hingham N	3	0
3	John TIDD	19	1618	1637	Sam Green-field	Weaver	?Norwich N	Wells	No	Norwich N	?30	?0
3	Edm TOWNE	18	1619	1637	Hen Skerry	Cordwainer	Gt.Yarmouth N	Gt.Yarmouth N	No	Gt.Yarmouth N	0	0
8	John TUFTS			1638	Thos Cooper				N1	Hingham N		
8	Wm WALKER			1637	John Gedney	Weaver			1593B	Norwich N		
8	Thos WARD			1630					N1	Bedingham N		
3	John WARNER	c19	c1616	1635	Matt Marvin	Agriculture	?Wrabness E	Manningtree E	1523B	Gt.Bentley E	5	7
2	John WHIPPLE	15	1617	1632	Isr Stoughton	Carpenter	Coggeshall E	Coggeshall E	c1570A	?Bocking E	0	?5

*Indentured servant.

Table 20. Age, Roots, and Mobility of Emigrant Male Servants

AG	Age	No.	Distance, BP:FR						Distance, BP:WP					
			0–4	5–9	10–14	15–19	20+	UK	0–4	5–9	10–14	15–19	20+	UK
1	6–10	2	2						2					
2	11–15	14	3	4				7	7	1		1	1	4
3	16–20	13	7	1			1	4	7	1	1		1	3
4	21–25	7	3	1	1			2	3		1		1	1
5	26–30	3	2	1					3					
6	31–35													
7	36–40	1							1					1
8	UK	15	7	2				6	7	2				6
	Total	55	24	9	1	0	1	19	30	4	2	1	3	15

Table 21. Emigrant Women Servants

Age	Name	DOB	DOE	WP	Master
20	Ann Alexarson	1617	1637	Norwich N	John Baker
24	Mercy Alexarson	1613	1637	Norwich N	John Baker
?	?Mary Ball	?	?	Bury St.Edmunds S	?
32	Bridget Bull	1605	1637	Norwich N	John Baker
27	?Martha Carter	1608	1635	Nazeing E	?
15	?Faith Clarke	1619	1634	Gt.Baddow E	?
c16	?Anne Coleman	1623	c1639	Colchester E	?
24	Eliz Cooper	1611	1635	Sudbury S	Rich Haffield
?	——— Crane	?	1637	Hatfield B.Oak E	?
24	Mary Denny	1611	1635	Gt./Lit.Baddow E	?
18	Alice Eden	1619	1637	Ormesby N	John Moulton
13	Mary Eliot	1622	1635	Nazeing E	?
13	Eliz Epps	1622	1635	Wickford E	?
17	Mary Fuller	1618	1635	Sudbury S	Mart Sanders
c26	Eliz Goffe	1609	c1635	?Bradwell S	Wm Ballard
18	Anne Goodwin	1619	1637	Yarmouth N	Abr Toppan
?	Frances Goodwin	?	1637	Yarmouth N	Abr Toppan
15	?Dorcas Greene	1619	1634	Gt.Baddow E	?
22	?Martha Hubbard	1613	1635	Tendring E	?
20	Mary Hubbard	1615	1635	Tendring E	?
c26	Alice Jones	1609	c1635	Bradwell S	Wm Ballard
?	Joanna King	?	1631	Groton S	John Winthrop Jr
19	Anne Leake	1616	1635	Gt./Lit.Baddow E	?
17	Ann Manning	1620	1637	Ormesby N	John Moulton
?	Mary Morton	?	1630	?Colchester E	?
23	Marion Moulton	1614	1637	Ormesby N	?
20	Ruth Moulton	1617	1637	Ormesby N	?
14	Thomasine Munson	1621	1635	Cold Norton E	Thos King
23	Lucy Poyett	1614	1637	Norwich N	John Gedney
?	?Ellen Robinson	?	1637	Norfolk	?
?	Marie Rudd	?	1631	Groton S	John Winthrop Jr
?	——— Salmon	?	c1638	Hatfield B.Oak E	?
12	Mary Sape	1625	1637	Norwich N	Thos Oliver
30	?Sarah Simes	1605	1635	Earl's Colne E	Rog Harlakenden
40	Alice Smith	1595	1635	Sudbury S	Rich Haffield
19	Anne Smith	1618	1637	Norwich N	Fran Lawes
20	Mirabel Underwood	1617	1637	Scratby N	Rich Carver
15	Anne Ward	1622	1637	Ormesby N	Rob Page

Table 21. *Continued*

Age	Name	DOB	DOE	WP	Master
38	Eliz Ward	1597	1635	Roxwell E	Thos Josselyn
15	Anne Williams	1622	1637	Norwich N	?
15	Mary Winch	1619	1634	Bocking E	Rowl Stebbings
23	Anne Wood	1612	1635	Earl's Colne E	Rog Harlakenden
?	Eliz Wybert	?	1631	Groton S	John Winthrop Jr

Notes: (1) Eight (with a question mark against their names) of the 43 are not specifically designated servants. (2) Four were aged 10–14, sixteen 15–20, seven 21–25, seven over 25, and nine were unknown. (3) Due to lack of background evidence in the majority of cases, further analysis about personal mobility prior to emigration has proved pointless.

Bay Company, may have so engaged, but only three young servants can now be definitely identified as indentured. These were Matthew and Richard Coys and their shipmate Hanniel Bosworth. These three Lincolnshire "servants in husbandry" were recruited in 1638 by John Whittingham, a landowner and merchant. He arranged for transportation down to London, their stay there, and their passage. Once in Massachusetts their services for seven or ten years were bought by William Hubbard of Ipswich.[6]

Finally, there were older men designated servants, meaning trusted, skilled employees. In the cases of Thomas Bartlett (aged 36) and William Brown (aged about 23), their masters were the young gentlemen William Pelham and John Winthrop, Jr. The employer of Clement Coie (aged 30) was the extremely wealthy merchant Robert Keayne, whose business affairs in the hectic 1630s needed expert assistance. Two other employees, one Burgess (aged 26) and Thomas Doggett (aged 30), worked for masters in the textile industry. Matthew Irons, who emigrated with his wife in 1630, is described as servant to William Colbron of Boston, Massachusetts, in 1634. Irons may have been driven into service by economic necessity in the New World, rather than having made the trip as an employee.[7]

The number of those males specifically designated servants who made the voyage to New England was small, only 55 out of more than 2,100 East Anglians. As we saw, nondesignated youths might increase the ratio of servants to about one in six of adult male emigrants. This was far lower than the proportion of servants going to other colonies and helps explain frequent complaints about the chronic lack of help in seventeenth-century New England. The large number of men who waited till their mid-twenties to emigrate, often just after marrying, suggests that freedom from farm service or apprenticeship indentures, which opened up a person's earning power, may have been seen as a pre-requisite to economic success among this generation, especially when Massachusetts wage levels began to inflate after 1633.[8]

A few of our servants fit the youthful Dick Whittington myth. The 23-year-old carpenter William Storey had moved the 20 flat miles from Yarmouth westward to Norwich to work for the master carpenter Samuel Dix. Samuel Lincoln, Honest Abe's forebear, had traveled 11 miles in the opposite direction from Hingham to the city to train as a weaver under Francis Lawes. John Bill, a *Hopewell* servant who may have come from Nazeing, seems to have moved 16 miles west to St. Albans because the death of his father placed him under the guardianship of his uncle, Richard Tuttle, who also emigrated in 1635.[9]

William Hill's story realizes the legend of the apprentice prospering through marriage to his master's daughter. The Hill family had been settled in the neighborhood of High Ongar, west of Chelmsford, Essex, between the fifteenth and the early seventeenth centuries. However, William's father lived 12 miles south near the Thames Estuary in the village of Upminster, just east of London. He married Jane Scarborough there in 1598 and was chosen churchwarden in 1606. William was baptized in Upminster in 1608. Later he returned to his ancestral roots. He became a servant to Richard Lyman of High Ongar, a follower of the Reverend John Eliot, and about 1632 he married Phyllis, his master's 21-year-old daughter. William's brother Thomas also immigrated to Roxbury, where he died at the minister's house in 1634. William moved on to Hartford along with his father-in-law in 1636. He achieved the ripe but not unusual old age of 75, outlived three wives, and was survived by nine children.[10]

Traditionally, adolescents and young unmarried adults have been thought of as the most mobile members of the population, as they are today. A 1620s letter in the *Winthrop Family Papers* refers to "servantes whose residence cannott bee expected to bee constant." Although apprentices might move from countryside to town to follow a trade, they could expect to be residentially stable during their training. Servants in husbandry and maidservants hired by the year would be more occupationally mobile. As their skills increased, they might seek more advanced types of work at new farms or households. They might gladly exchange a harsh or niggardly or even an overinvolved master or mistress at the end of the agricultural year. Maids or men in love might change employers to stay near one another. Such mobility could, theoretically, produce the shake-up needed to precipitate change and adaptability.[11]

Tables 19 and 20, however, suggest that adolescent mobility was mainly small-scale. The general picture for the great majority of these adolescents, like their elders, is one of neighborhood rootedness. A few might move a few miles to an adjacent parish for their servant years, but it was unusual to move far. Only 7 out of 35 moved 10 miles or more from birthplace to workplace, whereas 24 moved less than five miles away.[12]

Other pointers confirm servant localism. Hiring fairs usually operated at the familiar level of the hundred, a subdivision of the county, or served a combination of parishes. Analysis of a large sample of English servants concludes that "movement over long distances was rare . . . mobility did not tend to be random and cumulative, but directed and bounded." Even in the eighteenth century the median distance for servant moves in Suffolk was only five kilometers. In England generally, "farm servants moved often but not far, and were no more accustomed to long journeys to strange places than were more sedentary workers." During the Civil War, a group of Suffolk servants and laborers had to travel to a military rendezvous at Saffron Walden in the northwest corner of their county. They complained of feeling "benighted . . . in a strange country." The triumph of local loyalties among our emigrant servants seems to have been typical of the whole group in preindustrial England.[13]

This servant parochialism is bound to call into question Bailyn's contention that the adaptable young might find themselves the leaders of their less flexible elders in a new environment.[14] Further doubt arises from the fact that servants usually traveled within the households of their masters and not as venturesome, individualistic indentured servants.

Labor to be hired was extremely scarce in New England throughout the first generation of settlement, and many letters to England sought recruitment of additional hands. English servants were understandably chary about committing themselves to wilderness life. They wanted to know "what shall be the most of their employment there, whether dairy, washing, &c. and what should be the wages, and for how many years tied." Those prepared to go were often more nuisance than they were worth. "It is not the multiplicity of bad servants (which presently eats a man out of house and harbour, as lamentable experience hath made manifest)," wrote the realistic William Wood, "but the industry of the faithful and diligent labourer that enricheth the careful master; so that he that hath many dronish servants shall soon be poor, and he that hath an industrious family shall soon be rich." In 1633 and 1635, the younger Winthrop's efforts to hire workers in England were frustrated because of lack of supply and lack of money to subsidize passages. Labor soon became notoriously "uppity" in New England, demanding "oppressive" wages, twice or three times English rates, and, following Wood's advice, those who could depended on family members for help. In 1645, Emmanuel Downing, foreseeing a perpetual servant problem, proposed that native Americans captured in just wars be exchanged for "Moores," who would form a slave-labor force.[15]

Though in New England, "servants will desire freedom to plant for themselves and not stay with masters but for very great wages," they usually remained among the lower orders after service was completed. They often had to move on to cheaper land or to become tenants of larger landowners, and their median wealth was only three-fifths of other householders'. Among servants from the eastern counties, only 12 of the 55 rose to positions of prominence in town, church, or colonial government, and only six of these were servants in husbandry. None became leaders until they were well into middle age.[16] Ann Kussmaul has concluded that "it is unlikely that farm service was a major factor in preconditioning English society to the mobility that modernisation would call for. . . . Servant mobility was not destabilising despite the fact that servants had no direct bonds to the community other than their temporary contracts. Their mobility occurred as if in a closed container of customs and agricultural practices." Later, innovative farmers confirmed this view. Modernizers like Jethro Tull found that servants bitterly resisted change rather than welcoming it.[17]

Emigrants of Unknown Occupation

Those adult males whose occupations cannot now be recovered total 270 (see Tables 22 and 23); statistically, this is a depressingly large number. Furthermore, evidence about their birthplaces and workplaces is often negligible, as the totals in Table 23 show. Prior mobility cannot even be estimated in a quarter of this group; I have been unable to discover ages for well over one in six. In 68 additional cases I have had to estimate one or both of the distances moved on pretty meager evidence—usually of place of birth where parish registers no longer survive. Although the fragility of these figures is commoner than in occupationally defined groups, the conclusion is still quite emphatic,

Table 22. Male Emigrants, Occupations Unknown

AG	Name	Age	DOB	DOE	BP		FR	WP	Distances	
									BP:FR	BP:WP
12	Wm AGAR			1630	Nazeing E	1536A	Nazeing E	Nazeing E	0	0
3	Thos ARNOLD	c30	c1605	1635	Kelsale S	1476B	Theberton area S	Kelsale S	3	0
3	Fran AUSTIN	c28	c1608	1636	?Beccles S	N1	Aldburgh S	Ringsfield S	?23	?2
12	Dan BACON			by 1640	Colchester E	1561A	Colchester E	Colchester E	0	0
12	John BAKER			1630	Norwich N	N1	Norwich N	Norwich N	0	0
5	John BARNARD	37	1597	1634	Burnham E	N1	Southminster E	Burnham E	3	0
3	John BARNARD	30	1604	1634	W.Bergholt S	1594A	W.Bergholt	Dedham E	0	7
3	Sam BASS	30	1600	1630	Lit.Chesterford E	1557A	Lit.Chesterford E	Saffron Walden E	0	3
2	Greg BAXTER	c25	c1605	1630	Sporle N	1469C	Swaffham N	Sporle N	3	0
12	John BEALE			1638	Hingham N	1473A	Lit.Ellingham N	Hingham N	2	0
2	Wm BEAMSLEY	c25	c1605	1630	Lincoln L	No	Lincoln L	Lincoln L	0	0
12	John BIGGS			1630	Glemsford S	1528A	Glemsford S	Groton S	0	?9
1	Jer BLACKWELL	18	1617	1635		No	Lincolnshire	Lincolnshire		
7	Edm BLOSSE	47	1587	1634	?Brandeston S	No	W.Ipswich S	Brandeston S	15	0
12	Rob BLOTT			1634		No		Waltham E		
12	John BOGGIS			1630	?Boxted E	1461A	Edwardstone S	Boxted E	?6	0
2	Thos BOYDEN	21	1613	1634	?Ipswich S	N1	Ipswich S	Ipswich S	0	0
3	Hen BRIGHT	28	1602	1630	Bury S	1539A	Bury S	Bury S	0	0
12	Hen BROCK			1638	?Stradbroke S	1558A	Stradbroke S	Fressingfield S	?0	?3

No.	Name	Age	Born	Year	Place	Place	Ref	Place		
4	John BROWNE	31	1601	1632	Hawkedon S	Hawkedon S	1538A	Hawkedon S	0	0
3	Rich BROWNE	c30	c1600	1630	Hawkedon S	Hawkedon S	1538A	Hawkedon S	0	0
4	Thos BROWNE	c32	c1605	1637	Hawkedon S	Hawkedon S	1538A	?Lavenham S	0	8
12	Jas BROWNE	c50		1630	Hawkedon S	Hawkedon S	1538A	Lavenham S	0	0
7	Rob BUFFUM	c50	c1588	1638	Gt.Yarmouth N	Gt.Yarmouth N	No	Gt.Yarmouth N	0	0
12	Edw BUMSTEAD			1640	Rattlesden S	Rattlesden S	1501A	Rattlesden S	0	0
2	John BURRAGE	21	1616	1637	Norton Sub-course S	Norton S	1572A	Norton S	0	0
12	John CABLE			1630	?S.Ockendon E	S.Ockendon E	N1	Essex	0	0
6	Aug CALL	c42	c1595	1637	Gt.Yarmouth N	Gt.Yarmouth N	No	Gt.Yarmouth N		
4	Chas CHADWICK	33	1597	1630			No	Woodham Ferrers E	0	0
5	Wm CHANDLER	c37	c1600	1637	?Bps.Stortford, Herts	Bps.Stortford, Herts	1559A	Hatfield B.Oak E	0	4
5	Wm CHEESEBOROUGH	c36	c1594	1630			No	Boston L	0	0
2	Wm CHILD	c25	c1605	1630	Bury S	Bury S	1462B	Bury S		3
3	Thos CHUBBOCK	c28	c1605	1633	Hardingham N		No	?Hingham N	2	0
12	John CLARKE			1630	?Groton S	Ed'stone/Boxford S	1449A	Groton S	2	0
2	John CLARKE	22	c1612	1634	?Risby S	Bury S	No	Risby S	?3	?o
5	John CLARKE	c37	c1600	1637			No	Braintree/Bocking E		
1	Jos CLARKE	20	1618	1638	Westthorpe S	Gt.Ashfield S	1440A	Westhorpe S	3	0
4	Thos CLARKE	33	1605	1638	Westthorpe S	Gt.Ashfield S	1440A	Westhorpe S	3	0
3	Wm CLARKE	c29	c1610	1639			No	Braintree/Bocking E		
6	Wm COLBRON	c45	c1585	1630	?Brentwood E	Brentwood area E	N1	Brentwood E	?2	?o

Table 22. *Continued*

AG	Name	Age	DOB	DOE	BP	FR		WP	Distances	
									BP:FR	BP:WP
4	Anth COLBY	35	1595	1630	?Fressingfield S	Brockdish S	1592A	Fressingfield S	?3	?0
2	John COLE	c25	c1605	1630	?Boxford S	Stoke by Nayland S	N1	Boxford S	5	0
4	Edw COLLINS	35	1603	1638	?London	Bramford S (9)	1594A	?Dedham E	63	54
5	All CONVERSE	c40	c1599	1639	Navestock E	Stapleford Abbots E	1488A	Navestock E	4	0
6	Anth COOPER	c45	c1590	1635	Hingham N	Hingham N	1469B	Hingham N	0	0
4	Thos COOPER	31	1607	1638	Hingham N	Hingham N	1469B	Hingham N	0	0
4	Rich CRABBE	c34	c1600	c1634	Boxford S	Boxford S	1595A	Boxford S	0	0
3	Gil CRACKBONE	c30	c1605	1635	Gt.Coggeshall E	N.Cent.Essex	1559A	Gt.Coggeshall E	5–8	0
3	Griffin CRAFTS	c28	c1602	1630			No	Essex		0
5	John CRAM	39	1597	1636	Bilsby L		No	Bilsby L		0
4	John CRANE	c32	c1605	1637		NW Suffolk	1445C	Suffolk		
4	Rob CUTLER	c34	c1602	1636	Hingham N	Hingham N	1591A	Hingham N	0	0
6	Rob DANIEL	c42	c1592	c1634			No	Redgrave S		
12	John DARROW			1637			No	Norfolk		
12	Wm DAVIES			1640	?Sudbury S	Sudbury S	N1	Sudbury S	0	0
5	God DEARBORN	c36	1603	c1639	Willoughby L	Hogsthorpe area L	1573A	Willoughby L	4	0
1	John DEVEREUX	16	1614	1630	?Rattlesden S		N1	?Rattlesden S		?0

2	Edw DIX	c25	1630	Rattlesden S	Lavenham/Lit. Melford S	1492B	Rattlesden S	8/6	0
3	John DOGGETT	1602	1630	Groton S	Groton/Boxford S	1565A	Groton S	0/2	0
4	John EDDY	1597	1630	Cranbrook, Kent	?Bristol	No	Boxted E	150	53
2	John EDMUNDS	c1605	1630		Gt.Hormead E	1559B	Essex		0
1	Sam ELDRED	1620	1635	?Ipswich S	?Knettishall S	No	Ipswich S	28	0
1	Rob ELDRED	1618	1635	Ipswich S	?Knettishall S	No	Ipswich S	28	0
1	Wm ELDRED	c1620	1635	Ipswich S	?Knettishall S	No	Ipswich S	28	0
12	Edw ELMER		1632			No	Braintree E		
5	Wm ESTOW	c1600	1637	Ormesby N	Martham area N	c1562A	Ormesby N	3	0
3	John FARROW	c1608	1635	Hingham N	E.Dereham area N	1401B	Hingham N	6	0
1	Nat FELTON	1615	1635	Gt.Yarmouth N	Gt.Yarmouth N	1558A	Gt.Yarmouth N	0	0
6	John FIRMAN	1588	1630	Nayland S	Sudbury area S	1441B	Nayland S	7	0
6	Dav FISKE Sr.	c1594	1637	?Wrentham S	Laxfield/Beccles S	1505A	?Wrentham S	14/6	0
12	Jas FISKE		c1640		Laxfield S	1435A	Suffolk		
12	John FISKE		1638	Laxfield S	Laxfield S	1435A	Laxfield S	0	0
12	Phin FISKE		c1640		Laxfield S	1435A			
2	Wm FISKE	c1605	1637	St.Jas.S.Elmham S	Laxfield S	1435A	St.Jas.S.Elmham S	6	0
5	Nat FOOTE	c1593	1633	?Shalford E	W.Essex/Herts	N1	Shalford E	c12	?o
5	Ren FOSTER	c1595	1635	Harlow E	Hi.Laver E	1550B	?Harlow E	4	?o

Table 22. Continued

AG	Name	Age	DOB	DOE	BP	FR		WP	Distances	
									BP:FR	BP:WP
5	Wm FREEBORNE	40	1594	1634			No	Suffolk		o
4	John FRENCH	c33	c1602	1635	Halstead E	Gt.Maplestead area	1599A	Halstead E	3	o
8	Thos FRENCH	c53	1584	c1637	Assington S	Sudbury S	1531A	Assington S	4	o
4	Wm FRENCH	32	1603	1635	Halstead E	Gt.Maplestead area E	1599A	Halstead E	3	o
12	Geo FROST			1635	Rattlesden S	Cent.Suffolk	1404B	Rattlesden S	10	o
2	John FULLER	24	1611	1635	Lavenham S	Lavenham S	N1	Lavenham S	o	o
5	Matt FULLER	37	1603	1640	?Redenhall N		No	Redenhall N		?o
2	Wm FULLER	25	1610	1635	Lavenham S	Lavenham S	N1	Lavenham S	o	o
4	Step GATES	33	1605	1638	?Norwich N		N1	Hingham N		13
5	Wm GODFREY	c38	c1600	1638	Ormesby N	Gt.Yarmouth N	1479A	Ormesby N	4	o
6	Hen GOLDSTONE	43	1591	1634	Wickham Skeith S		No	Bedingfield S		6
4	Rob GOODALE	33	1601	1634	Dennington S	Dennington S	1601A	Dennington S	o	o
5	Ozias GOODWIN	c36	c1596	1632	?Bocking E	Bocking E	1523B	Bocking E	?o	?o
6	Wm GOODWIN	c43	c1589	1632	Bocking E	Bocking E	1523B	Bocking E	?o	?o
12	John GOSSE	c20	c1620	1630	Lit.Waldingf'd S	Sudbury area	1470A	Lit.Waldingf'd S	4	o
1	Nat GOULD			1640	Bury S	Bury S	1471C	Bury S	o	o
5	John GRAVES	c39	c1594	1633	?Stanstead Abbots E	Stanstead Abbots E	1525A	Nazeing E	?o	?5
8	Thos GRIGGS	51	1585	1636	Boxted E	Boxted area	1562A	Boxted E	2	o
5	Wm GUTTRIDGE	c40	c1596	1636	Bury S	Hessett/Felsham S	1423A	Bury/Rattlesden S	5/7	o/8

#	Name									
2	Geo HADLEY	24	1615	c1639	Reydon S	Lowestoft/Southwold S	1512B	Reydon S	8/1	0
2	Thos HALE	c21	c1613	1634	?Gt.Maplestead E	Gt.Maplestead E	1595A	Gt.Maplestead E	?0	?0
2	Sam HALL	23	1610	1633	?Langford E	Maldon E	1582B	Langford E	?2	?0
5	Pet HALLOCK	c40	c1600	1640	?Hingham N		No	?Hingham N		?0
8	Wm HARRISON	55	1580	1635	Bramford S	Ipswich S	N1	Bramford S	3	0
3	Step HARTE	c27	c1605	1632	?Ipswich S	Harwich E	1569B	Dedham E	?10	?10
3	Thos HASTINGS	29	1605	1634			No	Suffolk?		
1	Abr HAWKINS	c17	c1618	1635	Braintree E	Gt.Waltham E	1537B	Braintree E	7	0
2	Rob HAWKINS	25	1610	1635	Braintree E	Gt.Waltham E	1537B	Braintree E	7	0
9	Isaac HEATH	59	1585	1634	Nazeing E	Sawb'worth, Herts	1594A	Nazeing E	7	0
6	Wm HEATH	c42	c1590	1632	Nazeing E	Sawb'worth, Herts	1594A	Nazeing E	7	0
3	Nat HEATON	c26	c1608	1634	?Alford L		No	Alford L		?0
5	Wm HERSEY	c36	c1600	1636			No	Wymondham N		
1	Thos HILL	c20	c1612	1632	Upminster E	Hi.Ongar E	1485A	Upminster E	12	0
10	Edm HOBART Sr.	63	1570	1633	Hingham N	Scoulton area N	1532A	Hingham N	3	0
3	Thos HOBART	27	1606	1633	Hingham N	Scoulton area N	1532A	Hingham N	3	0
6	Geo HOLMES	44	1594	1638	Nazeing E		No	Nazeing E		0
12	Sam HOSIER			1630		Boxted area	No	Colchester E	2	
12	Edw HOWE			c1634	Boxted E		1582A	Boxted E	0	0
1	Sam HOWES	c20	c1614	1634	Lavenham S	Lavenham S	1516A	Lavenham S	0	0
6	John HUNTING	c42	1597	c1639	Hoxne S	Hoxne S	1538A	Oakley S		2

Table 22. *Continued*

AG	Name	Age	DOB	DOE	BP	FR		WP	Distances BP:FR	BP:WP
12	Sam HUTCHINSON			c1638	Rudhams N	Rudhams area N	1584B	Rudhams N	3	0
4	Edw IRESON	32	1603	1635	?Hingham N	Scoulton N	No	Buckenham N?	?3	?0
3	Nich JACOB	c30	c1603	1633	?Southwold S	Lowestoft area S	1436C	Hingham N	10	?0
12	Dan JEGGLES			1639	?Southwold S	Lowestoft area S	1461A	Southwold S	10	?0
1	Thos JEGGLES	c19	c1620	c1639	?Southwold S		1461A	Southwold S		0
12	Rich JENNINGS			1636	Ipswich S	Ipswich S	1571A	Ipswich S	0	0
3	Rob JENNISON	c30	c1606	c1636	?Colchester E		No	Colchester E	?	?0
2	Thos KILBOURN	24	1610	1634	Wood Ditton C		No	Wood Ditton C		0
6	Aust KILLAM	c42	c1595	1637	Dennington S	Theberton S	1523B	Dennington S	8	0
4	Thos KING	31	1604	1635	Cold Norton E	Dengie Peninsula E	1490A	Cold Norton E	5–10	0
1	Thos KING	19	1615	1634	?Dedham E	Ardleigh E	1558A	Dedham E	?2	?0
6	Hen KINGSBURY	45	1585	1630	Boxford S	Cornard S	1459A	Boxford S	5	0
12	John KINGSBURY			1635	Boxford S	Cornard S	1459A	Boxford S	5	0
3	Jos KINGSBURY	c27	c1610	c1637	Boxford S	Cornard S	1459A	Boxford S	5	0
12	Nich KNAPP			1630		Bures S	1521A	Suffolk		0
8	Wm KNAPP	52	1578	1630	Bures S	Bures S	1521A	Suffolk	0	0
12	Geo KNIGHT			1638		NW Suffolk	1468B	Barrow S	0	0

n	Name									
12	Rich KNIGHT			1640			No	Norfolk		?o
2	Edw LAMB	c25	c1605	1630	?Stowlangtoft S	Bury area S	1473B	Stowlangtoft S	?5	?o
12	Wm LANE						No	Chelmsford E		
12	Wm LARGE			1635	?Beeston N	Fransham N	1467A	?Hingham N	?3	?11
2	Chris LAWSON	21	1616	1637	?Saleby L	Saleby L	1541A	?Saleby L	?o	?o
1	Thos LEAVITT	c17	c1620	1637	Lincolnshire	Lincolnshire	1565C	Lincolnshire		
4	Edm LEWIS	33	1601	1634			No	Suffolk		
5	Wm LEWIS	c38	1602	c1640	Stoke by Nayland S	Stoke by Nayland area S	1573A	Stoke by Nayland S	3/o	0
2	Dan LINCOLN	c21	1619	c1640	Hingham N	Hingham N (5)	1543A	Hingham N	0	0
3	Step LINCOLN	c28	c1610	1638		Hingham N (5)	1543A	Wymondham N		
3	John LIVERMORE	28	1606	1634	Lit. Thurlow S	Lit. Thurlow S	1612A	Lit. Thurlow S		0
5	Edm LOCKWOOD	36	1594	1630	?Combs S	Hitcham area S	1558A	Combs S	0	?o
3	Rob LOCKWOOD	30	1600	1630	Combs S	Hitcham area S	1558A	Combs S	?6	?o
2	Wm LONGLEY	c21	c1614	1635			No	Firsby L	?6	
3	Edw LOOMIS	27	1608	1635	?Braintree E		N1	Braintree E		?o
3	Geo LUDKIN	c29	c1606	1635	Norwich N	N'ch/E. Harling area N	1590A	Norwich N	0/20	0
9	Rich LUMPKIN	c56	1582	c1638	Boxted E	Colchester E	1570A	Boxted E	5	0
8	Rich LYMAN	51	1580	1631	Hi. Ongar E	Navestock E	1556B	Hi. Ongar E	4	0
3	John MARSH	27	1618	1635	Braintree E	?Rayne E	1552B	Braintree E	?2	0
2	Edw MELLOWS	c21	c1612	1633	?Boston L	Coningsby L	1582B	Boston L	10	0
2	Ol MELLOWS	c25	c1609	c1634	Boston L	Coningsby L	1582B	Boston L	10	0
3	Jos METCALFE	c29	1605	c1634	?Tatterford N	Wensleydale, Yks	No	Norwich	?165	?25
5	Geo MINOT	36	1594	1630	Saffron Walden E	Felsted E	No	Saff. Walden E	18	0

Table 22. Continued

AG	Name	Age	DOB	DOE	BP	FR		WP	Distances	
									BP:FR	BP:WP
2	Griff MONTAGUE	c25	c1610	c1635			N1	Chelmsford E		
7	Fran MOORE	c46	1593	c1639	Maldon E	Maldon E	1594A	Maldon E	0	0
1	Jer MOORE	c18	c1620	1638	Wymondham N	Wymondham N	1591A	Wymondham N	0	0
2	Thos MOORE	c21	c1615	1636	Southwold S	Aldeburgh S/Yarmouth N	No	Southwold S	15/19	0
6	Isaac MORRILL	c44	c1588	1632	Hatf'd B.Oak E	Takeley E	1605A	Hatf'd B.Oak E	3	0
6	Rich MORRIS	c43	c1587	1630	Boston L	Fishtoft L	1592A	Boston L	2	0
2	Dan MORSE	22	1613	1635	Redgrave S	Boxted E	N1	Burgate S	27	2
3	John MORSE	28	1607	?1635	Redgrave S	Boxted E	N1	Burgate S	27	2
1	John MORSE	c18	c1616	1634	Dedham E	Dedham E	1450A	Dedham E	0	0
7	Jos MORSE	49	c1585	1634	Dedham E	Dedham E	1450A	Dedham E	0	0
2	Jos MORSE Jr.	24	1610	1634	Dedham E	Dedham E	1450A	Dedham E	0	0
7	Sam MORSE	c50	1585	c1635	Hinderclay S	Boxted E	N1	Burgate S	27	4
2	Thos MOULTON	25	1606	1631	Ormesby N	Ormesby N	c1530A	Ormesby N	0	0
12	Jos MOYSE			c1639		Tendring 100 E	No	Hadleigh S		
5	Edm MUNNINGS	40	1595	1635	Maldon E	Maldon E	1609A	?Dengie E	0	10
3	John MYGATT	c26	c1607	1633	?Roxwell E	SE Essex	No	Nazeing E	?6	?14
2	Thos NICHOLS	c22	1615	c1637	Coggeshall E	Colne Valley E	1531B	Coggeshall E	5	0
5	Miles NUTT	c38	1598	c1636	Barking S	Norton area S	N1	Barking S	15	0

3	Sam PACKER	26	1612	Stonham Aspal S	1638	Rattlesden area S	No	?Wymondham N	5	?27
3	Nich PALMER	c27	c1610	Rattlesden S	c1637		1558A	Rattlesden S	5	0
7	Wm PALMER	c48	c1589	Ormesby N	1637	Gt.Yarmouth area N	1520	Ormesby N		0
2	Wm PARKE	24	1607	?Semer S	1631	Horkesleys E	1510C	Bures S	?10	?10
8	Geo PARKHURST	c52	c1587	Ipswich S	c1639	Ipswich S	N1	Ipswich S	0	0
2	Edw PAYSON	c22	1613	Nazeing E	c1635	?Thorley, Herts	1566B	Nazeing E	?8	0
3	Giles PAYSON	24	1609	Nazeing E	1635	Thorley, Herts	1566B	Nazeing E	?8	0
3	John PEASE	27	1607	Gt.Baddow E	1634	Gt.Baddow E	1534A	Gt.Baddow E	0	0
3	Rob PEASE	27	1607	Gt.Baddow E	1634	Gt.Baddow E	1534A	Gt.Baddow E	0	0
12	Jas PEMBERTON				1630		No	Lawford E		
3	Jas PENNIMAN	c25	c1605	?Ashen E	c1631		No	Widford E	?22	?0
3	Rich PEPYS	27	1607		1634	Cottenham area C	No	Ashen E		?0
9	John PICKRAM	60	1570		1630		No	Sudbury S	?6	
3	Wm PIERCE	c27	c1606	?Boston L	1633	Leake L	1591A	Boston L		
12	Thos PLIMPLIN				c1640	Gt.Cornard S	1543A	Sudbury S		
3	John POND	c28	c1602	Groton S	1630	Gt.Waldingfield S	1566A	Groton S	4	0
6	John PORTER	c44	c1595	Messing E	c1639	Messing E	1530A	Messing E	0	0
6	John PRATT	c49	?1584	Wood Ditton C	1633	Fulbourn C	1545B	Wood Ditton C	9	0
2	Rich PRATT	23	1615	Maldon E	1638	Burnham E	1553A	Maldon E	10	0
4	Val PRENTICE	c31	c1600		1631	?Shalford E	1598B	Chelmsford E		
4	Mark QUILTER	34	1602	Assington S	1636	Bures S	1472B	Assington S	4	0
6	Thurston RAYNER	41	1593	Elmsett S	1634	Wickham Market/Ipswich S	N1	Elmsett S	15/8	0
6	Edm RICE	c44	c1594	Sudbury S	c1638	Bures S	1521B	?Sudbury/Bury S	5	0/4

Table 22. Continued

AG	Name	Age	DOB	DOE	BP	FR		WP	Distances BP:FR	BP:WP
3	Edw RISHWORTH	29	1617	1636	Laceby L	Worlaby L	No	?Laceby L	15	?0
12	Jas ROGERS			c1640	?Haverhill S	W.Suffolk	1592B	Haverhill S	7	?0
12	John ROGERS			1630			1572B	?Dedham E		
6	Thos ROGERS	c42	1588	c1630			No	Dedham E		
5	Rob ROSE	40	1594	1634	?Elmswell S	Bury S	1390C	Elmswell S	?8	?0
12	Jeff RUGGLES	c36	c1594	1630	Sudbury S	Sudbury S	1447A	Sudbury S	0–4	0
5	John RUGGLES			1630	Glemsford S	Glemsford S	1447A	Glemsford S	0	0
8	Thos RUGGLES	c53	c1584	1637	?Nazeing E	Elsenham D	No	Nazeing E	?12	0
3	Thos SANDFORD	26	1608	1634	Stansted Mt. Fitchet E	Stansted Mt. Fitchet E	1591A	Hatfield B.Oak E	0	?6
2	Rich SANGER	c22	c1618	c1640			No	Norfolk		
3	Rich SAYERS	c28	c1610	1638	?Gt.Yarmouth N	Gt.Yarmouth N	N1	Gt.Yarmouth N	0–4	?0
2	Rob SCOTT	21	1613	1634	Glemsford S	Glemsford S	1498A	Glemsford S	0	0
7	Thos SCRUGGS	c50	c1585	1635	?Gt.Yarmouth N	Gt.Yarmouth N	N1	Gt.Yarmouth N	?0	?0
12	John SEAMAN			1630			No	Suffolk		
2	John SEVERANCE	c23	c1614	c1637			No	Ipswich S		
1	Rob SHARP	c20	c1615	c1635	?Roxwell E	?Chelmsford area E	N1	Roxwell E	?5–7	?6
12	Thos SHARP			1630	?Roxwell E	?Chelmsford area E	N1	Sandon E	5–7	?6

	Name	Age	Date	Place	Date	Place	Ref.	Place			
1	Amos SHEFFIELD	c20	c1619	Sudbury S	c1639	?Sudbury S	1598A	Sudbury S	?o	?o	o
3	Edm SHEFFIELD	c27	1612	Sudbury S	c1639	?Sudbury S	1598A	Sudbury S	o	o	o
2	Sam SHEPARD	22	1613	Towcester, N'hants	1635	?Towcester, N'ha'nts	No	Earl's Colne E	?o	?o	75
9	Edm SHERMAN	c57	c1575	Dedham E	1632	Dedham E	1590A	Dedham E	o	o	o
7	John SHERMAN	48	1587	Dedham E	1635	Dedham E	1590A	Dedham E	o	o	o
1	John SHERMAN	20	1614	Dedham E	1634	Dedham E	1590A	Dedham E	o	o	o
2	Phil SHERMAN	23	1610	Dedham E	1633	Dedham E	1590A	Dedham E	o	o	o
1	Sam SHERMAN	16	1618	Dedham E	1634	Dedham E	1590A	Dedham E	o	o	o
12	Edw SKINNER			Braintree E	1636	Braintree E	1591B	?Cambridge		0	o
12	Wm SKINNER				c1635	?Norwich N	1596A	Braintree E		0	o
3	John SMART	c30	c1605	?Hempnall N	1638		1507C	Norfolk			o
5	Hen SMITH	c38	c1600		1630	Hempnall area N	1420C	Hempnall N		2–4	o
3	—— SMITH	c30	c1600		c1640		No	Buxhall S			o
12	Rich SMITH	c27		Shropham N	c1639	E. Harling N	1479C	Shropham N		4	o
3	Hen SOMERBY	45	1612	Lit. Bytham L	1634	Greetham L	1538A	Lit. Bytham L		6	o
6	John SPRING	c35	1589	?Stoke by Nayland S	1630	Lavenham S (II)	No	?Pakenham S			?o
4	Isaac STEARNS	c33	c1595		1633	Stoke by Nayland S	No	Stoke by Nayland S			?o
4	Edw STEBBINGS	40	c1600	?Bocking E	1634	Stebbing/Gt. Dunmow E	1274C	Bocking E		6/8	?o
5	Rowl STEBBINGS	51	1594	?Bocking E	1631	Stebbing/Gt. Dunmow E	1274C	Bocking E		6/8	?o
8	Geo STEELE	c40	1580	Fairstead E	c1631	Fairstead E	1547A	Fairstead E		0	o
5	John STEELE	c38	c1591	Fairstead E	c1638	Fairstead E	1547A	Fairstead E		0	o
5	Aug STORRE		c1600	Bilsby L	1638	NE Lincolnshire	Ni	?Alford L		15	?2

Table 22. *Continued*

AG	Name	Age	DOB	DOE	BP	FR	WP		Distances	
									BP:FR	BP:WP
2	John STOWERS	c24	c1610	1634	Parham S		Parham S	N1		0
3	Nich STOWERS	c29	c1600	1629	Parham S		Parham S	N1		0
6	John SYMONDS	c41	c1595	1636	Gt.Yarmouth N	Gt.Yarmouth N	Gt.Yarmouth N	1532A	0	0
4	John TALCOTT	c32	c1600	1632	Braintree E	Colchester E	Braintree E	N1	15	0
3	Wm TAYLOR	c30	c1600	1630	Haverhill S	Haverhill S	Haverhill S	1500A	0	0
3	Josh TIDD	30	1607	1637	?Norwich N	Wells N	Norwich N	No	?30	?0
3	John TOWER	28	1609	1637	?Hingham N		Hingham N	No		?0
5	Wm TOWNE	36	1599	c1635	Gt.Yarmouth N	Gt.Yarmouth N	Gt.Yarmouth N	N1	0	0
3	Rob TUCKE	c26	c1610	1636	Gorleston S	Gorleston/Yarmouth N	Gorleston S	1523B	0/1	0
1	Pet TUFTS	c20	1617	c1637	Wilby N	Wilby area N	Wilby N	1515C	5	0
4	Hen TUTTLE	c32	c1605	1637	Tharston N	Saxlingham N	Tharston N	1558A	5	0
12	John TUTTLE			c1637	Tharston N	Saxlingham N	Tharston N	1558A	5	0
5	Wm WADSWORTH	c37	c1595	1632	?Braintree E	Wethersfield E	Braintree E	No		?0
1	John WAITE	c20	c1617	1637	Wethersfield E	Wethersfield E	Wethersfield E	N1	0	0
1	John WALL	19	1616	1635	Braintree E	Braintree area E	Braintree E	1552A	6	0
1	Thos WARD	c17	c1620	c1637	Ormesby N	Filby area N	Ormesby N	1520A	3	0
1	Rob WARE	c20	c1618	1638	Fressingfield S	Wingfield S	Fressingfield S	1509C	2	0
7	Wm WARNER	c49	1586	c1635	Boxted E	Boxted E	Boxted E	1536A	0	0
6	John WARREN	45	1585	1630	Nayland S	Nayland S	Nayland S	1544A	0	0
	Wm WARREN			c1637	?Nayland S	Nayland S	Gt.Horkesley E	1544A	?0	?3

1	John WATERBURY	c20	c1610	1630	Sudbury S	Sudbury S	N1	Sudbury S	0	0
5	Wm WATERBURY	36	1594	1630	Sudbury S	Sudbury S	N1	Sudbury S	0	0
7	John WATERS	c50	c1580	1630	Nayland S	?Bildeston S	1583B	Groton S	?7	5
2	Rich WEBB	c25	c1605	1630	Nayland S	Dedham E	1529A	Nayland S	5	0
12	Wm WEBB			1636	Rattlesden S	Woolpit S	1463C	Rattlesden S	3	0
12	Nat WELLES			1630	Colchester E	Colchester E	1535B	Colchester E	0	0
3	Jas WHITE	c27	c1613	c1640		E. Dereham area N	1505B	?Hingham N	?8	?
4	John WHITE	c32	c1600	1632	Braintree E	Coggeshall E	N1	Braintree E	5	0
5	John WHITMAN	c37	c1600	1637		?Wymondham area N	1488C	Norfolk		
5	Wm WILLIAMS	40	1597	1637	Gt.Yarmouth N	Gt.Yarmouth N	1479B	Gt.Yarmouth N	0	0
12	Hum WINCOLL			c1634	?Lit.Waldingfield S	Lit.Waldingfield S	1521A	Lit.Waldingfield S	?0	0
1	Barnaby WINDES	c20	c1615	1635	?Ipswich S	Ipswich S	1577A	?Ipswich S	?0	?0
1	Isaac WRIGHT	c20	c1617	1637		?Hingham/Wymondham N	1376C	Norfolk		
3	Nich WRIGHT	27	1609	1636		Norfolk	No	Norfolk		
12	Sam WRIGHT			c1639	Wrightsbridge E	Norfolk	1551A	Wrightsbridge E		0
3	Thos WRIGHT	c29	1610	c1639	S.Weald E	S.Weald/Kelveden Hatch E	1551A	S.Weald E	0/3	0
12	John WYATT			c1635		S.Weald/Kelveden Hatch E	No	Assington S		

Table 23. Age, Roots, and Mobility of Male Emigrants, Occupations Unknown

AG	Age	No.	Distance, BP:FR 0–4	5–9	10–14	15–19	20+	UK	Distance, BP:WP 0–4	5–9	10–14	15–19	20+	UK
1	16–20	25	14	2	2		3	4	22					3
2	21–25	38	14	9	4	1	1	9	31		1		1	5
3	26–30	50	18	10	1	1	6	14	35	2	2		2	9
4	31–35	24	10	4		1	2	7	15	1	1		2	5
5	36–40	34	20	3	1	3		7	26	2	1			5
6	41–45	23	9	7	1	1		5	19		1			3
7	46–50	10	6	2		1	1		9	1				
8	51–55	8	7		1				8					
9	56–60	4	1	2				1	3					1
10	61–65	1	1						1					
11	66–70													
12	UK	53	24	5	2			22	28	2	1			22
	Total	270	124	44	12	8	13	69	197	8	7	0	5	53

especially when uncertain cases are excluded. The great majority of emigrants were under 45, the 21–30 age group predominating. Although there appears to have been remarkably little migration from where the majority of this group had been born to where they worked, there had been a movement of more than five miles in the history of one-third of the families (82 out of 270) of these individuals. Much of this ancestral emigration had been on a local scale, however.

What of those in this group who personally had moved longer distances, or whose families had? Usually, they came from one of the wider-horizoned English classes. Several were from clerical families. For instance, the brothers John and Samuel Eddy, who sailed in August 1630 on the *Handmaid* from London, were the sons of the Reverend William Eddy. He had been born in Bristol, but after graduating from Trinity College, Cambridge, he had become curate of Thurston, Suffolk, near Bury St. Edmunds. From there he had moved south to become vicar of Cranbrook in Kent. His sons, however, had become residents of Boxted near Dedham in Essex before joining the pioneer settlers in the New World. George Phillips, curate of Boxted, was also an emigrant in 1630. Similar clerical preferments account for the English mobility of the Morse, Storre, Rishworth, Metcalfe, Shepard, and Minot families.[18]

The apparent rootedness of John Hunting conceals a preemigration life of considerable occupational mobility. The family genealogist has traced the Huntings to the north Suffolk village of Hoxne. During the 1620s, John is described as "a ruling elder in Norfolk and Suffolk"— probably some kind of itinerant lay preacher. This may help to explain why his wife, Esther (Seaborne), came from Hingham, Norfolk, 18 miles to the northwest. Unlike nearly all Norfolk Hinghamites, the Huntings did not settle in New Hingham, Massachusetts. Instead, they went to Dedham, new home of many emigrants from north Suffolk. There John became a pillar of the newly gathered church and its first ruling elder.[19]

Kinship with mercantile families might also explain English mobility. Thomas Moore emigrated in his twenties from the Suffolk port of Southwold. His wife was Martha (Youngs), daughter of the vicar, and sister of emigrants John, Christopher, and Joseph. The family roots of both families have been traced to several Suffolk and Norfolk coastal towns, bearing out the suggestion that migration along the littoral was a good deal more common and far-reaching than inland.[20]

A combination of commerce and religious devotion accounts for the restlessness of Edward Collins (1603–87) and for the mobility of his family. The Collinses were a north Essex/south Suffolk clan, with one branch settled in the sixteenth century around Wethersfield and another to the west and southwest of Ipswich, especially the village of Bramford. However, Edward's father was a salter in the city of London, and there the boy grew up. At some point in his twenties he was smitten with religious anxieties and sought solace back at his family's roots. One of the two soul salvers he turned to was the Reverend John Rogers of Dedham, just nine miles south of Bramford. He "through spiritual comfort wrought peace." Collins also attended some of the Reverend Thomas Shepard's lectures at Earl's Colne, 12 miles west of Dedham. In 1638, he was to become the deacon of Shepard's church in Cambridge, Massachusetts. His London background may have recommended him to the rich merchant Matthew Craddock, first governor of the Massachusetts Bay Company. Collins lived on Craddock's farm at Medford, just north of Cambridge.[21]

The lure of a provincial center is seen in the family history of the Eldreds. Three brothers, Robert, Samuel, and William, emigrated in 1635. The family originally flourished in the Norfolk/Suffolk border village of Knettishall, but by 1566 three ancestral brothers had migrated to Ipswich. There the family grew to wealth and prominence. Thomas Eldred, of Fore Street, Ipswich, served as chandler on the epic 1586–88 circumnavigation of the globe by the "Wonderful Suffolk Boy," Thomas Cavendish. After his safe return he had a fine chimney-piece built and decorated with his exploits.[22] A cousin, John, became immensely rich from the Levant trade in spices from Aleppo and Baghdad. He followed convention by buying a country estate. He built his famous "Nutmeg Hall" at Great Saxham, 10 miles south of the family's roots at Knettishall and conveniently close to Bury St. Edmunds. He died there in 1632. Our three emigrants appear to have lived at Ipswich. In 1640 Samuel married Elizabeth Miller of St. Mary at Quay parish, Ipswich, with whom he settled first at Cambridge, Massachusetts, and then at Wickford, Rhode Island.[23]

These longer-distance migrants represent some of the different types of movement around England that we distinguished earlier: clerical preferment, betterment migration to commercial and industrial centers, following personal religious needs, coastal intermarriage, and local occupational travel. Although their family and personal histories are highly revealing about sources of restlessness in Greater East Anglia, these examples of mobility were, as with those of known callings, the exception rather than the rule. For most of this large group some jolt was needed to shake them out of their previous settledness.

Several of these miscellaneous emigrants are known to have been summoned before church courts. Thomas Scruggs, of that hotbed of dissent, Great Yarmouth, was cited before the Archdeacon's Court in 1635 for "walking abroad on the sabbath day," no doubt in protest against Laudian innovations at St. Nicholas Church. His case is marked in the records, "Att Newe England." There his "heretical pravity" got him into further trouble, this time with the town meeting of Salem, which dismissed him from the ruling board of selectmen.[24] Thomas Sharp, who returned in 1631 to the Chelmsford area after a series of personal calamities in Massachusetts, was presented in 1636 at Ingatestone Surrogate's Court for the classic puritan offenses: absence from worship, refusal to kneel at Communion, wife unveiled at her churching after childbirth, and attacks on the orthodox Book of Common Prayer.[25]

Bearing in mind the heavy representation in this group of people from the cloth towns of north Essex, south Suffolk, and central Norfolk and from the east coast ports, we may infer that some element in the decision to emigrate to New England was economic, the push factor of the 1620s and 1630s depression.[26]

Once again, then, religious and economic misfortunes seem to have been a necessary uprooter of a group of overwhelmingly stable, not to say entrenched, easterners.

Selected Women Emigrants

Though opinions differ about the status of women in early Stuart England, especially those of puritan persuasion, no scholar has claimed that women had wrested the leadership of family or community from men. Their relocation in New England might or might not have benefited them, but any bonus stopped short of usurpation. When female subversion threatened, as with Anne Hutchinson in 1637, the male authorities crushed it decisively. In any case, there are serious doubts whether such theological challenges will bear a feminist interpretation. It is inherently unlikely, then, that women could provide radical impetus toward change.[27]

Women formed a uniquely large proportion of the 1630s East Anglian migration (see Tables 24 and 25). In the majority of cases it has proved impossible to discover more than a forename for wives and a name and master for most serving maids (listed in Table 21). Rather than

Table 24. Selected Women Emigrants

AG	Née	Name	Husband	Husband's Occupation	Age	DOB	DOE	BP	FR	MH (Marital Home)	Distances BP:FR	BP:MH
1	Fletcher	Joan AMES*	Wm	Clergy	50	1587	1637	?Yarmouth N	Winterton N	No Netherlands	?6	125
12	Everard	Jud APPLE-TON	Sam	Gentleman			c1634	?Glemsford S	Glemsford S	1517A L. Walding-f'd S	?6	6
12	Bland	Isab AUSTIN	Fran				1636	Colchester E	Ringsfield S	No Ringsfield S		47
12	Read	Mary BACON	Dan				c1639	Colchester E	Colchester E	1504B ?Colchester E	0	0
4	?Perkins	Eliz BAKER	John	Grocer	31	1666	1637		?Norwich N	1517C Norwich N		
5	Stacy	Mary BAR-NARD	John		38	1596	1634	Burnham E	?Mayland E	1573C Burnham E	?5	0
3	Wilson (Whiting)	Phebe BAR-NARD	John		26	1608	1634	Dedham E	?Ardleigh E	N1 Dedham E	?3	0
4	Savill	Ann BASS	Sam		31	1601	1632	Saffron Walden E	Saffron Walden E	1588A Saffron Walden E	0	0
5	Hobart	Nazareth BEALE	John	Shoemaker	c40	c1598	1638	Hingham N	Hingham area N	1532A Hingham N	3	0
12	Barker (Copper)	Christiana BEECHER	Thos	Sea captain			1634			No Wapping/Harwich E		

1	Blower	Alice BRACKETT	Rich	Schoolmaster	20	1614	1634	?Sudbury S	Bildeston S	c1510A	Sudbury S	?9	?o
1	Dudley	Anne BRADSTREET	Simon	Steward	18	1612	1630		Northamptonshire	No	Sempringham L		
3	Youngs	Mary BROWN	Wm	Merchant	26	1609	1635	Southwold S	Essex coast	No	Brandon S	19	45
12	Ward (Thompson)	Thomasine BUFFUM	Rob				1638	Yarmouth N	Filby N	1520A	Yarm/S. Walsham N	4	o/10
2	Harding	Ann BUTTOLPH	Thos	Glover	24	1611	1635	Boreham E	Chelmsford area E	1557A	L.Baddow E	6/9	1
6	Hinds	Sarah CHAPLIN	Clem	Chandler	c45	c1590	1635	Bury S	Bury S	No	?Semer/Bury S	0	14
4	Townley	Mary CHASE	Wm	Carpenter	c31	c1599	1630		Wivenhoe E	1518C	?Colchester area E		
4	Stevenson	Anne CHEESEBOROUGH	Wm		c33	c1597	1630		Boston area L	1563A	Boston L		
6	Fiske	Anne CHICKERING	Fran	Yeoman	c43	c1595	1638	S.Elmham S	Laxfield S	1435A	Fressingfield S	6	4
5	Gross	Anne CHICKERING	Hen	Yeoman	c35	c1603	1638	Darsham S	Kelsale S	1460B	Wrentham S	4	9
4	Bond (Palmer)	Eliz CHILD	Eph	Merchant	c35	c1595	1630	Bury S	Bury S	N1	Bury/Nayland S	0	o/20
3	Hobart	Alice CHUBBOCK	Thos		26	1607	1633	Hingham N	Hingham N	1532A	Hingham N	0	6
12	Baker	Rose CHUTE	Lion	Schoolmaster	12	1630	1630		Ardleigh E	N1	Dedham E		

Table 24. *Continued*

AG	Née	Name	Husband	Husband's Occupation	Age	DOB	DOE	BP	FR	MH (Marital Home)	BP:FR	BP:MH
												Distances
3	Harges	Eliz CLARKE	John	Doctor	c26	c1611	1637	Bedford-shire		No Westhorpe S		55
2	Moseley	Mary COD-DINGTON	Wm	Merchant	c25	c1605	1630	Ousden S		No Boston L		60
6	Dearsley	Hannah COE	Rob	Clothier	43	1591	1634	Assington S	Kirtling area S	No Boxford S	19	3
12	Green	Margt COLE	Sam	Innkeeper			1630	Mersea E	St. Osyth area E	No Navestock E	5	30
12	Hawkridge (Storey)	Sarah COTTON	John	Clergy			1633		Boston L	No Boston L		
10	Myles (Grey)	Cath COYTMORE*	Rowl	Merchant	61	1576	1637	Sutton L	Sutton L	No (1) Harwich E	0	10
										(2) Prittle-well E		48
										(3) Wapping E		68
2	Rainborough	Martha COYT-MORE	Thos	Merchant	c23	c1614	1637	Wapping E	Wapping E	No Wapping/ Pritlewell E	0	0/31
5	White	Hester CRAM	John		c36	c1600	1636		Bilsby L	1581A Bilsby L		
7	Hutchins	Eliz CURTIS	John	Yeoman	c46	c1585	1631		Ware, Herts (6)	1554A Nazeing E		

146

No.	Surname	Name	First	Occupation	Age			Origin 1	Origin 2	Ref.	Destination		
4	Eliot	Sarah CURTIS	Wm	Yeoman	32	1600	1632	Widford E	Bps.Stortford area E	1542A	Nazeing E	6	6
8	Pitcher	Nazareth CUSHING	Matt	Yeoman	52	1586	1638	Harding-ham N (3)		1449B	Hingham N	6	6
2	Clarke	Eleanor DANE	John Jr.	Tailor	c23	c1613	1636	Hatfield B.Oak E	Hatfield B.Oak E	1558A	Hatfield B.Oak E		0
12	Morse	Eliz DANIEL	Rob				c1634	Redgrave S	Boxted/ Dedham E	N1	Redgrave S	28	0
5	Winthrop	Lucy DOWN-ING	Emm	Gentleman	37	1601	1638	Groton S	Groton S	No	London	0	50
7	Yorke	Dot DUDLEY	Thos	Steward	c48	c1582	1630			No	Sempr'ham/ Boston L		
4	Doggett	Amy EDDY	John		33	1597	1630		?Groton/ Boxted S	1565A	Boxted E		
12	Welby	Olive FAR-WELL	Hen	Tailor		c1604			Fosdyke L	1547A	Boston L (7)		
3	Story	Mary FELTON	Benj	Turner	c30	c1605	1635	Yarmouth N	Yarmouth N	1590A	Yarmouth N		
7	Thrower	Ellen FEL-TON*	John	Merchant	c47	c1588	1635	Yarmouth N	Yarmouth N	N1	Yarmouth N	0	0
3	Cooper	Mary FILLING-HAM	Fran	Cordwainer	c30	c1607	1637	Brampton S	Southwold area S	1451C	Brampton S	5	0

Table 24. *Continued*

AG	Née	Name	Husband	Husband's Occupation	Age	DOB	DOE	BP	FR	MH (Marital Home)	Distances BP:FR	BP:MH
12	Blessing	Alice FIRMAGE*					1638			No Gt.Yarmouth N		
5	Doggett	Martha FIRMIN	Giles Sr.	Apothecary	39	1593	1632	Groton S	Groton/Boxford S	1565A Sudbury S	0/2	5
6	Fiske	Mary FISHER	Anth	Yeoman	c44	c1593	1637	St.Jas.S. Elmham S	Laxfield S	1505A Fressingfield S	6	4
3	Gibbs	Ann FISKE	John	Clergy	c28	c1609	1637	Diss N	Diss N	N1 St.Jas.S. Elmham S		12
5	Smith	Sarah FISKE	Dav Sr.		c40	c1597	c1637	Wrentham S	Wrentham S	1593A Wren'm/ St.Jas.S. Elmham S	0	0/11
3	Musket	Bridget FISKE	Wm		c30	c1607	c1637	Pulham N	Haughley area S	No St.Jas.S. Elmham S	19	8
3	Gibbs	Meribah FOLGER	John	Yeoman	c27	c1668	1635	Diss N	Diss N	N1 Diss N	0	0
5	Dening	Eliz FOOTE	Nat		38	1595	1633		Essex coast N (20–25)	No Shalford E		
7	Wetherall	Sarah FOSDICK	Step	Carpenter	46	1589	1635		L.Bromley E (6)	1556B Wenham S		

148

12	Wimes	Abig **FOSTER**	Thos	Soldier	c38	c1597	1634	Ipswich S	1577A	Ipswich S	Ipswich S	0	0
5	Wignol	Jud **FOSTER**	Ren				1635	Theydon Garnon E	N1	Chigwell E	Theydon Garnon E	6	0
2	Gilman	Mary **FOULSHAM**	John	Yeoman	c23	c1615	1638	Caston? N	1585A	Caston N	Hingham N	0	6
3	Symmes	Eliz **FRENCH**	Wm		30	1605	1635		1538C	?Bulmer E (6)	Halstead E		
7	Riddlesdale	Sus **FRENCH**	Thos Sr.		c50	c1587	c1637	Assington area S	1552A	Assington area S (5)	Assington area S	0–5	0
4	Veare	Ann **GATES**	Step		35	1603	1638		1457B	Attleborough N (5)	Hingham N		
7	Clarke	Mary **GILMAN**	Edw	Sawyer	c48	c1590	1638	Hingham N	1462B	Attleborough N	Hingham N	5	0
3	Kilham	Cath **GOODALE**	Rob		28	1606	1634	Earl Soham S	No		Dennington S		5
4	Woodward	Mary **GOODWIN**	Ozias		c34	c1598	1632	Braintree E	N1	Earl's Colne E	Bocking E	5	2
7	Moore	Sarah **GREENLEAF**	Edm	Dyer	c46	1588	c1634	Langford E	1594A	Maldon E	Ipswich S	3	30
3	Surrey	Grace **GRIDLEY**	Rich	Mason	c27	c1603	1630	Groton S	N1	Groton S	Groton S		
1	Sturgeon	Pru **GUTRIDGE**	John	Tailor	c20	c1617	1637		1488A	Whepstead S (7)	Rattlesden S		

Table 24. Continued

AG	Née	Name	Husband	Husband's Occupation	Age	DOB	DOE	BP	FR	MH (Marital Home)	Distances BP:FR	BP:MH
3	Dowsett	Thomasine HALE	Thos	Glover	c29	c1608	1637	Harlow E	Stanford Rivers E	No Watten at Stone, Herts	7	12
4	Cason	Eliz HAMMOND	Thos		c33	c1603	1636		?Long Melford S (5)	N1 Lavenham S		
8	Payne	Eliz HAMMOND Sr.	Wm	Trader?	c54	c1580	1634	Lavenham S	Lavenham S	1533A Lavenham S	0	0
12	Wyatt	Sarah HEARD	Luke	Weaver			c1639	Assington S	?W.Suffolk	No Assington S	?30	0
3	Freestone	Fran HILL	Val	Merchant	26	1610	1636	Alford L	Alford L	No Winthorpe/ Croft L	0	40/10
10	Dewy	Margt HOBART	Edm Sr.		c61	c1572	1633		?Hethersett N (8)	No Hingham N		
3	Elmer	Eliz HOBART	Edm Jr.	Weaver	c28	c1605	1633		Scoulton N	1557A Hingham N		
3	Ibrook	Eliz HOBART	Pet	Clergy	27	1608	1635	Hingham N	Hingham N	No ?Haverhill S	?0	?41
2	Plomer	Anne HOBART	Thos		c25	c1608	1633		?Swaffham area N (13)	No Hingham/ Wymondham N		

8	Bulkeley (Whittingham)	Eliz HOUGH	Ath	Merchant	c51	c1582	1633	Odell, Beds		No	Boston L	0	60
3	Dane	Eliz HOWE	Jas	Weaver	c30	c1606	c1636	Bps.Stortford, Herts	Bps.Stortford, Herts	1502A	Hatfield B.Oak E	0	4
2	Knapp	Jud HUBBARD	Wm	Husbandman	25	1610	1635	Ipswich S	Ipswich S	N1	Ipswich/ Tendring	0	0/12
12	Fiennes-Clinton	Lady Sus HUMPHRY	John	Gentleman			1634	Sempring- ham L	Sempring- ham L	No	London/ Sandwich, Kent	0	80/140
6	Seaborne	Esther HUNTING	John		c42	c1597	c1639	Hingham N	Morley N	No	Hoxne S	4	?18
12	Barrett	Margt HUNTINGTON	Sim	Grocer			1633	Norwich N	Norwich/ Blythborough S	N1	Norwich N	0/22	0
6	Marbury	Anne HUTCHINSON	Wm	Clothier	43	1591	1634	Alford L	Louth area L	N1	Alford L	10	0
3	Ingoldsby	Olive JAMES	Thos	Schoolmaster	28	1602	1630		?E of Louth L (25)	No	Boston L		0
3	Fiennes-Clinton	Lady Arbella JOHNSON	Isaac	Gentleman	c27	c1603	1630	Sempring- ham L	Sempring- ham L	1570A	Sem/Stam- ford L	0	0/10
8	Moody	Fran KIL-BOURN	Thos		51	1584	1635	Moulton S	Moulton S	1574A	Wood Ditton C	0	4

Table 24. *Continued*

AG	Née	Name	Husband	Husband's Occupation	Age	DOB	DOE	BP	FR		MH (Marital Home)	Distances BP:FR	BP:MH
4	Stone (Cutting)	Sus KIMBALL	Hen	Wheelwright	35	1599	1634	Gt.Bromley E	Gt.Bromley E	1350A	Mistley E	0	4
5	Scott	Ursula KIMBALL	Rich	Wheelwright	37	1597	1634	Rattlesden S	Felsham S	1475A	Rattlesden S	3	0
2	Ames	Mill KINGSBURY	Jos		c25	c1612	c1637			No	Boxford S		
12	Tutty	Anna KNIGHT	Alex	Innkeeper			1635	London		No	Chelmsford E		30
5	Reade	Margt LAKE*	John		c37	1598	c1635	N.Benfleet E	Wickford E	1534A	N.Benfleet E	3	0
12	Kelway	Mary LANE	Wm					Chelmsford E	Chelmsford E	N1	Chelmsford E		0
12	?(Greene)	Eliz LEAGER	Jacob	Tailor			1638			No	Hadleigh/Kersey S		
7	?Fisher	Ann LEVERETT	Thos	Lawyer	c47	c1586	1633		?Boston area L (6)	1552B	Boston L		
3	Morse	Lydia LEWIS	Wm		c30	c1602	c1632	Stoke by Nayland S	Dedham E	1450A	Stoke by Nayland S	4	0
3	Lane	Annis LINCOLN	Thos	Cooper	c28	c1607	c1635	?Shipdham N	Shipdham N	1592A	Hingham N	0	3
3	Norman	Sus LOCKWOOD	Rob		c28	c1602	1630			No	Combs S		

7	White	Mary LOOMIS	Jos	Woolen draper	48	1590	1638	Shalford E	Messing E	N1	Braintree E	12	5
4	Waite	Mary LORD	Rob	Yeoman?	c32	1604	c1636	?Finching-field E	Wethers-field E	No	Sudbury S	?3	?13
12	Wilson (Whiting)	Anne LOVE-RAN	John	Yeoman			c1636	Dedham E	Dedham E	1567A	Ardleigh E	0	3
8	Baker	Sarah LUMP-KIN	Rich		c54	c1584	1638		Ardleigh E (5)	1501B	Boxted E		
7	Osborne	Sarah LYMAN	Rich		c49	c1582	1631	Halstead E	Halstead	No	Hi. Ongar E	0	24
2	Welles	Esther MASON	Hugh	Tanner	22	1612	1634	Maldon E	Maldon E	1404A	Maldon E	0	0
9	Bulkeley	Martha MEL-LOWS	Abr	Gentleman	c48	c1585	1633	Odell, Beds	Woore, Sa-lop	No	Boston L	100	60
4	Bishop	Avis MER-RIALL	John	Yeoman	c35	c1601	1636		Tatting-stone S (3)	1596A	Wherstead S		
4	Willerton	Sus MER-RIALL	Nat	Yeoman	c33	c1603	1636			No	Wherstead S		
5	Elwyn	Sarah MET-CALFE	Mich	Clothier	39	1598	1637	Heigham N	Heigham N	1563A	Norwich N	0	1
2	Kelway	Margt MON-TAGUE	Griffin		c23	c1612	1635	Chelms-ford E		No	Chelmsford E	0	0
4	Cox	Sarah MOODY	John	Gentleman	35	1598	1633	Bury S	Bury S	N1	Bury/ Moulton S	0	0/10
2	Youngs	Martha MOORE	Thos		23	1613	1636	Southwold S	Gt.Yar-mouth N	1554A	Southwold S	18	0

Table 24. Continued

AG	Née	Name	Husband	Husband's Occupation	Age	DOB	DOE	BP	FR		MH (Marital Home)	Distances BP:FR	BP:MH
8	Jasper	Eliz MORSE	Sam		55	1580	1635	Redgrave S		N1	Burgate S		3
5	Green	Anne MOULTON	John	Husbandman	38	1599	1637	Ormesby N	Ormesby N	1450A	Ormesby N	0	0
3	Markiet	Mary MUNNINGS	Edm		30	1605	1635			No	Dengie E		
6	Grome	Eliz MUNNINGS	Geo	Cordwainer	41	1593	1634	Rattlesden S	L.Melford/Lavenham S	1471B	Rattlesden S	7/10	0
3	Busby	Ann NICKERSON	Wm	Weaver	29	1608	1637	Norwich N		No	Norwich N		0
5	Branson	Sarah NUTT	Miles		c36	c1600	1636			No	Barking S		
2	Stream	Eliz PACKER	Sam		c24	c1614	1638			No	Wymondham N		
4	Ward	Lucy PAGE	Rob	Husbandman	32	1605	1637	Filby N	Filby N	C1550A	Ormesby N	0	3
2	Payne	Phoebe PAGE	John	Yeoman	36	1594	1630	Lavenham S	Lavenham S	No	Boxted E	0	11
7	Stamforth	Mary PALMER	Wm	Husbandman	c50	1587	1637	Ranworth N	Gt.Plumstead N (11)	N1	Ormesby N	5	8
7	Chapen	Martha PARKE	Rob		c48	c1582	1630	Bury S		No	Bury/Bures? S		?19/0
6	Whiting	Ann PAYNE	Rob	Merchant	c42	c1597	1639	Hadleigh S	Boxford S	1567A	Naughton S	4	5

154

9	Lawrence	Anne PECK	Rob	Clergy	c56	c1582	1638	St.Jas.S. Elmham S	Rumburgh S	No	Hingham N	3	22
2	Eliot	Lydia PENNI-MAN	Jas		c21	c1610	1631	Nazeing E	Bps.Stort-ford area, Herts	1542A	Widford E	6	6
10	Cooke (Reade)	Eliz PETER	Hugh	Clergy	c65	c1570	1635	Gt.Yeld-ham E	Gt.Yeld-ham area E	No	Wickford/ Rayleigh E	5	30
6	Knapp	Ann PHIL-BRICK	Thos	?Fuller	c43	1593	c1636	Bures S	Bures S	1521A	Bures S	0	0
1	Ames	Eliz PHILLIP	John	Clergy	c48	c1590	1638	Norwich N	Costessey N	1563A	Wrentham S	3	24
4	Sargent	Ann PHILLIPS	Geo	Clergy	c35	c1595	1630			No	Boxted E		
3	Clement	Abig PINGRY	Moses	Saltmaker	c28	c1612	c1640	?Colches-ter E		No	Colchester E		?o
4	Bellingham	Sus PORT-MONT	Philem	Schoolmaster	33	1601	1634	?Alford/ Barton L	Barton L	No	Grimsby L	?39/0	?23/18
6	White	Ann PORTER	John		c42	c1597	c1639	?Shalford/ Messing E	Messing E	N1	Felsted E	12/0	14/0
4	Bedle	Abig POWELL	Mich	Schoolmaster	31	1608	1639	Woolver-stone S	Brantham S	N1	Woolver-stone S	5	0
5	Harper	Martha PROC-TOR	John	Husbandman	c38	c1597	1635			No	Groton S		
5	Andrew	Anne PYN-CHON	Wm	Gentleman	c38	c1592	1630		Springfield E	N1	Writtle/ Springf'd E		

Table 24. *Continued*

AG	Née	Name	Husband	Husband's Occupation	Age	DOB	DOE	BP	FR		MH (Marital Home)	Distances	
												BP:FR	BP:MH
3	Rowning	Mary RAY	Sim	Yeoman	c28	c1612	c1640	Hundon S	Hundon S	1392A	Hundon S	0	0
2	Lessie	Sarah READ	John	Yeoman?	c23	c1616	c1639	Blythborough S	Wenhaston S	1541A	Blythborough S	2	0
5	Frost	Thomasine RICE	Edm		38/39	1600	1638/39	Bury S	Bury S	No	Berkhamsted, Herts	0	66
12	Pitcher	Frances RICROFT*					1638		Hardingham N (3)	1449A	Hingham N	0	
12	Everard	Sarah ROGERS	Ezek	Clergy			1638	London	?Gt. Waltham E	No	Hatfield B.Oak E/Rowley, Yks	?28	30/
5	Crane	Margt ROGERS	Nat	Clergy	c36	c1600	1636	Coggeshall E	Chilton, Sudbury S	No	Assington S	12	11
8	Curtis	Mary RUGGLES	Thos		c51	c1586	1637	Nazeing E	Nazeing E	1585A	Nazeing E	0	0
3	Peaseley	Mary SAWYER	Edw	Yeoman	26	1610	1636	Rattlesden S	Rattlesden S	No	Lincolnshire	0	
9	Whatlocke	Martha SCOTT*	Hen		60	1574	1634	Rattlesden S	Rattlesden S	N1	Rattlesden S	0	0

2	Marbury	Kath SCOTT	Rich	Clothier?	24	1610	1634	London/Berkhamsted, Herts	Louth L	N1	Glemsford S	125/20	47/58
5	Strutt	Eliz SCOTT	Thos	Glover	40	1594	1634	Rattlesden S	Rattlesden S	1592A	Rattlesden S	0	0
2	Kimball	Abig SEVERANCE	John		21	1616	1637		Lawford E (8)	N1	Ipswich S		
3	Touteville	Margt SHEPARD	Thos	Clergy	29	1606	1635	?Buttercrambe, Yks		No	Heddon, N'umbl'd		77
2	Odding	Sarah SHERMAN	Phil		c21	c1612	1633/34		Braintree area E (19)	No	Dedham E		
4	Travis	Sus SKELTON	Sam	Clergy	32	1597	1629	Sempringham L		No	Sempringham L	0	0
3	Stoughton	Jud SMEAD*	John		c30	c1600	1630	Coggeshall E	Cant'b'y/Sandwich, Kent	No		45/50	
5	Cooper	Jud SMITH	Hen		c36	c1602	1638	?Hingham N	?Hingham N	No	Hempnall N	?0	?14
2	Kelway	Milcah SNOW	Thos	Barber	c24	c1612	1636	Chelmsford E		N1	Chelmsford E		0
5	Angier	Mary SPARHAWK	Nat	Merchant	c38	c1600	1638	Dedham E	NE of Colchester E	1518B	Dedham E	5/6	0

Table 24. Continued

AG	Née	Name	Husband	Husband's Occupation	Age	DOB	DOE	BP	FR	MH (Marital Home)	Distances BP:FR	Distances BP:MH
5	Clark	Eliz STACEY	Sim	Clothier	c38	c1597	1635/36	Theydon Garnon E	Theydon Garnon E	1550A Bocking E	0	24
3	Barker	Mary STEARNS	Isaac		c30	c1600	1630	Stoke by Nayland S	Nayland S	1537B Stoke by Nayland	2	0
6	Whiting	Sarah STEBBINGS	Rowl		43	1591	1634		Coggeshall E (7)	1589B Bocking E		
7	Sorrell	Margery STEELE	Geo		c49	c1582	1631	Fairstead	Leighs/Walthams E	N1 Fairstead E	3/4	0
5	Talcott	Rachel STEELE	John		c38	c1593	1631	Braintree E	Colchester E	N1 Fairstead E	14	4
5	Clark	Joan STONE	Sim	Husbandman	38	1597	1635	?Halstead E		No Gt.Bromley/Boxted E		17/11
5	Hutchinson	Sus STORRE	Aug		c38	c1600	1638	Alford L	Lincoln L	N1 Bilsby L	30	2
5	Fox	Ruth SYMONDS	John		c39	c1597	1636			No Gt.Yarmouth N		
8	Harlakenden	Dot/Deb SYMONDS	Sam	Merchant	c40	c1597	1637	Earl's Colne E	Kenardston, Kent/EC E	1602A Gt.Yeldham E	60/0	8

3	Mott	Dot TALCOTT	John		c30	c1602	1632	Braintree E	Braintree E	1554A	Braintree E	0	0
12	Fiske	Martha THOMPSON	Edm	Sea captain			1637	St.Jas.S. Elmham S	SJSE/ Laxfield S	No	Gt.Yarmouth N	o/6	21
3	Goodale (Taylor)	Sus TOPPAN	Abr	Cooper	c27	c1610	1637		Gt.Yarmouth N	1525B	Gt.Yarmouth N		
4	Blessing	Joanna TOWNE	Wm		c35	c1600	1635	Gt.Yarmouth N		No	Gt.Yarmouth N		
3	Newdigate	Mary TOWNSEND	Thos	Husbandman	c28	c1610	1638	Bury/Hessett S	Ickworth S	1530A	Gedding S	2/6	7/2
5	Fiske	Martha UNDERWOOD	Mart	Clothier	c36	c1598	1634	St.Jas.S. Elmham S	SJSE/ Laxfield S	1435A	SJSE/ Wrentham S	o/6	o/11
5	King	Anna VASSALL	Wm	Merchant	c37	c1593	1630	Cold Norton E	SE Essex	1490A	Pritlewell E	6	10
4	Talcott	Sarah WADSWORTH	Wm		c35	c1597	1632	Braintree E	Colchester E	N1	Braintree E	14	0
4	Edmunds	Alice WARD	John	Clergy	c31	c1608	1639	Skirbeck L	Boston area L	No	Hadleigh E	2-7	26
2	Woodruff	Eliz WARDALL	Thos	Shoemaker	c24	c1610	1634			No	Alford L		
5	Mayhew	Anne WATERHOUSE	Thos	Clergy	c37	c1602	1639	Coddenham S	NE of Coddenham S	N1	Coddenham S	10	0
4	Wise	Eliz WELD	Jos	Merchant	c35	c1600	1635			No	Sudbury S		
4	Dearesley	Margt WELD	Thos	Clergy	c35	c1597	1632			No	Terling E		

Table 24. Continued

AG	Née	Name	Husband	Husband's Occupation	Age	DOB	DOE	BP	FR		MH (Marital Home)	BP:FR	BP:MH
2	Warner	Abig WELLES	Thos	Husbandman	22	1614	1636	Boxted E	Boxted E	1536A	Boxted/Colchester E	0	0/5
4	Hawkins	Ann WHIPPLE	Matt	Merchant?	c32	c1600	c1632	Braintree E	Gt. Waltham E	1537B	Bocking E	7	1
4	St.John	Eliz WHITING	Sam	Clergy	31	1605	1636	Keysoe, Beds	Bletsoe, Beds	No	Skirbeck L	4	60
4	Smith	Ann WILBORE	Sam	Woolen draper	c35	c1598	1633	Sible Hedingham E	Sible Hedingham E	1560B	Sible Hedingham E	0	0
6	Stalham	Eliz WILLIAMS	Rob	Cordwainer	43	1594	1637	Norwich N	Heigham/N'ch N?	1465A	Norwich N?	1/0	?0
2	Bernard	Mary WILLIAMS	Rog	Clergy	23	1607	1630	Worksop, Notts	Epworth L	No	High Laver E	19	120
6	Mansfield	Eliz WILSON	John	Clergy	c42	c1590	1632	London	London	No	Sudbury S	0	50
2	Reade	Eliz WINTHROP	John Jr.	Gentleman	21	1614	1635	N.Benfleet E	N.Benfleet E	No	Groton S	0	32
2	Fones	Eliz WINTHROP	Hen	Gentleman	21	1610	1631	London		No	Groton S	0	50
6	Tyndal	Margt WINTHROP	John	Gentleman	41	1591	1632	Gt.Maplestead E	Gt.Maplestead E	1530A	Groton S	0	10

12	James	Lydia WRIGHT	Sam				c1639	London		No	Kelvedon Hatch E		17
3	Clarke	Margt WYETH	Nich	Mason	c30	1608	c1638	Westhorpe S	Ashfield S	No	Mellis/ Framl'm S	3	5/19
3	Elvin	Pris YOUNG	Chris	Weaver	c26	c1612	1638	Gt. Yarmouth N	Gt. Yarmouth N	1516A	Gt. Yarmouth N	?o	o
4	Gentleman (Harrington)	Joan YOUNGS	John	Clergy	34	1603	1637	Southwold S	Southwold S	1562A	Southwold S	o	o
3	Warren	Margt YOUNGS	Jos	Sea captain	c28	c1610	1638	Southwold S	Southwold S	N1	Southwold S	o	o

Notes: Names in parentheses in Née column are of first husbands. Marital home (MH) occasionally means husband's home. Phebe Barnard's and Ann Loveran's mother was twice married, dates unknown. Distances in parentheses in FR column are from FR to MH.
*Widows.

Table 25. Age, Roots, and Mobility of Selected Women Emigrants

AG	Age	No.	Distance, BP:FR						Distance, BP:MH					
			0–4	5–9	10–14	15–19	20+	UK	0–4	5–9	10–14	15–19	20+	UK
1	16–20	3		1				2	1					2
2	21–25	23	7	3		2	2	9	7	3	2		6	5
3	26–30	36	14	3		2	1	16	13	4	3	1	5	10
4	31–35	30	9	4	1		1	15	10	1	2		3	14
5	36–40	30	14	5	3		3	5	12	3	5	1	3	6
6	41–45	14	6	2	3	1		2	7	1	3	1	1	1
7	46–50	15	5	4	1			5	5	2			5	3
8	51–55	7	3					4	3			1	1	2
9	56–60	3	2				1		1				2	
10	61–65	3	1	1				1					2	1
11	66–70													
12	UK	23	4	3			5	11	7	1	1	1	6	7
	Total	187	65	26	8	5	13	70	66	15	16	5	34	51

presenting tables dominated by "unknowns," I have selected a group of 187 married or widowed women whose maiden names are recorded. This group is, of course, skewed toward those female emigrants over 20 years of age.[28]

If we omit those whose family or personal movements are unknown, certain trends very similar to the different male occupational groups become apparent. Most obviously, the great majority of women had not experienced any long-range migration before they sailed to New England. Sixty-three of the 114 whose family roots are known (55 percent) came from neighborhoods where their families had been established for several generations. A further 22 percent had grown up within 10 miles of the family's roots. Over three-quarters, in other words, came from districts with which they and their ancestors had long been familiar. Distances moved from birthplace to marital home demonstrate that most brides married local grooms. Half of the 136 whose personal movements are known moved less than five miles from their parental to their marital homes. A further 11 percent moved less than 10 miles. Courtship and marriage were predominantly local.[29]

The age groups of married women emigrants coincide with those of married male planters. Three-quarters were aged 40 or under, 122 of the 164 whose ages are known. Sixty-two were newly or recently married. The 60 in their thirties almost always had two or more children. The peaking of 26–30-year-olds matches that of married males, though the comparatively slight rise in numbers probably reflects the lower average marriage age of women. Marriage for a significant number of our East Anglian women represented not only a rite of passage but an imminent transatlantic passage as well.

It is particularly unfortunate that for over half of the 26–30 age group (20 out of 36) the distance between parental home and family roots is lost. Data on the extent of moves between parental and marital homes are similarly patchy for women in their early thirties. Where mobility is recoverable, at least a half of most age groups moved less than five miles when they got married, and at least half were born in the immediate neighborhood of their ancestral roots.

There are exceptions to this localism, involving more distant moves for brides. Overall, 30 women out of the known 131 moved more than 20 miles when they married. This leaving of familiar backgrounds is particularly marked in the 21–25 age group and among those whose ages are unknown.

The reasons for this unusual mobility become clearer when we learn the occupations of their husbands or fathers. The great majority of the 30 came from classes or occupational groups with the widest geographical horizons and social networks. Thirteen were wives or daughters of clergymen.[30] Thirteen were similarly related to men engaged in trade.[31] Four were married to professional men;[32] Elizabeth (St. John) Whiting came from one of the most distinguished legal families in England. Only three of these uprooted women were married to artisans or farmers, confirming the greater residential permanence and more local outlooks of such vocations.[33]

Some of this wifely mobility is explained by previous family movement, either by a branch or by a whole clan. In 1620 Elizabeth Clerk married the clothier Simon Stacey at her ancestral church in Theydon Garnon, Essex. Though Simon came from the north Essex textile center of Bocking, his family roots were in Epping, close to Theydon Garnon. We see proof of the linkage in the fact that both branches used the highly unusual male Christian name of Nymphas. Simon and Elizabeth's courting and betrothal would have owed a great deal to the encouragement of his Epping cousins.[34]

A somewhat similar picture emerges from family papers of Henry Winthrop's whirlwind romance and runaway marriage with his London cousin Elizabeth Fones. Henry had been staying with his kinsman Thomas Fones, who was a London apothecary. Both fathers bemoaned the headlong audacity of youth, little imagining that Elizabeth would achieve posthumous fame as Anya Seton's *Winthrop Woman.* In this case kinship provided opportunity if not encouragement.[35]

Sometimes patrons, rather than kinsfolk, might wittingly or unwittingly foster romantic attachments between couples born far apart. Roger Williams, chaplain to Sir William Masham at Otes, High Laver, Essex, met his future wife, Mary Bernard, in the household of Sir William's formidable mother-in-law, Joan Lady Barrington, at nearby Hatfield Broad Oak. Mary was the daughter of the Reverend Richard Bernard, a famous puritan antagonist to separatism from the Church of England. She was born at Worksop in Nottinghamshire where the patron of the living was Richard Whalley, brother-in-law of Lady Barrington. When she was four her father moved to Batcombe in Somerset. Mary was a maidservant to another of Lady Barrington's daughters when she met her future husband. Mary's brother, as we shall see, immigrated to Weymouth, Massachusetts, in 1636.[36]

Something similar was probably afoot in the marriage of the Reverend Samuel Whiting, rector of Skirbeck by Boston in Lincolnshire, to

Elizabeth, only daughter of Oliver and Sarah (Bulkeley) St. John of Keysoe, Bedfordshire, 60 miles to the west. Two of the most important burgesses of Boston, Abraham Mellows and Atherton Hough (both of whom immigrated to the New World), were already married into the Bulkeley family, another Bedfordshire clan. Mellows's son was an alumnus of Whiting's old college, Emmanuel.[37]

A magnatial patron explains Sarah (Everard) Rogers's move from Essex to Yorkshire. Her husband, Ezekiel, served Sir Francis Barrington, first as his domestic chaplain at Hatfield Broad Oak and then as his appointee to the northern parish of Rowley, where he was patron of the living. Sarah had grown up in London, but the Everards were a well-known Essex clan based at Great Waltham and Topsfield, quite close to Roger's own youthful home at Wethersfield. Separated family branches again facilitated apparently long-range courting.[38]

The English migrations of several clerical wives simply reflected their husbands' calling. Anne (Lawrence) Peck, who grew up at St. James South Elmham, must have come to know Robert when he was a young man at the nearby market town of Beccles, long before the 25-year-old minister moved the 20 miles northwest to take up his benefice at Hingham in 1605.[39]

Two migrations of ministers' wives were less routinely occupational. Margaret Touteville met Thomas Shepard at the house of her kinsman Sir Richard Darley in Buttercrambe, Yorkshire, when the young divine was on the run from the prohibitions of Bishop Laud of London. After her marriage she was hustled up to "barbaric" Heddon near Newcastle to escape further persecution and then smuggled back to East Anglia. She endured near shipwreck off Yarmouth, the death of an infant, and a winter spent in hiding near Norwich before she finally escaped with her hounded husband to Massachusetts. There she soon died.[40]

Hugh Peter's wife was Elizabeth (Cooke) Reade of Wickford, Essex, near the Thames Estuary. She was the widow of a leading puritan layman of the neighborhood. She had been born on the other side of Essex at Great Yeldham, a member of a large and influential family of gentlemen and clothiers. Her first husband, Edmund Reade, came from a family with roots in the same area, but his branch had migrated down to the Thames at the beginning of the sixteenth century. Some such intertwining of branches as occurred with the Staceys, Rogerses, and Henry Winthrops must have brought these far-flung lovers together. Hugh Peter was another matter. This hotheaded young minister from Cornwall via Cambridge, successively curate and schoolmaster at Laindon and minister at Rayleigh, both by Wickford, wooed and won a woman old enough to be his mother. From this mismatch (as then regarded) and his abrasive personality sprang the shoots of sexual innuendo which were to entangle Peter for much of his eventful life. Significantly, two of Elizabeth's Yeldham Cooke cousins emigrated in the same year, 1635. They traveled as part of a large company of relatives— Lakes, Eppses, and Winthrops. By his marriage, the Cornishman had established kinship with a network of East Anglian puritan gentlemen and merchants.[41]

For women as well as men, easier inshore water communications could turn quite extended sections of coastline into neighborhoods. Sarah Moore came from a long-established leatherworking family in Langford near Maldon on the Essex coast. Her grandfather was in the trade, and her Uncle Nicholas was a shoemaker on Fullbridge Street, Maldon. A cousin, Edward, was also a shoemaker. In 1611 she married Edmund Greenleaf, a dyer and hosier from an equally venerable Ipswich family. Between 1540 and 1560, his grandfather, Stephen, had been an alderman of the port, which lay 30 miles up the coast from Maldon. In 1613 Sarah and Edmund's first child was baptized at St. Mary le Tower Church in Ipswich. They remained there until emigrating in about 1634 with their five children. How they met is unknown. There were frequent coastal links between ports on the east coast. It seems probable that Edmund may have called in there, perhaps on a regular basis. Sarah seems to have kept in touch with her family, for her younger brother, Francis, also emigrated.[42]

Some women's removals reflected the pull of trading centers. Martha (Fiske) Thompson, of the numerous north Suffolk clan, migrated from St. James South Elmham north to the leading local port of Great Yarmouth, where her husband was a sea captain. She did not lose touch with her family, however. The Thompsons joined the Fiske emigrant contingent in 1637 and six years later moved with them from Salem to Wenham, Massachusetts.[43]

Similar urban attraction occurred in the background of Margaret (Barrett) Huntington, who sailed from Yarmouth in 1633 with her husband Simon, a Norwich grocer. The Barrett family had been settled in the northeast Suffolk village of Blythborough near the port of Southwold for between 200 and 300 years by the middle of the sixteenth century. In 1565, Margaret Barrett, the widow of William Barrett, married into the wealthy Norwich clothier family of Suckling. She brought with her the 20 miles to the city her five-year-old son, Christopher Barrett. He grew up in the Norwich parish of St. Andrew (the church has a famous Suckling memorial) and eventually became mayor of the city. It was his granddaughter who married Simon Huntington in 1623. The Huntingtons had also been attracted to Norwich in the sixteenth century. Intriguingly, their family roots were in a group of villages only three to six miles on the Norwich side of Blythborough.[44]

Occasionally marriage provided a counterattraction to town or city life. Elizabeth (Bond) Palmer Child immigrated in the Winthrop fleet to Watertown from the Groton area. Winthrop referred to her second husband as "my neighbour Childe." Elizabeth's birthplace had been the West Suffolk center of Bury St. Edmunds. Her first husband had taken her 30 miles south to the Stour textile town of Nayland. Her second marriage in 1625 to the merchant Ephraim Child brought her into the Winthrop circle. With her went her five-year-old nephew, William Bond, third son of her brother Thomas. William later had a distinguished career as a leader of Massachusetts, and his successor Thomas Bond wrote a justly famous nineteenth-century history of Watertown.[45]

A similar current carried Anne (Marbury) Hutchinson. She had been born in Alford in 1591 when her father was master of the grammar school and preacher at St. Wilfred's Church. When she was fourteen, however, the Reverend Francis Marbury was appointed preacher at St. Martin in the Vintry, London. She continued in London until 1612, when she married the 26-year-old mercer William Hutchinson (whose brother had set up as an ironmonger in the city) and returned with him to their joint birthplace. There she brought up her expanding family for the next 22 years.[46]

The reasons for some longer moves are lost. A deposition made at Hampton, New Hampshire, in 1671 stated that Isabella (Bland) Austin had formerly lived with her father, John, in Colchester, Essex. How she met Francis Austin, who witnessed the will of Henry Chickering in Ringsfield, near Beccles, almost 50 miles to the north, we shall probably never know.[47] Anne Hutchinson's younger sister Katherine was born in St. Margaret's New Fish Street parish, London, in 1610. In 1632 she married Richard Scott, son of Edward Scott, clothier, of Glemsford, Suffolk, where the family had long been settled. The wedding took place in Berkhamsted, Hertfordshire. I have uncovered no clues as to how or why they came to be there.[48]

These interesting exceptions should not blind us to the overwhelming localism of most marriages in the sample of emigrant wives. As with male occupational groups, a sense of rootedness, of local horizons, and of very modest, untraumatic moves of homes increases as we go down the social scale. Take, for instance, the case of Thomasine Buffum who married Robert Buffum in 1634 and emigrated in 1638. She had been born, like her husband Robert, in the port borough of Yarmouth, but her first husband came from South Walsham, 12 miles to the west. After her second marriage, she must have thought she would live out the rest of her life back in her birthplace, instead of spending only a four-year transition there before immigrating to Salem.[49] Unusually, in the case of Henry and Olive Farwell, married in Boston, Lincolnshire, in 1629, we know more about the wife's background than her tailor husband's. She was born a Welby; the Welbys had been settled at Fosdyke, seven miles south of Boston, since the early 1500s. The only Lincolnshire Farwells I have found came from central and western parishes of the county. It is therefore possible that Henry migrated eastward to set up a home with Olive, though he may have already moved to Boston to follow his trade. Certainly the wife remained close to her ancestral roots.[50]

Yet, even with gentlewomen and clergy wives, there were plenty who had enjoyed undisturbed lives before embarkation to America. Margaret Tyndal Winthrop must have known the elder John and his village of Groton long before she married him. Her father, assassinated by a disappointed suitor in 1616, had been a leading Jacobean lawyer. Her home at Great Maplestead was only 10 miles from Groton.[51] Anne (Mayhew) Waterhouse was the daughter of the lord of the manor of the mid-Suffolk village of Coddenham. When Thomas Waterhouse arrived as curate, the couple fell in love and married. Shortly after they had immigrated to Dorchester, Massachusetts, Anne's father died, leaving her his Coddenham lands. She and Thomas returned to England, where he successively ministered to the adjacent parishes of Ash Bocking and Brandeston, five miles from Coddenham. Apart from the New England adventure and a brief sojourn in Colchester on their return, Anne lived out her life within walking distance of her birthplace.[52]

In her settled, predeparture lifestyle, Anne Waterhouse was typical not only of the married women we have selected but also of the male occupational groups previously analyzed. In the great majority of cases, emigrants were not used to lives of upheaval and mobility. The experience of leaving home and ancestral neighborhoods must have had the most jarring and jolting effects. It is highly doubtful whether these people would have agreed with Bailyn's judgment that they "were normal Englishmen acting normally" or that their errand into the wilderness was "nothing remarkable . . . in the context of the mobility of the time." They did not step from one moving belt to another; they were wrenched off their firmly planted feet by sudden, unprecedented shocks to their lives.

By the same token, although Anne Bradstreet, Anne Hutchinson, and Elizabeth Sherman are questionably celebrated as progressive feminist prototypes,[53] most women appear to have continued their traditional way of life and outlook in the New World. The few cases where female motives for emigration are known show them following the leads of husbands and ministers. Lucy Downing, John Winthrop's sister, was blamed for delaying her family's departure because of her timorousness, and she ended her days back in the eastern counties, cooped up and half-starved in a tomb-cold fenland house in the depths of Cambridgeshire by her Scrooge-like son Sir George. This complaining and pathetic gentlewoman hardly gives the impression of a great innovator.[54]

Though, at first glance, breasting the Atlantic and wrestling with a new continent might lend credence to the picture of the eastern counties contingent as bravers of change, prototypes of the Turnerian frontiersman and woman, closer study suggests strong conservative, traditionalist elements in their lives. Apart from a few gentlemen, clergymen, and merchants, most voyagers from Yarmouth, Ipswich, or London had had to sever powerful personal ties to local neighborhoods. The men and women of Greater East Anglia were, for the most part, reluctant travelers. Unused to "Worlds in Motion," they are more accurately described as "The Uprooted."[55] As we shall now discover, those roots usually went very deep.

7

Ancestral Roots

MOST OF the tradition-dominated emigrants from the eastern counties were not used to moving outside their familiar neighborhoods. It is now time to examine two further questions about the English background. The main thrust of this chapter is a systematic analysis of the depth of the emigrants' roots. How long families had been settled in a particular district would affect a clan's sense of belonging and its interconnectedness with other clans. With each generation the web of relationships would become denser and more binding. On the other hand, it might take people from "away" decades or even generations to win full community acceptance.[1] This chapter also considers a subsidiary question: Were those whose backgrounds have been uncovered typical of other possible emigrants from Greater East Anglia?

I have investigated the English ancestries of the more than 400 families known to have left the eastern counties during the 1630s. The sources used include published and unpublished family histories, the findings of professional genealogists, parish registers, muster and lay subsidy records, borough apprenticeship indentures and freeman's rolls, manorial and municipal records, wills, and the probate indexes published by the British Record Society for the ecclesiastical divisions of the eastern counties and for the Prerogative Court of Canterbury.

This mass of evidence has to be treated with great care. The enthusiasm of some family historians for lengthening and aggrandizing their pedigrees is not always matched by necessary caution. Will indexes can often reveal strong concentrations of one family name in a circumscribed area over many generations. It would, for instance, be absurd to doubt that the Aldous family, with over 20 wills between 1499 and 1678, made and witnessed in or adjacent to Fressingfield, were deeply rooted in their north Suffolk locality. Problems emerge with probate sources when emigrants have common surnames like Palmer or Allen. Even a very marked clustering in one place must be handled gingerly. All those Brownes in Sudbury might have come from quite separate clans (though it seems highly improbable). Missing names create unexpected difficulties. The making of wills was normally reserved for some members of the yeomanry and artisanry and their superiors. Recent estimates suggest that not many more than 5 percent of the population of west Suffolk made wills in the 1630s.[2] Absence of names in the probate indexes does not therefore prove absence from a particular neighborhood. The Youngs family of Great Yarmouth, for instance, have no wills indexed in the Norwich Consistory Court Records between 1473 and 1611. We might assume that their line of residence had been broken for 138 years. However, the municipal records show that three members of the family were bailiffs between 1587 and 1610, and probate records have William Youngs witnessing a will in 1601.[3] The burden of proof of local ancestry has thus often been counterweighted quite heavily, especially against the lower classes. We could reasonably expect more to have deep local roots than we have been able to unearth.

The varying quality of the data on family settlement has had to be taken into account in arriving at average lengths of residence for different occupational groups. The evidence of ancestral longevity has therefore been rated. In Table 26, the letter *A* signifies reasonable certainty, as in the case of the Aldous family's presence in the Fressingfield district from 1499 to 1638 when Nathan Aldous immigrated to Dedham, Massachusetts (Table 16). Painstaking pedigrees by reputable professional researchers[4] or credible, well-grounded family histories also qualify for this rating. *B* means probability, such as when a common surname is represented by local clustering over time or when there are brief gaps in the generational run, in wills, say, or in parish registration. *C* means possibility. This is when a concentration of testators is one of several within the ecclesiastical jurisdiction, or when there are long gaps or where a common surname is widely spread. *C*-rated longevity has been disregarded in the statistical analysis. A later *A* rating has usually been preferred to an earlier *C* rating. For instance, it is well established that the grocer John Baker of Norwich (Table 9) was directly descended from the John Baker, Sr., grocer, who died there in 1566. However, there was a John Baker, a "raffman" or chandler, admitted to the city's freemanship in the third year of Henry IV's reign, or 1401–2. Given the similar kind of business and forename, it is feasible that the raffman was our emigrant's forebear. Because of the lack of intervening generations in the distributive trades and of proof of pedigree, the

Table 26. Emigrants' Ancestral Roots

Residence (in completed generations)	Residence (by will dates or deaths)	A (certain)	B (probable)	C (possible)	Total Completed Generations (A)	Total Generations (B) (counted as half)	Average Completed Generations
Gentlemen:							
10–13	1300s	1			11		
6–9	1400s	3	1		25	4	
4–5	1500–1550	8		[3]	36		
2–3	1551–1600	8			20		
N1	1600–1630	6			6		
No		[6]					
Col. totals		32	1	3	98	4	
Totals			36 emigrants			102 generations	2.8
Merchants:							
10–13	1300s	1			12		
6–9	1400s	2	2	[2]	15	8	
4–5	1500–1550	7	3		32	7	
2–3	1551–1600	13	1		33	2	
N1	1601–1630	8			8		
No		[15]					
Col. totals		46	6	2	100	17	
Totals			54 emigrants			117 generations	2.2

Professional
& entrepreneurial:

	generations		emigrants			
	1300s	1400s	1500–1550	1551–1600	c1601–1630	
10–13	12	10	1			
6–9	8	5	1		1	
4–5	27	4	6	3	1	
2–3	10		4	2	1	
N1	4		4	3		
No			[4]			
Col. totals	61	19	20	8	3	2.6
Totals	80 generations		31 emigrants			

Artisans:

	generations		emigrants			
	1300s	1400s	1500–1550	1551–1600	c1601–1630	
10–13	143	45				
6–9	81	27	19			
4–5	85	5	18	12	5	
2–3	13		34	12	1	
N1			13	4		
No			33			
Col. totals	322	77	117	28	6	2.6
Totals	399 generations		151 emigrants			

Table 26. Continued

Residence (in completed generations)	Residence (by will dates or deaths)	A (certain)	B (probable)	C (possible)	Total Completed Generations (A)	Total Generations (B) (counted as half)	Average Completed Generations
Farmers:							
10–13	1300s	5	1	1	61	6	
6–9	1400s	9	5	1	67	19	
4–5	1500–1550	24	6		108	14	
2–3	1551–1600	12	2	1	30	3	
N1	c1601–1630	8			8		
No		6					
Col. totals		64	14	3	274	42	
Totals		81 emigrants			316 generations		4
Male servants							
10–13	1300s	4		3	30	4	
6–9	1400s	7	1		32	9	
4–5	1500–1550	6	4		15	9	
2–3	1551–1600	8	7		8		
N1	c1601–1630	15					
No							
Col. totals		40	12	3	85	22	
Totals		55 emigrants			107 generations		2

Occupations unknown:

	10–13	6–9	4–5	2–3	NI	No
1300s		53	188	5	14	25
1400s		36	158	8	15	35
1500–1550		18	125	3	15	50
1551–1600			38	1		38
c1601–1630						61
Col. totals		107	509	17	44	209
Totals		\} 616 generations			\} 270 emigrants	
		2.2				

Selected women:

	10–13	6–9	4–5	2–3	NI	No
1300s		19	23	1	5	2
1400s		14	75	3	6	10
1500–1550		5	86	1	4	19
1551–1600			73			29
c1601–1630			33			33
						74
Col. totals		38	290	5	15	167
Totals		\} 328 generations			\} 187 emigrants	
		1.7				

definite 1566 ancestry has been entered.[5] Where the probate evidence has been inconclusive and it has not been possible to find other residential data, it has been assumed that emigrants were newcomers to their districts. In some cases it is positively known that people had indeed themselves moved into the localities from which they emigrated. Such men as Thomas Dudley (Table 11) are designated No. If their fathers had moved in, they are rated N1. Such is Simon Bradstreet, born and raised at Horbling, Lincolnshire (Table 11). His clergyman father had been born at Gislingham in south Norfolk about 1565, had been appointed curate, then vicar of Hinderclay nearby, but in 1596 he had been translated to the benefice of Horbling, only two miles from the earl of Lincoln's mansion at Sempringham.[6] An ancestral neighborhood has been defined as having a radius of 10 miles; as the occupational listings have shown, most ancestral neighborhoods had a far shorter radius.

The key measurement for the depth of family roots is the number of generations (here, 30-year periods) a clan had lived in the same neighborhood. Bearing in mind that the dates given are for *deaths* of a generation, it has been assumed that anyone dying in the second half of the sixteenth century would be an emigrant's grandparent or great-grandparent, the second or third *completed* ancestral generation. Those decedents of the period 1500–1550 would be either great-great- or great-great-great-grandparents, fourth or fifth completed generations, and so on. Table 26 shows both the actual totals of generations and the group averages for each occupational group.

The longest average residence belongs, not surprisingly, to the farmers, yeomen and husbandmen. Four completed generations, or over 120 years in the neighborhood from which they emigrated, was typical. Some farming families went back much further. The Stone brothers could claim family settlement in Tendring Hundred near Colchester, Essex, since 1300. Their near neighbors, the Marvins, had crossed the Orwell estuary from Ipswich in the 1400s. The Cushings—or Cushions, as the nearly 200 listed in the current Norwich telephone directory call themselves—appeared in the 1327 subsidy rolls as landholders in Hardingham, Norfolk, the next village to Hingham, and their continuing residence there is documented up to their emigration in the 1630s. The family of Matthew Cushing's wife, Nazareth Pitcher, had been in Hardingham since the late 1300s. Though such residential longevity was exceptional, a quarter of the group could trace their ancestries to before 1499, two-thirds to before 1550. More typical of farmer emigrants was Nicholas Danforth of Framlingham, Suffolk, whose 12-year-old son

Thomas would live out his life until 1699 in Cambridge, Massachusetts, and become deputy governor of the colony. Nicholas's New Street farm still survives on the edges of the busy market town. The mill at Saxstead, his wife's village, can be seen from the chamber windows. Danforths had been in and around Framlingham since the direct ancestor William had died there in 1512. Similarly, the Essex farming family of the Olmsteads had a pedigree stretching back to 1520 in the Fairstead–Great Waltham district. The Fressingfield company, which settled in Dedham, Massachusetts, had been in the wood-pasture area of High Suffolk for generations. The earliest Aldous will is dated 1499 at Stradbroke, three miles southwest, but the family was living in Fressingfield by 1550 at the latest. In all, 20 Aldouses from the Fressingfield district made wills in the sixteenth and early seventeenth centuries. Barber wills made in the village date from 1458 and are similarly numerous. Fishers were in the satellite village of Wingfield by 1523 and in Fressingfield by 1585.[7] Such examples could be often repeated, as a glance at Table 16 will show. It should be emphasized that these dates record the *deaths* of ancestors, so in most cases a further life or part of it should be added.

The selected group of women emigrants has the shallowest roots. On average, about three-quarters of them lived in the same locale as their grandparents. One reason for this apparent brevity is the high total about whom little or nothing could be discovered and who were therefore assumed to have been newcomers. Before moving for reasons of marriage, husband's occupation, or economic opportunity, several women had lived in dense webs of relations. Thus Thomasine Frost came from a family that had been settled in Bury St. Edmunds since about 1404; 107 Frost wills are indexed for central Suffolk before 1700. In 1618, at the age of 18, Thomasine married Edmund Rice, whose roots in the Sudbury area 15 miles south of Bury probably stretched back to 1521 or before. By 1627, however, the Rices seem to have moved to Berkhamsted in Hertfordshire, 66 miles westward. When they settled in Massachusetts, they chose as their new home the town of Sudbury, with its Suffolk minister and strong East Anglian contingent of settlers.[8]

Women from all over the region could replicate Frost neighborhood embeddedness. Nazareth Hobart Beale, the Hingham shoemaker's second wife, would make a typical Norfolk representative, with a direct pedigree traced to 1532 in the little town itself and adjacent villages like Scoulton, Deopham, and Great Ellingham. From Essex, the Reverend John Eliot's sister Sarah Eliot Curtis had found her husband in Nazeing, to which her parents had moved from the nearby village of Widford where she and John had been born. Eliot cousins from at least four generations of settlement were dotted about the locality centered on the nearby market town of Bishop's Stortford. William Cheeseborough's wife, Anne, had a family settled in Boston since the mid-sixteenth century and kinsfolk in four villages within two hours' walk of the port. The father of Frances Kilbourne, who emigrated with her husband Thomas and five children from Wood Ditton, Cambridgeshire, was George Moody, famous along the Cambridge–Suffolk border "for his housekeeping and honest and plain dealing." His father, in turn, was the yeoman Richard Moody, who likewise had lived out his life from 1530 to 1574 in the village of Moulton, just four miles from Wood Ditton.[9] If only we knew more about the women emigrants, it is highly probable that such patterns of ancestral longevity would be often repeated.

Our other occupational groups range between these two extremes of average ancestral longevity. The male servants, often temporary living-in apprentices or on other resident traineeships in the households of their masters, nonetheless averaged two-generational completed family residences in their vicinities. Had their indentures been fully served before emigration, many would probably have returned to their hometowns to practice their crafts, as John Dane had done.

Merchants and other traders, along with those whose occupations are unknown, had, as groups, 60-year roots. On average, these 324 emigrants inhabited the same locales as their grandparents. The longest-settled of the mercantile group was the Coggeshall family. Between 1337 and 1553 their ancestors had inched their way from Hundon in south Suffolk the nine miles southeast to the cloth town of Halstead in north Essex, where the emigrant John was baptized in 1601. They had already reached Gosfield on the outskirts of Halstead by 1480. John's grandfather, also John, a clothier, bought the land and dwelling called "Munchensis" in Halstead in 1553. Many others in commerce came from families settled in the ports, industrial centers and market towns of the region since the reign of Queen Elizabeth or before.[10]

The pedigrees of the gentle emigrants often, as with the Winthrops, originated in fortunes made in the cloth industry. Their families had often been in their neighborhoods for many generations. The two Gurdon brothers came from Assington, three miles southeast of Groton. The family had prospered in the cloth town of Dedham, eight miles to the southwest, where they are recorded as early as 1406. They had acquired the manor of Assington by 1556.[11] Other armigerous clothier families with long records of residence were the Appletons of Little Waldingfield, there from 1416 to the death of the last male in 1676,[12] the Brands of Edwardstone (Winthrop's birthplace) since at least 1530,[13] and the Coes of Boxford (another Groton neighbor) since 1452. Before then, they have been traced to Gestingthorpe, nine miles east of Boxford, in 1340, eight generations back.[14] The Parkes of Bures went back even further, to Roger atte Parke of Gestingthorpe (six miles distant) in 1293.[15] The Cookes of Great Yeldham in north Essex had flourished in the wool town of Coggeshall (five miles southward) since the mid-1400s.[16] From south-central Essex, where cereals and livestock were raised for the London market, came two distinguished emigrant families. The Pynchons had been in Writtle and Springfield near Chelmsford since 1465. Sir Edward Pynchon's lavish memorial in the Writtle church underlines the family's roots in the vicinity.[17] Across the fields in Roxwell stood Turrell's Hall. Josselyns had owned the hall since the 1540s, having lived previously at High Roding, three miles to the west. From 1248 to the late fifteenth century they were located seven miles farther west at Sawbridgeworth, just over the border in Hertfordshire. The family base had crept 10 miles in 400 years.[18]

Families that remained active in the seventeenth-century textile industry as clothiers—with senior branches sometimes absorbed in the gentry—duplicated neighborhood affinities. For instance, the Fitches had been within 14 miles of their Tudor–Stuart base of Bocking since at least 1400. From Widdington just south of Saffron Walden they edged seven miles east to Lindsell by the end of the fifteenth century. Thomas Fitch of "Brasenhead" in the parish was buried in the center aisle of the Lindsell church with his wife, Agnes (Alger), in 1514. His son Roger acquired land in Panfield five miles east and then in Bocking itself before he died in 1559. Through marriage to the French family (also contributors of emigrants), George Fitch, Roger's son, added land in Winthrop's birthplace of Edwardstone. George Fitch was the emigrant brothers' grandfather. Their father, Thomas, and mother, Anne (Reeve), from Gosfield up the road toward John Coggeshall's home of Halstead lived among the tightly woven network of kin and neighbors in the north Essex vicinity. They could hardly fail to meet cousins in any village they might visit to the north or west of Bocking. Such would be the case with the Warners in western Essex, Shermans in the Dedham area, or Parishes in the central Stour Valley.[19]

Like gentlemen and entrepreneurs, the vicinage roots of professional men normally went back to great-grandparents' generations. This was the case with the Tyndals, lawyers and landowners in Great or Much Maplestead, north Essex, since the 1530s.[20] Margaret Tyndal was married to John Winthrop in the Great Maplestead church, and her brother Arthur left there in 1630 to join the *Arbella* at Southampton. Wills locate the forebears of Dr. John Clarke in the wood-pasture villages of Great Ashfield, Badwell Ash, and Finningham around Westhorpe in north Suffolk from the death of his yeoman namesake of Ashfield in 1440.[21] Another doctor, Richard Palsgrave of Wymondham, Norfolk, who was hired by the Massachusetts Bay Company in 1630, traced his lineage back to the misty past of 1400 in the villages of Little Palsgrave and Thruxton. The family can be safely located in Thruxton by the time of Richard's great-grandfather Henry, who lived from 1470 to 1516.[22] Most gentlemen, clothiers, and professional men lived in the same neighborhood as their great-grandparents.

Two out of every three artisans traced local pedigrees back three generations from their own. Of this stable group, the allied families of Kimball and Scott from Rattlesden in central Suffolk are not untypical. The emigrant Richard Kimball was a wheelwright, as was his kinsman Henry, and Thomas Scott was a glover. The Kimballs, who still thrive in the district as "Kembles," not only trace their ancestry to Thomas Kembold (*c.*1525) of Hitcham five miles to the south but also repeat the emigrants' baptismal names back down the line. Wills and parish registers show them in the neighboring villages of Elmsett, Bildeston, and Kettlebaston throughout the sixteenth century. Farming and craftsmanship were in their blood. Richard's brother-in-law Thomas Scott came from a line of farmers and leatherworkers originating in the probate records with John Scott of Felsham, three miles southwest of Rattlesden, who died in 1475. The intervening four generations, intermarried with local families like Strutts, Lockwoods, and Whatlocks, all stayed close to Rattlesden, farming, pursuing their crafts, and serving as parish officers.[23] Many other examples could be given of craftsmen embedded in the life and communities of their localities. In his ancestral background, like his personal life, the shoemaker John Beale was a typical emigrant.

With the possible exception of some of the clergy, it is clear that most of the great contingent of emigrants from the eastern counties were not just a previously settled people. They were a *long*-settled people. The very "middling-sort" composition of their exodus excluded those like "the meaner sort of people . . . whose residence cannot be expected to be constant."[24] The great majority of them must have known their neighborhoods like the backs of their gnarled hands. They must have been familiar too with their fellow villagers, many of whom would be related, and with local folklore and traditions handed down from generation to generation. Though class, education, occupation, and personal characteristics might produce considerable variations of individual horizons and breadth of outlook, these people were normally firmly rooted in place.

The most recent research has uncovered the English origins of only 4,557 (31 percent) of a possible 14,573 immigrants to New England between 1620 and 1650. Of these 4,557, 2,138 or 47 percent have been shown to have come from the five eastern counties. If this percentage were projected on to the possible 10,016 immigrants whose origins are not known, a further 4,708 people would be added to the Greater East Anglian contingent. A more conservative estimate would produce 2,533 putative Greater East Anglians.[25]

In the very nature of the case, there is no way of telling whether either of these figures is accurate. It is, indeed, not beyond the bounds of possibility that none of those of unknown origin came from eastern England. However, a plausible case could be made that the "other" Greater East Anglians cannot be traced precisely because they were geographically mobile and economically marginal. Their absence from the listings, analyses of mobility, and ancestral computations throws into doubt generalizations about personal and lineage stability. Were their movements and possible rootlessness to be discovered, a very different picture of the eastern counties founders of New England might emerge.

There can be no conclusive answer to this objection, but, quite apart from the weaknesses of contentions based on the absence of evidence, other reservations should be entered. First, there is emerging from recent research a sense that the emigration to New England from different regions of England varied in personnel and motivation. Many of those whose origins cannot be traced were young single people, who may well have been footloose in old England. From the origins or ports of embarkation of those singles with known backgrounds, it is far more likely that the majority came from the West Country than from the eastern counties. Whereas 40 percent of the married emigrants came from Norfolk, Suffolk, Essex, and Kent, these counties produced only 27 percent of the known single men. A far higher proportion sailed from the south coast and West Country ports; it would be reasonable to expect a similar proportion of the unknowns to have done likewise. This supposition is supported by research on West Country emigration to New England and Virginia, which finds the decision to emigrate to have been a last desperate seeking for subsistence after all other resorts had failed.[26] A disproportionate number of unknown young singles also left from London. Some may have been Greater East Anglians, but there are no grounds for arguing that more unknown London embarkers originated from the five counties than from the other 36 English counties furnishing immigrants to New England. The capital, after all, was a magnet for the whole country. Though East Anglia might be the heartland of English puritanism, all of England shared the Caroline recession, and other regions had fewer reserves than the eastern counties. Finally, young singles are by no means the only emigrants whose home parishes have been lost. Except in the case of seven complete lists of 693 passengers between 1635 and 1638, occasional references in letters or diaries, and lists of arrivals such as Matthew Cushing's, the connection of early New Englanders with English roots has depended on painstaking analyses of tens of thousands of wills, parish register entries, court records, and borough or manorial rolls. Since much of this research is genealogical, the random misfortune of childlessness could reduce the impetus for searching the English records. Settlers with common names are notoriously difficult to place. John and Mary Smith might have led uninterrupted lives in the same neighborhood as generations of forebears, but disentangling them from their namesakes and then matching them to specific parish registers is often well-nigh impossible. Greater East Anglia has suffered its fair share of loss of records, which, similarly, may have listed long-settled families who supplied New England settlers. The English origins of New England founders are being recovered all the time. There are plenty of entrenched emigrants emerging, thanks to more systematic searching.[27] There are more to be found, no doubt, in Greater East Anglian records. It is inherently improbable that new personnel will invalidate the overall conclusion that the 2,138 emigrants from Lincolnshire, Norfolk, Suffolk, Essex, and Cambridgeshire were wrenched from aged and complex family trees.

P A R T   I I I

New World Communities

IF, INDEED, the emigrant experience was one of sudden and unprecedented transplantation for most Greater East Anglians, how are we to
explain the paradox of extraordinary social cohesion and discipline in
the main New England colonies? Traumatizing displacement often
produces group fragmentation and atomization. Why was early Massachusetts or Connecticut not wracked by anarchic individualism, rejection of community values and family obligations, rootless opportunism, and widespread flouting of authority? Why was the social life of
New England so different from that of early Virginia?

There are many answers to this multifaceted question. Within the
scope of this study, only two explanatory sets of evidence can be presented: (*a*) the social cohesion of the actual emigration process; (*b*) the
regional clustering and comparative geographic stability of the early
New England settlements. These form the basis of the two chapters of
Part III.

183

8

Company Travel

IT IS a truism that 1630s migration to New England was a family enterprise, in stark contrast to the planting of Virginia with its mob of unattached younger men.[1] The fact that over 80 percent of the 1635–38 listed passengers were related is also pretty widely known.[2] What is less commonly appreciated is the extent to which people in the eastern counties migrated not just in families but in coalitions of families. They called them "companies."[3]

These companies were assembled in three different ways. Some were the clients and neighbors of a gentle emigrant. Some were devoted followers of a puritan preacher. Most, however, were groups of relatives (often including servants) moving to the New World together or in series.

Gentlemen's Companies

Gentle leaders of Greater East Anglian companies were commoner at the beginning of the 1630s. This reflected the organizational dominance of the Massachusetts Bay Company, which came to be controlled by gentlemen in 1629. The 1630 Lincolnshire company looked to the wealthy Isaac Johnson, brother-in-law of the earl of Lincoln, as their leader and focal point. Apart from his own relatives, like the Lady Arbella, Charles Fiennes, and John Johnson, his party was made up of the earl's clients, like Thomas Dudley and his son-in-law Simon Bradstreet, William Coddington, William Cheeseborough, and their families and servants. Johnson's early death may have contributed to the subsequent dispersal of the company.[4] William Pynchon of Springfield, near Chelmsford, Essex, had, like Johnson, been an early backer and assistant of the Massachusetts Bay Company. He, too, led a group of families from the villages around Chelmsford in the 1630 flotilla.[5] It seems probable that William Pelham led another company from the vicinity of the Stour Valley textile town of Bures, Suffolk; most of them joined the Saltonstall group in Watertown, but some settled in neighboring Newton (later Cambridge).[6]

The papers of the Winthrop family give us the most vivid detail about the formation of a gentleman's company. From August of 1629 and the signing of the Cambridge Agreement to emigrate, Winthrop's life was a frenzy of gathering people and stores until embarkation the following March. Some of his own large company were sons of neighboring gentry, like Robert Sampson,[7] Brampton Gurdon, Jr., or Benjamin Brand, young men who were contemporaries of Winthrop's emigrant son, Henry. James Downing was the stepson of Winthrop's sister Lucy, and Arthur Tyndal was the governor's brother-in-law. Henry Gosnall or Gosnold was probably related to the Edwardstone Gosnolds, childhood neighbors of Winthrop. Apart from these relatives and social equals, there was a large group of craftsmen and farmers who were Winthrop's tenants or clients at Groton. Many of these families are mentioned in the correspondence between John and his wife, Margaret[8]—"goodman Cole," "my neighbour Childe," "Coles kinsman," "Kingesbury," "Brice, Mr. Huggens son in law," "Old Waters of Nayland," "Jeffrey Ruggles of Sudbury," "Smith of Buxhall." During the first sickly months in America, Winthrop bemoaned to Margaret the loss of 12 of his family or company. Other friends and neighbors had written to the governor to reserve places. Francis Burrowes of Colchester asked that his son Samuel "go over in [Winthrop's] ship and be in his family" when they arrived. Samuel, in turn, wrote about a friend, James Boosey, who had been "inclind to that voyadg a gret wile." A youth from Halstead traveled the 11 miles to Groton in January 1630, only to be told that there were no berths left. Some companions were recommended by interested clergy like John Rogers of Dedham or Nathaniel Ward of Stondon Massey, Essex. Others of Winthrop's "family" were specially recruited experts like Dr. William Gager, the physician from nearby Little Waldingfield. Thirty-eight people left Groton alone in 1630, with another 13, mainly women, children, and servants, following in 1631. Thirty-six more planters came from neighboring villages.[9]

The Winthrop Papers also show the recruitment of a company by a gentleman who, though tempted, finally pulled back from emigrating himself. This was Winthrop's friend and correspondent Sir Simonds D'Ewes, the famous diarist and antiquarian. D'Ewes lived at Stowlangtoft east of Bury St. Edmunds in Suffolk but was also a major landowner at Lavenham near Winthrop's Groton. Twenty people in four families from these two places were in the *Arbella* fleet. They were followed in 1632 by another D'Ewes client, William Hammond of Lavenham, whose extended family joined him in 1635. This migration may have been activated by Winthrop's 1633 proposal to D'Ewes about "sending over some poore godly familyes with a years provision . . . if you will please to raise a colonye [i.e., a 'particular plantation'] heere in that manner (which would not be difficult for your self with such godly frends as you may have with you)." Sir Simonds records in his auto-biography how he began "to consider that a higher providence might ere long call me to suffer for His name and gospel or might prepare a way for my passage to America," but the personal summons never came. The D'Ewes company numbered 38 in all; most of them settled in Watertown.[10]

Most of these 219 East Anglian companions came from families who had lived for generations in the same neighborhoods and served the fathers, grandfathers, and great-grandfathers of the men who led them. They were bound together by the intersecting vines of kinship, clien-tage, and neighborliness.[11]

Clerical Companies

It was a persistent complaint of the English authorities that puritan lay people were subversively prone to "gadding to sermons," especially if their local parish priest failed to satisfy their exacting standards. John Rogers, lecturer at Dedham and leader of the north Essex puritans, drew crowds of as many as 1,200 to his weekly Tuesday morning addresses. When he died in 1636, so many people flocked from 20 miles or more to his funeral that the gallery in the church at Dedham came close to collapsing. A few years earlier, the vicar of Braintree had bemoaned the fact that "our people's pallats are grown so out of taste that no food contents them but of Mr. Hooker's dressing." A lieutenant of Archbishop Laud wrote that "lecturers [preachers] abounded, espe-cially in Suffolk. Not a market, or a bowling green or an ordinary [inn] could stand without one." An Ipswich housewife envied the New Englanders their access to good preaching. Once settled in Massachu-setts, the emigrants' appetites for sermons continued so ravening that the authorities had to place limits on the number each week.[12]

Puritan ministers were also expected to provide therapy for "cases of conscience," as they termed the daunting terrors of sin and damnation that beset scrupulous souls. Hooker had begun his pastorate ministering to the suicidally depressed Mrs. Drake at Esher in Surrey. Edward Collins, as we saw, sought reassurance at the feet of John Rogers. The spiritual confessions of other East Anglian applicants for membership in the Cambridge, Massachusetts, church demonstrate the powerful influence of puritan ministers in both alarming complacent and salving tender consciences.[13]

Finally, certain families and certain parishes had long reputations for dissent. Back in Queen Elizabeth's reign, Dedham and Braintree had been the centers of groups of subversive puritan ministers who met regularly there. Secret cells of dissenters were reported even earlier in Colchester and Bocking. Hingham and Norwich had provided martyrs in the persecution of the Lollards, the fifteenth-century proto-Protestants, and many more East Anglian religious radicals died at the stake when the breach with Rome was briefly healed under Queen Mary (1553–58).[14]

With such potency through preaching and soul saving, and with so many emigration catchment areas puritanically inclined, it is hardly surprising that when clergy decided or were driven to emigrate they usually influenced others to join them.

The ministerial companies are numerous: John Wilson's (1630), George Phillips's (1630), John Eliot's (1631), Thomas Hooker's (1632), John Cotton's (1633), Thomas Shepard's (1636), John Wheelwright's (1636), Nathaniel Rogers's (1636), John Phillip's and John Youngs's (1637), John Allen's and John Fiske's (1637), and Robert Peck's (1638). Some of these companies are justly famous. Eliot, pastor at Roxbury, Massachusetts, had 59 people in his congregation there who came from the west Essex district around his home at Nazeing. When Boston tried to lure the young minister, who arrived in the colony in November 1631, he informed the church that he was "committed to joining friends coming from England."[15] An advance party of Hooker's devotees traveled over in the *Lyon* in 1632. Fifty-eight of them hailed from the Braintree–Bocking textile mecca of north Essex. Fifty-three followed in succeeding years, including Hooker himself and John Haynes, later governor of both Massachusetts and Connecticut, in 1633. Many of the family names of this company appear in the records of the Company of Four-and-Twenty, which ruled the twin Essex towns. Almost all of them were well established, and several of the families had intermarried.[16] Cotton's followers sailed with him (and Hooker) in the *Griffin* in 1633 and settled mainly at Shawmut, renamed Boston in 1630, probably in Cotton's honor. The rear guard of the company, bringing the total to 59, arrived the following year and included his most notorious fan, Anne Hutchinson. Her reasons for leaving England are suggestive of more widely held motivations: "The Lord carrying Mr. Cotton to New England . . . I must go thither also. . . . When our teacher [Cotton] came to New England, it was a great trouble with me, my brother Wheelwright being put by [silenced] also, I was then much troubled concerning the ministry under which I lived." This company, again, was widely interrelated.[17] "Mr. Shepard's Company" in the *Defence* included several gentlemen from the Earl's Colne area, like Roger Harlakenden and the Cooke brothers. Shepard had lectured there before being forced to flee northward by Bishop Laud. The Danforth family was among the party of 38. They came from New Street Farm, just outside Framlingham, east Suffolk, where Shepard had also preached. This group took over land and houses vacated by Hooker's company in Newtown.[18] Wheelwright came from Bilsby, close to his kinsman Hutchinson's home at Alford, Lincolnshire. His 29 followers can be traced from their Lincolnshire villages to Boston, Massachusetts. Most continued to stick together in subsequent moves.[19] John Phillip's Company of 31 from Wrentham in northeast Suffolk and Youngs's group of 18 from nearby Southwold on the coast traveled in the *Mary Ann* in 1637,[20] with another northeast Suffolk and south Norfolk company of 62 following John Allen and John Fiske.[21] Youngs himself was barred from embarking at Great Yarmouth but appears to have somehow smuggled himself across to Salem in 1637. In 1640 his group founded Southold on Long Island, while the Fiske group moved west to Wenham.

By far the largest company to follow church leaders came from Hingham, Norfolk. In all, 143 people emigrated from the parish of St. Andrew between 1633 and 1640; a further 62 left neighboring towns and villages. Their ministers were the Reverend Robert Peck and the Reverend Peter Hobart. Peck had a long record of nonconformity. A man of Presbyterian leanings, like his younger Hingham-born colleague, "the old fox," as he was known to the bishop's officials, had been convicted as far back as 1615 of teaching the puritan scruples against the requirement "to kneel when they came into church" and of saying, "It is superstition to bow at the name of Jesus." In 1622 he and 22 "saints" were charged with "conventicling." Like Cotton at Boston, Lincolnshire, he appears to have been acknowledging a church of the elect within the wider St. Andrew's congregation. This elite of the saved probably obeyed the summons of a special ringing of the church bell when the vicar was to pray and preach. A different toll signified the despised Book of Common Prayer services. The last straw for the church authorities was Hingham's response to the Laudian injunction that proper altars at the east end should replace the central Communion tables. To puritans this smacked of the return of the papist mass. In St. Andrews an altar was obediently placed at the east end, in a specially dug pit! Even after his suspension in 1636, Peck continued to hold secret services for the elect. According to the family pedigree, his grandfather had similarly gone underground during the Catholic persecutions of Queen Mary's time. The faithful supported him and his family with voluntary tithes. Only the threat of summons before the draconian Court of High Commission in London drove the elderly minister and his devoted followers into exile in 1638. Some fellow villagers had already moved to New England, notably Edmund Hobart, who in 1633 had settled with his family at Bear Cove on the south shore of Massachusetts Bay. There he was joined in 1635 by his son, the Reverend Peter Hobart, who had ministered at Haverhill, Suffolk.[22] That year Bear Cove was renamed Hingham. "New Hingham" would prove as independent and ornery as the old. The church retained its Presbyterian bias among its Congregationalist neighbors and fiercely asserted its local rights in the 1645 militia case, creating a constitutional crisis in the colony.[23]

All in all, some 667 emigrants can be counted in the various companies that followed persecuted ministers across the Atlantic.[24] In some cases, there is evidence that these pastors had formed cadres of committed puritans in their English parishes, an elite or gathered church within a larger Anglican congregation. It is probable that this practice was common.[25] The sense of camaraderie and election was transplanted to the New World; "companionship" conferred a sense of belonging and value to the uprooted.

Extended Family Companies

However powerful mutual clientage or church membership might be, the tie that bound most tightly was kinship, through either blood or marriage.[26] Within the companies of gentlemen or clergymen, or among those traveling independently, there were extended families of sometimes extraordinary complexity (see Table 27).

In January 1637 Ann (Skinner) Wall, widow, of Felsted in Essex made her will. She was a widow twice over, which was not all that unusual.

Table 27. Extended Families

Note: (1) First parentheses contain town of origin, year(s) of emigration, and town of settlement in New England. (2) First name in parentheses after women's names is maiden surname; second is surname of first husband. (3) Relationships follow from immediately preceding name, but "and" refers back to original name in the sequence. (4) c = child(ren), svt = servant, km/kw = kinsman/kinswoman, m = mother; other kin abbreviations are obvious. (5) Relationships in brackets are either listed elsewhere or uncertain. (6) Figures in bold at end of each listing are totals of kin and household servants.

1. Walter ALLEN (Bury by 39 Newbury), bro-in-law Mr. CUTTING (Ipswich 36 Newbury 42) w 2c. **5**

2. John BARNARD (Dedham 34 Watertown) w Phebe (WILSON/WHITING) 2c 1svt, sis of Anne (W/W) LOVERAN, w of John (Ardleigh by 36 Wtrtn), unc of Thomas L (? 43 ?); A & P cous of Samuel SHERMAN (Dedham 34 Wtrtn) [and Philip SHERMAN; see no. 41]; nieces of Capt. John SHERMAN (Dedham 34 Wtrtn). **10**

3. Robert BUFFUM (Yarmouth 38 Salem) 1st w Margaret (BLESSING) 2c, sis of Alice (B) Vermais, 6c, kw of Joanna (B), w of William TOWNE (Yarmouth 35 Salem), 6c, km of Edmund TOWNE (Yarmouth 37 Salem). **20**

4. Edward GILMAN (Hingham 38 Hingham) w Mary (CLARKE) [?kw Rebecca (CLARKE) Peck] 5c 2svts; EG bro of Mary (G) FOULSHAM w of John (Hingham 38 Hingham), 1c, 2svts, bro of Adam F (Hingham 39 Hingham). **17**

5. Dr. John CLARKE (Westhorpe 37 Boston) w Elizabeth (HARGES), bro of Carew C, Joseph C, Thomas C, Mary C, and Margaret (C) WYETH w of Nicholas (?Mellis 38 Cambridge), 2c. **10**

6. Robert COE (Boxford 34 Wethersfield) w Hannah (DEARSLEY) 3c; RC cous of Samuel & Thomas HALE (Gt.Maplestead 34 Hartford). **7**

7. John COGGESHALL (Castle Hedingham 32 Boston) w Ann (BUTTER) 3c, kw of Brampton GURDON (Assington 30 Boston), bro of Edmund G (Ass'n 35 Ipswich), bro of Muriel (G) SALTONSTALL, w of Richard (Ass'n 35 Ipswich) 1c; A(B)C kw of Samuel APPLETON (Lt.Waldingfield 35 Ipswich) w Judith (EVERARD) 5c, sis of Sarah (E) ROGERS w of Rev. Ezekiel (Rowley 38 Rowley); Gurdons k of John, Humphrey, & Elizabeth WINCOLL (Lt.Waldingfield 35 Watertown). **22**

8. Edward COLLINS (Bramford 38 Cambridge) w Martha 4c, km of Abigail (BEDLE) POWELL w of Michael (Woolverstone 39 Dedham). **8**

Table 27. *Continued*

9. Edward CONVERSE (Navestock 30 Charlestown) w ?Sarah 4c, km of Allen C (Navestock by 39 Salem), km of John PARKER, km of Sarah SMITH. **9**

10. Benjamin COOPER (Brampton 37 died at sea) w Elizabeth (YOUNGS) 4c, 1sis, and d Mary (C) FILLINGHAM w of Francis (Brampton 37 Salem); E(Y)C kw of Christopher YOUNG (Yarmouth 38 Salem), bro of Rev. John YOUNGS (Southwold 37 Salem) w Joan (GENTLEMAN) 6c, and of Joseph Y (Southwold 38 Salem) w Margaret (WARREN), and of Mary (Y) BROWN w of William (?Yarmouth 35 Salem) and of Martha (Y) MOORE w of Thomas (Southwold 36 Salem) [YOUNGS k to PECKS; see no. 38.] **25**

11. Catherine (MYLES GREY) COYTMORE (Prittlewell 37 Charlestown) m of Thomas C (P'well 37 Chstn) w Martha (RAINBOROUGH), sis of William R (Wapping 39 Chstn); CC mother of Parnell (GREY) w of Increase NOWELL (London 30 Chstn) and of Catherine (GREY) w of Thomas GRAVES (Ratcliffe 30 Chstn) 2c. **10**

12. Theophilus CUSHING (Hingham 33 Hingham), bro of Matthew C (Hingm 38 Hingm) w ?Nazareth (PITCHER) 5c, sis of Frances (P) RICROFT (Hingm 38 Hingm). **9**

13. John EDDY (Boxted 30 Watertown) w Amy (DOGGETT) [?kw of John D, see no. 53] 2c, bro of Samuel E, and of Abigail (E) BENJAMIN, w of John (? 32 Boston) 4c, and of Anna (E) WINDES, w of Barnaby (Ipswich 35 Watrtn), km of Abigail (W) FOSTER, w of Thomas (Ipswich 34 Boston), and ?km of Faintnot W (? 35 Charlestown). **16**

14. Rev. John ELIOT (Nazeing 31 Roxbury), bro of Philip E (Nazg 35 Roxy) w Elizabeth (SIBTHORPE) 4c 1svt (John RUGGLES), and bro of Francis E (Nazg 40 Braintree) w Mary (SAUNDERS), and bro of Jacob E (Nazg 31 Boston), and bro of Lydia (E) PENNIMAN, w of James (Nazg 31 Boston), and bro of Sarah (E) CURTIS, w of William (Nazg 32 Roxy) 4c, bro of John C (Nazg 31 Roxy) w Elizabeth (HUTCHINS) 3c, bro of Thomas C, and bro of Mary (C) RUGGLES, w of Thomas (Nazg 37 Roxy) 2c, bro of John R (Nazg 35 Roxy) w Barbara 1c. **32**

15. William ESTOW (Ormesby 37 Hampton) w Mary (MOULTON) 2c, kw of William, Mary, & Ruth M (Orm 37 Ham), and of John M (Orm 37 Ham) w Anne (GREEN) 5c 3svts, bro of Thomas M (Orm 37 Ham) [?k of Robert M (?Yarmouth 29 Charleston) & Thomas M (Orm 31 Chstn)] **18**

16. David FISKE (Wrentham 37 Watertown) w Sarah (SMITH) 1c, bro of Nathaniel F (Wren 42 Wtrtn) w Susan, and bro of Martha (F) UNDERWOOD, w of Martin (Wren 34 Wtrtn) [?km of Mirabel U (Scratby 37 Wtrtn]. **7**

Table 27. *Continued*

17.   John FISKE (S.Elmham 37 Salem) w Ann (GIBBS) 2c, sis of Meribah (G) FOLGER, w of John (Diss 35 Watertown) 1c; JF bro of William F (S.Elm 37 Salem) w Bridget (MUSKET) 3c, km to John F (Laxfield 38 ?) w, bro of Anne (F) CHICKERING, w of Francis (Fressingfield 38 Dedham) 2c, bro of Henry C, w, 2c; JF km to Phineas F (? by 41 Salem) w 3c, bro of James F (? by 41 Salem) w; JF bro of Martha (F) THOMPSON, w of Edmund (?Yarmouth 37 Salem); JF km of Mary (F) FISHER, w of Anthony (Fressingfield 37 Dedham), bro of Joshua F (Fress ?40 Dedham) w 2c.   **37**

18.   John FRENCH (Halstead 35 Cambridge) w Joan, 2c, bro of William F (Hals 35 Cam) w Elizabeth (SYMMES) 3c; J & WF cous of Ann WOOD (Earl's Colne 35 Cam) [svt to Roger HARLAKENDEN].   **10**

19.   Thomas FRENCH (Assington 37 Ipswich) w Susan (RIDDLESDALE) 7c, fa of Thomas F Jr. (Assn 37 Ips) w Susan, 4c [Fs k to WARRENS; see no. 40].   **15**

20.   Henry GOLDSTONE (Bedingfield 34 Watertown) w 2c, km of Sarah (G) MERRIAM, w of Joseph (London 38 Charlestown) 1c, bro of George M (? 41 Concord) w.   **9**

21.   William HAMMOND (Lavenham 34 Watertown) w Elizabeth (PAYNE) 3c, bro of Thomas H (Lavm 36 Wtrtn) w 2c, fa of Thomas H Jr. (Lavm 33 Wtrtn) w Elizabeth (CASON) 2c; WH bro-in-law of William PAYNE (Lavm 35 Wtrtn) w Ann, 5c, bro of Phoebe (P) PAGE, w of John (Boxted 30 Wtrtn) 2c, sis of Robert PAYNE (Naughton 39 Ipswich) w Ann (WHITING), kw to William W (Boxford ?33 Cambridge) w 1c, bro-in-law of Thomas WIGGIN (? 34 Dover) w Catherine; A(W)P sis of Dorothy (W) AYRES, w of Simon (Lavm 35 Wtrtn) 8c; Wm Payne km of Samuel HOWES (Lavm by 34 Yarmouth).   **42**

22.   Robert HARDING (Boreham 30 Boston), bro of Abraham H (Bhm 35 Bos), bro of Ann (H) BUTTOLPH, w of Thomas (Lit.Baddow 35 Bos), and bro of Elizabeth (H) BRIDGHAM, w of Henry (Feltam ?41 Bos).   **6**

23.   Atherton HOUGH (Boston 33 Boston) w Elizabeth (BULKELEY/WHITTINGHAM) 1c, m of John W (Sutterton 38 Ipswich), ?bro of Thomas W, 5svts; E(B/W)H sis of Martha (B) MELLOWS, w of Abraham (Bos 33 Bos) 6c, km of Oliver M (Bos 34 Bos) w; E(B/W)H kw of Elizabeth (ST. JOHN) WHITING, w of Rev. Samuel (Skirbeck 36 Lynn) 2c.   **24**

24.   James HOWE (Hatfield Broad Oak 36 Roxbury) w Elizabeth (DANE) 1c, sis of John D (Hatfd 36 Roxy) w Eleanor (CLARKE), son of John D Sr. (Hatfd 36 Roxy) 3c; JH bro of Abraham H (Hatfd 38 Roxy) w 3c [?kw of WARNERS; see no. 50].   **14**

Table 27. *Continued*

---

25. William HUTCHINSON (Alford 34 Boston) w Anne (MARBURY) 11c, son of Susan H, bro of Samuel H, Edward H, and Mary (H) WHEEL-WRIGHT, w of Rev. John (Bilsby 36 Boston) 3c; WH bro of Susan (H) STORRE, w of Augustine (Bilsby 38 Boston) 1c, and unc of Edward Rishworth (Laceby 36 Boston); A(M)H sis of Katherine (M) SCOTT, w of Richard (Glemsford 34 Boston) 4c, km of Robert S (Glemsford 30 Boston); A(M)H aunt of William WENTWORTH (Alford 34 Boston), cous of Christopher LAW-SON (Lincs 37 Bos), cous of Christopher HELME (Long Sutton by 39 Exeter); WH km to Frances (FREESTONE) HILL, w of Valentine (Winthorpe 36 Bos), Ann and Frances F (34 Bos), and Elizabeth F (36 Bos). **40**

26. Isaac JOHNSON (Sempringham 30 Boston) w Lady Arbella (FIENNES-CLINTON), kw to Charles F (? 30 Bos); IJ km to John J (? 30 Bos) w Margery, 2c. **7**

27. Henry JOSSELYN (Roxwell 34 Maine), cous of George and John COOKE (Earl's Colne 35 Cambridge) and cous of Thomas J (Roxwell 35 Hingham) w Rebecca, 5c 1svt. **11**

28. Thomas KILBOURN (Wood Ditton 35 Wethersfield) w Frances (MOO-DY) 5c, sis of John M (Moulton 33 Hartford) w Sarah (COX) 6c 2svts, and sis of Elizabeth (M) PRATT, w of John (Wood Ditton 33 Hartford) [k of John BLODGETT, Reynolds and Matthew MARVIN]. **19**

29. Austin KILLAM (Dennington 37 Salem) w Alice, 3c, cous of Robert GOODALE (Dennington 34 Salem) w Catherine, 3c [Gs k of DOWNINGS; see no. 53]. **10**

30. Richard KIMBALL (Rattlesden 34 Watertown) w Ursula (SCOTT) 7c, km of Henry K (Mistley 34 Wtrtn) w Susan (STONE/CUTTING) 3c; RK bro-in-law of Thomas SCOTT (Rattlesden 34 Wtrtn) w Elizabeth (STRUTT) 3c, son of Martha (WHATLOCK) S; E(S)S sis of Susan (S) LOCKWOOD, w of John (Combs), km of Edmund L (Combs 30 Cambridge) w Elizabeth 1c, bro of Robert L (Combs 30 Wtrtn); RK km of Thurston RAYNER (Elmsett 34 Wtrtn) w Elizabeth 6c, and Elizabeth K (in household). **33**

31. Edward LOOMIS (Braintree 35 Windsor), km of Joseph L (Braintree by 38 Windsor) w Mary (WHITE) 8c, sis of Ann (W) PORTER, w of John (Messing 38 Windsor) 8c, sis of Elizabeth (W) GOODWIN, w of William (Braintree 32 Hartford). **23**

32. Robert LORD (Sudbury c36 Ipswich) w Mary (WAITE), sis of John W (Wethersfield 37 Malden) w, bro of Anne (W) BELL, w of Philip [kw of

Table 27. *Continued*

WHITINGS of Hadleigh; Ws' m kw of Rev. Nathaniel Ward (Haverhill 34 Ipswich)]; RL km of Simon STACEY (Bocking *c*36 Ipswich) w Elizabeth (CLARK); and km of Ann (STACEY) FITCH, w of Thomas (Bocking *c*38 Hartford), bro of John and James F; SS km of John WHIPPLE (Bocking 36 Ips) w, bro of Matthew W (Bocking 32 Ips) w Ann (HAWKINS), kw of Abraham H (Braintree 35 Charlestown) and of Robert H (Brt 35 Charlestown) w Mary [?RL km of Thomas L (Wethersfield 35 Cambridge) w Dorothy 7c]. **19**

33. Richard LUMPKIN (Boxted *c*38 Ipswich) w Sarah (BAKER), niece of Sarah B and sis of Abigail (B) WARNER, w of William (Boxted *c*35 Ips) 3c; their dau Abigail (W) WELLES w of Thomas (Colchester 35 Ips). **10**

34. Griffin MONTAGUE (Chelmsford by 35 Brookline) w Margaret (KEL-WAY), sis of Mary (K) LANE, w of William (Chelmsford *c*40 Dorchester), and sis of Milcah (K) SNOW, w of Thomas (Chmsfd 36 Boston). **6**

35. Samuel MORSE (Burgate 35 Dedham) w Elizabeth (JASPER) 3c 1grc, fa of Elizabeth (M) DANIEL, w of Robert (Redgrave *c*35 Watertown); SM km of Joseph M (Dedham 34/35 Wtrtn) w Dorothy 3c. **13**

36. Robert PAGE (Ormesby 37 Salem) w Lucy (WARD) 3c, sis of Anne W svt and Thomas W (Orms *c*37 Salem); RP cous of Ann, Frances, and Adam GOODWIN (Orms 37 Salem). **10**

37. Robert PARKER (Woolpit *c*34 Cambridge) w Martha (CHAPLIN), sis of Clement C (Semer 35 Cam) w Sarah (HINDS); CC unc of William CLARKE (? ? Roxbury). **5**

38. Rev. Robert PECK (Hingham 38 Hingham) w Anne (LAWRENCE) 2c 2svts [?kw of Thomas L (Hingham 38 Hingham)], bro of Joseph P (Hing 38 Hing) w Rebecca (CLARK) 4c 5svts. **17**

39. William PELHAM (Bures/Boston 30 Cambridge) 5c, bro of John P (?Bures/Bos 35 Cam), Penelope P, and Herbert P (Bures/Bos 38 Cam) 1c, bro-in-law of John HUMPHREY (Sempringham 34 Lynn) w Lady Susannah (FIENNES-CLINTON) [sis of Lady Arbella (F-C) Johnson; see no. 26] 3c; HP km to James OLMSTEAD (Fairstead 32 Camb) w 5c [Ps k to Winthrops, Gurdons; see nos. 54, 7]. **22**

40. Thomas PHILBRICK (Bures *c*36 Watertown) w Ann (KNAPP) 7c, dau of William K (Bures 30 Wtrtn) w 7c, A(K)P kw of Nicholas K (Bures 30 Wtrtn) w 4c; TP km of John WARREN (Nayland 30 Wtrtn) w 4c [JW ?km to John

Table 27. *Continued*

SCARLET (Nayland by 40 Springfield) and Samuel S (Kersey 45 Boston)].
31

41. William PYNCHON (Springfield 30 Roxbury) w Anne (ANDREW) 4c, cous of John PORTER (Broomfield 30 Roxbury) w (ODDING) 4c, m or sis of Sarah (O) SHERMAN, w of Philip (Dedham 34 Roxy). **14**

42. Simon RAY (Hundon 39/40 Braintree) w Mary (ROWNING) 2c [km of John BIGG; see no. 47; and km of Rev. Nathaniel ROGERS; see no. 44]. **4**

43. William SAVILL (Saffron Walden by 40 Braintree) w Hannah, bro of Ann (S) BASS, w of Samuel (Saff W 32 Roxbury/Brtree) 3c. **7**

44. Richard SHERMAN (Dedham 34 Boston) w Elizabeth 2c, bro of Edmund S (Dedham/Colchester 32 Bos) w Judith (ANGIER) 8c, aunt of Edmund A (Dedham 34 Cambridge) w Bridget (ROGERS), sis of Rev. Nathaniel R (Assington 38 Ipswich) w 4c [km of Rev. Ezekiel R; see no. 7], and km of Mary (A) SPARHAWK, w of Nathaniel (Ded 38 Cam) 8c; ES aunt of Edmund GREENLEAF (Ipswich 34 Newbury) w Sarah (MOORE) 5c, sis of Francis M (Maldon by 39 Cam) w 2c. **42**

45. Judith (STOUGHTON) SMEAD (Coggeshall 30 Dorchester) 1c, sis of Thomas S (born Naughton 30 Dorchester) w, and sis of Israel S (born Coggeshall 30 Dorchester) w Elizabeth (KNIGHT), ?sis of John K (Rotherhithe 30 Dorchester), and E(K)S's m and 4c. **12**

46. Gregory STONE (Gt.Bromley 35 Watertown) w Lydia (COOPER) 8c, bro of Simon S (Boxted 35 Wtrtn) w Joan (CLARK) 5c. **18**

47. John TALCOTT (Braintree 32 Cambridge) w Dorothy (MOTT) 2c, bro of Rachel (T) STEELE, w of John (Fairstead 32 Cam) 3c, bro of George S (Fstd 32 Cam) w 3c; D(M)T kw of Adam MOTT (? 35 Roxbury) w 5c; JT bro of Sarah (T) WADSWORTH, w of William (Braintree 32 Cam) 4c, and km of John BIGG (Groton 30 Boston) w. **29**

48. Abraham TOPPAN (Yarmouth 37 Newbury) w Susannah (GOODALE/ TAYLOR) 2c, dau of Elizabeth G 1c, kw of Mirabel UNDERWOOD (Scratby 37 Watertown) and of John MARSTON (Ormesby 37 Salem). **8**

49. William VASSALL (Prittlewell 30/35 Scituate) w Anna (KING) 6c, sis of Thomas K (Cold Norton 35 Scit) w 1svt. **11**

50. Andrew WARNER (Hatfield Broad Oak 31 Cambridge) w 2c, bro of Rose (W) SAMFORD, w of John (?High Ongar 30 ?Boston). **6**

Table 27. *Continued*

51.   Rev. Roger WILLIAMS (High Laver 30 Salem) w Mary (BARNARD),
sis of Masachiel B (Batcombe 35 Weymouth) w.   **4**

52.   Rev. John WILSON (Sudbury 30 Boston) w Elizabeth (MANSFIELD)
2c, sis of Anne (M) KEAYNE, w of Robert (London 35 Boston) 1c, and of John
M (London 34 Boston) w Mary (GOVE) 2c, dau of John G, w.   **13**

53.   John WINTHROP Sr. (Groton 30 Boston) w Margaret (TYNDAL) 3c, fa
of [John W Jr.; see no. 54] w1 Martha (FONES), and fa of Henry W w Elizabeth
(FONES), and bro-in-law of Arthur TYNDAL (Gt.Maplestead 30 Bos), and
uncle of Robert SAMPSON (Kersey 30 Bos), and cous of John DOGGETT
(Boxford 30 Watertown) w 2c, bro of Martha (D) FIRMIN, w of Giles (Sud-
bury 32 Bos) 1c; JW sr. bro of Lucy (W) DOWNING, w of Emmanuel
(London 38 Salem) 7c, uncle of Abigail GOAD (Lond 38 Ipswich), sis of
Thomas G (London 35 Ips).   **28**

54.   John WINTHROP Jr. (Groton 31/35 Boston/Ipswich) w2 Elizabeth
(READE), sis of Thomas R (Wickford ?35 Salem) and of Martha (R) EPPS and
of Margaret (R) LAKE, 2c; their m is Elizabeth (COOKE/READE) PETER,
w of Rev. Hugh P (Rayleigh 35 Salem) [E(C/R)P aunt of George and Joseph
COOKE; see no. 27].   **9**

55.   John WYATT (Assington by 35 Ipswich), fa of Sarah (W) HEARD, w of
Luke (Claxton by 39 Ips).   **3**

Her first husband had been John Talcott, who had died in 1604. She was
remarried to Moses Wall, who, in turn, died in 1623. Both her husbands
belonged to leading Braintree textile families. Her bequests to friends
and kinsfolk in New England reveal how the Braintree company—
many of them shipmates on the *Lyon* in 1632—were linked together
like a great chain by blood and marriage ties: her son John Talcott,
daughters Sarah Wadsworth (wife of William) and Rachel Steele (wife
of John), nephews both named John Skinner, sons respectively of her
brothers Richard and John. She also left gifts to former neighbors
William Goodwin, Edward Stebbings, and John Clarke. Her emigrant
Wall relations had already had their legacies when old Moses died. So
had some of his employees and friends whose families later emigrated,
like the Ventrises or his apprentice John Jacob or friend Thomas Fitch.
The Skinner–Talcott–Wall–Wadsworth–Steele extended family accounted for 23 emigrants. Braintree–Bocking neighbors—some of
whom had numerous emigrant relations not counted here—added another 21. Two wills uncover a congeries of kinship and neighborliness.[27]

The kinship tentacles of Mistress Catherine Coytmore are similarly octopodous. The daughter of Robert and Parnell (Reeve) Myles of Sutton on the Deben estuary in east Suffolk, Catherine had been born in 1576. Her family had been in Sutton since at least 1459. She married her first husband, the merchant Thomas Grey, when she was only 16 in 1593 and moved with him to the port of Harwich a few miles down the coast in Essex. Grey died in 1607, and three years later she married Rowland Coytmore. The Coytmore family came from Ipswich, near both Harwich and Sutton, but Rowland lived in Wapping in London's dockland, and he had a country house 30 miles downstream at Prittlewell. He was a widower; his previous wife had been the widow of William Harris, a Wapping mariner. Rowland died in 1626. Catherine had seven children by her first marriage. One daughter married Increase Nowell in 1628, and another married an east London neighbor, Thomas Graves, mariner of Ratcliffe. He was the mate on the *Talbot*, which sailed to Salem in 1629, and on the *Arbella* in 1630. Catherine's son Thomas Coytmore married Martha Rainborough, daughter of a sea captain from Wapping. Another daughter allied with the Tyng family. Thus, when the 61-year-old matriarch immigrated to Charlestown in 1637, she found herself surrounded by a company of children and grandchildren. Her children's spouses had relatives in the town too. Even several relatives of her husband's first wife, the Harrises, and their kinsfolk the Bournes were there. A large and complicated network had been transferred from one port to another.[28]

One more example must suffice: the Hutchinson clan. William and Anne had a fair crowd of their own on the *Griffin* in 1634 to start with. There were 11 children ranging in age from 21 to one, along with two spinster cousins, Anne and Frances Freestone. Thanks to the marriages of siblings and cousins, however, the couple were related to Scotts from Glemsford in Suffolk and Lincolnshire emigrant neighbors like the Wheelwrights, Rushworths, Storres, Wentworths, Lawsons, Helmes, and Hills. This company of 38 emigrants were all linked together before emigration. Once in New England, they established further alliances— Edward Rushworth's son married a daughter of John Wheelwright, for instance—and sent out tendrils to bind them to other networks.[29]

The simplest of these extended families is found when two or more adult siblings emigrate. In tracing kinship the major problem is ignorance of wives' maiden names, which, as we have seen, is all too common among the East Anglian contingent. Any number of brother–sister or sister–sister relationships may have escaped us. I have counted 78 pairs of adult emigrant brothers, 6 trios, and 4 quartets (one of which

Table 28. Adult Sibling Emigrants

A. Brothers and Stepbrothers

Note: (1) Names in brackets are uncertain. (2) Names with asterisks are counted in Table 27.

Michael & William BACON; Richard & William BELLINGHAM; Abraham & Richard BROWNE; James & John BUCK; [?Edward & Thomas BUM-STEAD]; Francis & Henry CHICKERING; Carew, John, Joseph, & Thomas CLARKE*; [?Allen & Edward CONVERSE]; George & Joseph COOKE*; Matthew & Richard COYS; John, Philip, & Thomas CURTIS*; Matthew & Theophilus CUSHING*; [?James & John CUTLER]; Philemon & Rev. Timothy DALTON; Nathaniel, Samuel, & Theophilus EATON; John & Samuel EDDY*; Robert & Samuel [& William] ELDRED; Francis, James, Rev. John, & Philip ELIOT*; Anthony & Joshua FISHER*; David & Nathaniel FISKE*; James & Phineas FISKE*; John & William FISKE*; James, Joseph, & Thomas FITCH*; Adam & John FOULSHAM*; John & William FRENCH*; Ozias & William GOODWIN; Brampton & Edmund GURDON*; John & William GUTTRIDGE; Samuel & Thomas HALE*; Abraham & Robert HARDING*; [?Abraham & Robert HAWKINS]; Isaac & William HEATH; Thomas & William HILLS; Edmund, Rev. Peter, & Thomas HOBART; Abraham & James HOWE*; Justinian & Richard HOLDEN; Edward, Samuel, & William HUTCHINSON*; Edmund & Francis INGALLS; Francis & Philip JAMES; Daniel, Francis, & William JEGGLES; Robert & William JENNISON; [?Isaac & John JOHNSON]; John & Joseph KINGSBURY; [?Edward & Thomas LAMBE]; Samuel & Thomas LINCOLN; Daniel, Stephen, & Thomas LINCOLN; Edmund & Robert LOCKWOOD*; George & William LUDKIN; Matthew & Reynold MARVIN; [?Edward & Oliver MELLOWS]; John & Nathaniel MERRIALL; Abraham & Isaac MORRILL; Daniel & John MORSE*; John & Joseph MORSE; John & Thomas MOULTON*; Robert & William PAYNE*; Edward & Giles PAYSON; Herbert, John, & William PELHAM*; Aaron & Moses PINGRY; [John & James PEMBERTON]; Joseph & Rev. Robert PECK*; Edmund & Leonard PITTS; Daniel, John, & Robert POND; Abraham & John PRATT; [?John & Robert REYNOLDS]; John & Thomas RUGGLES*; [Robert & Samuel SAMPSON]; Richard & Robert SCOTT*; Amos, Edmund, Ichabod, & William SHEFFIELD; Samuel & Rev. Thomas SHEPARD; Rev. John & Samuel SHERMAN*; Philip & Samuel SHERMAN*; Francis & Henry SKERRY; Anthony & Henry SOMERBY; George & John STEELE*; Gregory & Simon STONE*; Israel & Thomas STOUGHTON*; John & Joshua TIDD; Henry & John TUTTLE; Moses & William VENTRIS; James & Rev. John WARD*; Thomas & William WARDALL; John & William WATERBURY; Daniel, Joseph, & Rev. Thomas WELD; John & Matthew WHIPPLE*; Edward & William WILSON; Henry & John (Jr.) WINTHROP*; Christopher, Rev. John, & Joseph YOUNGS*.

Table 28. *Continued*

B. *Sisters or Brothers and Sisters* (not in Table 27)

Note: Names in parentheses have been listed in Part A.

Ann & Mercy ALEXARSON; Mary (R) BACON & Thomas READ; Alice (H) CHUBBOCK & (Edmund, Rev. Peter, and Thomas HOBART); Martha (S) CLARKE & Richard SALTONSTALL; Judith, Margaret, & Nathaniel FEL-TON; Mabel & Roger HARLAKENDEN; John HOOD & Mary (H) TRUES-DALE; Martha (H) PECK & (Samuel & Thomas HALE); Susanna (B) PORT-MONT & (Richard & William BELLINGHAM); Mary (R) SEYMOUR & William RUSCOE; John STRATTON & Elizabeth (S) THORNDIKE; ?Eliza-beth (T) LYNDE & Peter TUFTS; Richard TUTTLE & Dorothy (T) BILL; Elizabeth & William WILLIAMS; Elizabeth & (Moses and William) VEN-TRIS.

is composed of Eliots!). The totals of brother–sister and sister–sister emigrants are 55 pairs, 13 trios, and 2 quartets (Table 28). Where one, both, or all siblings are married, the people drawn into the extended family network would be at least doubled. If some of their spouses also had emigrant siblings, a highly complex web of emigrant relationships is woven.

We have already met the extended emigrant family of five Braintree surnames uncovered in the legacies of Moses and Ann Wall. If we intertwine the spouses' relations to this skein, five more families are added: Motts, Biggses, Loomises, Porters, and Goodwins. The extended family thereby grows from 23 to 57 people, a company indeed. All of this group came from the Braintree–Bocking district, which produced another, the Lord–Stacey–Whipple–Mears–Fitch company. Hardly anyone who left the twin towns for the New World was not some other emigrant's relation.[30]

If we dig below the surface of the groups who followed a gentle or clerical leader, we often find these adhesive family interconnections cementing the companies. The Hinghamites supporting Robert Peck were widely intermarried. Thomas Chubbock's wife was Alice Hobart, daughter of the large emigrant Hobart clan, which intermarried with the Beales and the Pecks. Eight different Lincoln adult males (four of them confusingly named Thomas) set up households in New England. Despite the family's later fame, their 1630s interrelations have proved almost impossible to plumb. The surname of only one Lincoln wife is known. We learn from his will that Thomas Lincoln the weaver called fellow emigrants Nicholas Jacob "cousin"and Samuel Lincoln "brother." It seems likely that this numerous clan was related to members of the Gilman–Foulsham–Ricroft–Cushing–Pitcher company. Indeed, given the many generations that most of the Hingham families had lived in the district, it is well within the bounds of probability that all of them were interrelated.[31]

Sometimes the leaders of companies were themselves clan members. Winthrop's nuclear family of nine people was extended to 30 by kinship with Brand, Tyndal, Gurdon, Brown, Sampson, Downing, Doggett, Firmin, and Bright families before emigration. Subsequent marriages of his children in New and old England attached many more patches to the quilt.[32] Many of the Eliot company from the Nazeing area on the Essex–Hertfordshire border were siblings, in-laws, or cousins, making a known network of Eliot–Curtis–Penniman–Abbott–Perry–Payson–Ruggles families, 32 strong.[33] The same pattern can be found in the Fiske company from north Suffolk. The seven men of that surname who went with their families to New England were related to Chickerings, Thompsons, Underwoods, Coopers, Stones, Fishers, Aldouses, Allens, Gibbses, and Folgers.[34]

In all, I have found 55 extended emigrant families composed of 215 nucleated families (see Table 27). Most of these kinship companies had been neighbors in the eastern counties. Occasionally, however, it has been possible to discover farther-flung connections. The Reverend Roger Williams's brother-in-law was the clothier Masachiel Bernard, who had moved from his Nottinghamshire birthplace to Batcombe in Somerset when his father, the Reverend Richard, had been translated there. He immigrated to Weymouth, Massachusetts, in 1636.[35] The Reverend John Wilson of Sudbury, Suffolk, married Elizabeth, daughter of Sir John Mansfield, goldsmith and lord mayor of London. Her brother John and her sister, who had married the London merchant Robert Keayne, also emigrated.[36] As we saw, the wives of the Reverend Samuel Whiting, Atherton Hough, and Abraham Mellows, Lincolnshire Bostonians, all came from Bedfordshire; they were, in turn, kinswomen of the Reverend Peter Bulkeley of Odell, Bedfordshire, who became the first minister in Concord, Massachusetts.[37] Allen has posited Hingham kinship links for Matthew Hawke of Cambridge, England, Thomas Thaxter of Brigham, Norfolk, and the Ludkins of Norwich. John Winthrop's servant and agent, John Sandford, married Elizabeth Webb, also of Groton. Her brother Henry lived in Salisbury, Wiltshire, and is mentioned in correspondence from the West Country to Winthrop. He, too, immigrated to Boston where he became a merchant.[38] It is only through the chance survival of family letters that this distant and unguessable link has been uncovered.

Over one-third of the East Anglian emigrants have been connected to larger extended families or "companies" of kinsfolk. It should be stressed that this is a *minimal* figure, including only those who were close relations and whose female maiden names have survived. Adding these 853-strong kinship networks to 120 brother-and-sister emigrants and the 403 not listed in Table 27 who traveled as members of gentle or clerical companies, we arrive at a grand total of 1,376 emigrants known to have traveled in companies. Given undoubted underrecording, it is likely that few people from the eastern counties had to tackle the challenge of leaving old haunts, braving the voyage, and taming a wilderness on their own.

The effects of this group cohesion were momentous. The decision to leave a long-settled neighborhood would have been less traumatic when taken by a company rather than by a solitary individual or a nuclear family. John and Nazareth Beale must have been heartened when Ripley and Hobart kinsmen agreed that a move to the New World could no longer be delayed, and their cousin and neighbor Edmund Hobart was already over there establishing a bridgehead at Bear Cove. Having nearly grown-up children and two servants in the family would have added the reassurance of strong pairs of hands for the daunting tasks ahead.

The presence of community leaders was of the utmost importance. There was a marked shift over the decade from predominantly lay-led companies to clerically inspired groups. The Winthrops, Pynchons, Dudleys, and Johnsons—along with Rossiters, Saltonstalls, Endecotts, Ludlows, or Humphreys from other areas—provided gentry leadership in England, on the voyage, and during the initial wave of mass migration. Used to exerting control in their local districts, investors in the Massachusetts Bay Company, recruiters of craftsmen and specialists as well as kinsfolk and clients, organizers of provisioning, equipment, transport, and embarkation, they naturally assumed command once in the Bay. They chose town sites and supervised their companies; they reached crucial decisions with their peers and prior friends and acquaintances on the Court of Assistants. They behaved much as local justices in Essex or Norfolk were accustomed to, especially in the last two decades of ecological and economic disasters. Thus was a sense of hierarchy transferred. Clients followed and deferred to patrons. Gentlemanly obligations of hospitality and good neighborhood persisted. Winthrop obeyed the same sense of noblesse oblige as generations of lords of the manor of Groton when he shared his flour supply with the hungry during the starving time of 1630–31. The Cambridge Agreement signed by these early gentle and lay leaders must have been a powerful persuasion to yeoman and artisan neighbors or tenants and servants concerned about the way their world was deteriorating.[39]

It was not until the second surge, heralded by the arrival of Cotton, Hooker, and Samuel Stone in the *Griffin* in 1633, that clerical leadership of companies took over. Previous ministerial emigrants had usually been young and little known, but names like Shepard, Ward, Rogers, Knowles, or Peck enjoyed greater celebrity. Their companies, already formally or informally "gathered" in Greater East Anglia, predated the "wandering congregations" identified in New England. The nature of the cement of these second- and third-wave godly companies was subtly different from that of the earlier lay-led cohorts. This may help explain the marked rise in the evangelical temperature of the Bay after 1633. Religious enthusiasm is explosively released as godly company after godly company arrived to breathe freer and purified New World air.[40]

This breaking free should not be exaggerated. The "wandering congregations" were also carefully graded by rank and often also related by blood or marriage. Kinship networks, the third and most pervasive basis of company travel, would have a restraining as well as a reassuring component. The extended family group under a single patriarch or an oligarchy of clan leaders would transfer the elaborate pecking order of the Old World to the New. It could be expected to nurture the continuance of "English ways" in the new homes. Indeed, home sites might even be chosen because they reminded the group of what had been left behind.[41] The company nature of emigration would tend to dampen eagerness for change or experimentation. It would also discourage mobility in the new environment and encourage a clannishness in individual settlements. This might result in feuding among "mixt multitudes," as happened between East Anglians and West Countrymen in New Hingham and later at Marblehead and Gloucester. It is possible that other New England conflicts, like the Antinomian Crisis, the Child Remonstrance, the Half-Way Covenant, even Salem witchcraft, had some basis in intra- or interregional rivalries exacerbated by company solidarity.[42]

It is impossible to imagine the migration of the 1630s being "Great" without company travel. The staggering achievement of transporting

13–20 thousand people within a decade contrasts with the stuttering start of Virginia or the ineffectiveness of earlier New England plantations. Rather than having to marshal individual, disconnected migrants, the recruitment of one Greater East Anglian for New England pulled in a network of others—like digging up one buttercup only to find its root system crisscrossing the soil to other plants. Even a transfer of individual nuclear families would have reduced the flow and, more important, the ardor toward New England.[43]

The uncovering of the widespread nature of company travel calls into question several recent hypotheses. There is, first, the suggestion that the transatlantic voyage had transforming effects on the passengers. This is variously described as a rite of passage, the beginnings of the process of creating New Englanders, or the formation of "communitas." All rely on the action of the watery wilderness on seriously disoriented and frightened individuals who have had to divest themselves of all but their basic needs. Without discounting the terrors of the deep or the sense of group solidarity that grows from enduring and surviving such dangers, the norm of company travel gives a quite different context to the experiences of the voyage. Traveling with a supporting clan or godly brothers and sisters or neighbors and fellow clients would bolster the weak-hearted, provide continuity, and pool resources. The passage, in such familiar company, might lose its quality of traumatized transformation that "rite of passage" implies. Travelers would be reminded of old England by the presence of friends and neighbors, offsetting their sense of loss and alienation. The soldering effect of horrors overcome would *further* solidify communitates already linked, not newly joined.[44]

The existence of these "daisy chains" of kinship suggests, second, that the oft-asserted "death" of the extended family has been "altogether exaggerated." Though demographic research in early modern England and colonial America finds that the customary residential unit was the nuclear family, the pulling power of clan tentacles revealed here argues that the emotional and affinal loyalties did not stop at the garden gate. Much other evidence from an array of English and American sources supports this powerful persistence of extended-family interreliance. The claims and obligations proper to quite distant kin continued across the Atlantic and successfully spanned that vast barrier. Changes in familial and personal dynamics seem to have been slower than some commentators had thought. Certainly the claim that "the American family was born modern" now has a very hollow ring.[45]

The third proposition undermined by the group system of migration is that of "The Great Reshuffle" in the early years after arrival in New England.[46] This thesis argues that communities created on shipboard are essentially temporary. When new arrivals step ashore in Boston, according to this account, they are on their own again, and they have to find communities to join or, with other strangers, set about forming new ones. It is unfortunate that the couple chosen to illustrate this process were John and Anne Moulton from Ormesby, Norfolk. There were not only five other adult Moultons on their ship but also 36 neighbors and kinfolk from east Norfolk. Furthermore, there were Moulton kin already established in Massachusetts and fellow villagers preparing temporary accommodation before the Ormesby company could move up the coast to found Hampton the following year. There is little evidence that the Greater East Anglian companies reshuffled in New England. They may have perched briefly like exhausted swallows on telephone lines, but they soon rejoined their family groups. This New England experience is the subject of our next chapter.

9

꙰

New England

SO FAR, we have observed the Greater East Anglians pulling up their deeply sunken and intertwined roots. How did they fare after this transplantation? We saw, in the discussion of the historiography of mobility and migration in Chapter 1, that the effects of this early experience in New England have been variously interpreted. Some historians see it as a confrontation with an "Atlantic frontier" where, in Turner's oft-repeated words, "the environment overmastered the man," rapidly transforming the Old World European into a New World American. Others have stressed the powerful persistence of the "cultural baggage" or "English ways" of traditional, local responses and attitudes in unfamiliar surroundings. Where did the behavior of eastern counties arrivals fit on this spectrum? Perhaps patterns of stability, community, localism, kinship loyalty, and conservatism were copied in New England. Conversely, the unprecedented challenge might have triggered new ways of responding, wider-ranging, more adaptable, individualistic, and opportunist.[1]

I have employed two measures of response to the new environment among these planters in New England: (1) the frequency of people's moves, and (2) the distances they moved. The shorter the time individuals stayed in any one town, the greater the sense of displacement and change; the farther people went, the more disorienting and isolating the sense of the unfamiliar.

I have also followed the emigrant companies in the New World. They would have been a major source of communal reassurance if they held together. Of course, there are many other variables apart from residential mobility and group cohesion feeding into the pioneers' responses— religion, for instance, or economics. Nevertheless, measurements of movements and companionship should provide important indications of settler mentality.[2]

Even a cursory look at our mass movement reveals certain patterns of transatlantic settlement. Thus we quickly come to expect any family who left the Fressingfield area in northeast Suffolk to end up at Dedham, Massachusetts, or its daughter town of Medfield.[3] The great majority of people who left Great Yarmouth on the Norfolk east coast clustered together at Salem, Massachusetts. So did the large group of kinsfolk from the South Elmham hamlets who later moved out to Wenham and then settled Chelmsford, Massachusetts, in 1655.[4] The intermarried company that sailed from the Ormesby district near Yarmouth moved from temporary quarters at Salem up the coast to settle Hampton in the early 1640s.[5] Hinghamites from Norfolk went en masse to "New" Hingham, as they initially called their South Shore town.[6] The *Lyon* company from Braintree and its Essex hinterland tried initially to settle Mount Wollaston southwest of Boston (later called Braintree) but were ordered to move up to Newtown because of problems of colonial security. In 1635–36 they decided to move with their pastors Hooker and Stone to the richer meadowlands of the Connecticut Valley. The names carved on the Founders' Memorial in Hartford are a roll call of north Essex families. When William Lingwood of Braintree, Essex, wrote in 1652 to his cousin Nicholas Clarke, who had emigrated in the *Lyon* in 1632, he sent his love to "my cosen Loomis, cosen Cullick, John Talcott, John Steele and the rest of my cosens and friends there with you." Some of this company, later disagreeing with the policies and teachings of the Reverend Samuel Stone, swarmed a third time at Hadley, Massachusetts, in 1659 under their lay leader of two decades, William Goodwin of the ancient Braintree, Essex, clothier family.[7] People from Eliot's Nazeing district went together to Roxbury. There too settled Pynchon's company. They came from Essex neighborhoods adjacent to Eliot's followers. Many Pynchonites from Chelmsford, Essex, must have come to know Eliot during his residence at Little Baddow just outside their town. A group of them also moved westward in 1636 and settled Springfield on the east bank of the Connecticut River.[8] Most of the men who signed the Exeter Combination in 1639 had known each other in Lincolnshire before their stay in Boston, Massachusetts, was so rudely interrupted by the colonial crisis over their old-country neighbors, Anne Hutchinson and the Reverend John Wheelwright.[9] Many other examples of Massachusetts clustering could be given: Sudbury, Ipswich, Watertown, and Cambridge—where Mr. Shepard's company stepped into the shoes of Mr. Hooker's—were all predominantly East Anglian towns.[10] On the other hand, it is very unusual—and raises doubts about correct attributions of origins—if an East Anglian settles at Weymouth or Rowley or Gloucester or Dorchester or Concord.

Before chalking up "companionship" on the side of stability in the New World, we need to know how enduring it was. If groups split up after a few years or were quickly decimated by death, the shock of the new would be all the more devastating. One crucial clue is the extraordinary longevity of many members of the first generation. Table 29 shows the length of time 718 adult and adolescent males lived in New England before they either died or, in some 60 cases, returned to England. Of the 621 whose death or departure dates are known, 315 survived for more than 30 years. It would not, therefore, have been at all unusual for children to have grandparents still alive.[11] Indeed, I have counted 126 first-generation men who lived to 80 or beyond, a phenomenal age in that period, and usually over the threshold into great-grandparenthood.[12] We can expect these long-livers to have been guardians of ancient traditions who could ensure cultural continuities and social cohesion. It was particularly important that 66, or two-thirds of settlers arriving in their forties, should survive into their sixties and beyond. These were often the natural leaders of the migration, experienced, well-established family men at the height of their powers. The "transit of civilization" had its best chance of success in their hands. The same pattern of survival can be seen in the large group of men arriving in their twenties and thirties, the leadership successors of the "founding fathers."

The well-known social harmony of Dedham, Massachusetts, owed much to the survival of its East Anglian planters. Of the adult males who traveled from Fressingfield, Henry Brock was the briefest resident; he died after 10 years. Robert Ware, who arrived as a young servant, spent 61 of his 80 years in Dedham. Most of the remaining eight immigrant householders lived there for over 30 years, the average for the entire 10 being 34 years. All except Brock held town, church, and often colony offices for long periods. Their pastor, the Reverend John Allen, who came from neighboring St. James South Elmham, ministered to the congregation until his death in 1671, at the age of 74. His 34 years of service made him, residentially at least, an average inhabitant.[13]

Mere longevity would not on its own guarantee social stability. Given his long life and his calling, one might expect the Reverend William Leveritch to be a steadier of giddy spirits in the New World. A 30-year-

Table 29. Survival Rate in New England

Age at Emigration	Years of Life in New England									Totals
	0–4	5–9	10–19	20–29	30–39	40–49	50–59	60+	UK	
15–19	3	1	6	1	4	8	9	10	15	57
20–29	14	12	25	25	30	47	39	14	28	234
30–39	12	7	40	24	36	32	22	3	10	186
40–49	9	8	18	29	25	10	2	0	9	110
50–59	9	6	4	14	10	1	1	0	4	49
60–69	2	1	3	0	0	0	0	0	0	6
UK	7	8	8	10	8	4	0	0	31	76
Totals	56	43	104	103	113	102	73	27	97	718

Table 30. New England Mobility and Residence

Age at Emigration	No.	No. of Moves	Return	Length of Stays (in years)					
				0–5	6–10	11–20	21–30	31+	UK
0–19	73	157	6	28	26	20	20	28	29
20–29	231	445	19	96	54	87	42	80	67
30–39	185	348	21	89	57	59	33	63	26
40–49	109	182	5	46	26	41	19	20	25
50–59	50	77	4	25	11	11	15	5	6
60–69	6	6	0	2	1	3			
UK	83	141	8	34	19	21	9	6	44
Totals	737	1,356	63	320	194	242	138	202	197

old graduate of Emmanuel College, he had already had pastoral experience as rector of Great Livermere, near Bury St. Edmunds, Suffolk. He survived to the ripe old age of 74. However, during his 44 years in America he lived in no less than six different places, and these were often far apart—Maine, Cape Cod, Long Island, and finally Connecticut. With the exception of 13 years based at Sandwich on the Cape and 12 at Huntington, Long Island, his stays were usually brief, five years or less.[14] John Wheelwright, although he lived to be 81, was a similarly itchy-footed minister, only finding a sense of permanence at Salisbury, Massachusetts, in the last 17 years of his long life. Before 1662 he had moved five times in 26 years, including a five-year return visit to England. This kind of gadding from place to place would be deeply unsettling, even if it were done by groups of people.[15]

How typical were these wills-o'-the-wisp? The evidence from Table 30 seems at first sight ambiguous. On the one hand, the average of just under two moves each for the 737 males listed, with young arrivals moving more often than established family men, suggests a stability in strong contrast to the roving ministers. This is confirmed by the finding that half of the known group had lived in the same town for more than 20 years and nearly a third for more than 30. On the other hand, the largest single total is that for shortest stays in one place, under five years. On the face of it, the fact that 43 percent perched in one place for such a brief period negates the evidence of individual longevity. Nearly half the East Anglians seem to have experienced a quick move, which could have been potentially unsettling and destabilizing.

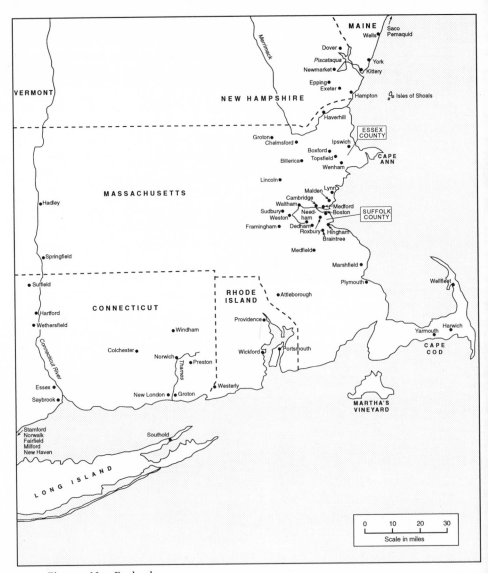

Figure 2. New England

Individual cases help identify several distinct reasons for short stays in one place in New England, and they also reveal certain patterns during a typical adult life.

Many of those who returned to England had only been away a short while. Some East Anglians saw New England as a temporary refuge or an adventurous place to visit, not as a place of permanent settlement at all. The elderly persecuted ministers Robert Peck and John Phillip both came late and probably reluctantly to the wilderness in 1638. Both were back in their old English parishes three years later, after the Long Parliament had begun its campaign of cutting back royal and episcopal prerogatives. A lay refugee who quickly returned was Ferdinando Adams, puritan shoemaker of St. Mary le Tower, Ipswich, who had fled the wrath of Bishop Wren and Archbishop Laud after insulting their authority and barring the church door to the diocesan officers. Several of the young gentlemen in the *Arbella* fleet returned to England within a year.[16]

Others who went back to England may have intended permanent planting but had their minds changed by New England conditions or altered circumstances in Britain. A letter to William Pond in Edwardstone, Suffolk, from his son in Watertown in 1631 gives a strong sense of the common disillusionment at the gulf between the advertised and the actual life of a pioneer: "There come back again [to England] four score and odd persons and as many more would have come if they had wherewithal to bring them home." Those who went back to England in the 1640s, like the ministers Thomas Weld and Hugh Peter, or the Harvard class of 1642, or gentlemen like John Humphrey and George Cooke, were partly responding to a fear that they might "miss the apocalyptic boat."[17]

Within New England itself, some migration was involuntary. The followers of such East Anglian "heretics" as Roger Williams, Anne Hutchinson, or John Wheelwright would no doubt have much preferred to have stayed in the modest comfort of Salem or Boston rather than be expelled to Providence or Portsmouth or Newport or Exeter. When Massachusetts annexed Exeter in 1642 the antinomians had to move yet again up to Wells, Maine. Wheelwright's problems were less itchy feet than bruised buttocks.[18] Others had personal failings or disagreements that forced them to move. The dismissed first head of Harvard, Nathaniel Eaton, typified the former, and Henry Vane or William Vassall, who fell out theologically or politically with the regime, the latter.[19] Sometimes whole groups moved on because of disagreements. The breakaway group from Sudbury who founded Marlborough were bitter about land policy. The *Lyon* company dissidents who felt impelled to abandon Hartford in 1659 could not see eye to eye with their minister, Samuel Stone.[20] There were a few families whose "uncomfortable living" or general fecklessness led to vagabond existences, with town selectmen only too glad to see the back of them. Such was the family of Samuel Hutchinson (he came originally from the Rudhams, north Norfolk), who riotously and shiftlessly moved from Lynn to Reading to Andover. The wife of Thomas Boyden, Jr., presented a pitiful petition in 1685 about her husband's wandering and improvidence. His role model, the elder Thomas, a 1634 emigrant from Ipswich, Suffolk, had moved seven times in his 50 years in Massachusetts. Such drifters were very rare in early New England, however.[21]

The Indians forced people to move. The *Lyon* company's chosen place of settlement at Mount Wollaston had to be abandoned, as we saw, because of its exposed situation. The frontier savagery of King Philip's War (1675–76), which reached within 20 miles of Boston, drove many settlers to flight. Older settlers—among them several of our 1630s planters—never returned. Their short stays came at the end of long lives.[22]

Perhaps the most obvious reason for moving was economic privation and cramped locations. This was the reason given by Hooker's company for their trek to the Connecticut Valley, and there is little doubt that Pynchon's followers from Roxbury to Springfield were similarly motivated. The Ormesby men who moved up the coast from Salem to Hampton after 1639 needed the space to survive and prosper. So did the Fiske party from northeast Suffolk who founded Wenham and then moved on to Chelmsford.[23] As Hooker and Pynchon show, first-comers to Massachusetts could reswarm, but most of the second-wave plantations on the frontier were settled by later arrivals after 1635 who found the original towns crowded.[24]

Artisans, professionals, or merchants might find that they needed to move to a central town for custom or facilities. Thus, as we saw, William Ludkin, the locksmith from Norwich, moved after a few years from the outlying town of Hingham and set up his shop in Boston. His fellow Norwich emigrant, Dr. Simon Ayres, spent the last 13 years of his professional life in the colony capital after eight years in Watertown. Richard Kimball, the wheelwright, who led a large company from Rattlesden in Suffolk in 1634, was soon wooed away from Watertown to Ipswich by a generous offer of land. Such occupational mobility was often affected by age. Single immigrants, newlyweds, young tenant farmers who had accumulated capital, and servants just out of their time were more likely to move on from their first settlement, as Table 30 shows. Unless their parents were proprietors of the town, these recruits to independence might, like later arrivals, have to look to new plantations for sufficient land and available proprietorships. Isaac Hart and Thomas Doggett arrived as servants but then moved on after three and four years respectively to less congested settlements at Lynn and Concord. Thomas Boyden, arriving in 1634 at the age of 21, spent only a year in Watertown before moving to the more remote Scituate. This age-occupation movement is corroborated by other recent studies. It was usually short-range and was often followed by the long-term settledness of independent landownership.[25]

The commonest reason for short residence in one town was the great leveler, death. Forty-two male settlers from East Anglia lived for five years or less in the New World. Winthrop's early letters home record the Grim Reaper's bumper harvest during the first months of danger, morbidity, exposure, and malnourishment: "So many have died and many yet languish . . . I have lost twelve of my family [company], Walters, Gager, Smith of Buxall, William Taylor of Haverhill . . . Jeffery Ruggles of Sudbury . . . and principal persons, Mr. Johnson and the lady Arbella, mr. Rossiter, mrs. Phillips."[26] A further 21 East Anglian emigrants perished within nine years of landing. It is most likely that many of the 97 whose length of survival in New England is not known also died soon after arrival. Some voyagers like Simon Huntington, wealthy grocer from Norwich, or Benjamin Cooper, husbandman of Brampton, who left an estate valued at £1,278, never saw the promised land, dying en route. Anthony Cooper from Hingham died almost immediately after landing, leaving a wife, eight children, and four servants.[27]

Short stays usually came at the start or toward the end of the individual's New England experience. A settler, a clan, a company would perch for a while before moving off to a more permanent settlement. Thus Emmanuel Downing wrote to John Winthrop in October 1637: "I follow your councell in coming to the Bay before I resolve where to pitche. I pray helpe me to hire or buy some howse (so as I may sell yt againe if I shall remove) in some plantation above the Bay." Downing's clerk, contemplating emigration in 1633, had lower expectations: "I hope I shall find with you or Mr. Sandford a wadd of straw to lye on until I may buye or buyld a howse . . . a tent . . . I conceive a necessary

Table 31. New World Moves by
Adult Males

Stayed put	287	(287)
Moved once	244	(488)
Moved twice	85	(255)
Moved three times	29	(116)
Moved four times or more	16	(80)
Totals	661	(1,226)

Note: Figures in parentheses represent
number of residences.

thinge with you."[28] Several families who founded Sudbury had spent a
few years at Watertown.[29] The Ormesby and South Elmham parties
squatted briefly at Salem before branching out. The discovery, surveying, laying out, and partial clearing of a new settlement was a huge
undertaking. If there was temporary accommodation to be had, pru-
dence dictated delay before moving out to permanent homes.

Near the end of a long life, an infirm parent might have to move in
with a son or daughter for care and sustenance. This explains why the
84-year-old Samuel Appleton of Ipswich, Massachusetts, died at Rowley. His daughter Sarah had married Rowley's minister, the Reverend
Samuel Philips. The same pattern holds for the 94-year-old Simon
Bradstreet, the octogenarians James Fitch, William Goodwin, Anne
(Veare/Gates) Woodward, Ichabod Sheffield, Andrew Warner, and the
mere stripling in his early seventies, Abraham Howe, who died at his
daughter's home in Boston.[30]

Loss of neighbors through death or departures for England would be
emotionally upsetting for townspeople who remained. Fleeing from the
Indians would be terrifying. Exile of "subversives" or splintering off of
dissidents would be bound to dislocate the refugees, but it would also
defuse overcharged emotions and help restore social harmony for those
who remained. Without discounting the effects of these short stays, it is
hard to see them as being so destabilizing as to turn settlers into "New
Men." The only moves that might be seen as "Turnerian" responses
were those to less constricted town sites. Yet to interpret the move to the
Connecticut Valley solely in terms of economic opportunism would
oversimplify to the point of travesty.[31]

The 320 men who spent less than five years in one place do not
therefore necessarily represent a society in flux. Their brief sojourns are

Table 32. Age and Mobility in America

Age at Emigration	Stayed Put	Moved Once	Moved Twice	Moved Thrice	Moved 4 or More Times	Totals
15–19	12	19	10	3	1	45
20–29	79	84	33	8	6	210
30–39	82	65	24	9	3	183
40–49	57	34	11	3	0	105
50–59	27	14	2	2	0	45
60–69	6	0	0	0	0	6
Totals	263	216	80	25	10	594

more likely to have arisen from close-knit communities coming to terms with their new environment.

The most persuasive evidence in support of persistent cohesion and cooperation is the strong pattern of residential stability shown in Tables 31–33. Table 31 lists the movements of 661 adult males about whom sufficient information exists. The great majority either stayed put where they originally settled or moved only once.

The relationship between age and mobility in America emerges from Table 32. The older a planter was when he landed, the less likely was he to move. Servants and other adolescents commonly moved at least once away from their first setting down. Relocation was somewhat less likely with arrivals in their twenties, the usual marriage decade. By the thirties cohort, it has become normal to stay put, and thereafter the proportion of standpatters increases with each decadal group. This pattern essentially replicated the experience of Englishmen.[32] A small number of men in their twenties and thirties make up the most mobile of the immigrants. Philip Taber, a 25-year-old Essex carpenter who emigrated in 1630, holds the record with eight moves covering four different jurisdictions and the offshore island of Martha's Vineyard during his 42 years in America.[33]

The best-rooted residents were the 106 men who remained in one town for a period of 40 years or more—10 of them for 60 or more (Table 33). The record holder, Nathaniel Felton, arrived in Salem in 1635 and stayed there for the next 70 years, dying at the age of 90. Although 10 arrivals in their forties lived on in one place to their eighties, the great majority of long-established townsmen were, like Felton, in their twenties (55) or thirties (30) when they landed. Most striking is the fact that

Table 33. Long-Settled Residents in New England

Name	Date Arr.	Age at Arr.	Occupation	Long Residence	Years	Dates	Death	Other Res. and Dates
John ALLEN	1635	30	Merchant	Charlestown	40	1635–75	1675	
Edm ANGIER	1636	24	Innkeeper	Cambridge	57	1636–93	1693	
Theo ATKINSON	1632	20	Hatter/merchant	Boston	69	1632–1701	1701	
Sam AYRES	1637	15		Ipswich	40	1637–77	1677	
Sam BASS	?1630	30		Braintree	54	1640–94	1694	Roxbury 1632–40
John BEALE	1638	45	Shoemaker	Hingham	50	1638–88	1688	
John BIGELOW	1637	20	Blacksmith	Watertown	66	1637–1703	1703	
Edm BLOSSE	c1634	47		Watertown	c47	c1634–81	1681	
Hanniel BOSWORTH	1638	c23		Ipswich	45+	1638–83+		
Rich BRACKETT	1630	19	Schoolmaster	Braintree	50	1641–91	1691	Boston 1630–41, married London 1634
Thos BRADBURY	1634	23	Schoolmaster/gent.	Salisbury	55	1639–94	1694	York 34–39
Thos BRICE	1630		Ship carpenter	Gloucester	49	1642–91	1691	?1630–42
Walt BRIGGS	1639	27	Yeoman	Scituate	45	1639–84	1684	
Hen BRIGHT Jr.	1630	28		Watertown	56	1630–86	1686	
Thos BROWN	1638	33		Concord	48	1640–88	1688	Sudbury 38–40, died at Cambridge
John BUCK	1638	c18		Scituate	47	1650–97	1697	Hingham 1638–50
John BURRAGE	1637	21	Ferryman	Charlestown	41	1637–78	1678	
Thos CARTER	1635	25	Minister	Woburn	44	1640–84	1684	Watertown 1635–38; Dedham 1638–40
Chas CHADWICK	1630	33		Watertown	52	1630–82	1682	
Thos CHUBBOCK	1633	c28		Hingham	41	1635–76	1676	Charlestown 1633–35

Name		Age	Occupation	Place			Notes
Wm CODDINGTON	1630	29	Merchant	Newport	1637–78	1678	Boston 1630–37; England 1631–33; 1648–51
John COGGESHALL	1632	31	Merchant	Newport	1638–89	1689	Roxbury 1632; Boston 1635–38
Edw COLLINS	1638	35		Cambridge	1638–89	1689	
John COOLIDGE	1636	c32	Gentleman	Watertown	1636–91	1691	
Thos COOPER	1638	31		Rehoboth	1643–90	1690	Hingham 1638–43
Griffin CRAFTS	1630	28		Roxbury	1630–90	1690	
John CRAM	1636	39		Exeter	1638–82	1682	
Wm CURTIS	1632	40	Yeoman	Roxbury	1632–72	1672	
Theoph CUSHING	1633	49	Yeoman	Hingham	?1633–79	1679	May have been Charlestown 1633–35
Jas CUTLER	1634	28	Yeoman	Cambridge Farms	1648–94	1694	Watertown 1634–48
Wm DADY	1630	25	Butcher	Charlestown	1630–82	1682	
John DANE Jr.	1636	23	Tailor	Ipswich	1636–84	1684	
John DEVEREUX	1630	16	Fisherman	Marblehead	1648–94	1694	Salem 1630–48
Thos DOGGETT	1637	30		Marshfield	1652–92	1692	Salem 1637–42; Concord 1642; Weymouth 1643–52
John EDDY	1630	29		Watertown	1633–84	1684	Plymouth 1630–33
John ELIOT	1631	27	Minister	Roxbury	1631–90	1690	
John FARROW	1635	27		Hingham	1635–87	1687	
Benj FELTON	1635	31	Turner	Salem	1635–88	1688	
Nat FELTON	1635	20		Salem	1635–1705	1705	
Thos FLEGGE	1637	21		Watertown	1637–98	1698	
Renald FOSTER	1635	40		Ipswich	1635–81	1681	
John FULLER	1635	24		Newton	1635–99	1699	Returns to Eng to marry 1635, 2nd crossing

Table 33. *Continued*

Name	Date Arr.	Age at Arr.	Occupation	Long Residence	Years	Dates	Death	Other Res. and Dates
Wm FULLER	1635	25		Hampton	54	1639–93	1693	Ipswich 1635–39
John GEDNEY	1638	34	Weaver	Salem	50	1638–88	1688	
Hen GIBBS	1633	20		Hingham	?43	?1633–76	1676	?Charlestown c1633–35
Rob GOODALE	1634	33		Salem	49	1634–83	1683	
Ozias GOODWIN	1632	36		Hartford	48	1635–83	1683	Cambridge 1632–35
Rich GRIDLEY	1630	29	Mason	Boston	44	1630–74	1674	
Rob HAWKINS	1635	25		Fairfield	54	1650–1704	1704	Charlestown 1635–50; died at Charlestown
Wm HILL	1632	24		Hartford	47	1636–83	1683	Roxbury 1632–36
Edm HOBART Jr.	1633	29	Weaver	Hingham	51	1635–86	1686	Charlestown 1633–35
Peter HOBART	1635	31	Minister	Hingham	44	1635–79	1679	
Thos HOBART	1633	27		Hingham	54	1635–89	1689	Charlestown 1633–35
Jas HOWE	1635	31	Weaver	Ipswich	61	1641–1702	1702	Roxbury 1635–41
Edw IRESON	1635	32		Lynn	40	1635–75	1675	
Rob JENNISON	1636	c30	Yeoman	Watertown	54	1636–90	1690	
Thos KING	1635	31		Scituate	56	1635–91	1691	
Thos LEAVITT	1637	c17		Hampton	54	1644–96	1696	Boston 1637–39; Exeter 1639–44
Rich LEEDS	1637	32	Mariner	Dorchester	56	1637–93	1693	Salem 1637
Dan LINCOLN	1640	21	Boatman	Hingham	59	1640–99	1699	
Sam LINCOLN	1637	18	Mariner	Hingham	53	1637–90	1690	
Thos LINCOLN	1636	30	Cooper	Hingham	55	1636–91	1691	

Name								
Thos LINCOLN	1638	22	Husbandman	Hingham	54	1638–92	1692	
Hen LOOKER	1639	c19	Glover	Sudbury	49	1639–88	1688	
John MARSTON	1637	20	Carpenter	Salem	44	1637–81	1681	
Hugh MASON	1634	28	Tanner	Watertown	44	1634–78	1678	
Thos MOORE	1636	21	Shipowner	Southold	40	1651–91	1691	Salem 1636–51
Jos MORSE Jr.	1634	24		Watertown	57	1634–91	1691	
Thos MOULTON	1637	29	Husbandman	York	45	1654–99	1699	Newbury 1637–39; Hampton 1639–54
Jos MYGATT	1633	37	Merchant	Hartford	44	1636–80	1680	Cambridge 1633–36
Thos NICHOLS	1637	22		Hingham	59	1637–96	1696	
Nich PALMER	1637	27		Windsor	52	1637–89	1689	
Wm PARKE	1631	24		Roxbury	54	1631–85	1685	
Rob PAYNE	1639	44	Merchant	Ipswich	44	1640–84	1684	
Aaron PINGRY	c1640	c20	Husbandman	Ipswich	56	1640–96	1696	
Moses PINGRY	c1640	c30	Saltmaker	Ipswich	55	1641–96	1696	
Edm PITTS	1637	24	Weaver	Hingham	48	1637–85	1685	
Rich PRATT	1638	23		Malden	53	1638–91	1691	
John READ	1639	41	Yeoman	Rehoboth	40	1645–85	1685	Dorchester 1639; Braintree 1640–45
Thos SANDFORD	1634	26		Milford	41	1640–81	1681	Dorchester 1634–40
Rich SCOTT	1634	29	Merchant	Providence	42	1638–80	1680	Boston 1634–38
John SEVERANCE	c1637	23	Innkeeper	Salisbury	43	1639–82	1682	Boston c1637–39
Edm SHEFFIELD	1639	27		Braintree	60	1645–1705	1705	Roxbury 1639–45
John SHERMAN	1634	20		Watertown	57	1634–91	1691	
Fran SKERRY	1637	29	Husbandman	Salem	47	1637–84	1684	

Table 33. *Continued*

Name	Date Arr.	Age at Arr.	Occupation	Long Residence	Years	Dates	Death	Other Res. and Dates
Hen SKERRY	1637	31	Cordwainer	Salem	54	1637–91	1691	
Hen SMITH	1637	30	Husbandman	Dedham	43+	1637–80+		
Anth SOMERBY	1639	29	Schoolmaster	Newbury	47	1639–86	1686	
Isaac STEARNS	1630	c35		Watertown	41	1630–71	1671	
Wm STOREY	1637	23	Carpenter	Ipswich	56	1637–93	1693	
John STOWERS	1634	c24		Newport	c47	1638–85+		Watertown 1634–38
Sam SYMONDS	1637	c42	Merchant	Ipswich	41	1637–78	1678	
John THURSTON	1637	30	Carpenter	Dedham	49	1637–86	1686	
Josh TIDD	1637	30	Merchant	Charlestown	41	1637–78	1678	
Peter TUFTS	1637	20	Ferryman	Malden	63	1637–1700	1700	
John TUTTLE	1637			Southold	40+	1641–81		New Haven 1637–41
John WAITE	1637	20		Malden	56	1637–93	1693	
John WARD	1639	33	Minister	Haverhill	48	1645–93	1693	Maine 1639–45
Thos WARD	1638	17		Hampton	42	1638–80	1680	
Rob WARE	1638	20		Dedham	61	1638–99	1699	
Wm WENTWORTH	1637	21	Gentleman	Dover	48	1650–98	1698	?1637–39; Exeter 1639–42; Wells 1642–50
Sam WHITING	1636	39	Minister	Lynn	43	1636–79	1679	
Rob WILLIAMS	1637	44	Cordwainer	Roxbury	56	1637–93	1693	
Rog WILLIAMS	1631	27	Minister	Providence	47	1636–83	1683	Salem 1631; Plymouth 1631–33; Salem 1633–36
Nich WYETH	1638	43	Mason	Cambridge	42	1638–80	1680	

only 18 of the 106 reached New England before 1635. Twenty-six did not start their long residence until 1640 or after. The better established a settlement was, it seems, the better chance of a long life. There were exceptions, though. Hingham was not founded until 1635, yet 14 men who settled there between 1635 and 1638 (mostly in the first year) survived in the town for 40 years or more. Four of Watertown's 11 long-dwellers arrived in 1630. These two towns and Ipswich (10) had far and away the most East Anglian standpatters. Hingham's lead was aided by the (genetic?) longevity of four Lincolns and three Hobarts. Other towns to which considerable numbers of East Anglians went had much lower totals.[34]

The fact that most of these patriarchs lived into the late 1670s or 1680s and that they were distributed around 37 New England towns would help to preserve a sense of continuity with English traditions into the third and fourth generations in New England, especially when so many of them held positions of power and influence in church or town, county or colony. They helped to shape the collective memory of New England.[35]

Despite this impressive evidence of residential permanence, there is one more factor we need to examine before reaching a verdict on the relative stability or unsettledness of East Anglian New Englanders. Table 31 shows that 374 men out of 661 moved once or more during their lives in New England. The distances involved and the manner of moving are, as in the English experience, crucial evidence. There is a world of difference between a group of families forming a daughter settlement in a large town grant and a lone individual like Philip Taber who moved long distances to remote and marginal outposts.

Of the 661 men about whom sufficient data survive, 197 (30 percent) moved over 30 miles from their original New England homes.[36] These long-distance migrators can be divided into three groups: religious refugees and first- and second-wave frontiersmen. The "heretics" with East Anglian backgrounds numbered 46 men and their families, devotees of Roger Williams who fled 53 miles to Providence, Rhode Island, of Anne Hutchinson (65 miles to Rhode Island), or John Wheelwright (43 miles to Exeter, New Hampshire).[37] Their banishment was intended to safeguard religious orthodoxy and social cohesion, and, if the subsequent shambles in Rhode Island is anything to go by, it probably did.[38]

We have already discussed the first-wave frontiersmen. These were the large group of 66 East Anglians and their families who migrated in the late 1630s from the Massachusetts Bay beachhead the 100 miles west to the Connecticut Valley towns of Hartford (35 men), Wethersfield (14), and Springfield (6), or the 150 miles to eastern Long Island (10 families) in the early 1640s.[39]

The second-wave dispersal took place after the 1640s and, conditioned by such deterrents as the impenetrability of the inland wilderness and fear of Indians, was coastal or estuarine.[40] Eighty-five families from the Connecticut Valley or directly from Massachusetts settled the coves, creeks, and bays of the Connecticut coast to the south or the Maine shore to the north. Thus did ports and havens like Norwich, Fairfield, and Milford, Connecticut, or Wells, York, and Kittery, Maine, acquire an East Anglian flavor. All of these migrations were over 30 miles. Seventeen moves exceeded 100 miles.[41]

One might expect some kind of Wild West abandon among these twice-displaced migrants, destabilizing vagabondage triggering frontier lawlessness and disorder. Sometimes it happened, as in the excessive atomization of early Rhode Island. Some Maine toeholds, bases for commercial fishing like the Isles of Shoals, or trading posts with the Indians earned notorious reputations among right-thinking puritans.[42]

Social harmony was the norm, however, even for these displaced persons. Why? The main reason seems to be that these migrations were not fissiparous dispersals but cases of established companies reswarming. This has already been demonstrated for the Connecticut Valley. Followers of Hutchinson and Wheelwright often had kinship links and neighborhood connections from English days. The same linkages operated in the settlement of the Connecticut coastlands. For example, the brothers Samuel and Thomas Hale, who with their families helped to found Norwalk in 1651, had been neighbors in north Essex, England, of Thomas Fitch, Norwalk's richest and most powerful townsman, and of his brother Joseph. They had continued their proximity in the Hartford, Connecticut, area during the 1640s. Like Hartford, Norwalk was, to adapt a phrase, a "company town."[43]

Additionally, coastal expansion was less isolating than inland. Communication by water was a good deal easier than overland. In such ways were the alienating effects of even long-distance treks minimized.[44]

Without underplaying these examples of long-distance New World migrants, we should keep their restlessness in proportion. For every adventurous or disappointed or disapproving individual or family who moved away from his or her New England base, nearly three stayed put or moved only to adjacent settlements. Seventy percent of the East

Anglian male sample preferred rooting to trailing. This is confirmed by the fact that early Massachusetts settlement was so relatively dense. The farthest inland the first generation penetrated was only about 25 miles from Boston. Even frontier outposts like Groton or Lancaster or Chelmsford were connected to their less exposed neighbors by trails or rivers, and so back to the core of the colony. This more settled majority thus kept in touch with family, old friends, and neighbors and with the ordered, structured, and interlinked life of their jurisdictions. If they moved, they rarely moved alone. The founders of Sudbury had previously perched together at Watertown, as we saw; subsequently, a dissident company of Sudbury men founded Marlborough. Such sprouting of offshoots was common and "organic."[45]

Although there was considerable shaking-down and some distant resettlement among the Greater East Anglians in the New World, then, it is abundantly clear that this did not occur at the expense of order or social consensus. There were too many counteragents of continuity, cohesion, community: persistent companionship, widespread first-generation longevity, residential stability, and intraneighborhood movement and family formation. Those who returned to England or fled Massachusetts persecution or were drawn by faraway places or simply failed to survive wilderness conditions did not undermine this stable core.

Conclusion

OVER THE last 30 years mobility and migration studies have enjoyed an extraordinary renaissance. Early revisions of the "Merrie Englande" myth suggested that all England was restlessly on the move with people skittering about all over the place. This alleged fluidity, combined with other volatile changes, produced the following epitome: "a dynamic, mobile, loose, open . . . society." These exuberant upsettings of the model of stability, including the new portrait of the early modern English parish as "a geographical area through which very large numbers of people flowed," have been more recently tempered and refined. Some relocation was normal at certain phases of life, but it was customarily short-distance and often temporary. Education, status, and occupation could all expand individual horizons, but for many of the middling sort a neighborhood of a 5–10-mile radius was reassuringly familiar territory beyond which they rarely strayed. These core populations of towns and villages were the social sheet anchor, a source of stability and communal continuity in a world of change. For change was certainly in the air in early Stuart England, not least in Greater East Anglia. Long-term population growth, short-term ecological disasters, economic recessions, and foreign policy miscalculations all combined to thrust vulnerable groups below the poverty line. Nonetheless, the pace of change and social disintegration so bleakly recorded by some revisionists has been exaggerated. Despite a swelling underclass of rogues and vagabonds, young and not-so-young men and women on the road in search of survival, localism, rootedness, and custom were still the norm for those Englishmen who enjoyed a competency.[1]

Certainly, in the case of the 2,138 emigrants from England's eastern counties during the 1630s, "Worlds in Motion" is a serious misnomer. Although Greater East Anglia was one of the most advanced regions of England with diverse, commercially oriented agriculture, a renowned textile industry producing for overseas customers, and an active land market, most of its emigrants, its many women included, came from established, often long-established, residential backgrounds. Some of the contingent's natural leaders, regionally recognized clergymen, gentlemen with wide county, regional, or London connections, and members of successful entrepreneurial and mercantile families, had experience of moving and broad horizons. Much more typical, though, were emigrants of the middling sort, small traders in country market towns, village craftsmen, minor members of the textile industry, yeomen and husbandmen from the wood pasture, all commanding a modest competency and a more or less secure independence. A majority lived in the same Essex, Suffolk, Norfolk, Lincolnshire, or Cambridgeshire neighborhoods as their great-grandparents or, in the case of farmers, their great-great-grandparents. They usually grew up among complex networks of relatives, trained and married locally, and lived out their lives in the districts where they had been born. It was to such people in the *Arbella* fleet that John Cotton preached his "God's Promise to His Plantations." The rhythmically recurring refrain of his sermon is the desirability of rooting, abiding, continuing, planting, and the horrors of being moved, plucked up, or rooted out.[2] I have argued in Chapter 7 that these well-embedded people were probably representative of the "hidden" emigrants from the eastern counties whose English origins are unknown. However, they were less typical of contingents from other parts of the country, especially London and the West Country. Both of these places had far higher proportions of young single men, some of whom had tried every other possible route to survival before the last resort of America. Such desperate drifters formed the bulk of the passengers bound for the Chesapeake. The Greater East Anglian contingent studied here total only 10 to 15 percent of the Great Migration but, I would argue, typify more than a third. Supplying, as they did, more than their fair share of lay and spiritual leaders and established married men who would run local government, the long-settled people from eastern England would likely prove influential in the New World.

The prospect of transatlantic emigration for such people would have been akin to a voyage to the moon for us. Indeed, it was even more daunting than a space shot. Most seventeenth-century embarkers knew that they would never see the old country, family, or friends again. The craftsmen and farmers and small traders who made up the bulk of the contingent would have sunk most of their capital into fares for family and cargo.

Yet, by and large, New England settledness followed the traumatic uprooting from East Anglia. Extended kin groups, neighborhood companies, and "gathered" groups of saints transferred East Anglian stability to the New World. Although there was an initial period of instability and shaking-down for some, especially adolescent, less affluent arrivals, the typical emigrant's world was only jarred, not thrown into motion. Notwithstanding the considerable outmigration among younger people during the 1650s, there were more than enough settled planters to establish an enviable social order during the first generation.

These first planters had two important early tasks: the distribution of land and the naming of their settlements. How they went about these brings us back to the interpretational debates that form the context of this study. They parceled out land freehold to all households. This marked a distinct break from the highly complex system of land tenure in England. However, the size of grants reflected the socioeconomic pecking order within the group, a retention of old-country hierarchical values. In town naming, they often used East Anglian precedents (see Figure 2), a symbol of continuity. Yet relatively few of them adopted the name of the English parish from which they had come. Yeomen from Fressingfield had to get used to living in Dedham. Both continuity and change inhere in these and other New World decisions.[3]

The prevailing geographic stability of the East Anglian contingent in the Old and New Worlds gives an impression of continuity during colonization. Mobility is but one factor in the complex process of change; other findings in this study about attitudes to age, the philosophies of leaders, community values, and persistent localism tend to reinforce the sense of conservatism during the first two decades of settlement.

In New England, age continued to be venerated, and an unprecedented number of the East Anglian contingent survived in their towns to their seventies and eighties. Anne Bradstreet from Lincolnshire described long lives as God-given. Her widower, Simon, was elected to the governorship even into his eighties. Many annually reelected magistrates, deputies, town and church officials, as well as ministers, continued in harness until they dropped. Thomas Danforth, who arrived in Cambridge as a boy of 11 with his father and six siblings from Framlingham, Suffolk, in 1635, was elected to the colony council well into his seventies and rode circuit as a judge a few weeks before he died in 1699. Colonial mores reflected popular trust in experience. Preferential seating for elderly people in the meetinghouse symbolized this respect for age. Longevity and wisdom were conventionally equated. Ancient inhabitants preserved community memories. They were consulted by the courts to help settle disputes over wills, land, and rights-of-way. There is little evidence that arrival in the New World opened up opportunities for leadership among more flexible younger men. Except for the very poor or the senile or the disabled, "older meant better and oldest meant best" in early New England, as it had in Greater East Anglia. The sense of superiority elders felt is reflected in contemporary generational comparisons. When, in 1649, old William Knapp, who had emigrated from Bures in Suffolk to Watertown in 1630, paid young Phoebe Page, daughter of his fellow passenger in the *Arbella* fleet, John Page from Dedham in Essex, five shillings for a kiss, he asserted "that young men would only give a touch, but he (aged *71*) would give her a cleaving kiss and old Knapp did afterward desire to kiss her again upon that five shillings and she answered no." Disparagement of the rising generation may well reveal a society resistant to change. Such self-confidence in and reverence for age and seniority would help to foster tradition and long-held values.[4]

The traditional leaders of local communities, gentlemen and clergy, were mostly conservative in their backgrounds, training, and attitudes. The more radical among them either returned to England, like Henry Vane or Hugh Peter, or ended up in exile like Roger Williams or John Wheelwright. The wilder experiments of the English Interregnum were not for the first-generation rulers. From the vantage point of the old country during the 1650s, New England, with its intolerance, its exclusivity, and its narrow-minded rigor seemed painfully old-fashioned and parochial—"a forlorn and distant sideshow," "a backwater," "the outskirts of the world." Their greatest first-generation leader, John Winthrop, habitually interpreted events as providences of God, the causer of all things. He was typical of all those emigrant laymen and clergy whose perceptions have survived. The church year was punctuated by days of humiliation and thanksgiving, placating or expressing gratitude to an unpredictable deity. *Pace* Darrett Rutman, the ideals proclaimed in 1630 by the governor were by no means blasted by the time of his death in 1649.[5]

The major finding that so many Greater East Anglians traveled in companies that held together in the plantations suggests that community probably continued to exert strong influence over family and personal consciousness. Several local and legal studies confirm the impression that the interests of the group were rated more highly than the wishes of its constituent parts. The emigration of the extended family and its clannish strength in the wilderness tended to deflate individual aspirations. The persistence of the endogamous marriage patterns of East Anglian towns and villages in the New World would have further thickened the network of kinship. Moral controls continued to be externalized rather than being considered matters of personal or family conscience. Public shaming punishments survived the sea change, as did the communal scapegoating of deviants. Fear and suspicion of "strangers" and mistrust of people from other English regions point to a group need for consensus, conformity, and familiarity. Obedience and the acceptance of group norms were enforced by the "Holy Watchfulness" of neighbors. Habitual close supervision and lack of privacy persisted in the wilderness. The "Commonwealth" ideals of Winthrop's "Model of Christian Charity" seem to have reflected the attitudes of many of the early planters.[6]

One other enduring import from England was localism, the resistance of those in "the provinces" to central direction and pretensions. The eastern counties had a long tradition of such "country" opposition, which may be said to have culminated in the Eastern Association of the Great Rebellion.[7] Similar resentments and suspicions have been detected among emigrants in New England. As early as 1631, the men of Watertown under George Phillips, born in Norfolk and officiating in Essex, enunciated the principle of no taxation without representation. East Anglians had only four years earlier resisted Charles I's forced loan with similar determination.[8] The Massachusetts freemen in 1634 put a stop to Winthrop's ambition to rule the colony summarily. Dissatisfied in 1635 with their allocation of meadowland from the General Court, a large number of settlers in Cambridge, Massachusetts, decided to move to the Connecticut Valley. Nothing the central authorities could do would stop them. Ironically, once in the valley they lost Springfield to Massachusetts because of a spat with the Connecticut central government. Perhaps the loudest outburst of localism was registered by the ex-Norfolk men in New Hingham over their right to choose their own militia officers.[9]

Persistent localism, persistent companionship, and persistent leadership were fortuitously helped by the New England environment in reinforcing continuity. A generally austere climate and soil, the lack of an agricultural staple, shortages of capital as well as labor, and isolation from conflict all conspired to reduce opportunities for change. All these factors coincide with our main conclusion of persistence of Old World rootedness in the New.

228

However, there is no denying that radical alterations did occur in planters' new lives. New England saw major changes in both spiritual and secular areas. The creation of the exclusive, semiindependent gatherings of the godly, calling their own ministers, cleansing the liturgy, morality, and daily life of Old World corruptions, may have been presaged in England and may have been dressed up in the conservative language of return to the primitive and pristine Christianity of the first churches. Nonetheless, as the dominant orthodoxy of a semiautonomous society, it was revolutionary. So too was the release of pent-up religious energy evident in Massachusetts in the revivalist atmosphere of the mid-1630s and its concomitant surge of spiritual liberation and experimentation. The repercussions of the ecclesiastical changes were everywhere in daily life: long-agitated legal reforms, wholesale reformation of manners, unqualified and unpolluted sabbatarianism, the harrying out of such "rags of Rome" as Christmas, pagan names for days and months, and the luxury of a cornucopia of "means"—sermons, catechizings, lectures, prayer meetings, and "conventicles." Over all this reform and purification loomed the ideal of the restoration of order— the curbing of excess, self-assertion, extravagance, corruption, exploitation, and arrogance. The incipient chaos and collapse they feared and fled in England would be replaced by well-ordered families, well-ordered communities, and a well-ordered commonwealth.[10]

Equally striking changes occurred in emigrants' secular lives. The emigration of the General Court of the Massachusetts Bay Company transported political accountability at the colonial level. Although these former freemen in Norwich and other boroughs like Great Yarmouth, Ipswich, Bury, or Boston had had some voice in the local political process, most of the settlers would have been accustomed to having their magistrates appointed by the crown. Although individual New England towns might continue their hierarchical and oligarchic traditions from the Old World, they had far more autonomy in the new decentralized regime. However, the absence of the hated ecclesiastical courts and chancery brought much more legal business before lay magistrates, who further officiated at the civil contract of marriage. Many temporal changes resulted from radical simplification of institutions. The population of Massachusetts Bay at the end of the Great Migration was smaller than that of the city of Norwich; its evolving system of government was not dissimilar.[11]

Shortly before he sailed to America, Governor Winthrop asked, "Why then should we stand striving here for places of habitation &c (many men spending as much labour and cost to recover and keep sometimes an acre or two of land as would procure them many hundred acres as good or better in another country [America] and in the meantime suffer a whole continent as fruitful and convenient for the use of man to lie waste without any improvement?" Unquestionably, the belief in the abundance of land was the greatest temporal change in people's lives. Actuality might bring disappointment to some; marsh or meadow might be short, rock, ice, and sand depressingly plentiful, forest impenetrable, rivers uncontrollable, climate trickily unfamiliar. Towns would respond in varied ways to this sudden affluence of land. Hingham and Dedham might act to conserve reserves for future generations; Watertown and Ipswich might rapidly divide it among proprietors; Boston might argue, Cambridge complain, Springfield develop into a company town. These responses would depend on interaction between inherited English ways and American environment and opportunities, but all reflected revolutionized circumstances. Land abundance exacerbated incipient labor shortages. "Workmen for being restrained would either remove to other places where they might have more," complained John Winthrop in 1641, "or else, being able to live by planting and other employments of their own they would not be hired at all."[12] So those English institutions of service in husbandry and day labor collapsed and withered. In a capital-starved economy, tenancy, under greatly improved terms, might continue for young families getting started, but the family farm wholly reliant on the labor of two or three generations became the norm. This purely familial reliance produced subtle changes in group dynamics, in the power balance between parents and children, in adolescence, in young married adulthood and its sense of independence.[13]

New England was, to these newcomers, new. The younger Winthrop described this vast wilderness "as in the beginning of the world." Its very primeval qualities produced striking transformations, not only in the physical but also in the psychic world of the new arrivals. No longer were their homes surrounded by the associations that went back beyond "the memory of man." In terms of local customs, lore, and folkways, they were cultural castaways. Nothing in their new world was "time-honored." This has been suggested as a powerful reason for the immigrants' eagerness for written contracts, for codifications of laws, for platforms of belief. It has also been advanced as a motive for the settlers' apparent conservatism: People subjected to dramatic changes "take refuge in the familiar . . . cling to the past and try to recapture it." Paradoxically, this very absence of the time-honored and the associational may, in some, have acted as a liberating force, a freer of energies.[14]

The Greater East Anglian planters were thus inevitably both conservers and innovators. David Grayson Allen, the subtlest tracer of the persistence of English ways in New England, mounts his analysis within the framing assumption that "To emigrate . . . meant a startling transformation. . . . The townsmen had to change or abandon almost every formal institution which they had taken for granted. This was indeed a 'new' England." Yet his findings bear out the contention of another expert that emigrants took with them to America "a vast array of social and cultural assumptions, implicit structures of organization and ideals of order. . . . If they could depart religious persecution and economic dislocation, they could not escape those culturally engrained habits that stamped them English."[15]

When spokesmen of the puritan diaspora considered motivation, they depicted themselves as "reformers." The word has clashing ambiguities, however. It can mean, as it usually did in the seventeenth century, the return to old forms, the recapturing of lost, pristine states. Its other sense, our usage, is of change for the better. "Reform" contains both reactionary and radical potential. Typically and typologically, puritan apologists compared the Great Migration to the flight of the Jews from Pharaoh's Egypt. They felt the compulsive push of persecution that inevitably followed their resistance to a rising tide of pollution and anti-Christian innovation. They were not called puritans for nothing. Despite their root-and-branch policy of tearing off the strangulating ivy of Roman Catholicism from the Church of England, they phrased this intention in highly conservative terms: "to lead ancient lives" and return to the purity of the early church. Our analysis of what can be discovered about the personal and ancestral backgrounds of the Greater East Anglian contingent suggests that the rhetoric of preservation and return to purity would appeal to people unused to moving away from long-familiar vicinities and deeply conservative in their outlook. They would require explosive threats of incipient catastrophe to blast out their resistant and intertwined roots. William Coddington, who was 29 when he fled one Boston for another in 1630, "a godly man of good estate," compared himself to Lot escaping from Sodom just before the cities of the plain were devastated by Jehovah's wrath.[16]

Yet the other meaning of "reform" had to be implicit in reasons moving the emigrants: change for the better. That change would include, along with purity and safety, material security, what Captain John Smith called "advancement of fortune." This promoters like John White and William Wood understood. It underpinned Winthrop's justification for leaving and his apprehensions about the new society. The

self-same William Coddington later became notorious as a land speculator as he expanded his good estate in New England. So many coils
bound people to the eastern counties that they had to feel the attraction
of powerful incentives.[17]

"Rewards there had to be." This book has illustrated the huge cost
"these traditionalist-minded folk were willing to pay to find a world free
of both prelates and the profane." Lucy Downing had to overcome her
terrors of sea and wasteland, her fears for her children's future and her
own health. It took her five years. Thomas Shepard recorded "lament-
ing the loss of our native country, when we took our last look of it," and
John Cotton lovingly called England "the womb that bare thee and the
breast that gave thee suck." The younger Winthrop never lost his
"persistent attachment" to the mother country. Unprecedented uprooting from long-familiar neighborhoods represented an enormous
sacrifice.[18]

When ordinary people sought to explain their reasons for emigration,
they habitually talked of lack of "means" in the eastern counties. What
they meant was the silencing of their beloved soul-saving and con-
science-stirring preachers and suppression of purified services and the
Lord's Supper—the means to salvation. "Lack of means" has an alternative sense, and from the financially straitened Winthrop downward
the New England inducement of the means to "competency," to an
ending of the recession fears of the 1620s and 1630s, to a sense of
economic independence and security, played a magnetic role in the
decision to abandon the overburdened homeland.

The extent of material betterment in the New World depended on a
range of factors, including age, temperament, capital, and, not least,
luck. The issue of a status revolution in the New World is hard to
resolve because status in the Old World is often difficult to discover. In
some cases English status seems to have been deliberately concealed or
downgraded to get past emigration barriers. We have already encountered "husbandmen" like William Payne of Lavenham or Benjamin
Cooper of Brampton who commanded far greater capital than their
given calling usually even dreamed of. Once safely in Watertown, Richard Carver styled himself yeoman, though to the port officer of Yarmouth he had been a mere husbandman.[19] Relatively few mature members of the Great Migration made any very striking gains in New
England. Even William Pynchon, a notable developer of the central
Connecticut Valley, fur trader, store owner, and moneylender of Springfield, Massachusetts, owned only 300 acres when he returned to En-

gland in 1652. Some failed, like the luckless D'Ewes client William Hammond or the ill-served elder Winthrop. Others like William Gault, Michael Metcalfe, William Nickerson, and Francis Lawes failed to thrive as they might have expected.[20] The last three were all weavers who might have suffered financially by leaving the specialized East Anglian industry. However, John Pierce of Watertown and Nicholas Busby of Boston both left "good estates," including their looms. Pierce had 50 yards of cotton shirt fabric, 62 yards of cotton cloth, and 170 skeins of cotton yarn as well as a treble viol and a looking glass in his 1661 inventory of £285. He also had land in Sudbury and Lancaster. Busby, also from Norwich, bequeathed £1,066, including haberdashery, dry goods, and 400 yards of fabrics. He described himself in his 1657 will as a merchant. Our friend John Beale had come from the middle of the old Hingham pecking order, like his Hobart and Cushing neighbors. Leading townsmen like Isaac Pitcher and Thomas Taylor did not emigrate. Beales, Hobarts, and Cushings would never have dominated old Hingham life as they quickly did the new Hingham's. It is likewise hard to imagine Samuel Symonds, 42 when he arrived in Ipswich, scaling heights equivalent to the Massachusetts deputy governorship, if he had remained in Great Yeldham, Essex, or accumulating 1,700 acres of land and an estate worth £2,534. His fellow townsman, Richard Kimball, the wheelwright from Suffolk, did similarly better in the New World, leaving an estate of £737, including 107 acres. Emigration for older men might open up opportunities in both officeholding and wealth, but such status improvement was far from guaranteed. For most, a competency was all they could hope for and probably all they wanted. This older generation of founders did not lack energy, but their efforts went into establishing continuities in the face of change.[21]

For some younger adult immigrants, New England's potential proved larger and the developmental drive more powerful. Arriving in Massachusetts in their twenties or even their teens, men like John Pynchon, John Leverett, the younger Winthrop, William Coddington, Simon Bradstreet, Valentine Hill and other merchants discussed in Chapter 4, Eleazer Lusher, Joshua Fisher, or Thomas Danforth, men of yeoman or artisan stock, were successful entrepreneurs in the wilderness.[22] Some like Pynchon or Leverett were building on foundations laid by parents, and some, notably merchants, were closely allied with London businessmen. A few like William Coddington and the older Richard Bellingham or the humbler Hugh Parsons of Springfield—"eager after the world"—betrayed the "unacceptable face of capitalism" by their acquisitiveness and ruthlessness, but, for many, prosperity came gradually and reflected onerous part-time careers in public service. By the end of the 1650s, they had helped finance the spread of settlement in some 45 towns up and down the coast and along fertile, fur-rich river valleys, organized highly profitable fishing, timber, and shipbuilding industries, raised capital for iron and saltmaking, and developed a sophisticated system of marketing, distribution, and external trade. According to Rutman, such were the complexities of commerce by the time of John Winthrop's death that "Boston wheat might be exchanged in Barbados for sugar delivered in London and credited against an earlier purchase of cloth and metal goods on the promise of delivering the wheat in Barbados."[23]

Men of such energy and drive were only a small minority of emigrants from Greater East Anglia, but the pattern of their success was followed in more modest style by humbler men. John Dane, the struggling tailor, died as a surgeon. John Moulton, the Ormesby husbandman, could bequeath ample farms to his two sons. Of the Hingham settlers, David Grayson Allen has written, "Men who in the East Anglian woods might have spent a lifetime building up a compact farmstead achieved the same thing in Massachusetts in a matter of years." He quotes Samuel Symonds's observation that "the poorer sort (held under in England)" enjoyed "inlargement" of their assets. Even some youths who arrived as servants climbed several rungs up the social ladder, most successfully Joshua Fisher, Jr. For most, the prospects in New England were a marked improvement over day laboring in Greater East Anglia. Luck, ability, help, and opportunity combined to enable considerable numbers of Greater East Anglians to share in the quiet and modest growth of New England's prosperity.[24]

This commitment to "improvement" and evidence of material benefit have led some historians to suggest that religious zeal played a brief or only a window-dressing role for many migrants. Declension began with the first footstep on Boston Dock. Yet, as we have suggested, prosperity and piety were not mutually incompatible. Indeed, in the rolls of most gathered churches, the two went together. Greater East Anglians, from a diversified and market-oriented region of England, saw taming wasteland, building docks, towns, ships, dams, mills, or highways as a God-given duty. They were obliged to work hard in their callings, to provide for their posterity, to husband God's blessings. A competency signaled divine approbation in their providential world, and they habitually accepted the concept that they were only stewards and had responsibilities to their less fortunate fellows. To men and women from the early Stuart eastern counties, poverty meant ignorance, indolence, and impiety. They had needed inducement, "rewards" or "remedies," to loosen their deep-seated roots. Provided concern for this world did not overshadow their hopes for the next, the Greater East Anglians need feel no guilt about their "profits in the wilderness."

Monocausal explanations of motivation are simplistic and unhistorical. "Tools for agriculture and books for religion tossed together in those long sea journeys—a combination in various proportions that has provided the traditional explanation of the Great Migration." Every active decision maker had his or her personal mix of reasons for leaving, not least "means." In a few cases we can infer these complex motivations. John Dane, the tailor, saw life in western Essex as full of temptations. It was also full of tailors. Colonization was in the air of the Barrington estates. The Reverend John Norton, Dane's spiritual mentor, was following his predecessor Roger Williams into exile. Dane's parents were persuaded by biblical revelation, and his brother-in-law was eager to go. Williams had not been able to get a benefice. He had recently married and had blotted his copybook with Joan Lady Barrington. John Fiske was likewise professionally frustrated when his father's death released capital that paid for his young family's passage. The Reverend Samuel Rogers's agonies over whether or not he had a call to New England were cured by an attractive job offer. Nicholas Danforth was a devotee of the Reverend Thomas Shepard. His wife, the mother of his six children, had recently died. His local minister at Framlingham was a threatened reformer. Winthrop's similar indecisions involved a whole raft of considerations. For many worried souls, the fact that, "the times being bad, and good people departing [they] thought to come to New England." The Great Migration acquired its own dynamic.[25]

John Beale has left us no reason why he and his family left. His particular mix of motives, of pulls and pushes, is lost. What we can say with some assurance for him and many of his fellow travelers from Greater East Anglia is that the transatlantic migration was an uncharacteristic uprooting for otherwise sedentary lives in old and New England.

Abbreviations

AgHE, 4	Joan Thirsk, ed., *The Agrarian History of England*, vol. 4 (Cambridge: Cambridge University Press, 1967)
BRS	*British Record Society*
CSPD	*Calendar of State Papers, Domestic*
Colket	Meredith D. Colket, *Founders of Early American Families* (Cleveland: Founders' Project, 1985)
DNB	*Dictionary of National Biography*
Essex Wills	Wills at Chelmsford, *British Record Society* 82 (1966), 86 (1973), 92 (1981)
Ferris	Mary W. Ferris, *Dawes–Gates Ancestral Lines* (Privately printed, 1943), 2 vols.
Hale, House	D. L. Jacobus and E. Waterman, *Hale, House Families* (Baltimore: Genealogical Publishing, 1979)
Lincs Wills	Calendar of Wills Proved at Lincoln, *BRS* 28 (1902), 41 (1910)
MHS Colls	*Massachusetts Historical Society Collections*
NEHGR	*New England Historical Genealogical Register*
NEQ	*New England Quarterly*
Norwich Wills	Index of Wills Proved at Norwich, *Norfolk Record Society* 16 (1943), 21 (1950), 28 (1958), 29 (1959)
PCC	Wills Proved at the Prerogative Court of Canterbury, *BRS* 10 (1893), 11 (1895), 18 (1897), 25 (1901), 43 (1912), 44 (1912)
Roberts	Gary Boyd Roberts, ed., *English Origins of New England Families* (Baltimore: Genealogical Publishing, 1984), 6 vols. in two series
Savage	James Savage, *Genealogical Dictionary of New England* (Boston: Little, Brown, 1860–64)
SPD	Public Record Office: State Papers, Domestic Series
Sudbury Wills	Archdeaconry of Sudbury Probate Records, *BRS* 90 (1979), 91 (1980)
Suffolk Wills	Archdeaconry of Suffolk Probate Records, *BRS* 94 (1984), 95 (1984)
Tyack	N. C. P. Tyack, "Migration from East Anglia to New England, 1620–60" (University of London Ph.D. dissertation, 1951)
Venns	J. and J. A. Venn, *Alumni Cantabrigienses* (Cambridge: Cambridge University Press, 1922), Pt. I, to 1751, 6 vols.

Waters   H. F. Waters, *Genealogical Gleanings in England* (Boston: NEHGS, 1901), 2 vols.

WMQ   *William and Mary Quarterly*

WJ   J. K. Hosmer, ed., *John Winthrop's Journal: History of New England* (New York: Barnes and Noble, 1946), 2 vols.

WP   Allyn P. Forbes, ed., *Winthrop Family Papers* (Boston: MHS, 1929–47), 5 vols.

Wyman   T. B. Wyman, *Charlestown Genealogies and Estates* (Boston: Clapp, 1879)

Notes

Preface

1. M. Halsey Thomas, ed., *The Diary of Samuel Sewall* (New York: Farrar, Straus and Giroux, 1974), 163; Savage; Norwich Wills; Tyack, rev. App. B; *Hobart Genealogy* (n.p., n.d.), chap. 1. Since completing the preface, I have learned from Mrs. Alys Chubbock Monod that Beale was probably born in 1593.

2. *WP*, 2:207, 3:126; Sudbury Wills.

3. See Chapter 5, n. 3, herein.

4. For instance, see the names John Cullick and Edmund Thompson discussed in Chapter 4, n. 10, herein, or William Browne in Chapter 6, n. 30, or Thomas Boyden, Sr. and Jr., in Chapter 9, n. 21.

5. Philip Battell, "William Hammond," *NEHGR* 130 (1976):75–79, and 106 (1952):83–87; W. E. Barton, *Lineage of Lincoln* (Indianapolis: p.p., 1929), Pt. I; J. H. Lea and J. R. Hutchinson, *Lincoln Family* (Boston: p.p., 1909), 3–14; Waldo Lincoln, *History of the Lincoln Family* (Worcester MA: p.p., 1926), chap. 1; J. E. Morris, *Stephen Lincoln* (Hartford: p.p., 1895), passim; B. L. Palcie, *Genealogy of the Robert Lincoln Family* (p.p., 1985), 1–5; G. A. Morrison, *Clarke Families of Rhode Island* (New York: Bland, 1903), chap. 1.

6. *Hale, House*, 550–51.

7. Summarized in P. McC. Morse, *Know Your Ancestors* (p.p., 1967), chap. 1, and B. M. Federico, *Pioneers* (Washington DC: p.p., 1977), 28–32.

8. For example, there are no parish registers or bishops' transcripts for Hingham before 1600, no registers for Southwold before 1603 or for Ormesby before 1670; these were all important catchment areas for emigration. For an ambiguous shipping list, the *Hopewell*'s, see *NEHGR* 14 (1860):304; on New England church records, see Robert G. Pope, *The Half-Way Covenant* (Princeton: Princeton University Press, 1969).

9. Chapter 7, herein.

Chapter 1. Mobility, Migration, and Change

1. George Wilson Pierson, "The M-Factor in American History," *American Quarterly* 14 (1962):275–93; George Rogers Tyler, ed., *The Turner Thesis* (Boston: Heath, 1956).

2. Bernard Bailyn, *Education in the Forming of American Society* (Chapel Hill: University of North Carolina Press, 1960); Louis B. Wright, *The Atlantic Frontier* (New York: Knopf, 1947).

3. Bernard Bailyn, *The Peopling of British North America* (New York: Knopf, 1986), 17–26.

4. E. E. Rich, "The Population of Elizabethan England," *Economic History Review*, 2nd ser. 2 (1950):264–65.

5. Wilbert E. Moore, "The Social Framework of Economic Development," in Ralph Braibanti and Joseph J. Spengler, eds., *Tradition, Values, and Socio-Economic Development* (Chapel Hill: University of North Carolina Press, 1971), 71; Peter Clark and David Souden, eds., *Migration and Society in Early Modern England* (London: Hutchinson, 1987), 29; David Riesman, *The Lonely Crowd* (Garden City, NY: Anchor Doubleday, 1953), 29–30.

6. H. A. Gemery, "Emigration from the British Isles to the New World, 1630–1700," *Research in Economic History* 5 (1980):179–231; E. A. Wrigley and Roger Schofield, *The Population History of England* (London: Routledge, 1981).

7. Bailyn, *Peopling*, chap. 1; J. A. Jackson, ed., *Emigration* (Cambridge: Cambridge University Press, 1969), 3.

8. Clark and Souden, *Migration*, 22; T. D. Bozeman, *To Live Ancient Lives* (Chapel Hill: University of North Carolina Press, 1985); Andrew Delbanco, "The Puritan Errand Re-viewed," *Journal of American Studies* 18 (1986):343–60; Michael Zuckerman, "The Fabrication of Identity in Early America," *WMQ* 34 (1977):194.

9. Clark and Souden, *Migration*, 10.

10. Ibid., 22; C. G. A. Clay, *Economic Expansion and Social Change* (Cambridge: Cambridge University Press, 1984), 2:10, 17, 40.

11. Peter Clark, "Migration to Kentish Towns," in Peter Clark and Paul Slack, eds., *Crisis and Order* (London: Routledge, 1974); A. L. Beier, *Masterless Men* (London: Methuen, 1985); J. F. Pound, *Poverty and Vagrancy in Tudor England* (London: Longmans, 1971); David Souden, "Indentured Servitude in English Migration," in Clark and Souden, *Migration*, 150–71.

12. Clay, *Economic Expansion*, 1:82, 98, 191; Margaret Spufford, *Contrasting Communities* (Cambridge: Cambridge University Press, 1974).

13. E.g., Ralph Hakluyt, "Discourse of Western Planting," in Merrill Jensen, ed., *American Colonial Documents* (London: Eyre and Spottiswood, 1964), 102–6.

14. See Chapter 2, herein.

15. Christopher Hill, *A Nation of Change and Novelty* (London: Routledge, 1990), 42–44, 53, 104; *WP*, 2:91–92, 117–18, 121–23, 130, 142, 146.

16. See Chapter 3, herein.

17. Jack Goody and Ian Watt, "The Consequences of Literacy," in Jack Goody, ed., *Literacy in Traditional Societies* (Cambridge: Cambridge University Press, 1964), 67–68; David D. Hall, *Worlds of Wonder, Days of Judgment* (New York: Knopf, 1989), chap. 1; D. W. Jaffee, "Village Enlightenment," *WMQ* 47 (1990): 327–46; Rous quoted in David Cressy, *Coming Over* (Cambridge: Cambridge University Press, 1987), 8.

18. A. Hassell Smith, "Labourers in Late Sixteenth-Century England," *Continuity and Change* 4 (1989):381; Clark and Souden, *Migration*, 16; Stephen Foster, *Notes from the Caroline Underground* (Hamden CT: Archon, 1978), 47.

19. Clay, *Economic Expansion*, 2:88, 93.

20. Ibid., 1:171.

21. John Berger, *Pig Earth* (London: Writers' Cooperative, 1974), 56, 74–75, 196.

22. Sidney L. Paine, "The English Ancestry of Stephen Paine," *NEHGR* 144 (1989):299.

23. Clark and Souden, *Migration*, 22, 213–14.

24. Roger Thompson, "State of the Art: Early Modern Migration," *Journal of American Studies* 25 (1991):59–69.

Notes to Mobility, Migration, and Change

25. Peter Laslett and John Harrison, "Clayworth and Cogenhoe," in H. E. Bell and R. L. Ollard, eds., *Historical Essays Presented to David Ogg* (London: Black, 1963); Clark and Souden, *Migration*, has further examples, 29, 31, 50, 53, 96, 223, 315; Alan Macfarlane, *The Culture of Capitalism* (Oxford: Blackwell, 1987), 20.

26. E. J. Buckatzsch, "Constancy of Local Population before 1800," *Population Studies* 5 (1951):62–69; Julian Cornwall, "Evidence of Population Mobility in the Seventeenth Century," *Bulletin of the Institute of Historical Research* 40 (1967):142–52; Peter Spufford, "Population Mobility in Seventeenth-Century England," *Local Population Studies* 4 (1970):41–50; Ann Kussmaul, *Servants in Husbandry in Early Modern England* (Cambridge: Cambridge University Press, 1981); W. R. Prest, "Stability and Change in Old and New England," *Journal of Interdisciplinary History* 6 (1976):359–74; Virginia de John, "To Pass beyond the Seas: The Background of East Anglian Emigration to New England, 1620–1660" (University of East Anglia M.A. dissertation, 1978); E. A. Wrigley, "A Simple Model of London's Importance in Changing England's Society and Economy," *Past and Present* 37 (1967):45–63; Clark and Souden, *Migration*, 24–25, 315.

27. John Patten, "Patterns of Migration and Movement of Labour in Three Pre-industrial East Anglian Towns," *Journal of Historical Geography* 2 (1976):111–29.

28. Jeremy Boulton, "Neighbourhood Migration in Early Modern London," and Peter Clark, "Migrants in the City," both in Clark and Souden, *Migration*, 107–49, 270.

29. Keith Wrightson and David Levine, *Poverty and Piety in an English Village: Terling* (London: Academic Press, 1979); Peter Laslett and Karla Oosterveen, "Long-Term Trends in Bastardy in England," *Population Studies* 27 (1973):255–84; Peter Laslett, *Family Life and Illicit Love* (Cambridge: Cambridge University Press, 1977); P. E. H. Hair, "Bridal Pregnancy," *Population Studies* 20 (1966):233–43, and "Bridal Pregnancy Further Examined," ibid., 24 (1970):59–70; Edward Shorter, *The Making of the Modern Family* (London: Panther, 1976); Lawrence Stone, *Family, Sex, and Marriage in England, 1500–1800* (New York: Harper and Row, 1977).

30. Ursula Brumm, "Transfer and Arrival in the Narratives of the First Immigrants to New England," in Winfried Herget and Karl Ortseifen, eds., *The Transit of Civilisation from Europe to America* (Tubingen: Narr, 1986), 29–36; Sacvan Bercovitch, *The Puritan Origins of the American Self* (New Haven: Yale University Press, 1975), 109, 115, chap. 4; Patricia Caldwell, *The Puritan Conversion Narrative* (Cambridge: Cambridge University Press, 1983), 129–30, 135–37; Cressy, *Coming Over*, chap. 5.

31. Kenneth Lockridge, *A New England Town* (New York: Norton, 1970); Michael Zuckerman, *Peaceable Kingdoms* (New York: Knopf, 1970); Philip Greven, *Four Generations* (Ithaca: Cornell University Press, 1970); John Murrin, "Review Article," *History and Theory* 11 (1972):226–75; James Henretta, "The Morphology of New England Society," *Journal of Interdisciplinary History* 2 (1971–72):379–98; David Hackett Fischer, *Growing Old in America* (New York: Oxford University Press, 1977); John Demos, "Old Age in Early New England," in Demos and Sarane Boocock, eds., *Turning Points* (Chicago: Chicago University Press, 1978), 248–87.

32. Sumner Chilton Powell, *Puritan Village* (Middletown CT: Wesleyan University Press, 1963); John Demos, *A Little Commonwealth* (New York: Oxford University Press, 1970); Linda Auwers Bissell, "From One Generation to Another: Windsor CT," *WMQ* 31(1974):79–110; Steven Innes, *Labor in a New Land: Springfield* (Princeton: Princeton University Press, 1983).

33. Innes, *Labor*; Daniel Vickers, "Work and Life on the Fishing Periphery of

Essex County, Massachusetts, 1630–1675," in David D. Hall and David Grayson Allen, eds., *Seventeenth-Century New England* (Boston: Colonial Society of Massachusetts, 1984); Christine Heyrman, *Commerce and Culture: Maritime Communities in Colonial Massachusetts, 1690–1750* (New York: Norton, 1984); Virginia de John Anderson, *New England's Generation* (Cambridge: Cambridge University Press, 1991); John F. Martin, *Profits in the Wilderness* (Chapel Hill: University of North Carolina Press, 1991).

34. Harry S. Stout, "The Morphology of Remigration: New England University Men, 1640–60," *Journal of American Studies* 10 (1975):151–72; Delbanco, "Puritan Errand"; idem, *The Puritan Ordeal* (Cambridge MA: Harvard University Press, 1989).

35. Bailyn, *Education*; Wright, *Atlantic Frontier*.

36. Herbert Baxter Adams, *Germanic Origins of New England Towns* (Baltimore: Johns Hopkins University Press, 1882); Edward Eggleston, *The Transit of Civilization* (Boston: Appleton, 1900); David Grayson Allen, *In English Ways: The Movement of Societies and the Transferal of English Local Law and Custom to Massachusetts in the Seventeenth Century* (Chapel Hill: University of North Carolina Press, 1981); idem, "Both Englands," in Hall and Allen, *Seventeenth-Century New England*; David Hackett Fischer, *Albion's Seed* (New York: Oxford University Press, 1989); N. C. P. Tyack,"The Humbler Puritans of East Anglia and the New England Movement," *NEHGR* 138 (1984):79–106; Kenneth A. Shipps, "Puritan Emigration to New England: A New Source on Motivation," *NEHGR* 135 (1981):83–97; T. H. Breen and Steven Foster, "Moving to the New World," *WMQ* 30 (1973): 189–222; Virginia de John Anderson, "Migrants and Motives," *NEQ* 58 (1986): 339–83.

37. There is a huge scholarly literature on the relationship of puritanism to continuity and change, summarized in Lawrence Stone, *The Past and the Present Revisited* (London: Routledge, 1989), on which this study will touch.

38. Fischer, *Albion's Seed*, and Zuckerman, "Fabrication of Identity," could be cited as deterministic in their approach.

39. Joyce Appleby, "Value and Society," in Jack P. Greene and J. R. Pole, eds., *Colonial British America* (Baltimore: Johns Hopkins University Press, 1984), 305–9; Jack P. Greene, *Pursuits of Happiness* (Chapel Hill: University of North Carolina Press, 1988), 1–80; Allen, *In English Ways*; Darrett B. Rutman, *Winthrop's Boston* (Chapel Hill: University of North Carolina Press, 1965), 274–79; Jon Butler, "Magic, Astrology, and the Early American Religious Heritage," *American Historical Review* 84 (1979):317–46.

Chapter 2. Greater East Anglia

1. Tyack, rev. App. B; John Camden Hotten, *Original Lists of Persons of Quality Who Went to the American Plantations* (Baltimore: Genealogical Publishing, 1962); Charles E. Banks, *Topographical Dictionary of 2,885 English Emigrants to New England* (Philadelphia: Bertram, 1937); idem, *The Winthrop Fleet* (Boston: Houghton Mifflin, 1930); Charles B. Jewson, "Transcription of Three Registers of Passengers, 1637–39," *Norfolk Record Society* 25 (1954); Eben Putnam, "Two Early Passenger Lists, 1635 and 1637," *NEHGR* 75 (1921):221–26; Savage; C. H. Pope, *The Pioneers of Massachusetts* (Boston: Wilson, 1900); *NEHGR* (1846–) is a storehouse of genealogical research.

2. Clive Holmes, "The County Community in Stuart Historiography," *Journal of British History* 19 (1980):66. Tyack's dissertation remains the most thorough and detailed examination of the economic, religious, and political background to East Anglian emigration.

3. Joan Thirsk, "The Farming Regions of England," in *AgHE*, 4:38–62; Eric Kerridge, *The Farmers of Old England* (London: Methuen, 1973), 84–87, 104; idem, *Textile Manufactures in Early-Modern England* (Manchester: Manchester University Press, 1985), 9, 10, 187–93, 201–14, 232; Diarmaid MacCulloch, *Suffolk and the Tudors: Politics and Religion in an English County, 1500–1600* (Oxford: Clarendon, 1987); William Hunt, *The Puritan Moment: The Coming of Revolution in a Puritan County* (Cambridge MA: Harvard University Press, 1983); Clive Holmes, *The Eastern Association in the Civil War* (Cambridge: Cambridge University Press, 1974), 1, 7, 8, 13–21, 46–51, 54–55; idem, ed., "Suffolk Committees for Scandalous Ministers," *Suffolk Record Society* 13 (1970); David Cressy, *Literacy and the Social Order* (Cambridge: Cambridge University Press, 1980), 73; Robert I. Butterfield, "East Anglia, 1645–60" (University of Michigan Ph.D. dissertation, 1981), 2–22, 35, 41, 65, 114; Lord Francis Hervey, ed., *Suffolk in the Seventeenth Century: "The Breviary of Suffolk" by Robert Ryece, 1618* (London: Murray, 1902); Alan Everitt, "Suffolk and the Great Rebellion," *Suffolk Record Society* 3 (1960):8–18, 36; Patrick Collinson, *The Religion of Protestants* (Oxford: Oxford University Press, 1982), 78–258; J. H. Pound, *Tudor and Stuart Norwich* (London: Phillimore, 1988); R. W. Ketton-Cremer, *Norfolk in the Civil War* (Hamden CT: Archon, 1970); Peter King, "Bishop Wren and the Suppression of the Norwich Lecturers," *Historical Journal* 11 (1968):237–54; John T. Horton, "Two Bishops and the Holy Brood," *NEQ* 40 (1967):339–63.

4. J. T. Cliffe, *The Puritan Gentry: The Great Families of Early Stuart England* (London: Routledge, 1984), chap. 5; *WP*, 2:239.

5. Thirsk, "Farming Regions," 38–62; Kerridge, *Farmers*, chap. 1.

6. Kerridge, *Textile Manufactures*; K. J. Allison, "The Norfolk Worsted Industry," *Yorkshire Bulletin of Economic and Social Research* 12 (1960):73–83, and 13 (1961):61–77.

7. Allen, *In English Ways*, 117–18; Cliffe, *Puritan Gentry*, 63; Anderson, *New England's Generation*, 28–30.

8. Spufford, *Contrasting Communities*, 65–85; Kerridge, *Farmers*, 89–94; Allen, *In English Ways*, 57–61.

9. W. K. Jordan, *The Charities of Rural England* (London: Allen and Unwin, 1961), 92, 150–54, 196–97; Cressy, *Literacy and the Social Order*, chap. 3.

10. Collinson, *Religion of Protestants*, 67–80; Allen, *In English Ways*, 9–10, 88, 172; Hunt, *Puritan Moment*; Holmes, "County Community," 68–73; Mark Spurrell, *The Puritan Town of Boston* (Boston: Kay, 1972), 10; Cliffe, *Puritan Gentry*, 12, 94–101; Cressy, *Coming Over*, 132–34; Henry Swinden, *The History and Antiquities of Great Yarmouth* (Norwich: Crouse, 1772), 7–10.

11. Holmes, "County Community," 73; *NEHGR* 36 (1882):327.

12. Peter Bowden, "Agricultural Prices, Farm Profits, and Rents," in *AgHE*, 4, 676–79; Hunt, *Puritan Moment*, 160–74, 235–50; Tyack, 102–68, 196–223; Clay, *Economic Expansion*, 1:18; Allen, *In English Ways*, 174, 187.

13. *WP*, 2:118, and cf. 91, 123–24, 133–34, 141. Emigrants would have suffered a series of lean years rather than starvation.

14. Tyack, "Migration," chap. 1; Robert C. Anderson, "A Note on the Changing Pace of the Great Migration," *NEQ* 109 (1986):406–7.

15. E.g., Anderson, *New England's Generation*; Breen and Foster, "Moving to the New World," and Cressy, *Coming Over*, 65–73.

16. Michelle Leung, "New England's Call" (University of Western Ontario M.A. dissertation, 1991). My thanks to David Flaherty.

17. The ratio of artisans to farmers in England in 1688—the famous Gregory King calculation—was 1 : 7 + ; the emigrant ratio is −2 : 1, but if half the unknowns

were added the ratio would change to 1 : 1.4. For other English socioeconomic ratios, see Peter Laslett, *The World We Have Lost* (London: Methuen, 1971), 36–37.

18. Breen and Foster, "Moving to the New World," 194–98; Anderson, "Migrants and Motives," 347–59.

19. See Chapter 6, "Servants," herein.

20. Cressy, *Coming Over*, 66, Table 1. Converted to my categories, his full occupational list reads: Gents 0%, Mercantile 2%, Professional 2%, Entrepreneurs 2%, Artisans 47%, Farmers 22%, Servants 25%. Cf. Leung, "New England's Call," 154, Table 5–8: Artisans 36%, Farmers 10%, Gents 1%, Servants 43%.

Chapter 3. The Better Sort

1. J. A. Sharpe, *Early Modern England: A Social History, 1550–1760* (London: Arnold, 1987), 127–51, has an excellent survey; T. M. Breen, *The Character of a Good Ruler* (New York: Norton, 1974), chaps. 1, 2.

2. J. H. Hexter, "Storm over the Gentry," in idem, *Reappraisals in History* (London: Longmans, 1961); Cliffe, *Puritan Gentry*; G. E. Mingay, *The Gentry* (London: Longmans, 1976). Sir Thomas Barrington had invested the enormous sum of £1,025 in the Providence Island Company by 1633; Cliffe, *Puritan Gentry*, 117.

3. A. W. Simpson, *The Wealth of the Gentry* (Cambridge: Cambridge University Press, 1961), 216; Overbury quoted in Kerridge, *Farmers*, 66; cf. T. B. Macauley, *History of England* (London: Dent, 1906), 1:216, on "The English esquire of the seventeenth century . . . His ignorance and uncouthness, his low tastes and gross phrases . . . indicating a nature and a breeding thoroughly plebeian . . . a man with the deportment, the vocabulary and the accent of a carter."

4. *WP*, vol. 1, "Introduction" and passim, 2:1–233; Edmund S. Morgan, *The Puritan Dilemma: The Story of John Winthrop* (Boston: Little, Brown, 1958), 3–53; Richard S. Dunn, *Puritans and Yankees* (New York: Norton, 1971), 3–57; Samuel Eliot Morison, *Builders of the Bay Colony* (Boston: Houghton Mifflin, 1958), 51–104; Allen, *In English Ways*, 123.

5. Great Stambridge was four miles from the family lands of John's mother at Prittlewell.

6. See Table 27, no. 53, for his kinship links with emigrant families.

7. *WP*, 2:106.

8. Ibid., 133.

9. Ibid., 1:18; 289; Cressy, *Coming Over*, 217: Winthrop received 93 letters from England during the 1630s.

10. F. J. Simmons, *Emmanuel Downing* (p.p., 1958). Downing (1585–1660) appears frequently as a correspondent in *WP*.

11. Three children by this wife, Anne (Ware), went to Massachusetts prior to their father: James in 1630, Mary and Susan in 1633. *WP*, 3:75–76, 82, 113, 376–77.

12. Francis Kirby and John Goad, skinners, and Richard Hill, merchant.

13. George probably obtained a post for his father in Scotland from Cromwell.

14. The letter is addressed from Layer Marney in Essex.

15. J. L. Chester, "Herbert Pelham," *NEHGR* 133 (1979):284–96; *DNB* cites Herbert and other members of the Pelham family. The Pelhams were related to the Winthrops through Margaret (Tyndal), whom Herbert described as "my cosen your wife." *WP*, 3:228. He was also the brother-in-law of John Humphrey. After Elizabeth (Pelham) Humphrey died, Humphrey, deputy governor of the Massachusetts Bay Company in 1629, married Lady Susannah Fiennes-Clinton in 1626, thus

becoming the brother-in-law of Isaac Johnson and the earl of Lincoln. Humphrey (1596–1653) was a Dorset man by birth, a collaborator with the Reverend John White as treasurer of the Dorchester Company in 1624, and subsequently a member of the earl of Lincoln's circle at Sempringham. When John Winthrop, Jr., took his party to embark for New England in 1631, they stayed at Humphrey's house, "The Dolphin," at Sandwich, Kent.

16. *WP*, 2:222.

17. *WJ*, 2:43–44. "Mr. Walgrave," an absentee proprietor, had 25 acres of meadow in Sudbury MA. Powell, *Puritan Village*, 153. Holmes, "County Community," 57.

18. *Hale, House*; Waters, 2:861; *NEHGR* 94 (1940):387; *MHS Colls*, 5th ser. 6:369; John H. Upton, *A History of Writtle Church* (p.p., 1930), 72–78; Joseph M. Smith, *Pynchon Court Record*, 6–9; Innes, *Labor*, 3–5. My thanks to the Reverend Peter Nokes, vicar of Writtle.

19. Simmons, *Downing*, 11; *WP*, 3:75–76; *MHS Colls*, 5th ser. 1:203 n.

20. Dunn, *Puritans and Yankees*, 59–187; R. C. Black, *The Younger John Winthrop* (New York: Columbia University Press, 1966), 1–40; John Jr.'s early career can be followed in *WP*, 1 and 2.

21. *WP*, 1:333, 338, 357, 382, 2:66, 79, 84, 94. Henry, who drowned in Massachusetts in 1630, had caused his father considerable heartache and outrage, especially by his illicit and impetuous marriage with Elizabeth Fones in 1629.

22. J. H. Adamson and H. F. Folland, *Sir Harry Vane: His Life and Times (1613–1662)* (Boston: Gambit, 1973), 3–120; *DNB*.

23. *NEHGR* 8 (1854):359–62; Waters, 2:1032–33.

24. Winifred Lovering Holman, "Notes on the Appletons," ms in NEHG Library, 101 Newbury Street, Boston. *WP* 3:2, 346; *NEHGR* 39 (1885):66, 67, 56 (1902):184, 57 (1903):219; Harry Clive, *Beyond Living Memory* (Little Waldingfield: p.p., 1979), 4–9.

25. Waters, 2:957; *NEHGR* 94 (1940):74–78, 95 (1941):69–71.

26. Sir Anthony Wagner, "A New Harlakenden Line," *NEHGR* 120 (1966):1–15.

27. J. B. Threlfall, *The Ancestry of Thomas Bradbury* (p.p., 1988); Roberts, 2nd ser. 3:742.

28. Warner F. Gookin, "The Ancestry of Bartholomew Gosnold," *NEHGR* 115 (1961):5–22, Gookin and Philip Barbour, *Bartholomew Gosnold* (Hamden CT: Archon, 1963), 36–48.

29. Waters, 1:96; *Hale, House*.

30. Waters, 2:896–97.

31. Samuel Appleton, for instance, was related to the Crane, Spring, Mountney, Ryece, Rookwood, Sexton, and Gurdon families. Appletons owned land in Kersey, Groton, Great and Little Waldingfield, Capel, Glemsford, Chilton, all in Suffolk, and in Great Canfield, Essex.

32. Of those known, 47 percent were born at or within four miles of their family roots, 69 percent within nine miles; similarly, 69 percent lived in adult life within four miles of their birthplaces.

33. Eleven were eldest sons, 10 younger, and 15 unknown. Cf. Martin H. Quitt, "The Immigrant Origins of the Virginia Gentry," *WMQ* 45 (1988):632–35.

34. Winthrop and Haynes were frequently governors; from their base in Springfield, Pynchons ran the Massachusetts territory in the Connecticut Valley for most of the seventeenth century; Innes, *Labor*. Pelham was treasurer of Harvard College (1643) and an assistant (1645); Chester, "Herbert Pelham," 291–92; Powell, *Puritan Village*, 115, 153, 157, 160, 210. Humphrey, like Winthrop, Pelham, and

Pynchon, had been a member of the Massachusetts Bay Company in England and brought £2,000 and supplies to Massachusetts in 1634. He was sergeant-major-general of the colony in 1641; Frederick Humphreys, *Humphreys Family* (New York: p.p., 1883).

35. Morgan, *Puritan Dilemma*, 175; Bernard Bailyn, *The New England Merchants in the Seventeenth Century* (New York: Harper, 1964), chap. 1; Dunn, *Puritans and Yankees*, 56; *WJ*, 1:169–72; Rutman, *Winthrop's Boston*, 76, 81, 173.

36. Dunn, *Puritans and Yankees*, 60, 62, 64, 106–7, 130–31, 142, 168, 169–71, 201; Black, *Younger Winthrop*, 248–56; *WP*, 3:101, 141, 292; Mitchell Robert Breitwieser, *Cotton Mather and Benjamin Franklin* (Cambridge: Cambridge University Press, 1984), 136, 144, 145–52, 165, 188, 240, 291; Martin, *Profits*, 22, 53–56.

37. Innes, *Labor*, 3–18, 29, 147.

38. Allen, *In English Ways*, chap. 5, 184. Other East Anglians in Ipswich were William Hubbard, Thomas Dudley, Simon Bradstreet, Samuel Symonds, Giles Firmin, the Whipple brothers, William Payne, and Dr. John Ward; Edward S. Perzel, "First Generation of Settlement in Colonial Ipswich" (Rutgers University Ph.D. dissertation, 1967).

39. Bailyn, *New England Merchants*, chaps. 2, 3.

40. Most of Martin's expansionists flourished in the period after 1660; *Profits*, passim.

41. The standard biographical dictionaries for clergy such as Venns; S. E. Morison, *Founding of Harvard College* (Cambridge MA: Harvard University Press, 1936), App. B; F. L. Weis, *Colonial Clergy of New England* (Baltimore: Genealogical Publishing, 1977); Savage; and *DNB* are not cited and should be taken as read. Darrett Rutman, *American Puritanism* (New York: Norton, 1977); Breen, *Character of a Good Ruler*, 37–47.

42. Rosemary O'Day, *The English Clergy: The Emergence and Consolidation of a Profession, 1558–1642* (Leicester: Leicester University Press, 1979); Michael Hawkins, "Ambiguity and Contradiction in the 'Rise of Professionalism': The English Clergy, 1570–1730," in A. L. Beier, David Cannadine, and J. M. Rosenhaim, eds., *The First Modern Society: Historical Essays for Lawrence Stone* (Cambridge: Cambridge University Press, 1989), 241–70.

43. Keith Wrightson, "The Puritan Reformation of Manners" (Cambridge University Ph.D. dissertation, 1973); Larzer Ziff, *The Career of John Cotton: Puritanism and the American Experience* (Princeton: Princeton University Press, 1962), 43–46. Frank Shuffelton, *Thomas Hooker* (Princeton: Princeton University Press, 1972), 71; Collinson, *Religion of Protestants*, 63–68; Arthur Searle, ed., "Barrington Family Papers," *Camden Society*, 4th ser. 28 (1983):63–68; W. J. Sheils, "Puritans and the Diocese of Peterborough," *Northampton Record Society* 30 (1979):100; Cliffe, *Puritan Gentry*, 44, 78; Allen, *In English Ways*, 197.

44. Morison, *Builders of the Bay Colony*, 217–43; Roberts, 2:3, 617; Michael McGiffert, ed., *God's Plot: . . . Autobiography and Journal of Thomas Shepard* (Amherst: University of Massachusetts Press, 1972), 7–8; Raymond P. Stearns, *The Strenuous Puritan . . . Hugh Peter* (Urbana: University of Illinois Press, 1954), 89–90.

45. *CSPD*, 1634–35, 537–39; Everett Emerson, ed., *Letters from New England: Massachusetts Bay Colony, 1629–38* (Amherst: University of Massachusetts Press, 1976), 180; *WJ*, 1:328; *WP* 3:390, 4:86.

46. Morison, *Founding of Harvard*, 226–41; *WJ*, 1:310–14; *WP*, 4:142–43.

47. See Chapter 6, herein. Some children of ministers who emigrated had similarly shallow English roots, e.g., James and Samuel Eddy, Henry Goldstone, Michael Metcalfe, Samuel Morse, Simon Bradstreet, and John Newcomen.

48. G. A. Moriarty, "Bernard of Epworth," *NEHGR* 113 (1959):189; ibid., 43 (1889):299, 317, 445; *WP*, 3:237, 240; James W. Jones, *The Shattered Synthesis* (New Haven: Yale University Press, 1973), 3–31.

49. Ola E. Winslow, *John Eliot* (Boston: Houghton Mifflin, 1968), 18–22; *NEHGR* 107 (1953):245–57; Waters, 2:904.

50. Wyman; Ralph J. Crandall and Ralph J. Coffman, "From Emigrants to Rulers: The Charlestown Oligarchy in the Great Migration," *NEHGR* 131 (1977):8.

51. Norwich Wills.

52. J. Wentworth, *Wentworth Genealogy* (Boston: p.p., 1878), 72–74; Roberts, 2nd ser. 3:723–4.

53. J. R. S. Whiting, "Rev. Samuel Whiting," *NEHGR*, 123 (1969), 161–8.

54. Roberts, 2nd ser. 3:19–37; John Rogers dedicated his influential *Doctrine of Love* (1627) to, inter alios, Muriel Gurdon.

55. Kenneth W. Shipps, "Lay Patronage of East Anglian Clerics" (Yale University Ph.D. dissertation, 1971); Richard Waterhouse, "Reluctant Emigrants: The New England Clergy," *Historical Magazine of the Protestant Episcopal Church* 44 (1975):481.

56. David Cressy, "Social Composition of Caius College, Cambridge, 1580–1640," *Past and Present* 47 (1970):114–18.

57. J. S. Ibish, "Emmanuel College" (Harvard University Ph.D. dissertation, 1985); Rebecca S. Rolfe, "Emmanuel College and the Puritan Movement in Old and New England" (University of Southern California Ph.D. dissertation, 1979); Cliffe, *Puritan Gentry*, 94–97, 100–101.

58. C. F. Robinson, *Weld Collections* (p.p., 1938); John Winthrop, Sr., John Humphrey, and Charles Chauncy were also Trinity men.

59. *WP*, 1:243–47; Nesta Evans, ed., "Wills of the Archdeaconry of Suffolk, 1630–35," *Suffolk Record Society* 29 (1987):627; Paul S. Seaver, *The Puritan Lectureships* (Stanford: Stanford University Press, 1970).

60. Laud was promoted from the bishopric of London (which covered Essex) to the archbishopric of Canterbury in 1633; his enthusiastic adjutant, Matthew Wren, became bishop of Norwich (which covered Norfolk and Suffolk) in 1636. John Williams, the anti-Laudian bishop of Lincoln, was suspended in 1637. Horton, "Two Bishops," 356–63.

61. Stout, "Morphology of Remigration," 151–72.

62. *NEHGR* 42 (1888):27; *MHS Colls*, 4th ser. 1:100 n.

63. A. G. Matthews, ed., *Calamy Revised* (Oxford: Clarendon, 1934), 425; *NEHGR* 45 (1891):234, 62 (1908):168.

64. *NEHGR* 57 (1903):197; *MHS Colls*, 3rd ser. 10:170.

65. *MHS Colls*, 3rd ser. 10:169–70, and 4th ser. 8:590–91; Roberts, 2nd ser. 3:901.

66. Seven were sons of merchants or entrepreneurs, eight of yeomen; three came from gentle families, nine from clerical.

67. Skelton, George Phillips, Williams, Wilson, Eliot, Weld; *WP*, 1:102–17; *WJ*, 1:165, 168, 178; Morison, *Builders of the Bay Colony*, 21–50, 235; Shipps, "Puritan Emigration," 86.

68. Southold, Long Island; Sudbury; Wenham and Chelmsford, Massachusetts.

69. David D. Hall, *The Faithful Shepherd* (New York: Norton, 1974), 121–57.

70. Waterhouse, "Reluctant Emigrants," 478–79, 482; Michael Walzer, "Puritanism as a Revolutionary Ideology," *History and Theory* 3 (1961):59–90.

71. Jesper Rosenmeier, "John Cotton on Usury," *WMQ* 47 (1990):548–65; Harry S. Stout, *The New England Soul* (New York: Oxford University Press, 1986), 1–66.

72. The case for the deep-seated traditionalism of the clergy has most recently been made by John Morgan, *Godly Learning* (Cambridge: Cambridge University Press, 1986), esp. 90–96.

73. Waterhouse, "Reluctant Emigrants," 485–86.

74. Fifteen had fallen afoul of the church courts, and three cited the 1633 reissue of the Book of Sports as the last straw.

Chapter 4. The Enterprising Sort

1. In the tradition of Marx and Weber, the great British exponents of this view have been R. H. Tawney, *Religion and the Rise of Capitalism* (London: Murray, 1929), and Christopher Hill, *Century of Revolution* (London: Nelson, 1961); cf. Greene, *Pursuits of Happiness*, 7–27; Perry Miller, *The New England Mind: From Colony to Province* (Boston: Beacon, 1956).

2. Frances Rose-Troup, *The Massachusetts Bay Company* (New York: Grafton, 1930); N. B. Shurtleff, ed., *The Records of the Massachusetts Bay Company*, vol. 1 (Boston: White, 1853); Bernard Bailyn, ed., *The Apologia of Robert Keayne* (New York: Harper, 1965); Rutman, *Winthrop's Boston*.

3. Bailyn, *New England Merchants*; Dunn, *Puritans and Yankees*.

4. Totals exceed 54 because some followed dual callings.

5. Allen, Coytmore, Hill, Hills, Newgate, Scott, Vassall.

6. The only rural exceptions are Coggeshall, Cullick, Knapp, and Scott.

7. Friedrich Tonnies, *Community and Society* (New York: Harper, 1963); Thomas Bender, *Community and Social Change in America* (Baltimore: Johns Hopkins University Press, 1982).

8. *WP*, 3:22; *NEHGR* 36 (1882):123–27; Spurrell, *Puritan Town*, 12; A. J. Willett, *Willett Families* (p.p., 1985), 1–6; *NEHGR* 61 (1907):157–59.

9. On Coytmore, see Chapter 5, herein. C. H. Calder, "Alderman John Vassall," *NEHGR* 109 (1955):91–98; Waters, 2:1319; *WP*, 2:153n, 265n, 276.

10. Thompson was the son of John and Anne (Hastings) Thompson of Holkham, north Norfolk. However, his wife was the sister of John Fiske of South Elmham, Suffolk. The name was common in Great Yarmouth and northeast Suffolk and was also that of a Norwich fish merchant family. There may be elision here. Cullick, identified with both Felsted and Upminster 35 miles to the south on equally persuasive evidence, may likewise be two different emigrants, or there may be a link between two branches of the family.

11. Of those with known birth- and workplaces (34 out of 51), 66 percent had either stayed put or moved less than four miles.

12. Knapp's trade is based on his being convicted by the General Court on 1 March 1631 for selling a cure for scurvy which proved worthless. Edmund S. Morgan, ed., *The Founding of Massachusetts* (Indianapolis: Bobbs-Merrill, 1964), 402.

13. Alan Everitt, "The Marketing of Agricultural Produce," *AgHE*, 4:467, 474–78, 588.

14. Ibid., 489, 537, 543; Clay, *Economic Expansion*, 1:170–71.

15. T. S. Willan, *The English Coasting Trade, 1600–1750* (Manchester: Manchester University Press, 1938); Neville Williams, "Maritime Trade of the East Anglian Ports" (Oxford University Ph.D. dissertation, 1953); David Beers Quinn, *England and the Discovery of America* (London: Allen and Unwin, 1974), 199–200; D. W. Waters, *The Art of Navigation* (London: 1958), 111; Ralph Davis, *English Merchant Shipping and the Dutch Rivalry of the Seventeenth Century* (Greenwich: National Maritime Museum, 1975), 1, 7–8; George Selement and Bruce Woolley, eds.,

Thomas Shepard Confessions (Boston: Colonial Society of Massachusetts, 1981), 110–13; Patten, "Patterns of Migration," 97.

16. See Table 27, no. 10, herein. The Fosters of Ipswich had mariner relatives in Aldburgh, and the Scarlets had branches in Lowestoft, Ipswich, and Southwold; Suffolk Wills.

17. *NEHGR* 98 (1944):66–72, 101 (1947):292; Bailyn, *New England Merchants*, 80.

18. Norwich Wills.

19. *NEHGR* 52 (1898):42–44; Edward E. Hale, ed., *Notebook Kept by Thomas Lechford, 1638–41* (Cambridge MA: Wilson, 1885), 18–19; *WP*, 4:161.

20. NEHGR 56 (1902):183; Sudbury Wills, IC 500/1/77 (116), IC 500/1/87 (12).

21. NEHGR 99 (1945):285–96, 57 (1903):402–3, 100 (1946):14.

22. Millses, four miles from Cockfield to Lavenham; Paynes, four miles from Lawshall to Lavenham; Welds, four miles from Long Melford to Sudbury, all in Suffolk; and Whittinghams, six miles from Swinehead to Sutterton, Lincolnshire.

23. E. A. Wrigley, "Simple Model of London's Importance"; see also nn. 19 and 9 to this chapter.

24. *NEHGR* 37 (1883):106; R. J. Allen, *Valentine Hill Genealogy* (Mandarin FL: p.p., 1973), 1–6; Bailyn, *New England Merchants*, 35.

25. B. F. Wilbore, "English Ancestry of Samuel Wilbore," *NEHGR* 112 (1958): 108, 250–55, 113 (1959):55–60, 98–103.

26. Three came from gentle backgrounds, one clerical, and one from the yeomanry.

27. See Chapter 6, "Selected Women Emigrants," herein.

28. Angier–Sparhawk, Payne–Hammond, Hough–Whittingham, Scott–Hutchinson, Sherman–Sparhawk. See Table 27, herein.

29. Wade's father, Thomas, had invested £50 in the Massachusetts Bay Company. Wade's own estate was worth £7,859 in 1684; Wyman.

30. Hills had £33 in the joint stock. W. S. Hill and T. Hill, *Hill Family* (New York: p.p., 1906); J. W. Hill, *Genealogy of Isaac Hill* (p.p., 1927).

31. Paine's father-in-law, John Whiting, a mercer of Hadleigh, Suffolk, lent him £100 and bequeathed him a house. *NEHGR* 50 (1896):126, 7; H. D. Paine, *Paine Family Records* (p.p., 1880–83).

32. Symonds bought John Winthrop, Jr.'s farm "Argilla" in Ipswich in 1637. He left £2,534 in 1678; *WP*, 3:518, 4:12.

33. Hill, who had liberal credit from his brother John in London, left £2,532; Bailyn, *New England Merchants*, 35.

34. Mills, £211; Knight, £164; Loomis, £178; Whipple, £114.

35. *NEHGR* 106 (1952):83–87. Henry Dade, Laud's commissary in Suffolk, wrote on 4 February 1634 about the connection between the depression and emigration: "As soon as any one purpose to break [go bankrupt] he may fly to New England and be accounted a religious man"; *CSPD*, 1633–34, 450–51.

36. Allen (West Indies), Brown (fish), Coytmore (shipmaster, £1,266), Davison (agent, West Indies, Maine, England, money-lending, £1,896), Hill (Maine, fish, fur, £2,532), Leeds, (fish, £963), Symonds (fur, £2,534), Wade (£7,859), Weld (England, £2,028), Whiting (fur, £2,854), Willett (fur, £2,798); Coytmore, Weld, and Whiting survived only to the 1640s; the rest had business careers lasting 30 to 50 years.

37. Rutman, *Winthrop's Boston*, 138, 194–95, 199; Bailyn, *New England Merchants*, 35–36, 84.

38. Allen, *In English Ways*, 117–45; Martin, *Profits*, 52–53.

39. Coddington, Coggeshall, Harding, Sales, Scott, Throckmorton, Wilbore. Martin, *Profits*, 125.

40. *WJ*, 2:271; Jack P. Greene, ed., *Settlements to Society* (New York: Norton, 1966), 90, 102–3.

41. Bailyn, *New England Merchants*, 44, 105–10. Miller, *New England Mind*, investigates the puritan idea of declension, of which the undermining of spiritual values by materialistic drives is a major ingredient.

42. William Pynchon's *Meritorious Price of Christ's Redemption* (1650) is discussed in Morison, *Builders of the Bay Colony*, 369–75.

43. Rutman, *Winthrop's Boston*, 223.

44. Sons: Firmin, Allen, Hough, Whittingham; kin: Angier, Brown, Mills, Sparhawk, Youngs, Weld.

45. *NEHGR* 56 (1902):183; *WP*, 2:276, 3:22; Ferris; Martin, *Profits*, 118, 124; Leung, "New England's Call," 22.

46. Selement and Woolley, *Shepard Confessions*, 63–64, 113.

47. Heyrman, *Commerce and Culture*, 12–18, 203; Martin, *Profits*, 111; Vickers, "Work on the Fishing Periphery," 84–89; Greene, *Settlements to Society*, 75, 94; James Lemon, "Spatial Order," in Greene and Pole, *Colonial British America*, 98–110; Jordan, *Charities*, passim.

48. Anderson, *New England's Generation*, 44, 123, 125, 175, 189, 203; Everitt, "Marketing," 467, 499; Paul Seaver, "The Protestant Work Ethic Revisited," *Journal of British Studies* 19 (1980):35–53; Rutman, *Winthrop's Boston*, 180.

49. Elizabeth Wade White, "The Tenth Muse," *WMQ* 8 (1951): 357.

50. Dunn, *Puritans and Yankees*, 134–41, 146–47; Colket, 68; Morrison, *Clarke Families*; *NEHGR* 75 (1921):273, 279–80.

51. E. G. Sanford, "Early Years of John Sanford," *NEHGR* 114 (1960):83; Moriarty, "John Sanford in New England," *NEHGR* 103 (1949):189–97; *NEHGR* 105 (1951): 304–7.

52. Morison, *Founding of Harvard*, 157.

53. Sharpe, *Early Modern England*, 190–92; G. S. Holmes, *Augustan England: Professions, State, and Society, 1680–1730* (London: Allen and Unwin, 1982).

54. John Demos, ed., *Remarkable Providences* (New York: Braziller, 1972), 79–88; *NEHGR* 96 (1942):298.

55. Dudley: *WP*, 3:6, 37; Cotton Mather, *Magnalia Christi Americana* (New York: Russell, 1967), 132–35; Emerson, *Letters*, 66–83. Bradstreet: *NEHGR* 65 (1911):69–74; Masters: Emerson, *Letters*, 83–85.

56. Bridge: W. D. Bridge, *Genealogy of the John Bridge Family* (Cambridge MA: Murray, 1924), 1–12; McGiffert, *God's Plot*, 55; Rayne Workers Education Association, *Rayne* (Rayne: p.p., 1977), 37. Corlett: Morison, *Founding of Harvard*, 373; Powell: Michael G. Hall, *Increase Mather* (Middletown CT: Wesleyan University Press, 1988), 39–40.

57. C. W. Brooks, *Pettyfoggers and Vipers of the Commonwealth* (Cambridge: Cambridge University Press, 1986); G. L. Haskins, *Law and Authority in Colonial Massachusetts* (New York: Macmillan, 1960), 186.

58. Tyndal: F. L. Weis, *Ancestral Lines of Sixty Families* (Baltimore: Genealogical Publishing, 1976); Waters, 2:1035. Leverett: A. M. Cook, "Boston Migrants to Massachusetts," *Lincolnshire Magazine* 2 (1949):305. Bellingham: Spurrell, *Puritan Town*, 12–15; Pishey Thompson, *History of Boston* (Boston: Noble, 1856), 428–29; Mather, *Magnalia*, 137; *WP*, 4:71.

59. The Reverend Simon Bradstreet, Sr. (*c*1565–1621), was born at Gislingham near Diss, Norfolk, and served a cure at nearby Hinderclay before moving to Horbling near the earl of Lincoln's seat at Sempringham in 1596. Dudley's father,

Captain Roger, was killed at the Battle of Ivry in 1590. Thomas (1574–1653) served with the Protestant army of Henri IV of France and was a page to the earl of Lincoln before becoming steward in 1619.

60. Kerridge, *Textile Manufactures*, 9–17, 187–93, 201–14.

61. Coe: Ferris; *NEHGR* 52 (1898), 65; Peter Northeast, ed., "Boxford Church-wardens' Accounts," *Suffolk Records Society*, 23 (1982):85. Fitch: R. C. Fitch, *History of the Fitch Family* (p.p., n.d.), 5–17; Waters, 1:593; C. Poteet, "Fitch Ancestry," *NEHGR* 133 (1979):91–105. Hutchinson: *NEHGR* 20 (1866):355–67; Thomas Hutchinson, *The History of the Colony and Province of Massachusetts-Bay*, ed. Lawrence Shaw Mayo (Cambridge MA: Harvard University Press, 1936), 1:49–50, 62–65. Sherman: Roberts, 2nd ser. 3:209–21; Waters, 2:1166–67, 1171, 1188.

62. Mills, Collins, Goodwin, Gosse, Guttridge, Hawkins, Marsh, Nichols, Scott, Doggett, Biggs, Morse.

63. Stacey: Ferris; Roberts, 2nd ser. 3:296.

64. Warner: F. F. Starr, *Ancestral Lines of James Goodwin* (Hartford: Brown and Gross, 1915), 38–42; L. C. Warner, *Descendants of Andrew Warner* (New Haven: Tuttle, Morehouse and Taylor, 1919), 3–7.

65. *Discovering Bradford Street* (Bocking: Friends of Bradford Street, 1977), unpaginated; I am indebted to Mr. Dixon Smith for lending me Xerox copies of Lyons Hall papers, 1548–1678.

66. Metcalfe: *NEHGR* 16 (1862):184–89, 78 (1924):63–65, 80 (1926):312–13; Breen and Foster, "Moving to the New World," 203; Ketton-Cremer, *Norfolk*, 78–79; Kerridge, *Textile Manufactures*, 189. Underwood: *MHS Colls*, ser. 10 (1839):158; Nesta Evans, *The East Anglian Linen Industry* (Aldershot: Gower, 1985).

67. Selement and Woolley, *Shepard Confessions*, 86–88; *MHS Colls*, 6th ser. 4 (1865):7–11. Stansby's uncle was vicar of Westhorpe, Suffolk, and a correspondent of John Wilson.

68. John Sherman, John Cotton, and John Fiske.

69. Tyack, "Migration," 187–223; Pound, *Norwich*, 112, shows that by far the highest vagrancy totals occurred in the periods 1600–22 and 1625–45. Breen and Foster, "Moving to the New World," 201–22; Anderson, "Migrants and Motives," 369–81; Bailyn, *New England Merchants*, 71–74.

70. Rutman, *Winthrop's Boston*, 192–93, 247; Allen, "Both Englands," 68–69; Martin, *Profits*, 52–53.

71. Innes, *Labor*, 32; Rutman, *Winthrop's Boston*, 31, 73, 74, 80; Martin, *Profits*, 57–58, 90–96, 106, 261; James Poteet, "More Yankee than Puritan: James Fitch," *NEHGR* 133 (1979):102–16; Bailyn, *New England Merchants*, 80.

Chapter 5. The Industrious Sort: Artisans and Farmers

1. Greene, *Settlements to Society*, 8; Mark Kishlansky, "Community and Continuity," *WMQ* 37 (1980):145.

2. Whittington (1358–1423) was in fact the younger son of a Gloucestershire knight. The myth was popular in the seventeenth century; see Roger Thompson, ed., *Samuel Pepys' "Penny Merriments"* (London: Constable, 1976), 54–55, 60–64, 281; R. H. Tawney, *Business and Politics under James I: Lionel Cranfield as Merchant and Minister* (Cambridge: Cambridge University Press, 1958), 11.

3. J. T. Gilbert, *Toppan Family History* (p.p., 1969), 1–6; Roberts, 2nd ser. 3:507–8. On links between Yorkshire and Norfolk cloth industries, see Patten, "Patterns of Migration," 93.

4. Margaret Spufford, *Small Books and Pleasant Histories* (London: Methuen, 1981), 182–83; Thompson, *Penny Merriments*, 200–208.

5. Leager: *NEHGR* 59 (1905):353–55. Pingry: R. and J. Carpenter, *Pengry Family* (Coon Rapids IA: p.p., 1979), 3–9; idem, *Pengry Genealogy* (p.p., 1984).

6. L. Keyser, *Keyser Family* (Portland ME: p.p., 1983), 2–4; *NEHGR* 41 (1887):55; Clay, *Economic Expansion*, 1:183.

7. G. A. Moriarty, "English Connection of Thomas Felbrigg," *NEHGR* 108 (1954):252–58; Alan Macfarlane, *Diary of Ralph Josselin* (London: British Academy, 1976), 697.

8. Walter Rye, ed., *L'Estrange's Calendar of Norwich Freemen* (Norwich: p.p., 1888); Percy Millican, ed., *Register of Freemen of Norwich, 1548–1713* (Norwich: Jarrold, 1934); idem, ed., "An Index of Indentures of Norwich Apprentices," *Norfolk Record Society* 29 (1959); W. L. Sachse, "Minutes of Norwich Mayoralty Court, 1630–1635," *Norfolk Record Society* 15 (1947) and 36 (1967); Norwich Wills.

9. Millican, "Index of Apprentices"; G. Towne, *Ancestry of R. F. and E. C. Towne* (p.p., 1974); F. L. Weis, *Robert Williams* (p.p., 1945), 3–9.

10. Rye, *Norwich Freemen*; Millican, *Register of Freemen*; idem, "Index of Apprentices"; Norwich Wills; Cressy, *Coming Over*, 175, 267.

11. Pound, *Norwich*, chap. 3, calculated the city's population as 1611–20: 22,467; 1621–30: 25,086; 1631–40: 21,318.

12. Ferris; J. S. Herbst, *Storrs–Moulton–Smith Connection* (p.p., 1981), 7–11; *Massachusetts Bay Records*, 1:27–37.

13. Sachse, "Mayoralty Court"; Rye, *Norwich Freemen*; Millican, *Register of Freemen*; Norwich Wills.

14. Allen: A. H. Bent, *Walter Allen* (Boston: p.p., 1900); *WP*, 4:97–98. Atkinson: *NEHGR* 89 (1935):47. Bumstead: *NEHGR* 57 (1903):332; Waters, 1:751. Moody: *Hale, House*; Waters, 1:96; Sudbury Wills.

15. J. G. Hunt, "Welles Ancestry," *NEHGR* 113 (1959):73–82; Essex Wills.

16. M. W. Otten, *Wardwell Family* (Del Mar CA: p.p., 1985), 1–8; Lincs Wills.

17. Demos, *Remarkable Providences*, 79–88; Ferris; *NEHGR* 96 (1942):298.

18. L. A. Morrison, *History of the Kimball Family* (Boston: Wilson, 1897), 1–11; Waters, 2:1412. I am most grateful to Robert and the late Margaret Kemball for their help.

19. Beale: Norwich Wills. Barrell: E. French, "Genealogical Research in England," *NEHGR* 65 (1911). Hood: Waters, 2:1210; Essex Wills.

20. "The village craftsman working in wood or iron—carpenters, wheelwrights, ploughwrights—had both a workshop and a stake in the land. . . . The wealthier entrepreneur . . . a Norfolk brewer, a tanner, was usually a farmer as well." M. W. Barley, "Rural Housing in England," *AgHE*, 4:760; Ralph J. Crandall, "Family Types, Social Structure, and Mobility in Early America: Charlestown, Massachusetts, a Case Study," in Virginia Tufte and Barbara Meyerhoff, eds., *Changing Images of the Family* (New Haven: Yale University Press, 1979), 61–81; Anderson, *New England's Generation*, 64–65.

21. Kerridge, *Textile Manufactures*, 193. Remaining clothworkers were 12 tailors. Pound, *Norwich*, chap. 2.

22. George P. Winship, ed., *In Boston in 1682 and 1699* (Providence: Club for Colonial Reprints, 1905), 73.

23. *WP*, 4:97.

24. Oliver: Savage; Cressy, *Coming Over*, 267. Adams: *WP*, 3:439–40. Metcalfe: *NEHGR* 16 (1862):183–87.

25. Roberts, 1st ser. 1:37; *NEHGR* 53 (1899):277, 56 (1902):178.

26. Patrick Collinson, *The Elizabethan Puritan Movement* (London: Cape, 1967); R. G. Usher, "Presbyterian Movement in the Reign of Queen Elizabeth," *Camden*

Society, 3rd ser. 8 (1905); T. J. Hosken, *History of Congregationalism in Suffolk* (Ipswich: Clowes, 1920); Tyack, "Humbler Puritans," 79–106.

27. SPD, 400, no. 67; *NEHGR* 61 (1907):69; Kishlansky, "Community," 143; Holmes, "County Community," 73.

28. K. L. Roper, *The Ropers* (Baltimore: p.p., 1983).

29. See Chapter 2, herein. A contemporary ballad, "The Zealous Puritan," significantly cites religious causes for emigration among artisans: "Tom Taylor is prepared, / And the smith as black as coal; / Ralph Cobler too with us will go, / *For he regards his soul*; / The weaver, honest Simon . . . / Professeth to come after" (my italics); cited in Fischer, *Albion's Seed*, 30; *WP*, 1:295–98, 2:115, 122–23; Allen, *In English Ways*, 174.

30. Everitt, "Marketing," 588; Kerridge, *Textile Manufactures*, 187; Ursula Priestley, *The Fabric of Stuffs* (Norwich: Centre of East Anglian Studies, 1990), 11; Clay, *Economic Expansion*, 1:62–63; Sharpe, *Early Modern England*, 207.

31. Sharpe, *Early Modern England*, 270; Clay, *Economic Expansion*, 2:65.

32. Sharpe, *Early Modern England*, 242.

33. Ibid., 301.

34. Kerridge, *Textile Manufactures*, 187; Anderson, *New England's Generation*, 140.

35. Rutman, *Winthrop's Boston*, 52; Allen, *In English Ways*, 132; Demos, *Remarkable Providences*, 86.

36. Sharpe, *Early Modern England*, 143; Anderson, *New England's Generation*, 137–40; Seaver, "Protestant Work Ethic," 57.

37. *WJ*, 2:348; Sharpe, *Early Modern England*, 49–52.

38. There are a few anomalies in the styling of some emigrants, perhaps employed to deceive royal emigration officials. For instance, William Payne of Lavenham is called a husbandman on the *Increase* shipping list of 1635, but he had shares in five ships and two mills, large sums at venture in England and later in Jamaica and the Saugus ironworks, and he left a staggering £4,329. Similarly ranked was Benjamin Cooper of Brampton in northeast Suffolk, who died on the voyage to New England. He too was a shareholder in a ship. He had £400 in cash, and his estate was valued at £1,278 in 1637. Such wealth and commercial enterprise were hardly usual or possible for the average husbandman. The average value of 470 husbandman inventories between 1580 and 1700 was £76. Sharpe, *Early Modern England*, 201.

39. The classic account is Mildred Campbell, *The English Yeoman* (New York: Barnes and Noble, 1960); G. Batho, "Landlords in England," *AgHE*, 4:301–4; Sharpe, *Early Modern England*, 199–202. Batho estimates that the average wealth of the yeomanry doubled between 1560 and 1640.

40. Kerridge, *Farmers*, 104; W. G. Hoskins, "The Rebuilding of Rural England," *Past and Present* 4 (1958):44–59.

41. Danforth: John Booth, *The Home of Nicholas Danforth in Framlingham, Suffolk, England, 1635* (Framingham MA: Historical Society, 1954); John M. Merriam, "Nicholas Danforth, the Puritan Layman," in John Booth, ed., *Nicholas Danforth and His Neighbours* (Framingham MA: Historical Society, 1935), 5; Marvin: *Hale, House*; G. F. and W. T. R. Marvin, *Descendants of Reynold and Matthew Marvin* (Boston: p.p., 1904); Waters, 2:1103–4. Wrightson and Levine, *Poverty and Piety*.

42. Laslett, *World We Have Lost*, 36–37. Sharpe, *Early Modern England*, 201.

43. Michael and William Bacon of Winston; Henry and Francis Chickering of Ringsfield; Theophilus and Matthew Cushing of Hingham; John Curtis of Nazeing; John Cutler of Sprowston; Joseph Peck of Hingham; Anthony Fisher of Fressing-

field. The elder John Page was the brother of Phoebe (Page) Payne, who married William Payne of Lavenham.

44. Chickerings, Cushings, Peck, Olmstead, Fisher, Danforth, Curtises.

45. As in n. 44, above, with the addition of Page.

46. Peck: *NEHGR* 92 (1938):234, 93 (1939):178, 109 (1955):268; Waters, 1:934; Bacon: T. W. Baldwin, *Michael Bacon* (Cambridge MA: p.p., 1915); *NEHGR* 63 (1909):282–83, 69 (1915):229, 79 (1925):339, 100 (1946):79; Roberts, 1st ser. 1:11; *CSPD*, 1638, 64.

47. Clay, *Economic Expansion*, 1:63–65.

48. Aldous, Barber, Brock, Fisher, Lusher, Chickering. Nesta Evans et al., *Looking Back at Fressingfield* (Fressingfield: Workers Education Association, 1979), 3–55; Kerridge, *Farmers*, 86, 104.

49. Suffolk Wills.

50. Martin, *Profits*, 15–16, 300.

51. See Table 27, no. 17.

52. Kerridge, *Farmers*, 55–57; Sharpe, *Early Modern England*, 135, 201–2; Spufford, *Contrasting Communities*.

53. Moulton, Godfrey, Page, Dow, Palmer, Carver.

54. On servants, see Chapter 6, "Servants," herein. I am grateful to Barbara MacAllen for sharing her scholarly findings on Ormesby farming.

55. Dow/Nudd: J. J. Dow, *Dow Genealogy* (p.p., 1981), 1–10; R. B. Dow, *Book of Dow* (Rutland VT: Tuttle, 1929), chap. 1; *NEHGR* 9 (1855):335–37, 112 (1958):138, 142 (1988):255–58; Norwich Wills. Moulton/Green: W. H. Jones, "Ormesby Emigrants," *NEHGR* 141 (1987):313–29, 142 (1988):260–63; Herbst, *Storrs–Moulton–Smith*; Norwich Wills. Page/Ward: M. B. Thompson, *Some New Hampshire Families* (p.p., 1977); W. Chamberlain, "Page Genealogy," *NEHGR* 66 (1912):145; Norwich Wills. Palmer: *NEHGR* 69 (1915):342–43. Goodwin: Jones, "Ormesby Emigrants," 122; Norwich Wills. Underwood: Norwich Wills.

56. Sharpe, *Early Modern England*, 135, 201; Kerridge, *Farmers*, 55–57. MacAllen is finding widespread geographical stability in the Ormesby area between 1530 and 1630.

57. Tyack, "Humbler Puritans"; *CSPD*, 1634–35, 537–39. The Scruggs and Felton families, influential religious radicals in Yarmouth, also left in 1635. Barbara MacAllen is unearthing serious conflict about taking Communion at the railed altar at Hemsby.

58. J. Dow, *History of Hampton* (Salem MA: p.p., 1893); V. C. Sanborn, "Grantees and Settlement at Hampton, N.H.," *Essex Institute Historical Collections* 53 (1917):228–49.

Chapter 6. Dependents

1. Kussmaul, *Servants in Husbandry*, 27, 77; Alan Everitt, "Farm Labourers," *AgHE*, 4:461–70; Sharpe, *Early Modern England*, 210–13; J. Morgan, *Godly Learning*, 86; Edmund S. Morgan, *The Puritan Family* (New York: Harper, 1966), 109–32; Steven R. Smith, "The London Apprentices as Seventeenth-Century Adolescents," *Past and Present* 61 (1966):149–61; Anne Yarborough, "Apprentices as Adolescents in Sixteenth-Century Bristol," *Journal of Social History* 13 (1979):67–82; Margaret G. Davies, *The Enforcement of English Apprenticeship* (Cambridge MA: Harvard University Press, 1956); O. J. Dunlop and R. D. Redman, *English Apprenticeship and Child Labour* (New York: Macmillan, 1912).

2. Morgan, *Puritan Family*, 77; Kussmaul, *Servants in Husbandry*, 29–33; Thompson, *Penny Merriments*, 116–20.

3. Servants are the least well documented of the emigrants. In nearly one-third of the cases ages cannot be estimated; birthplaces and family roots are too often irrecoverable. There is ambiguity in the 1635 *Hopewell* list: John Bill, Thomas Greene, Edward Keele, Isaac Morris, and John Goadby may not have been Nazeing residents. *NEHGR* 14 (1860):304.

4. Dunlop and Redman, *English Apprenticeship*, chap. 1; Davies, *Enforcement*, 1–14, 271–74; Morgan, *Puritan Family*, 120–21.

5. Kussmaul, *Servants in Husbandry*, 57–77. Hiring in Lincolnshire and other grazing areas often occurred in May; ibid., 47.

6. Abbott Emerson Smith, *Colonists in Bondage* (New York: Norton, 1971), 3–66; Mildred Campbell, "Social Origins of Some Early Americans," in James Morton Smith, ed., *Seventeenth-Century America* (Chapel Hill: University of North Carolina Press, 1959), 63–89; David Galenson, *White Servitude in Early America* (Cambridge: Cambridge University Press, 1981); J. Hunt, "Matthew and Richard Coys," *NEHGR* 113 (1959):236; Richard Rutyma, "Richard Coys," *Essex Institute Historical Collections* 104 (1968):75–79. William Hubbard was Whittingham's father-in-law.

7. Brown: *WP*, 4:165; Cole: *NEHGR* 50 (1896):419–22; Irons: *NEHGR* 11 (1857):36.

8. Roger Thompson, *Women in Stuart England and America* (London: Routledge, 1974), 28–30, 71; idem, *Penny Merriments*, 119.

9. Storey: Norwich Wills; he was related by marriage to the Feltons who emigrated from Great Yarmouth in 1635. Lincoln: Lincoln, *History of Lincoln Family*, chap. 1; Barton, *Lineage of Lincoln*, 5–14; Lea and Hutchinson, *Lincoln Family*, chap. 2. Bill: L. Bill, *History of the Bill Family* (New York: p.p., 1867), 1–11.

10. *Hale, House*; Essex Wills; W. L. Holman, *Ancestry of Colonel J. H. Stevens* (Concord NH: p.p., 1948–52).

11. *WP*, 2:63; Kussmaul, *Servants in Husbandry*, chap. 4.

12. Two cases of servant migration remain a mystery. Thomas Flegge, servant to Richard Carver of Scratby near Yarmouth, appears from Norwich Wills evidence to have come 30 miles, halfway across Norfolk, from Hardingham near Hingham. There may have been some kinship connection. However, Scratby is in the hundred (a county division) of Flegge, and Thomas may have been a local lad. Even more extraordinary was the presence of Thomas Comberbatch in the company of Michael Metcalfe, the dornick weaver and clothier from Norwich. I have been unable to find any prior instance of this unusual name in the local records. The only clue to Thomas's origins is that Comberbatch is the name of a village on the other side of England, just north of Northwich in Cheshire.

13. Kussmaul, *Servants in Husbandry*, 57–62, 66; Everitt, "Farm Labourers," 464, 467; Kerridge, *Farmers*, 88; P. J. Bowden, *The Wool Trade in Tudor and Stuart England* (London: Macmillan, 1961), 501.

14. Bailyn, *Education*, 22–23.

15. *WP*, 3:124, 125, 208, 211, 5:207. Daniel Vickers, "Working in the Fields in a Developing Economy: Essex County MA, 1630–75," in S. Innes, ed., *Work and Labor in Early America* (Chapel Hill: University of North Carolina Press, 1988), 49–69; Alden T. Vaughan, ed., *New England's Prospect* (Amherst: University of Massachusetts Press, 1977), 70–71.

16. *Albro, Andrew, Atkinson, Bartlett, *R. Coys, Doggett, *Flegge, *Goodwin, Hale, *Moore, *Moulton, Whipple. (* indicates probable servants in husbandry.)

17. Kussmaul, *Servants in Husbandry*, 66–70.

18. J. and S. Eddy, *Eddy Family* (Boston: p.p., 1881), Pt. I; R. S. D. Eddy, *Eddy Family* (Boston: p.p., 1930), 11–20. Morse: G. A. Moriarty, "Morse Family," *NEHGR* 83 (1929):70–78, 278–94, 106 (1952):137; P. McC. Morse, *Your Ancestors* (p.p., 1967), 15. Storre: Savage; Lincs Wills. Rishworth: Savage. Metcalfe: see Chapter 4, "Professionals and Entrepreneurs," herein. Shepard: half-brother of the Reverend Thomas; G. F. Shepard, *Shepard Families* (New Haven: p.p., 1973), chap. 1. Minot: J. Leach, *Family of Levi Morton* (Cambridge MA: p.p., 1894); *NEHGR* 1 (1847):171, 52 (1898):98–99; Essex Wills.

19. T. D. Hunting, *Descendants of Abraham Hunting* (p.p., 1910), iii–ix; *NEHGR* 61 (1907):360–61; Robert C. Anderson kindly shared with me his discovery that Hunting moved to the parish adjacent to Hoxne, Oakley, where the famous preacher and soul salver William Greenhill was vicar. Greenhill was silenced in 1637. See Chapter 5, herein.

20. See Chapter 4, n. 16, herein.

21. The second soul salver was the Reverend William Greenhill of Oakley; see n. 19, above. Selement and Woolley, *Shepard Confessions*, 81–84; Suffolk Wills; C. L. Collens, *Collins Memorials* (p.p., 1959), 1–9; *NEHGR* 89 (1935):73–79, 148–50.

22. Now in Christchurch Museum, Ipswich, Suffolk.

23. G. E. Saulters and H. E. Smith, *Eldred Genealogy* (p.p., 1987), chap. 1; *DNB*.

24. *WP*, 3:484; Ferris; C. E. Banks, "Persecution and Prosecution," *MHS Proceedings* 63 (1932):148.

25. Banks, "Persecution and Prosecution," 146; Tyack, "Humbler Puritans," 105. Others presented were Edward Howe, Richard Lumpkin, Edmund Sheffield, and Samuel Sherman.

26. Tyack, "Migration," 189–237.

27. Lyle Koehler, *A Search for Power* (Urbana: University of Illinois Press, 1980), sees puritanism as hyperpatriarchal and oppressive; in his view, immigration to New England worsened women's lot. For less gloomy interpretations, see Laurel Thatcher Ulrich, *Good Wives* (New York: Knopf, 1982), or Thompson, *Women*.

28. Despite this limiting of the sample, there are still many gaps. The ages of 23 are not available; for 73, or 39 percent, of the total the distance between birthplace or childhood home and family roots is irrecoverable; the same holds for 28 percent in the case of distance of moves from family roots to marital home.

29. These findings are corroborated in de John, "To Pass beyond the Seas," 42–50.

30. Joan (Fletcher) Ames, widow of the distinguished puritan exile, the Reverend William Ames, who taught at the Dutch University of Franeker, *DNB*. Mary (Youngs) Brown was the daughter of the Reverend Christopher Youngs, vicar of Southwold, Suffolk; her brother John led a group of emigrants from the town. Identification of her husband with Brandon is in doubt. It seems strange that a resident of an inland Suffolk town should have been a member of the Fishmongers' Company; there may be elision of two emigrants with this common name; Ferris; E. D. Hines, *Browne Hill* (Salem: p.p., 1897); Waters, 1:242, 280; Bailyn, *New England Merchants*, 122. Elizabeth (Ibrook) Hobart. Martha (Bulkeley) Mellows was the daughter of the Reverend Edmund Bulkeley, vicar of Odell, Bedfordshire, and sister of Peter, first minister of Concord; M. L. Holman, *Bulkeley Notes* (p.p., 1934), passim. Anne (Lawrence) Peck. Elizabeth (Cooke/Reade) Peter. Elizabeth (Ames) Phillip was a sister of the Reverend William Ames; she returned to England with her husband in 1641. Sarah (Everard) Rogers. Margaret (Touteville) Shepard. Judith (Stoughton) Smead was the daughter of the deprived vicar of Coggeshall.

Elizabeth (St. John) Whiting. Mary (Barnard) Williams. Elizabeth (Mansfield) Wilson. Elizabeth (Daniel) Morse married the son of a clergyman.

31. Mary (Moseley) Coddington. Margaret (Green) Cole. Catherine (Myles/ Grey) Coytmore. Martha (Rainborough) Coytmore; the 31-mile distance entered in Table 24 is from their townhouse to their country house down the Thames Estuary. Frances (Freestone) Hill. Elizabeth (Bulkeley/Whittingham) Hough. Margaret (Barrett) Huntington. Anna (Tutty) Knight came from the famous London puritan parish of St. Stephen's, Coleman Street; *NEHGR* 48 (1894):142–43. Katherine (Marbury) Scott was Anne Hutchinson's younger sister. Elizabeth (Clark) Stacey. Dorothy (Harlakenden) Symonds's family had moved from Kent to north Essex in the middle of the sixteenth century. Susannah (Hutchinson) Storre was the sister of the merchant William Hutchinson. Martha (Fiske) Thompson.

32. Elizabeth (Harges) Clarke. Lucy (Winthrop) Downing, who also lived for four years in Dublin, 1622–26, when first married. Lady Susannah (Fiennes-Clinton) Humphrey. Susannah (Bellingham) Portmont.

33. Sarah (Wyatt) Heard. Elizabeth (Woodruff) Wardall. Margaret (Clarke) Wyeth.

34. Ferris; Roberts, 2nd ser. 3:296; Essex Wills.

35. *WP*, 2:79, 84.

36. Searle, "Barrington Letters," 63–68; Moriarty, "Bernard of Epworth," 189.

37. See Table 27, no. 23, herein; Holman, *Bulkeley Notes*; G. W. Hough, *Hough Families* (p.p., 1974), vol. 2, chap. 1; *DNB*, s.v. Peter Bulkeley.

38. *NEHGR* 41 (1887):163, 178–79; Searle, "Barrington Papers," 5, 13, 28–30, 167–68, 187, 198–99, 225–26, 257–58; Shipps, "Puritan Emigration," 83–97; *DNB*; Waters, 1:226.

39. *NEHGR* 107 (1953):268.

40. McGiffert, *God's Plot*, 52–65.

41. *WP*, 3:234, 236, 366, 376, 4:109; Waters, 1:673; Roberts, 2nd ser. 3:6; Stearns, *Strenuous Puritan*, 31–33, 56, 88, 94–95, 127–28.

42. Dorothy Boynton, *Edmund Greenleaf* (p.p., 1980); *NEHGR* 38 (1884):299–301, 122 (1968):28–35.

43. *NEHGR* 62 (1908):303–4; *Calendar of the Freemen of Great Yarmouth*, 1429–1800 (Norwich: Norfolk and Norwich Archaeological Society, 1910); Norwich Wills.

44. M. M. Howland, "English Barrett Records," *NEHGR* 110 (1956):312, 111 (1957):153, 114 (1960):70; E. B. Huntington, *Genealogical Memorials of the Huntington Family* (Stamford CT: p.p., 1863), Pt. I.

45. *WP*, 2:157, 3:7, 142, 143–44; E. C. Child, *Child Genealogy* (Utica, NY: p.p., 1881), 1–4; W. H. Whitmore and W. K. Watkins, eds., *Aspinwall Notarial Records, 1644–51* (Boston: City of Boston, 1903), 85; Waters, 1:744.

46. Selma R. Williams, *Divine Rebel* (New York: Holt, Rinehart, Winston, 1981), 9–76; *NEHGR* 20 (1866):355–67.

47. Thompson, *New Hampshire Families*, 14; Roberts, 1st ser. 1:43.

48. A. Scott, *Genealogical Notes* (p.p., n.d.), 6; Waters, 2:1287. Cf. Thomasine (Frost) Rice and her husband, Edmund, who also emigrated from Berkhamsted, discussed in Chapter 7, herein.

49. W. G. Davis, *The Ancestry of Sarah Johnson* (Portland ME: p.p., 1960), chap. 1.

50. *NEHGR* 91 (1937):296; Lincs Wills.

51. Waters, 2:1035–36. Cf. Judith (Everard) Appleton, Lady Arbella (Fiennes-Clinton) Johnson, Dorothy (Harlakenden) Symonds, Martha (Rainborough) Coytmore, Anna (King) Vassall, and Anne (Dudley) Bradstreet.

52. Venns; *NEHGR* 50 (1896):130–31; Roberts, 2nd ser. 3:901; *MHS Colls*, 4th ser. 8 (1847):590–91; Suffolk Wills. Cf. Margaret (Crane) Rogers, Susannah (Travis) Skelton, Joan (Gentleman/Harrington) Youngs, Ann (Gibbs) Fiske.

53. Koehler, *Search for Power*, 56, 219–34.

54. F. J. Simmons, *Emmanuel Downing* (p.p., 1958), passim; *WP*, 3:131, 311, 312, 369; Dunn, *Puritans and Yankees*, 126. Lucy Downing wrote to her brother: "I am but a wife and therefore it is sufficient for me to follow my husband"; Simmons, *Downing*, 43.

55. Cf. Lucy Downing: "For my own part, changes are ever irksome to me"; Simmons, *Downing*, 43; cf. Fischer, *Albion's Seed*, 55–57.

Chapter 7. Ancestral Roots

1. It is still said in rural Norfolk that locals start accepting "strangers" after 20 years.

2. Evans, "Wills of Sudbury," x.

3. *Calendar of Freemen of Great Yarmouth*, 1519, 1547, 1587, 1595, 1610, 1636. Will of John Felton the elder, PCC, 1602, 56 Montague.

4. E.g., Henry F. Waters, Elizabeth French, J. Gardner Bartlett, Col. J. H. Lester, Mary and Winifred Lovering Holman, D. L. Jacobus, M. W. Ferris, G. A. Moriarty, J. B. Threlfall, H. W. Jones, Robert C. Anderson, and the current staff of the New England Historical Genealogical Society.

5. Rye, *Norwich Freemen*; Norwich Wills; W. S. Appleton, *Ancestry of Priscilla Baker* (Cambridge MA: p.p., 1970), chap. 1.

6. *NEHGR* 65 (1911):69–74.

7. Stone: J. G. Bartlett, *Gregory Stone Genealogy* (p.p., 1918); idem, *Simon Stone Genealogy* (p.p., 1926); Waters, 1:819, 2:1123; Roberts, 1st ser. 1:45; Essex Wills. Marvin: *Hale, House*; Ferris; Marvin and Marvin, *Descendants*, Pt. I; Essex Wills. Cushing/Pitcher: J. S. Cushing, *Cushing Family Genealogy* (Montreal: p.p., 1905), 1–12; Norwich Wills. Danforth: Chapter 5, n. 41, herein. Fressingfield: Evans et al., *Looking Back*; Suffolk Wills. Olmstead: H. K. Olmstead, *Genealogy of the Olmstead Family* (New York: p.p., 1912).

8. Robert C. Anderson, "English Origins of Philemon Whale of Sudbury MA," *The Genealogist* 6 (1985):131–41, demonstrates that Edmund and Thomasine Rice are recorded in 1619–25 in the parish registers of Stanstead, Suffolk, nine miles south of Bury. Thomasine's widowed sister Elizabeth (Frost/Rice) married Philemon Whale in 1622. The Whales also lived in Stanstead and moved to Berkhamsted in 1627. However, they did not emigrate until after our period, c1643, but predictably settled with the Rices in Sudbury MA. Sudbury Wills; N. S. Frost, *Frost Genealogy* (West Newton MA: p.p., 1926), chap. 2.

9. Beale: *Hobart Genealogy* (n.p., n.d.), NEHGS; *NEHGR* 15 (1861):3–25; Norwich Wills.

10. *NEHGR* 99 (1945), 100 (1946); Suffolk Wills; Essex Wills.

11. *NEHGR* 94 (1940):74–76.

12. Holman, "Notes on the Appletons"; Clive, *Beyond Living Memory*, 4.

13. *MHS Colls*, 3rd ser. 10:154–55; Northeast, "Boxford Churchwardens' Accounts," 85.

14. Ferris.

15. Towne, *Ancestry*, 7–13; *Parke Society Newsletter* 23 (1986):33; Waters, 1:145–46; *WP*, 2:276.

16. Waters, 1:673; Essex Wills; Shipps, "Puritan Emigration," 90.

17. *Hale, House*; Waters, 2:861; *NEHGR* 94 (1940):387; *MHS Colls*, 4th ser.

6:369; Upton, *Writtle Church*, 72–78. I am indebted to the Reverend Peter Nokes, vicar of Writtle, for his scholarly help.

18. *NEHGR* 71 (1917):19–33, 227–57; Waters, 1:765; Wyman.

19. Fitch, *Fitch Family*, chaps. 1, 2; Waters; 1:593; Essex Wills.

20. Waters, 2:1035–37; *WP* 3:30; Weis, *Ancestral Lines*; Essex Wills.

21. Morrison, *Clarke Families*, 1–20; Colket, 60–69; Suffolk Wills.

22. *NEHGR* 102 (1948):87–98, 312–13, 107 (1953):269.

23. Morrison, *Kimball Family*, 1–37; J. R. Olorenshaw, *Notes on the History of Rattlesden* (p.p., 1900), 3–16; Waters, 2:1412; Sudbury Wills; J. B. Threlfall, "Scott Family," *NEHGR* 141 (1987):34–37.

24. *WP*, 2:63.

25. The total is based on Richard Archer's computer analysis of 22,164 names with the addition of 275 Greater East Anglians not counted in his contingent; "New England Mosaic," *WMQ* 47 (1990):477–502. The lesser number of possible additional emigrants from East Anglia was reached by taking the percentage of Archer's known eastern counties emigrants of the known total, 36 percent, and calculating that ratio of half the unknowns (assuming the other half was born in New England), or 2,481, plus the unknown emigrants, 4,757.

26. Ibid., 483–87; Anthony Salerno, "Social Background to Seventeenth-Century Emigration to America," *Journal of British Studies* 19 (1979):31–52; James Horn, "Servant Emigration to the Chesapeake," in Thad Tate and David Ammerman, eds., *The Chesapeake in the Seventeenth Century* (Chapel Hill: University of North Carolina Press, 1979), 94–95.

27. See, for instance, new findings on the Ormesby group in recent issues of *NEHGR* and early results of the Great Migration Project described in its *Newsletter*.

Chapter 8. Company Travel

1. Horn, "Servant Emigration," passim; Greene, *Pursuits of Happiness*, 7–54.

2. Anderson, "Migrants and Motives," 339–83; idem, *New England's Generation*, 21.

3. For instance, Robert Parke to John Winthrop: "I do propose to go with you and all my company"; *WP*, 2:213. On 31 December 1638, the Salem town meeting resolved that village lands should be granted to "Mr. Phillips and his Company"; quoted in Waters, 1:280. Fischer, *Albion's Seed*, 25–26, quoted "The Zealous Puritan," a 1639 ballad: "Stay not among the Wicked, / Lest that with them you perish, / But let us to New-England go, / And the pagan people cherish . . . / For Company I fear not, / There goes my cousin Hannah, / And Reuben so persuades to go / My cousin Joyce, Susanna. / With Abigail and Faith, / And Ruth no doubt comes after; / And Sarah kind, will not stay behind; / My cousin Constance daughter." The word "company" was used in England to describe gatherings of the godly who were not joint members of one parochial congregation; Paul S. Seaver, *Wallington's World* (London: Routledge, 1985), 187.

4. The Johnson company numbered 21; it included Isaac and the Lady Arbella, John Johnson family of four, Thomas Dudley family of seven, William Coddington and wife, William Cheeseborough family of four, Simon Bradstreet and wife.

5. The Pynchon company numbered 35: Jehu Burr family of three, Matthew Irons and wife, John Cable, William Chase family of three, William Crafts family of three, John Samford, John Edmunds and wife, Robert Cole, John Porter family of six, William Blake family of seven, Pynchon family of six. Tyack, rev. App. B, unpaginated; hereafter cited as Tyack listing.

6. The Pelhams were intermarried with the Waldegraves, lords of the manor of

NOTES TO COMPANY TRAVEL

Bures. "Mr. Walgrave" invested in the Massachusetts Bay Company and acquired land, as an absentee, in Sudbury MA; Powell, *Puritan Village*, 153. The Pelham company numbered 42: Pelham family of six, John Warren family of six, John Waters family of five, Lawrence Waters, Isaac Stearns family of seven, Robert Parke family of six, William Knapp family of nine, Nicholas Knapp and wife; Tyack listing.

7. Sampson was the son of Winthrop's sister-in-law, Bridget Clopton.

8. Margaret remained at Groton while John visited London and after he sailed in 1630. She joined him at Boston in the spring of 1631. Winthrop included in his "family" people who were unrelated to him.

9. From Groton in 1630: John Winthrop, Sr.'s household of 14, Richard Gridley family of four, three Pond brothers, Lewis Kidby family of three, Edward Kidby, John Bigg and wife, John Clarke, John Cole and wife, John Doggett family of four, Henry Kingsbury family of four. In 1631: Margaret Winthrop, John Jr. and five siblings, five servants, and Joanna King. Neighboring parishes: Assington—Brampton Gurdon and Thomas French family of nine; Boxford—Robert Reynolds family of six; Edwardstone—Benjamin Brand, Thomas Brease; Sudbury—the Reverend John Wilson, Jeffrey Ruggles and wife, William Waterbury and wife, John Waterbury, John Pickering family of four; Buxhall, Smith family of four; Little Waldingfield—Dr. William Gager and servant, John Gosse and wife; Tyack listing. The gathering of this company is recorded in *WP*, 2:161–213.

10. John Mills family of eight, John Sales family of three, Edmond Onge family of four, Thomas Lambe family of four, William Hammond family of five, William Payne family of seven, William Fuller family of three, Thomas Hammond family of four; Tyack listing; *WP*, 3:139, 270–71; *NEHGR* 106 (1952):83–87. D'Ewes, like Winthrop, had married a Clopton. Emerson, *Letters*, 104, 224–30.

11. 136 emigrants in gentlemen's companies are not listed in Tables 27 and 28.

12. Collinson, *Religion of Protestants*; Seaver, *Puritan Lectureships*; Hunt, *Puritan Moment*; Shipps, "Lay Patronage of East Anglian Clerics"; Evans, "Wills," will 627; *WP*, 1:243–47.

13. Shuffelton, *Thomas Hooker*, chap. 2; Selement and Woolley, *Shepard Confessions*; Hall, *Faithful Shepherd*, 14–20; Robert C. Anderson, "English Origins of John Hunting," *National Genealogical Society Quarterly* 78 (1990):85–97; *WP*, 2:315.

14. Collinson, *Elizabethan Puritan Movement*; idem, *Godly People* (London: Oxford University Press, 1982); Usher, "Presbyterian Movement"; Hosken, *Congregationalism in Suffolk*, 18–132; Swinden, *History of Great Yarmouth*, 852–56; *WP*, 3:439.

15. Thomas Rawlins family of seven, William Agar, Isaac Morrill family of five, William Heath family of three, William Curtis family of seven, John Curtis family of five, the Reverend John and Philip Eliot family of six, John Graves family of seven, John Mygatt and wife, John Ruggles family of four, Mary Eliot, Giles and Edward Payson, Isaac Heath, Thomas Ruggles family of four, George Holmes family of three. Tyack listing. Eliot must have come to know William Pynchon, his coleader at Roxbury, during his stay at Little Baddow; Rutman, *Winthrop's Boston*, 103.

16. The *Lyon* company of 1632; William Goodwin and wife, Ozias Goodwin family of three, John and Matthew Whipple, James Wall, John Talcott family of four, William Wadsworth family of six, John White family of four, Edward Elmer, John Coggeshall family of five, John Steele family of five, George Steele family of five, James Olmstead family of seven, Nicholas Clarke, Richard Lyman family of seven, John Bridge, Andrew Warner family of four. Later emigrants: three Fitch

brothers, Thomas Wilson family of five, Rowland Stebbings family of seven, Mary Clarke, Simon Stacey, John Amies, Robert Hawkins family of three, Joseph Loomis family of 11, John Wall, Francis Skinner, John Marsh, Robert Hawkins and wife, Nathaniel Sparhawk family of 10; Tyack listing. F. G. Emmison, ed., *Early Essex Town Records* (London: Jenkins, 1971), 1–103; W. F. Quin, *A History of Braintree and Bocking* (Lavenham: Phillimore, 1981), 58–128. John Corley and Dixon Smith were most helpful in identifying the *Lyon* company.

17. The Cotton company: the Reverend John Cotton and wife, Abraham Mellows family of nine, Thomas Leverett family of four, William Dinely and wife, Valentine Hill family of three, William Hutchinson family of 15, Richard Scott family of eight, Atherton Hough family of three, Richard Bellingham family of four, Nathaniel Heaton and wife, Thomas Marshall family of five, William Pearce, and Richard Truesdale; Hutchinson, *History of Massachusetts-Bay*, 2:384.

18. The Shepard company: the Reverend Thomas Shepard family of four, Roger Harlakenden family of four, George and Joseph Cooke, William French family of seven, John French and wife, Sarah Symmes, Samuel Symonds family of seven, Nicholas Danforth family of seven, Nicholas Wyeth family of four, totaling 38; Tyack listing.

19. The Wheelwright company: the Reverend John Wheelwright family of five, Christopher Helme, Edward Rushworth, John Cram and wife, Godfrey Dearborn family of five, Philemon Portmont family of three, Thomas Wardall family of three, Christopher Lawson, Thomas Leavitt, Jeremiah Blackwell, Gabriel Fish, Augustine Storre family of three, Richard Morris and wife.

20. The Phillips–Youngs company: the Reverend John Phillip and wife, Henry Chickering family of four, Thomas Paine family of eight, John Thurston family of four, Austin Killam family of five, Hugh Stacey, Thomas West, Nicholas Pacy, William Brown and wife, the Reverend John Youngs family of eight, Joseph Youngs family of three, William Cockram family of six, William, Daniel, and Thomas Jeggles, Thomas Moore; Tyack listing.

21. The Fiske–Allen company: John Fiske family of six, the Reverend John Allen family of three, Tuttle family of six, Edmund Thompson and wife, George Barrell family of five, John Fiske family of three, Martin Underwood and wife, Henry Chickering family of four, Francis Chickering family of four, David Fiske family of three, Nathan Fiske and wife, William Fiske family of six, Phineas Fiske family of five, Benjamin Cooper family of 11; Tyack listing.

22. *NEHGR* 121 (1967):254; Allen, *In English Ways*, 171–75.

23. The Peck company: the Reverend Robert Peck family of six, Joseph Peck family of six, John Foulsham family of four, Edward Gilman family of nine, Matthew Cushing family of eight, Thomas Cooper family of six, John Beale family of nine, Francis James family of four, Philip James family of 11, Henry Chamberlain family of seven, Thomas Lincoln, Stephen Gates family of five. Other Hingham emigrants: Theophilus Cushing, Edmund Hobart family of nine, Nicholas Jacobs family of four, Ralph Smith, Thomas Lincoln, Thomas Hobart family of five, Edmund Hobart and wife, Thomas Chubbock and wife, Anthony Cooper family of 14, John Farrow family of three, William Large and wife, Thomas Lincoln family of four, Robert Cutler, Thomas Lincoln family of three, John Tower and wife, Thomas Barnes and wife, Adam Foulsham, Daniel Lincoln, Edmund Pitts family of three, the Reverend Peter Hobart and wife. Neighboring parishes: Stephen Lincoln family of four, Samuel Packard family of three, Jeremy Moore, Thomas Lincoln, William Ripley family of six, John Cutler family of eight, John and Henry Tuttle families of seven, John Sutton family of six, Henry Smith family of four, Henry Smith family of twelve, Stephen Paine family of 10, William Hersey and

wife; Tyack listing. John J. Waters, "Hingham, Massachusetts, 1631–61: An East Anglian Oligarchy in the New World," *Journal of Social History* 1 (1967):351–70; M. E. Lonsdale, *In the Heyday of Their Strength* (Wymondham: Reeve, 1979); idem, *Hingham, in History* (Wymondham: Reeve, n.d.); Robert E. Wall, *Massachusetts Bay: The Crucial Decade* (New Haven: Yale University Press, 1972), chap. 7; David Grayson Allen, "A Tale of Two Towns," in H. C. Allen and Roger Thompson, eds., *Contrast and Connection* (London: Bell, 1976), chap. 1. The third Thomas Lincoln listed, "the cooper," may have come from the Dorset town of Beaminster; F. J. Nicholson, "A Clue to the English Origins of Thomas Lincoln the Cooper and William Lane of Hingham MA," *American Genealogist* 64 (1989):214–15.

24. Further clerical companies were John Wilson's from Sudbury and Glemsford, totaling 20 for his first two crossings. In 1630, George Phillips led a party of 17 from Boxted–Dedham in north Essex. Assington and Little Waldingfield contributed 20 people to the company of Nathaniel Rogers in 1636; Tyack listings. Of the total of 667 in the clerical companies, 267 are not listed in Tables 27 and 28.

25. Spurrell, *Puritan Town*, 9–15; Wrightson and Levine, *Poverty and Piety*, 132; Waters, "Hingham," 357–59; Frank Thistlethwaite, *Dorset Pilgrims* (London: Barrie and Jenkins, 1989), 27.

26. Wrightson and Levine, *Poverty and Piety*, play down the importance of kinship networks in Terling. However, their conclusions have been called into question by David Cressy, "Kinship in Early Modern England," *Past and Present* 113 (1986):38–69, and by my *Sex in Middlesex: Popular Mores in a Massachusetts County, 1649–1699* (Amherst: University of Massachusetts Press, 1986), 167–68.

27. J. J. Goodwin, *The Goodwin Family* (Hartford: p.p., 1891), 36; *Hale, House*, s.v. Talcott.

28. Savage; Wyman. When Catherine Coytmore died in her eighties, she left such luxury items as two Persian carpets, two boxes of East India dishes, a Turkish carpet, two fair window cushions, and a great looking glass. Cf. Crandall and Coffman, "From Emigrants to Rulers," 11; E. C. Nichols, "Myles Family," *NEHGR* 138 (1984):40–41.

29. For instance, Wheelwright daughters married into the families of Parsons, Maverick, Bradbury, Checkley, Nanny, Naylor, and Crispe. Wentworth, *Wentworth Genealogy*, 72–4; Williams, *Divine Rebel*, 24–78; A. M. Cook, *Lincolnshire Links with the United States* (Lincoln: Kay, 1956), 36–50.

30. See Table 27, nos. 31, 32.

31. See Table 27, nos. 4, 12. The Beale family is regularly recorded in the Diocese of Norwich Probate Records from 1473 (27 Paynot) as resident in the Hingham area. Cushings first appear in the Lay Subsidy Rolls for Hardingham, the neighboring parish, in 1327. Pitchers regularly appear as testators there after 1449. Hobarts had lived in neighboring parishes since at least 1532 and Lincolns since 1543. Thomas Lincoln, the cooper, may have come from Beaminster in Dorset. See Source Notes to Table 14.

32. See Table 27, no. 53. John Sr.'s fourth wife was a member of the Coytmore clan. John Jr.'s second marriage linked Winthrops with the Reade–Lake–Epps–Peter–Cooke clan. This may help explain why when in 1701 Samuel Reade in England wished to sell his father's farm in Salem he chose his cousin Wait Winthrop as his attorney. The buyer was another cousin, Daniel Epps. Table 27, no. 54.

33. See Table 27, no. 14. Winslow, *John Eliot*, 28.

34. See Table 27, nos. 16, 17. Simon Fiske, "The Fiske Family of Laxfield," *NEHGR* 92 (1938):177–83, 287–88; Robert G. Pope, ed., "The Notebook of Rev. John Fiske," *Colonial Society of Massachusetts Publications* 47 (1974):xxxviii–ix.

35. Moriarty, "Bernard of Epworth," 189; Thistlethwaite, *Dorset Pilgrims*, 52.

36. Thompson, *Sex in Middlesex*, 117, 125; Bailyn, *Apologia of Robert Keayne*, 41, 43.

37. Holman, *Bulkeley Notes*; Hough, *Hough Families*, 2:5–27; Allen, *In English Ways*, 179.

38. Sanford, "Early Years of John Sanford," 83; Moriarty, "John Sanford in New England," 271–77; *WP*, 3:109.

39. Edward Johnson, *Wonder-Working Providence of Sion's Saviour*, ed. J. F. Jameson (New York: Barnes and Noble, 1967), 77.

40. Hall, *Faithful Shepherd*, chap. 3; idem, *The Antinomian Crisis* (Middletown CT: Wesleyan University Press, 1991), Introduction; Stephen Foster, *The Long Argument* (Chapel Hill: University of North Carolina Press, 1991), chap. 5. I thank Gerald Moran for introducing me to "wandering congregations."

41. I owe this insight to Barbara MacAllan's surveying of the sites of Ormesby, Norfolk, and Hampton NH.

42. Heyrman, *Commerce and Culture*, 37; Emory Battis, *Saints and Sectaries* (Chapel Hill: University of North Carolina Press, 1962), App. I; some of the most famous "witches" had East Anglian origins; Rebecca Nurse, Bridget Bishop, John Procter, Martha Corey, and Sarah Cloyse.

43. Anderson, *New England's Generation*, chap. 5.

44. Brumm, "Transfer and Arrival," in Herget and Ortseifen, eds., *Transit of Civilisation*, 29–36; Bercovitch, *Puritan Origins*, 109, 115, chap. 4; Caldwell, *Puritan Conversion Narrative*, 129–30, 135–37; Cressy, *Coming Over*, chap. 6; Anderson, *New England's Generation*, chap. 2. An additional benefit of company travel among Greater East Anglians was a low shipboard mortality rate; Cressy, *Coming Over*, 148. The only adult deaths recorded among East Anglian passengers en route were those of Benjamin Cooper and Simon Huntington.

45. Laslett, *World We Have Lost*, 93; Shorter, *Making of the Modern Family*, 103; Cressy, *Coming Over*, chaps. 9, 11; Miranda Chaytor, "Household and Kinship," *History Workshop Journal* 10 (1980):3–29; Smith, "Labourers in Late Sixteenth-Century England," 11–52, 367–94; Hall, *Worlds of Wonder*, chap. 4; Thompson, *Sex in Middlesex*, 167–68.

46. Anderson, *New England's Generation*, 100–103.

Chapter 9. New England

1. See Chapter 1, herein. Within the scope of this study, it has not proved possible to devote equivalent space to individual emigrants' movements in New England. This will be treated in greater depth in a further study.

2. Fischer, *Albion's Seed*, 184–85, offers various persistence rates for eight New England towns which confirm my findings.

3. Don Gleason Hill, ed., *Early Records of the Town of Dedham* (Dedham: Dedham Historical Society, 1886), 1:iii–xvi.

4. Richard P. Gildrie, *Salem, a Covenant Community, 1626–83* (Charlottesville: University of Virginia Press, 1975), chap. 2; Christine A. Young, *From "Good Order" to Glorious Revolution: Salem MA, 1628–1689* (Ann Arbor: University of Michigan Press, 1980), 35–37; Pope, "Notebook of John Fiske," xxix–xxxvi.

5. Dow, *History of Hampton*, chap. 1; Sanborn, "Grantees at Hampton," 228–49; Jones, "Ormesby Emigrants," 118–26.

6. Waters, "Hingham"; *NEHGR* 15 (1861):26–35 has Daniel Cushing's contemporary list of Hingham settlers; *NEHGR* 121 (1967):228–36, has the Reverend Peter Hobart's register.

7. Goodwin, *Goodwin Family*, 42; I am most grateful to John Corley of Brain-

tree, Essex, for sharing his facsimile list of "The Original Proprietors of Hartford" memorialized in the Center Church Burying Ground, Hartford CT, in 1837. Thirty-six families joined 22 from Wethersfield to form Hadley; A. Raymond, "Porters of Hadley," *NEHGR* 133 (1979):198–220.

8. Innes, *Labor*, 3–9; Joseph H. Smith, *Colonial Justice in Western Massachusetts: The Pynchon Court Record, 1639–1702* (Cambridge MA: Cromwell Foundation, 1961), 10–31; *NEHGR* 14 (1860):304–5; 33 (1879):370–77, and 39 (1885): 365–68, have extracts from Eliot's account of the early history of Roxbury. Walter Eliot Thwing, *History of the First Church of Roxbury* (Boston: p.p., 1908), 1–46.

9. J. T. Perry, *History of the First Church of Exeter, 1638–1888* (Exeter NH: p.p., 1898), Pt. I.

10. Powell, *Puritan Village*, 206–12; E. S. Perzel, "The First Generation of Settlers in Ipswich MA, 1633–60" (Rutgers University Ph.D. dissertation, 1967); Allen, *In English Ways*, App. VI; Lucius Paige, *History of Cambridge* (Cambridge MA: Cambridge Historical Society, 1877), 11–15.

11. Cf. Murrin, "Review Article," 236–39; Demos, "Old Age," 252–61.

12. Octogenarians: John Albro (1617–1712), Walter Allen (1601–81), Nathaniel Aldous (c1595–1676), Theodore Atkinson (1612–1701), Edmund Angier (1612–93), Samuel Appleton (1586–1670), John Beale (1593–1688), Samuel Bass (1600–94), Edmund Blosse (1587–1681), Joseph Bixby (1621–1701), Richard Bellingham (1592–1672), John Bigelow (1617–1703), Thomas Bradbury (1611–94), Simon Bradstreet (1603–97), Richard Brackett (1611–91), Henry Bright, Jr. (1602–86), Thomas Browne (1605–88), Robert Buffum (c1588–1669), Charles Chadwick (1597–1682), Henry Chickering (1588–1671), Robert Coe (1596–c1676), John Coggeshall (1601–89), Edward Collins (1603–89), Alan Converse (c1599–1679), John Coolidge (1604–91), Thomas Cooper (1607–90), William Crafts (1602–90), John Cram (1597–1682), William Curtis (1592–1672), Theophilus Cushing (1584–1679), James Cutler (1606–94), Godfrey Dearborn (1603–86), John Devereux (1614–95), Thomas Doggett (1607–92), John Eddy (1597–1684), Samuel Eddy (1608–c88), John Eliot (1604–90), Benjamin Felton (c1604–88), Nathaniel Felton (1615–1705), Joshua Fisher (1585–1674), David Fiske, Jr. (c1623–1711), Nathaniel Fiske (c1592–1676), James Fitch (1622–1702), Joseph Fitch (c1624–c1713), Thomas Fitch (1612–c1704), Thomas Flegge (1616–98), Stephen Fosdick (1583–1664), Renald Foster (c1595–1681), John Fuller (1611–99), Thomas Fuller (c1618–98), William Fuller (1610–93), John Gedney (c1603–88), Robert Goodale (1601–83), Ozias Goodwin (c1596–1683), William Goodwin (c1589–1673), Edmund Greenleaf (c1586–1671), William Hammond (1575–1662), Thomas Hastings (1605–85), Robert Hawkins (1610–1704), Joseph Hill (1602–88), Edmund Hobart, Jr. (1604–86), Thomas Hobart (1606–89), Justinian Holden (1611–91), Richard Holden (1609–96), James Howe (1604–1702), William Hubbard (1622–1704), John Hunting (1597–1689), Gawdy James (1604–84), Robert Jennison (c1606–90), Richard Kimball (1595–1675), William Knapp (1578–1658), Francis Lawes (c1586–c1666), Richard Leeds (1605–93), Daniel Lincoln (1619–99), Thomas Lincoln, the miller (1600–83), Thomas Lincoln, the cooper, (c1605–91), Robert Lord (1603–83), Matthew Marvin (1600–87), John Mills (c1592–1678), Isaac Moore (1622–1705), John Morse (c1616–97), Joseph Morse, Jr. (1610–91), Thomas Moulton (1608–99), Joseph Mygatt (1596–1680), John Newgate (1580–1665), Thomas Nicholls (1615–96), William Nickerson (1605–90), Robert Payne (1595–1684), Robert Parke (1580–1665), Robert Parker (1603–85), Thomas Parker (1609–90), John Parmenter (1588–1671), Giles Payson (1609–89), Moses Pingry (1610–96), Thomas Philbrick (1584–1667), William Roscoe (1594–1682), Amos Sheffield (c1619–1708), Edmund Sheffield (1612–1705), Samuel Sherman (1618–99), Henry Skerry (1606–91),

George Steele (1580–1664), Gregory Stone (1592–1672), Simon Stone (1585–1665), John Stratton (c1606–86), Samuel Symonds (c1595–1678), John Throckmorton (1601–c87), John Thurston (1607–86), John Tower (1609–1702), Thomas Townsend (1595–1677), Peter Tufts (1617–1700), John Ward (1606–93), Robert Ware (c1618–99), Andrew Warner (1594–1684), John Warren (1585–1667), Lawrence Waters (1602–87), Thomas Webster (1631–1715), Daniel Weld (1585–1666), William Wentworth (1616–98), John Wheelwright (1598–1679), John White (c1595–1683), John Whitman (c1600–92), Samuel Whiting (1597–1679), Robert Williams (c1593–1693), Roger Williams (c1603–1683), Deane Winthrop (1623–1704), Nicholas Wyeth (c1595–1680). Octogenarian women: Mary Blosse (1594–1675), Christian Chamberlain (1578–1659), Catherine Coytmore (1576–1659), Elizabeth Hammond (1587–1670), Ann Pollard (c1620–1725), Anne Woodward (1603–83). It has proved far harder to recover women's vital records than men's.

13. Lockridge, *New England Town*, 43 n. 10, 45, 84; Hill, *Records of Dedham*, vol. 1, passim; Wall, *Massachusetts Bay*, 28–29; Prest, "Stability and Change," 359–74; Archer, "New England Mosaic," 497; Philip J. Greven, "Family Structure in Seventeenth-Century Andover, Massachusetts," *WMQ* 23 (1966):135–54; Anderson, *New England's Generation*, 180.

14. Weis, *Colonial Clergy*; Savage; Morison, *Founding of Harvard*, 387.

15. Roberts, 2nd ser. 3:723–74; Wentworth, *Wentworth Genealogy*, 74–76; C. H. Bell, *John Wheelwright* (Boston: Prince Society, 1876), passim.

16. Peck was 58 in 1638, Phillip 56. On Adams, see *WP*, 3:439–40; Thomas G. Barnes, "Thomas Lechford and the Earliest Lawyering in Massachusetts, 1638–41," in Daniel R. Coquillette, ed., *Law in Colonial Massachusetts* (Boston: Colonial Society of Massachusetts Publications, 1984), 3–38; Adams, a churchwarden, had resisted the requirement to install a railed altar at the east end of St. Mary's in 1635. He had also scrawled over the episcopal commissary's seat, "My house shall be called the house of prayer; but ye have made it a den of thieves." After refusing to remove his graffito, he had been excommunicated. In his subsequent action he had been represented by William Prynne, notorious antagonist of Laud, and by Lechford. After losing the case, both Adams and Lechford fled to Massachusetts in 1637. Cf. *CSPD*, 1636–37, 420. On young gentlemen who returned—Sampson, Fiennes, Tyndal, Gurdon, and Brand—see Table 5.

17. Emerson, *Letters*, 63–66, 15 March 1631. Stearns, *Strenuous Puritan*, 175–82; Stout, "Morphology of Remigration," 151–72; Delbanco, "Puritan Errand," 343–60; Cressy, *Coming Over*, 178–212.

18. *WJ*, 1:162–63, 169, 239–40, 26, 2:42–44. Irwin H. Polishook, ed., *Roger Williams, John Cotton, and Religious Freedom* (Englewood Cliffs, N.J.: Prentice-Hall, 1967), 4–18; Battis, *Saints and Sectaries*, 184–86, 208.

19. Eaton: *WJ*, 1:310–14; *WP*, 4:142–43; Morison, *Founding of Harvard*, 226–41. Vane: *WJ*, 1:229; Adamson and Folland, *Vane*, 107–8, 119–20. Vassall: *WP*, 2:153n., 265 n., 276; Waters, 2:1319; *WJ*, 2:271, 339. Cf. Thomas Goad, an unsatisfactory servant (and distant kinsman) of John Winthrop, Jr., sent home after only a few weeks in Massachusetts (*WP*, 3:258), or Josiah Plaistow, a gentleman convicted of stealing corn from an Indian in 1631, who after degradation left the colony (*WJ*, 1:68).

20. Powell, *Puritan Village*, chaps. 8–9; Goodwin, *Goodwin Family*, chap. 3.

21. Thompson, *Sex in Middlesex*, 116–17, 123–25; W. C. Boyden, *Thomas Boyden* (Boston: p.p., 1901), passim. It is possible that the moves of father and son may have been elided. Cf. Walter Allen, the scandalous fornicator, who moved or was moved four times; Bent, *Allen*, chap. 2; *WP*, 4:97–98.

22. *WJ*, 1:90. Refugees from King Philip among our contingent were Richard

Holden, Daniel Hovey, William Longley, John Roper, John Tower, Lawrence Waters, and John Page (?). Douglas Leach, *Flintlock and Tomahawk* (New York: Norton, 1966), 187–88.

23. Hooker: *WJ*, 1:132–34; Shuffelton, *Thomas Hooker*, 197–214. Pynchon: Innes, *Labor*, 5–9; Smith, *Colonial Justice*, 18–26. Ormesby: Dow, *History of Hampton*, chap. 2. Barbara MacAllen has pointed out to me the extraordinary similarity of the terrain at Hampton NH and Ormesby, Norfolk, with the invaluable addition in New England of marshland. Fiske: Pope, "Notebook of Fiske," ix–xvi; Adeline P. Cole, *Notes on Wenham History* (Wenham: Wenham Historical Society, 1943), chap. 1; W. P. Upham, *Wenham Town Records* (Wenham: Wenham Historical Society, 1927), vol. 1.

24. E.g., Sudbury, Dedham, Ipswich, Hingham; Anderson, *New England's Generation*, 100.

25. Ludkin and Ayres: Savage. Kimball: Morrison, *Kimball Family*, chap. 2; Perzel, "Settlers in Ipswich," 176, 193. Others who moved into Boston were John Amye (ship captain), Bozoun Allen (yeoman), Richard Bellingham (lawyer and official), Thomas Bumstead (pewterer), Simon Bradstreet (merchant and official), Nicholas Busby (merchant and weaver), John Coggeshall (mercer), Giles Firmin, Sr. (apothecary), Edmund Greenleaf (innkeeper), Gawdy James (cordwainer), George Munnings (cordwinder and prison keeper), Thomas Mount (bricklayer and mason), William Payne (merchant and shop owner), Thomas Rucke (innkeeper), Robert Reynolds (shoemaker), Michael Powell (scrivener and teacher), John Scarlett (mariner), Francis Smyth (card maker), John Ward (doctor), Samuel Wilbore (merchant), and Richard Woodward (miller), Archer, "New England Mosaic," 485–89; Anderson, *New England's Generation*, 108–14; Vickers, "Working the Fields," 64–67.

26. *WP*, 2:312, 319–20.

27. *WP*, 3:485; *NEHGR* 15 (1861):25; Huntington, *Huntington Family*, chap. 1. On passenger mortality, see Cressy, *Coming Over*, 148.

28. *WP*, 3:400, 138; cf. 3:410.

29. Powell, *Puritan Village*, 92–101.

30. Appleton: Holman, "Notes on the Appletons," 17; Bradstreet, Fitch, Goodwin, Sheffield, Howe, Warner: Savage; Woodward: Ferris.

31. Robert J. Taylor, *Colonial Connecticut: A History* (Millwood NY: KTO Press, 1979), 3–9; Shuffelton, *Thomas Hooker*, chap. 6; Sidney E. Ahlstrom, "Thomas Hooker and the Settlement of Connecticut," *Church History* 32 (1962–63):415–18.

32. Chapter 6, "Servants," herein.

33. G. L. Randall, *Taber Genealogy* (p.p., 1924), chap. 1. Taber's moves: Plymouth 1630, Watertown 1634, Yarmouth 1639, Martha's Vineyard 1653, New London CT 1654, Portsmouth RI 1659, Tiverton RI 1667–72. Cf. Thomas Boyden, seven moves, and Richard Holden and Thomas Willett, six moves.

34. Sixty-six of the 106 lived in only one town in New England, but 28 had moved once, five twice, four three times, and one man four times before they settled. No one moved away from where they had spent four decades or more, though two died while visiting children in other towns. Two men who had arrived as bachelors, Thomas Brown of Cambridge and Robert Hawkins of Charlestown, had returned briefly to London to marry, and William Coddington twice remarried there on trips back to England (1631–33 and 1648–51). Where the occupations of these town survivors are known, it appears that men whose callings were least physically exposed generally had the best chances of a long life. Thus 6 ministers, 3 schoolmasters, 10 merchants, 2 innkeepers, and 15 workshop artisans bulk large among the 59 whose occupations are known. Three points should give us pause, however. First, 10 farmers and a surprising 6 sea- or watermen lived to great ages in one place,

despite hazardous vocations. Second, many of the 47 whose occupations are unknown were probably subsistence farmers. Third, several described on shipping lists as indoor artisans, weavers especially, would have had to turn their hands to farming to survive. It is also remarkable how few gentlemen or professionals made it in the residential marathon.

35. Kenneth A. Lockridge and Alan Kreider, "The Evolution of Massachusetts Town Government, 1640 to 1740," *WMQ* 30 (1961):549–74.

36. A radius of 30 miles has been chosen—in contrast with the 10-mile East Anglian neighborhood radius—because New England settlement was so much thinner.

37. Wheelwright and Hutchinson followers are listed in Battis, *Saints and Sectaries*, 301–28. Their male supporters of East Anglian origin numbered 39. Eastern counties migrants from Massachusetts to Williams's Providence Plantation were Robert Cole, Adam Goodwin, Richard Scott, Thomas Sucklin, John Throckmorton, John Whipple, and Williams himself.

38. Sidney V. James, *Colonial Rhode Island, a History* (New York: Scribners, 1975), 1–118.

39. **Hartford:** Allyn, Barber, Barnard, John Clarke, Nicholas Clarke, Elmer, Edmunds, Ozias Goodwin, William Goodwin, Samuel Hale, Thomas Hale, Hart, Hills, Hooker, Haynes, Lord, Lyman, Marsh, Matthew Marvin, Reynold Marvin, Moody, Mygatt, Olmstead, Pratt, Roscoe, Edward Stebbings, George Steele, John Steele, Talcott, Wadsworth, Andrew Warner, John Warner, Webb, White, Whiting. **Wethersfield:** Chaplin, Coe, Foote, Hubbard, Plumbe, Rayner, Reynolds, Rose, Seaman, Edmund Sherman, Sr., Samuel Sherman, Jr., Wright, Kilbourne Sr., Kilbourne Jr. **Windsor:** Taylor. **Springfield:** Burr, Cable, Pynchon, Rowland Stebbings, Ufford, S. Wright. **Long Island:** Dickerson, Hallock, Peter Hobart, Moore, Townsend, Henry Tuttle, John Tuttle, Windes, John Youngs, Joseph Youngs.

40. Ralph Crandall, "New England's Second Great Migration," *NEHGR* 133 (1979):198–220.

41. **Connecticut coast:** Astwood, Becket, Burr, Cable, John Clarke, John Clarke, Coe, Crabbe, John and Thomas Fitch, Samuel and Thomas Hale, Hubbard, James, Knapp, Leveritch, Livermore, Lockwood, Matthew Marvin, Moore, Plumbe, Rayner, Roscoe, Rose, Royce, Seaman, Edmund Sherman, Sr., John Sherman, Samuel Sherman, Sandford, Ufford, Waterbury, Webb, Wright. **Connecticut Valley:** Babcock, Cheeseborough, Joseph Clarke, William Clarke, James Fitch, Hovey, Huntington, Reynold Marvin, Parke, Royce, Taber, Winthrop. **Cape Cod and islands:** Crowe, Doggett, George, Large, Leveritch, Nickerson, Pease, Smith, Taber. **New Hampshire and Maine coast:** Baker, Brock, Burdett, Colby, Philemon and Timothy Dalton, Dawson, Dixon, Foulsham, Godfrey, Hill, Hood, Jenner, Josselyn, Lawson, Leveritch, Mason, Montague, Palmer, Willett, Wincoll. **Within Massachusetts (over 30 miles):** Cromwell, Eddy, Gilman, Guttridge, Greenleaf, Hills, Page. **Remigration to Massachusetts:** Cullick, Forster, Reynolds, Scarlet, John Sherman. **Rhode Island:** Eldred, Helme, Palmer, Taber. **Note:** All long-distance moves are included; thus restless individuals like Leveritch or Taber are listed more than once.

42. Henry S. Burridge, *Beginnings of Colonial Maine* (Portland: State of Maine, 1914), chap. 3; Charles Clark, *Maine: A Bicentennial History* (New York: Norton, 1977), 16–52; John G. Reid, *Maine, Charles II, and Massachusetts* (Portland: Maine Historical Society, 1977), 1–11. Vickers, "Work on the Fishing Periphery," 83–117, describes the "frontier" ambience of fishermen based in Essex County MA, as does Heyrman, *Commerce and Culture*, 29–51, 209–30.

43. Fitch: Poteet, "More Yankee than Puritan," 102–23; *Hale, House.*

44. David C. Klingaman, "The Coastwise Trade of Colonial Massachusetts," *Essex Institute Historical Collections* 108 (1972):217–34.

45. William Haller, Jr., *The Puritan Frontier* (New York: AMS Press, 1968); Pope, *Pioneers*, 522.

Chapter 10. Conclusion

1. Keith Wrightson, *English Society, 1580–1680* (London: Macmillan, 1982), and Allan Macfarlane, *The Origins of English Individualism* (London: Arnold, 1978), have depicted early modern England as highly individualistic, mobile, and acquisitive. More moderate views are offered in Sharpe, *Early Modern England*, and Clay, *Economic Expansion*. Greene's influential *Pursuits of Happiness*, 30–35, adopts the Wrightson–Macfarlane line.

2. Greene, *Settlements to Society*, 64–66.

3. E.g., Waters, "Hingham," 361; Wall, *Massachusetts Bay*, 26–34; Paige, *Cambridge*, 11.

4. Thompson, *Sex in Middlesex*, 162–63, 176–77; Demos, "Old Age," 272–76.

5. Cressy, *Coming Over*, 28–29; Appleby, "Value and Society," 305–9. A recent rebuttal of Rutman, *Winthrop's Boston*, is Foster, *The Long Argument*.

6. Roger Thompson, "Holy Watchfulness and Community Conformity," *NEQ*, 56 (1983):504–22; Allen, "Both Englands," 80; Anderson, *New England's Generation*, 185.

7. T. H. Breen, "Persistent Localism: English Social Change and the Shaping of New England Institutions," *WMQ* 32 (1975):1–29.

8. Tyack, "Humbler Puritans," 101–3; *WJ*, 1:74–75.

9. *WJ*, 1:122–23, 124–33, 288–90, 2:229–45; Waters, "Hingham," 351–70.

10. Michael Walzer, *"Puritanism as a Revolutionary Ideology," History and Theory* 3 (1961):59–90; David D. Hall, "Religion and Society: Problems and Reconsiderations," in W. L. Joyce et al., eds., *Printing and Society in Early America* (Worcester: American Antiquarian Society, 1983), 317–39.

11. Allen, *In English Ways*, passim.

12. *WP*, 2:138–39.

13. *WJ*, 2:24.

14. Vickers, "Working the Fields," 51, 53, 55, 60, 66.

15. Butler, "Magic, Astrology, and Religious Heritage," 317–46; Heyrman, *Commerce and Culture*, 414.

16. Allen, *In English Ways*, 4; Kishlansky, "Community," 139.

17. *WP*, 3:22.

18. Greene, *Settlements to Society*, 65; McGiffert, *God's Plot*, 63; Cressy, *Coming Over*, 208.

19. Anderson, *New England's Generation*, 125.

20. Innes, *Labor*, 28; Anderson, *New England's Generation*, 126–24, chap. 4, 115–18.

21. Allen, *In English Ways*, 130–31; Perzel, "Settlers in Ipswich," 248; Daniel Vickers, "Competency or Competition," *WMQ* 47 (1990):3–29.

22. Anderson, *New England's Generation*, 107; Martin, *Profits*, passim; Innes, *Labor*, 17–43.

23. Rutman, *Winthrop's Boston*, 187.

24. Allen, *In English Ways*, 136, 142, 214; Martin, *Profits*, 15–16; Anderson, *New England's Generation*, 109; see Chapter 7, herein.

25. Mary R. McCarl, "Shepard's Record of Relations," *WMQ* 48 (1991):451.

Table Source Notes

Table 5. Gentlemen Emigrants

Appleton: See nn. 24 and 31, Chapter 3. **Bradbury:** n. 27. **Brand:** *NEHGR* 56 (1902):298; *MHS Colls*, 5th ser. 10:154–55; P. Northeast, "Boxford Church-wardens' Accounts," *Suffolk Records Society* 22 (1965); Sudbury Wills. **Cookes:** *NEHGR* 135 (1981):90; Waters, 1:673; *WMQ* 98 (1991):439, 460–61; Essex Wills. **Coolidge:** *American Genealogist* 62 (1954):65–67; F. C. Crawford, *One Branch of the Coolidge Family* (p.p., 1964); E. D. Coolidge, *Coolidge Genealogy* (Boston: p.p., 1931); Roberts, 2nd ser. 1:586–601. **Cope:** *NEHGR* 107 (1953):268; *WP*, 4:59. **Crowes:** Wyman; Norwich Wills; PCC. **Downings:** nn. 19, 10. **Gosnold:** n. 28. **Gurdons:** n. 25. **Harlakenden:** n. 26. **Haynes:** n. 30. **Helme:** Lincs Wills. **Humphrey:** F. Humphreys, *Humphreys Family* (New York: p.p., 1883); F. Rose-Troup, "John Humphreys," *Essex Institute Historical Collections* 65 (1929):293–308. **Johnson:** n. 23. **Josselyn:** F. L. Weis, *Ancestral Lines of Sixty Families* (Baltimore: Genealogical Publishing, 1976); Venns, Pt. I, 2:290; *NEHGR* 63 (1909):19–33, 490. **Moody:** n. 29. **Parke:** G. Towne, *Ancestry of R. F. and E. C. Towne* (p.p., 1974); *WP*, 2:276; *Parke Society Newsletter* 23 (1986):33. **Pelhams:** nn. 15–17. **Plaistow:** *WJ*, 1:68; Essex Wills. **Plumbe:** Waters, 2:1413–14; *NEHGR* 107 (1953):3–7; Wyman; Essex Wills. **Pynchon:** n. 18. **Sampson:** *WP*, 2:229, 276, 318; Norwich Wills; PCC. **Sams:** *NEHGR* 50 (1896):234, 64 (1910):168; Waters, 1:515–16; Essex Wills. **Thorndike:** *NEHGR* 53 (1899):129; Waters, 2:1267–70; Lincs Wills. **Vane:** n. 22. **Wentworth:** J. Wentworth, *Wentworth Genealogy* (Boston: p.p., 1878); Lincs Wills. **Winthrops:** nn. 4, 20, 21.

Table 7. Clerical Emigrants

J. Allen: Robert Charles Anderson, private communication; after consulting the Norwich Consignation Books and the Peterborough Ordination Books, he concludes that the John Allen baptized at Colby, Norfolk, curate at Denton and vicar of St. James South Elmham, is a different clergyman. **T. Allen:** see n. 50, Chapter 3. **Bright:** *Massachusetts Bay Records*, 1:34, 37*e, f*; Frances Rose-Troup, *John White of Dorchester* (Boston: Little, Brown, 1930), 139, 140, 144. **Brown:** *NEHGR* 58 (1904):184; S. C. Powell, *Puritan Village* (Middletown CT: Wesleyan University Press, 1963), 51–52. **Burdett:** n. 45. **Burr:** C. B. Todd, *Genealogical History of the Burr Family* (New York: p.p., 1902). **Carter:** *NEHGR* 41 (1887):335, 52 (1898):85; Waters, 1:142; H. W. Carter, *Carter Genealogy* (Norfolk CT: p.p., 1909); Suffolk Wills. **Cotton:** H. G. Somerby, "Cotton Family," *Heraldic Journal* 22 (1868):49–58. **Dalton:** *CSPD*, 1633–34, 450–51; *WP* 3:348; *NEHGR* 39 (1885):249. **Eaton:**

n. 46. **Eliot:** n. 49. **Fiske:** *NEHGR* 88 (1934):40–45, 141–46, 217–24, 367–74, 90 (1936):142–46, 265–73, 92 (1938):177–83; *WP* 3:394–95; Suffolk Wills. **Hobart:** *NEHGR* 11 (1857):15, 25; Norwich Wills; *WJ* 2:224; Wyman. **Hooker:** E. Hooker, *Descendants of Rev. Thomas Hooker* (Rochester NY: p.p., 1909). **James:** B. Swan, *Society of the Colonial Wars of Rhode Island* 48 (1963):1–15; *WJ*, 1:217; Waters, 2:1356–57; F. L. Weis, *Colonial Clergy of New England* (Baltimore: Genealogical Publishing, 1977). **Jenner:** Venns, Pt. I, 2:469; *WP*, 3:385; Essex Wills. **Knollys:** Venns, Pt. I, 2:503; *WJ*, 1:295; *WP*, 4:176–78. **Knowles:** Venns, Pt. I, 2:504; Lincs Wills. **Leverich:** n. 47. **Norton:** *WP*, 3:237; Essex Wills; Venns; Weis, *Colonial Clergy.* **Peck:** *NEHGR* 91 (1937):15, 92 (1938): 71–73, 93 (1939):178, 94 (1940):69–73; Norwich Wills. **Peter:** R. P. Stearns, *The Strenuous Puritan* (Urbana: University of Illinois Press, 1954), 5–9. **Phillip:** n. 51. **Phillips:** *NEHGR* 110 (1956):276; *WP*, 2:164–65, 250–51, 276, 319–20, 3:173; *MHS Colls*, 5th ser. 1:123. **Rogerses:** Roberts, 2nd ser. 3:19–37; Waters, 1:226; Essex Wills. **Shepard:** Michael McGiffert, *God's Plot* (Amherst: University of Massachusetts Press, 1972), 3–4. **Skelton:** Roberts, 2nd ser. 3:252–69. **Wards:** Roberts, 2nd ser. 3:617; *NEHGR* 33 (1879):160, 34 (1880):188; Waters, 2:1103–4; *WP*, 3:390; A. W. Simpson, *The Wealth of the Gentry* (Cambridge: Cambridge University Press, 1961), 127. **Waterhouse:** *NEHGR* 52 (1898):130–31; *MHS Colls*, 3rd ser. 10:169–70, 4th ser. 8:590–91; Roberts, 2nd ser. 3:901. **Weld:** n. 58. **Wheelwright:** n. 52. **Whiting:** n. 53. **Williams:** n. 48. **Wilson:** *DNB*; Weis, *Colonial Clergy.* **Youngs:** *NEHGR* 53 (1899):244–46, 102 (1948):89; *MHS Colls*, 4th ser. 1:101; *Great Migration Newsletter*, 1st ser. 2 (1990):16; Southwold Parish Register transcript (I am grateful to the vicar of Southwold for the loan of the transcript); Suffolk Wills; Sudbury Wills; Norwich Wills.

Table 9. Mercantile Emigrants

Allen: Wyman; Sudbury Wills. **Andrews:** G. Selement and B. Woolley, eds., *Thomas Shepard Confessions* (Boston: Colonial Society of Massachusetts, 1981); PCC. **Angier:** *NEHGR* 44 (1890):269, 52 (1898):400–406; *MHS Colls*, 3rd ser. 10:166; Essex Wills. **Baker:** Walter Rye, ed., *L'Estrange's Calendar of Norwich Freemen* (Norwich: p.p., 1888); Percy Millican, ed., *Register of Freemen of Norwich* (Norwich: Jarrold, 1934); idem, ed., "An Index of Indentures of Norwich Apprentices," Norfolk Record Society 29 (1959); Norwich Wills. **Brown:** E. D. Hines, *Browne Hill* (Salem: p.p., 1897); Waters, 1:242, 280; Suffolk Wills. **Chaplin:** see n. 20, Chapter 4. **Child:** E. C. Child, *Child Genealogy* (Utica NY: p.p., 1881); Waters, 1:744; *WP*, 3:7, 142; Suffolk Wills. **Cockram:** Southwold Parish Register transcript; *NEHGR* 54 (1900):242–43, 59 (1905):198; Waters 2:1407; *WP*, 4:128; Suffolk Wills. **Coddington:** n. 8. **Coggeshall:** n. 21. **Cole:** *NEHGR* 64 (1910):167–68; Essex Wills. **Coytmore:** nn. 9, 19. **Cromwell:** Suffolk Wills. **Cullick:** n. 10. **Davison:** Wyman; Norwich Wills; Waters, 1:635; *WP*, 4:128; W. L. Sachse, "Minutes of Norwich Mayoralty Court," *Norfolk Record Society* 15 (1947):6 July 1631. **Firmin:** *NEHGR* 17 (1863):53–56, 40 (1886):72; *MHS Colls*, 3rd ser. 10: 168, 5th ser. 1:199–200; *WP*, 4:164; Sudbury Wills. **Foster:** n. 16. **Hammond:** n. 35. **Harding:** G. F. Harding, *Abraham Harding* (Hartford: p.p., 1979); Essex Wills. **Hill:** n. 24. **Hills:** n. 30. **Hough:** G. W. Hough, *Hough Families* (p.p., 1974), vol. 2, chap. 1; *NEHGR* 47 (1893):284–88, 36 (1882):29–33, 28 (1874):133; Lincs Wills. **Huntington:** E. B. Huntington, *Genealogical Memorials of the Huntington Family* (Stamford CT: p.p., 1863); *NEHGR* 114 (1960):74, 110 (1956):312, 111 (1957):153; Sachse, "Norwich Mayoralty Court," 29; Suffolk Wills. **Knapp:** David

Cressy, *Coming Over* (Cambridge: Cambridge University Press, 1987), 171; Sudbury Wills; Essex Wills; Ferris. **Knight:** *NEHGR* 50 (1896):142–43, 53 (1899): 378; Philip Vincent, *True Relation of the War against the Pequots* (London: Barker, 1636), 34; Essex Wills. **Leeds:** Ferris; Norwich Wills; Norfolk and Norwich Record Office, Great Yarmouth Freemen's Rolls. **Loomis:** E. Loomis, *Descendants of Joseph Loomis* (New Haven: p.p., 1875); Waters, 1:466–67; *NEHGR* 92 (1938): 203; J. J. Goodwin, *The Goodwin Family* (Hartford: p.p., 1891); Essex Wills. **Mills:** n. 45. **Mygatt:** Essex Wills. **Newgate:** n. 19. **Onge:** Sudbury Wills; *Great Migration Newsletter*, 1st ser. 4 (1990):1; *WP*, 3:346. **Payne:** n. 31. **Rucke:** *NEHGR* 138 (1984):105; Waters, 1:515; Essex Wills; PCC. **Sales:** *WP*, 2:229, 276; PCC. **Scott:** *NEHGR* 96 (1942):3–27; Waters, 2:1287; A. Scott, *Genealogical Notes* (p.p., n.d.); *WP*, 4:59; Roberts, 2nd ser. 3:82–83; Sudbury Wills. **Sherman:** *NEHGR* 26 (1872):65, 52 (1898):390–93; Roberts, 2nd ser. 3:209; R. E. Wall, *Massachusetts Bay* (New Haven, 1972), 51–60; Essex Wills. **Smith:** R. H. Freeman, *Descendants of Ralph Smith* (Middlebury CT: p.p., 1975); *NEHGR* 17 (1863):25; Norwich Wills. **Sparhawk:** Waters, 2:1187–89, 1123–24; Selement and Woolley, *Shepard Confessions*; *WP*, 4:134–35; Roberts, 2nd ser. 3:282; Essex Wills. **Symonds:** Waters, 1:177; American Antiquarian Society, ms letters of John Hall, 1660s; Cressy, *Coming Over*, 181–82, 283; *WP*, 4:12; PCC. **Taylor:** Ferris; *WP*, 2:319–20; Sudbury Wills. **Tidd:** n. 18. **Thompson:** n. 10. **Throckmorton:** n. 17. **Vassall:** n. 9. **Wade:** F. Rose-Troup, *Massachusetts Bay Company* (New York: Grafton, 1930), 37; Norwich Wills. **Wainwright:** *NEHGR* 59 (1905):265–69; Vincent, *Pequot War*, 47. **Weld:** C. F. Robinson, *Weld Collections* (p.p., 1938); *NEHGR* 53 (1899):496, 95 (1941):204; Sudbury Wills. **Whipples:** H. B. Whipple, *Descendants of Matthew Whipple* (p.p., 1965); Waters, 1:465–67; *NEHGR* 98 (1944):79; D. G. Allen, *In English Ways* (Chapel Hill: University of North Carolina Press, 1981), 198; Essex Wills. **Whiting:** *WP*, 2:389; Sudbury Wills; Essex Wills. **Whittingham:** Waters, 1:112; C. H. Pope, *The Pioneers of Massachusetts* (Boston: Wilson, 1900); Lincs Wills. **Wilbore:** n. 25. **Willett:** n. 8. **Youngs:** Waters, 2:1410–12; *WP*, 4:142; Southwold Parish Register transcripts; and Source Notes to Table 7.

Table 11. Professional Emigrants

Ayres: *NEHGR* 67 (1913):248–52; Sudbury Wills; Suffolk Wills. **Bellingham:** *WP*, 4:71; Lincs Wills. **Brackett:** Savage; Pope, *Pioneers*; Sudbury Wills. **Bradstreet:** see nn. 55 and 59, Chapter 4. **Bridge:** n. 56. **Chute:** *NEHGR* 54 (1900):113; Waters, 2:1201; E. S. Perzel, "First Generation of Settlement in Colonial Ipswich" (Rutgers University Ph.D. diss., 1967); Essex Wills. **Clarke:** n. 50. **Dinely:** Johnson, *Wonder-Working Providence*, 192; E. Battis, *Saints and Sectaries* (Chapel Hill: University of North Carolina Press, 1962), App. I; Lincs Wills. **Dudley:** D. B. Rutman, *Winthrop's Boston* (Chapel Hill: University of North Carolina Press, 1965), 25; *WP*, 3:6, 57. **Foster:** F. M. Hawes, *Foster Records* (Somerville MA: p.p., 1889), x; Suffolk Wills; Norwich Wills. **Gager:** *WP*, 2:276; Sudbury Wills. **Leverett:** Waters, 1:109; Lincs Wills. **Masters:** *NEHGR* 93 (1939):69–71; Pope, *Pioneers*; E. Emerson, ed., *Letters from New England* (Amherst: University of Massachusetts Press, 1976), 83–85; Essex Wills. **Palsgrave:** *NEHGR* 102 (1948):87–98, 312–13; Norwich Wills. **Portmont:** Battis, *Saints and Sectaries*, App. I; Pope, *Pioneers*; Lincs Wills. **Powell:** *NEHGR* 50 (1896):239; M. G. Hall, *Increase Mather* (Middletown CT: Wesleyan University Press, 1988), 38; Suffolk Wills. **Pratt:** *NEHGR* 18 (1864):29, 46 (1892):127; Pope, *Pioneers*; Ely Wills, *BRS*. **Sandford:** n. 51. **Somerby:** Savage; Lincs Wills. **Tyndal:** n. 58. **Ward:** *NEHGR* 54 (1900):113, 261–62; Waters, 1:587; Essex Wills; Suffolk Wills.

Table 12. Entrepreneurial Emigrants

Coe: see n. 61, Chapter 4. **Fitch:** n. 61. **Hutchinson:** n. 61. **Metcalfe:** n. 66. **Parish:** Pope, *Pioneers*; Selement and Woolley, *Shepard Confessions*; Sudbury Wills. **Sherman:** n. 61. **Stacey:** n. 63. **Stansby:** *WP*, 3:381; Selement and Woolley, *Shepard Confessions*; *MHS Colls*, 6th ser. 4:7–11; Sudbury Wills. **Underwood:** n. 66. **Warner:** n. 64.

Table 14. Emigrant Artisans

Adams: *WP*, 3:439–40; Suffolk Wills. **Allen:** see nn. 14 and 23, Chapter 5. **Amye:** Waters, 1:466; *NEHGR* 56 (1902):276; Essex Wills. **Babcock:** Essex Wills. **Bacon:** *NEHGR* 50 (1896):42–44; Sudbury Wills; Norwich Wills. **Barber:** *NEHGR* 83 (1929):339; N. Evans et al., *Looking Back at Fressingfield* (Fressingfield: Workers Educational Association, 1979), 30; Suffolk Wills; Norwich Wills. **Barker:** E. F. Barker, *Barker Family* (New York: p.p., 1927; Allen, *In English Ways*, 245; Sudbury Wills. **Barnes:** T. C. Barnes, *Barnes Family Yearbook* (New York: p.p., 1907); Norwich Wills. **Barrell:** n. 19. **Beale:** n. 19. **Bigelow:** P. Bigelow, *Bigelow Family Genealogy* (n.p., 1986); *NEHGR* 67 (1913):363; PCC; Suffolk Wills, s.v. Beggerly. **Birde:** *WP*, 3:126; A. Searle, ed., "Barrington Family Papers," *Camden Society*, 4th ser. 28 (1983):146; Essex Wills. **Blodgett:** G. Limeburner, *Seth Blodgett* (Rutland VT: Tuttle, 1933); *NEHGR* 100 (1946):318; Suffolk Wills. **Boosey:** *Bradford Street, Bocking* (Bocking: Friends of Bradford Street, 1974), 12; *MHS Colls*, 5th ser. 1:192, 4; *WP*, 2:139; Essex Wills. **Brice:** *WP*, 2:207, 3:126; Sudbury Wills. **Browne:** *Massachusetts Bay Records*, 1:34, 37*e*, *f*, 51–54; Rose-Troup, *White*, 144–45, 153; Alexander Young, ed., *Chronicles of the First Planters of Massachusetts* (Gloucester MA: Smith, 1971), 61; Waters, 2:855–56; Essex Wills. **Buckland:** Savage. **Bumstead:** n. 14. **Burr:** Todd, *History of the Burr Family*; Hale, *House*; Essex Wills. **Burrows:** Great Yarmouth Freemen's Rolls; Norwich Wills. **Busby:** A. C. Kingsbury, *Historical Sketch of Nicholas Busby* (n.p., 1924); J. W. Hawes, "Genealogy of NB," *Library of Cape Cod History and Genealogy* 100 (1912); Sachse, "Norwich Mayoralty Court," 12 April 1631, 6 November 1631; Millican, *Register of Norwich Freemen*. **Buttolph:** Harding, *Abraham Harding*; *NEHGR* 52 (1898): 318; Bernard Bailyn, *New England Merchants in the Seventeenth Century* (New York: Harper, 1964), 37; Essex Wills. **Cakebread:** *NEHGR* 107 (1953):197; Essex Wills. **Chamberlain:** *NEHGR* 15 (1861):26; P. Glazier, *Chamberlain Families* (p.p., 1973); Colket; Norwich Wills. **Chase:** G. M. Chase, *William Chase of Yarmouth* (p.p., 1984); Essex Wills. **Church:** C. W. Church, *Gideon Church* (Waterbury CT: p.p., 1914); Essex Wills. **Clarke:** *NEHGR* 128 (1974); Savage. **Clough:** Suffolk Wills. **Converse:** Wyman; J. Converse, *Ancestry and Descendants of Samuel Converse* (Boston: p.p., 1905); W. M. Dixon, *Kith and Kin* (Los Angeles: p.p., 1922); Waters, 1:237; Essex Wills. **Dady:** Wyman; Waters, 1:143; Essex Wills. **Dalton:** Savage; see Timothy Dalton in Source Notes to Table 7. **Danes:** n. 17. **Dickerson:** W. L. Baker, *Descendants of Philemon Dickerson* (Chicago: p.p., 1978); Suffolk Wills. **Dix:** Millican, *Register of Norwich Freemen*; J. H. Pound, "The Norwich Poor, 1570," *Norfolk Records Society* 40 (1971):86; Sachse, "Norwich Mayoralty Court," 9; Norwich Wills. **Dixon:** Wyman; Sudbury Wills. **Eddy:** *NEHGR* 98 (1944):83, 101 (1947):64; J. and S. Eddy, *Eddy Family* (Boston: p.p., 1881); R. S. D. Eddy, *Eddy Family* (Boston: p.p., 1930). **Farwell:** *NEHGR* 95 (1941); Lincs Wills. **Felton:** *NEHGR* 56 (1902):236–37; Waters, 2:1402; Great Yarmouth Freemen's Rolls; W. R. Felton, *Genealogy of the Felton Family* (Rutland VT: Tuttle, 1935); PCC. **Fillingham:** *WP*, 3:484; Suffolk Wills; Norwich Wills.

Notes to Table 14

Fish: Battis, *Saints and Sectaries*, App. I; Lincs Wills. **Fishers:** A. F. Michels, *Roots of Fishers* (p.p., 1983); P. A. Fisher, *Fisher Genealogy* (Everett MA: p.p., 1898); *NEHGR* 85 (1931):339; *MHS Colls*, 3rd ser. 10:159–60; J. F. Martin, *Profits in the Wilderness* (Chapel Hill: University of North Carolina Press, 1991), 15–16; Suffolk Wills. **Fosdick:** *NEHGR* 97 (1943):169; Suffolk Wills. **Frost:** N. S. Frost, *Frost Genealogy* (West Newton MA: p.p., 1926); R. C. Anderson, "English Origins of Philemon Whale," *The Genealogist* 6 (1985):131–41; *NEHGR* 68 (1914); Suffolk Wills. **Fuller:** *Brief Sketch of Thomas Fuller* (Appleton WI: p.p., 1909); Rye, *Norwich Freemen*; Millican, *Register of Norwich Freemen*; Pound, "Norwich Poor," 51; Norwich Wills. **Gage:** D. M. Gage, *John Gage of Ipswich* (p.p., 1983); Sudbury Wills. **H. Garrett:** Suffolk Wills. **R. Garrett:** *WP*, 2:272; *WJ*, 1:40; Essex Wills. **Garrold/Ett:** n. 27. **Gault:** Great Yarmouth Freemen's Rolls; V. Anderson, *New England's Generation* (Cambridge: Cambridge University Press, 1991), 110; Norwich Wills. **Gedney:** H. F. Waters, *Gedney and Clarke Families* (Salem: p.p., 1880); Pound, "Norwich Poor," 69; Millican, *Register of Norwich Freemen*; Rye, *Norwich Freemen*; Norwich Wills. **George:** *NEHGR* 105 (1951):164; Sudbury Wills. **Gilman:** D. Q. Davis, *Gilmans of New Hampshire and Maine* (Providence: p.p., 1970); M. B. Thompson, *Some New Hampshire Families* (p.p., 1977); *NEHGR* 19 (1865): 26; Norwich Wills. **Greenfield:** V. C. Sanborn, *Essex Institute Historical Collections* 53 (1917):241–42; Rye, *Norwich Freemen*; Millican, *Register of Norwich Freemen*; Norwich Wills. **Greenleaf:** D. Boynton, *Edmund Greenleaf* (p.p., 1980); *NEHGR* 42 (1888):299–301; Waters, 1:71; Norwich Wills; Suffolk Wills. **Gridley:** *NEHGR* 80 (1926):240; *WP*, 4:213; Sudbury Wills; **Griggs:** Roberts, 1st ser. 1:44; Sudbury Wills. **Guttridge:** *NEHGR* 61 (1907):332; Sudbury Wills; Norwich Wills. **Haffield:** *NEHGR* 60 (1906):181. **Harding:** Harding, *Abraham Harding*; Essex Wills. **Hart:** *NEHGR* 98 (1944):80; Essex Wills. **Hayward:** Pound, "Norwich Poor"; Rye, *Norwich Freemen*; Millican, *Register of Norwich Freemen*; Norwich Wills. **Heard:** *NEHGR* 54 (1900):99; Waters, 2:1357; Northeast, "Boxford Churchwardens' Accounts"; Perzel, "Ipswich"; Essex Wills. **Hett:** *NEHGR* 64 (1910): 183; *Aspinwall Notarial Records* (Boston: Registry Commission, 1903), 85. **Hobart:** see Peter Hobart in Source Notes to Table 7. **Holden:** E. Putnam, *Holden Genealogy* (Boston: p.p., 1923); Ferris; Sudbury Wills. **Hood:** n. 190. **Hovey:** *Hovey Book* (Haverhill MA: p.p., 1913); Perzel, "Ipswich"; Essex Wills. **Howchen:** Rutman, *Winthrop's Boston*, 247; Wall, *Massachusetts Bay*, 183; Norwich Wills; Suffolk Wills. **Howe:** *NEHGR* 135 (1981); Cressy, *Coming Over*, 216; M. Halsey Thomas, ed., *The Diary of Samuel Sewall* (New York: Farrar, Straus and Giroux, 1974), 19 May 1702; Account Book in Ipswich Historical Society; Perzel, "Ipswich"; L. C. Warner, *Descendants of Andrew Warner* (New Haven: Tuttle, Morehouse and Taylor, 1919); Essex Wills. **Howlett:** Allen, *In English Ways*, 131, 136; Perzel, "Ipswich"; Suffolk Wills. **Ingalls:** C. Burleigh, *Genealogy and History of the Ingalls Family* (Baltimore: p.p., 1984); Lincs Wills. **James:** Wyman; B. MacAllen, private communication; Norwich Wills, s.v. Gawdy and James. **Jones:** n. 4. **Keyser:** n. 6. **Kidbys:** *WP*, 2:321; Savage. **Kimballs:** n. 18. **Lamb:** *WP*, 2:271, 276; Waters, 1:1; Sudbury Wills. **Lawes:** n. 8. **Leager:** n. 5. **Lincoln** (1): J. E. Morris, *Stephen Lincoln* (Hartford: p.p., 1895); B. L. Palcie, *Genealogy of the Robert Lincoln Family* (p.p., 1985); Norwich Wills. **Lincoln** (2): *NEHGR* 19 (1865):25; Norwich Wills. **Lincoln** (3): see Chaper 8, n. 31. **Looker:** *NEHGR* 143 (1989):325–31; Roberts, 1st ser. 1:40, 67; Essex Wills, s.v. Looker and Ridsdale. **Lord:** Pope, *Pioneers*; Waters, 2:1102–3; D. P. Corey, *Waite Family* (Malden MA: p.p., 1913); Allen, *In English Ways*; Sudbury Wills. **Ludkin:** n. 13. **Lusher:** *NEHGR* 83 (1929):339; Martin, *Profits*, 16; Johnson, *Wonder-Working Providence*, 143, 229; K. Lockridge, *A New England Town* (New York: Norton, 1970), 29, 43–46, 62, 84, 125; Pope,

Pioneers. **Marshall:** Rutman, *Winthrop's Boston*, 73, 247; Battis, *Saints and Sectaries*, App. I: Lincs Wills. **Mason:** n. 15. **Marston:** Great Yarmouth Freemen's Rolls; *NEHGR* 90 (1936):359; H. M. G. Hargrave, *Goodale–Goodell Forebears* (p.p., 1976), v; Norwich Wills. **Mixer:** n. 25. **Moody:** n. 14. **Merrill:** Pope, *Pioneers*; Essex Wills. **Mott:** *American Genealogist* 35 (1957):107–8; J. L. Mott, *Mott Street* (Baltimore: p.p., 1986); *Hale, House*, 749–51; *NEHGR* 135 (1981):86; Sudbury Wills; Essex Wills. **Moulton:** n. 12. **Mount:** *WP*, 2:272; Essex Wills. **Mulliner:** Waters, 2:1355; *NEHGR* 5 (1901):421; Suffolk Wills. **Nickerson:** Rye, *Norwich Freemen*, s.v. Nyker; Anderson, *New England's Generation*, 105; *NEHGR* 94 (1940):156; Pound, "Norwich Poor," 89; C. E. Nickerson, *From Pilgrims and Indians to Kings and Indentured Servants* (p.p., 1970), chap. 1; Norwich Wills. **Oliver:** n. 10. **Page:** T. P. Brigham, *Descendants of John Page* (Haverhill MA: p.p., 1972); L. M. Case and P. Sanderson, *Family of John Page* (Baltimore: Genealogical Publishing, 1978). **S. Paine:** *NEHGR* 143 (1989):291–302, 54 (1900):231; Norwich Wills. **T. Paine:** N. Paine, *Thomas Paine of Salem and His Descendants* (Haverhill MA: Record Publishing, 1928); Norwich Wills. **Palmer:** *NEHGR* 60 (1906):275; Waters, 2:1197; Essex Wills. **Parker:** Waters, 1:32; *NEHGR* 60 (1906): 184; *MHS Colls*, 3rd ser. 10:168; Sudbury Wills. **Parmenter:** *NEHGR* 67 (1913): 280–81, 68 (1914):136–37, 70 (1916):176, 72 (1918):262–73, 91 (1937):212–13; Essex Wills. **D. Pierce:** H. C. Pierce, *Seven Pierce Families* (Washington DC: p.p., 1936); Norwich Wills; Rye, *Norwich Freemen*; Millican, *Register of Norwich Freemen*. **J. Pierce:** F. C. Pierce, *Pierce Genealogy* (Worcester MA: p.p., 1880); *NEHGR* 90 (1936):258, 111 (1957):158–60; Rye, *Norwich Freemen*; Millican, *Register of Norwich Freemen*; Anderson, *New England's Generation*, 102–4; Norwich Wills. **Pemberton:** Waters, 1:461; *NEHGR* 43 (1889):61–62, 50 (1896):392–98; Suffolk Wills. **Philbrick:** n. 7. **Pingry:** n. 5. **Pickering:** Waters, 2:981; H. Ellery and C. P. Bowditch, *Pickering Genealogy* (p.p., 1897); R. H. Eddy, *Genealogical Data on John Pickering of Portsmouth, N.H.* (Boston: p.p., 1884); *WP*, 4:143; Sudbury Wills. **Pitts:** Pope, *Pioneers*; *NEHGR* 51 (1897):421; Norwich Wills. **Pond:** E. D. Harris, *Genealogical Records of Daniel Pond* (Boston: p.p., 1873); Pope, *Pioneers*; Sudbury Wills. **Rawlins:** Savage; Essex Wills. **Reynolds:** *WP*, 2:276; M. H. Reynolds, *Robert and Mary Reynolds* (p.p., 1928); Sudbury Wills; Norwich Wills. **Ripley:** *NEHGR* 19 (1865):27. **Rix:** Rutman, *Winthrop's Boston*, 193; Norwich Wills. **Robinson:** *WP*, 3:295–96; Sudbury Wills. **Rogers:** *NEHGR* 60 (1906):379; Waters, 1:204, 216, 232; Roberts, 2nd ser. 3:19–37; Essex Wills. **Roper:** n. 28. **Royce:** F. F. Starr, *Ancestral Lines of James Goodwin* (Hartford: Brown and Gross, 1915); M. R. Patton, *Royce Family Book* (n.p., n.d.); *NEHGR* 122 (1968):275; Sudbury Wills. **Ruggles:** *NEHGR* 18 (1864):304, 58 (1904):219; Essex Wills. **Salter:** Savage; Battis, *Saints and Sectaries*, 316; Sudbury Wills. **Sanders:** *NEHGR* 70 (1916):176–77; Pope, *Pioneers*; Sudbury Wills; Norwich Wills. **Savill:** Pope, *Pioneers*; Essex Wills. **Scarlet:** Roberts, 1st ser., 1:39; *WP*, 3:507; *NEHGR* 67 (1913):278–79; Pope, *Pioneers*; Suffolk Wills; Norwich Wills. **Scott:** n. 18. **Skerry:** Great Yarmouth Freemen's Rolls; E. Power and R. H. Tawney, eds., *Tudor Economic Documents* (London: Longmans, 1933), 268; Norwich Wills; Norwich Record Office, Filby Parish Registers, 12 February 1598, 3 July 1598; my thanks to Barbara MacAllan. **Smyth:** Essex Wills. **Snow:** *NEHGR* 51 (1897):414, 60 (1906):378; Essex Wills. **Sutton:** Savage. **Taber:** G. L. Randall, *Taber Genealogy* (p.p., 1924); Waters, 1:586; 2:1315; Suffolk Wills; Essex Wills. **Thurston:** Anderson, *New England's Generation*, 148; Waters, 1:280; Suffolk Wills; Norwich Wills. **Tidd:** Ferris; Rye, *Norwich Freemen*; Norwich Wills. **Toppan:** n. 3. **Truesdale:** Savage. **Ventris:** Ferris, 2:805. **Wall:** J. W. Pope, *A George Willard Wall Memorial* (p.p., 1959); *WP*, 2:79–81; Waters, 2:1130; Essex Wills. **Wardalls:**

M. W. Otten, *Wardwell Family* (Del Mar CA: p.p., 1985); Lincs Wills. **Warde:** Savage. **Waters:** *WP*, 4:43, 47–84; Sudbury Wills. **Williams:** n. 9. **T. Wilson:** Waters, 2:1112–14; *NEHGR* 39 (1885):243, 55 (1901):275–76; PCC; Essex Wills. **W. Wilson:** Savage: Lincs Wills. **Woodward:** N. S. Woodward, *Descendants of Richard Woodward* (Baltimore: Genealogical Publishing, 1982). **Wyeth:** Selement and Woolley, *Shepard Confessions*; Powell, *Puritan Village*, 80; Suffolk Wills. **Young:** Selah Young, *Young Family* (New York: p.p., 1907); Great Yarmouth Freemen's Rolls; *Essex Institute Historical Collections* 2:6; Norwich Wills; Cressy, *Coming Over*, 197.

Table 16. Farmer Emigrants

Aldous: See n. 48, Chapter 5. **Allen:** *NEHGR* 50 (1896):331–32; Waters, 2:1447; Norfolk Record Office, King's Lynn Freemen's Rolls; Norwich Wills, s.v. Bozoun. **Allyn:** not to be confused with namesake from Devon; Essex Wills. **Astwood:** *NEHGR* 18 (1864):304; Waters, 1:81. **Bacons:** n. 46. **Ballard:** C. F. Farlow, *Ballard Genealogy* (Boston: p.p., 1911); *CSPD*, 1638, lists him as ship-money defaulter "gone to New England"; Suffolk Wills. **Barber:** n. 48. **Billington:** Savage. **Bixby:** *NEHGR* 141 (1987):228–43; *WP*, 3:126; Suffolk Wills; Pope, *Pioneers*. **Bradstreet:** A. O. Kelly, *Bradstreet Genealogy* (p.p., 1976); *NEHGR* 69 (1915):69–74; Suffolk Wills; Norwich Wills. **Briggs:** L. Y. Briggs, *History and Genealogy of the Briggs Family* (Boston: p.p., 1938); Suffolk Wills. **Brown:** Waters, 1:89; *Watertown Records*, vol. 1, passim; Suffolk Wills. **Bullock:** Waters, 2:1128; Essex Wills. **Carver:** R. Carver, *Carver Family of New England* (p.p., 1935); Barbara MacAllan, private communication; Pound, "Norwich Poor"; Sachse, "Norwich Mayoralty Court," 194; Norfolk Record Office, Parish Registers of Filby, 1597, 1614, and Ormesby St. Margaret, 1628; *NEHGR* 2 (1848):262. **Chickerings:** n. 48. **Thos. Clarke:** *NEHGR* 79 (1925):273–80; Suffolk Wills. **Thurston Clarke:** *NEHGR* 73 (1919):252–53; Suffolk Wills. **Cooper:** *NEHGR* 61 (1907):198; *WP*, 3:485; Anderson, *New England's Generation*, 62–3, 68; Suffolk Wills. **Curtises:** Roberts, 2nd ser. 1:634–36; *NEHGR* 58 (1904):447–49; *National Society of the Descendants of John and Elizabeth Hutchins Curtiss* (p.p., 1983); Essex Wills. **Cushings:** *NEHGR* 19 (1865):26, 54 (1900):84; J. S. Cushing, *Cushing Family Genealogy* (Montreal: p.p., 1905); Waters, 1:81–82; Norwich Wills, s.v. Cushion. **Cutlers:** *NEHGR* 19 (1865):27, 44 (1890):302, 90 (1936):257; Rye, *Norwich Freemen*; Millican, *Register of Norwich Freemen*; Ferris; Norwich Wills. **Danforth:** n. 41. **Desborough:** Waters, 1:253; E. Johnson, *Desborough Families in England* (Martinsville IN: p.p., 1976); C. F. Dow, ed., *Essex County Court Records* (Salem: Essex Institute, 1936), 1:276, 283; Ely Wills. **Dow:** n. 55. **Eliots:** *NEHGR* 8 (1864):304–5, 30 (18678):145, 43 (1889):365–68, 107 (1953):29–40; Waters, 2:904; Rutman, *Winthrop's Boston*, 247; Essex Wills. **Fisher:** n. 48. **Folger:** Roberts, 1st ser. 2:429; *NEHGR* 90 (1936):257; Norwich Wills. **Foulshams:** Roberts, 1st ser. 1:7; E. K. Folsom, *Genealogy of the Folsom Family* (Baltimore: Genealogical Publishing, 1975); *NEHGR* 19 (1865):61, 185–86, 66 (1912):217; Norwich Wills. **Goffe:** *NEHGR* 100 (1946):218–19; Norwich Wills; Suffolk Wills, s.v. Gough. **Hammond:** *MHS Colls*, 5th ser. 1:125, 4th ser. 6:395; *NEHGR* 58 (1904):288–89, 59 (1905):107–8, 60 (1906):184, 83 (1929): 82–84, 106 (1952):83–87, 130 (1976):28–34; *WP*, 3:139, 256; *New York Genealogical and Biographical Record* 121 (1990):19–22; Suffolk Wills. **Harwood:** W. H. Harwood, *Genealogical History of Harwood Families* (Chasm Fall NY: p.p., 1911); Wyman; *WP*, 2:173; Essex Wills. **Howe:** Pope, *Pioneers*; Essex Wills; see James Howe in Source Notes to Table 14. **Hubbard:** H. P. Hubbard, *Hubbard History* (New York: p.p., 1895); Johnson, *Wonder-Working Providence*, 142–43; *WP*, 4:140;

Essex Wills. **Ingalls:** see Francis Ingalls in Source Notes to Table 14. **Jameses:** *NEHGR* 19 (1865):26; Norwich Wills. **Jenner:** Waters, 2:899; Essex Wills. **Josselyn:** Waters, 1:765; *NEHGR* 75 (1921):19–33, 227–57; Weis, *Ancestral Lines*; Essex Wills. **Lincolns:** Norwich Wills; W. E. Barton, *Lineage of Lincoln* (Indianapolis: p.p., 1929); J. H. Lea and J. R. Hutchinson, *Lincoln Family* (Boston: p.p., 1909); Waldo Lincoln, *History of the Lincoln Family* (Worcester MA: p.p., 1925; Norwich Wills. **Lord:** Waters, 2:1102–3; Corey, *Waite Family*; Allen, *In English Ways*, 89; Sudbury Wills. **Loveran:** *NEHGR* 60 (1906): 184; *WP*, 3:6; Essex Wills. **Manning:** W. H. Manning, *Manning Families of New England* (Salem MA: p.p., 1902); Selement and Woolley, *Shepard Confessions*; Essex Wills. **Marvins:** n. 41. **Merrialls:** H. W. Merriall, *Joseph Merriall* (p.p., 1984); Suffolk Wills. **J. Moulton:** nn. 55, 58. **T. Moulton:** n. 55. **Olmstead:** H. K. Olmstead, *Genealogy of the Olmstead Family* (New York: p.p., 1912); *MHS Colls*, 4th ser. 1:95; Fairstead and Terling Parish Register transcripts, kindly communicated by the Honorable Guy Strutt; Essex Wills. **J. Page** (1 and 2): *NEHGR* 101 (1947):242, 105 (1951):26; C. N. Page, *Page Family* (p.p., 1911); *WP*, 2:316; Sudbury Wills. **R. Page:** nn. 55, 58. **Payne:** *NEHGR* 58 (1900):125–32, 60 (1906):184; *MHS Colls*, 3rd ser. 10:170–71; Allen, *In English Ways*, 133; *WP*, 3:347; Lavenham Parish Register transcripts kindly communicated by the vicar of Lavenham; Sudbury Wills. **Peck:** n. 46. **Pingry:** R. and J. Carpenter, *Pengry Family* (Coon Rapids IA: p.p., 1979); idem, *Pengry Genealogy* (p.p., 1984). **Porter:** H. P. Andrews, *Descendants of John Porter of Windsor* (Saratoga Springs NY: p.p., 1893); Ferris; *NEHGR* 50 (1896):23–24, 28–29, 48; Essex Wills. **Procters:** L. H. Procter, *John Procter of Ipswich* (Springfield MA: p.p., 1985); Pope, *Pioneers*; Colket; Sudbury Wills. **Ray:** *NEHGR* 63 (1909): 357–60, 69 (1915):27–28, 86 (1932):325, 105 (1951):164; Waters, 1:223; Roberts, 1st ser. 1:56–66; Sudbury Wills. **Read:** Pope, *Pioneers*, Waters, 2:1354–55; *NEHGR* 57 (1903):197; Suffolk Wills. **Reade:** *NEHGR* 88 (1934):302; *WP*, 3:176, 194; Waters, 1:673–74; Roberts, 2nd ser. 3:6; Pope, *Pioneers*; Essex Wills. **Roscoe:** *NEHGR* 71 (1917):113–15; *MHS Proc* 63:147–48; Ferris, 2:727; Roberts, 2nd ser. 3:122; Essex Wills. **Sawyer:** F. E. Sawyer, *Sawyer Family* (p.p., 1983); *NEHGR* 98 (1944):181; Lincs Wills. **Sherman:** Battis, *Saints and Sectaries*, 316; *NEHGR* 14 (1860):65; Roberts, 2nd ser. 3:209; Essex Wills. **Skerry:** Pope, *Pioneers*; see Henry Skerry in Source Notes to Table 14. **Smith:** Norwich Wills. **G. and S. Stone:** J. G. Bartlett, *Stone Genealogy* (p.p., 1918, 1926); Waters, 1:189; Essex Wills. **J. Stone:** Waters, 2:1123; Essex Wills. **Townsend:** Sachse, "Norwich Mayoralty Court," March 1633; Norwich Wills. **Welles:** Colket; Ferris, 1:649; Essex Wills. **Wing:** *WP*, 4:68; Pope, *Pioneers*; Essex Wills.

Table 19. Emigrant Male Servants

Albro: Savage; Pope, *Pioneers*. **Andrew:** Tyack, App. B. **Arres:** Sachse, "Norwich Mayoralty Court," 143–44, 191; Millican, "Index of Apprentices"; J. C. Hotten, *Original Lists of Persons of Quality* (Baltimore: Genealogical Publishing, 1962), 11 May 1637. **Atkinson:** *NEHGR* 90 (1936):47; Rutman, *Winthrop's Boston*, 219–20, 247; Sudbury Wills. **Bartlett:** Tyack, App. B; *Watertown Records*. **Baxter:** Norwich Wills. **Beckett:** Essex Wills. **Bill:** see n. 9, Chapter 6. **Bosworth:** n. 6. **Brown:** n. 7. **Bucks:** *NEHGR* 19 (1865):26; Norwich Wills. **Burgess:** Pound, "Norwich Poor," 29; Rye, *Norwich Freemen*; Millican, *Register of Norwich Freemen*; Norwich Wills. **Cole:** n. 7. **Comberbatch:** Tyack, App. B; Hotten, *Persons of Quality*. **Coyses:** n. 6. **Doggett:** S. B. Doggett, *Doggett–Daggett Family* (Boston: p.p., 1894); Rye, *Norwich Freemen*; Norwich Wills. **Flegge:** E. Flegg, *Genealogical Notes on the Founding of New England* (Hartford: p.p., 1926); Norwich Wills. **Gedney:** see Gedney in

Source Notes to Table 14. **Gibbs:** *NEHGR* 19 (1865):25; C. Heyrman, *Commerce and Culture* (New York: Norton, 1984), 218; Norwich Wills. **Goad:** *WP*, 3:199, 232, 258; Essex Wills. **Goadby:** *NEHGR* 19 (1865):304. **Goodwin:** Great Yarmouth Freemen's Rolls; N. C. P. Tyack, "The Humbler Puritans of East Anglia," *NEHGR* 138 (1984):105; Norwich Wills. **Greene:** *NEHGR* 19 (1865):304; Waters, 2:907; Essex Wills. **Hale:** *Hale, House*; *NEHGR* 54 (1900):65; Essex Wills. **Hart:** Waters, 1:599; Great Yarmouth Freemen's Rolls; Norwich Wills. **Hawkins:** Tyack, App. B; Sudbury Wills. **Hayward:** Tyack, App. B; Essex Wills. **Hill:** n. 10. **Howes:** T. P. Howes, *Genealogical Sketch of the Howes Family* (Yarmouthport MA: p.p., 1914); J. C. Howes, *Genealogy of the Howes Family* (Yarmouthport MA: p.p., 1892); Rye, *Norwich Freemen*; Millican, *Register of Norwich Freemen*; Pound, "Norwich Poor"; Norwich Wills. **Irons:** n. 7. **Keele:** *NEHGR* 14 (1860):304. **Killin:** Hotten, *Persons of Quality*; Suffolk Wills. **Laverick:** Sudbury Wills. **Lincoln:** n. 9. **Mitchell:** *NEHGR* 15 (1861):27; Norwich Wills. **Moore:** L. E. de Forest, *W. H. Moore and His Ancestry* (New York: p.p., 1934); Essex Wills. **Morfield:** *NEHGR* 15 (1861):26. **Morris:** Pope, *Pioneers*; Essex Wills. **Moulton:** See J. Moulton in Source Notes to Table 16. **Pitts:** see Pitts in Source Notes to Table 14. **Ridley:** Pope, *Pioneers*. **Skoulding:** Waters, 1:819; Allen, *In English Ways*, 257; Millican, *Register of Norwich Freemen*; Norwich Wills. **Smiths:** Pope, *Pioneers*; Powell, *Puritan Village*, 156. **Storey:** n. 9. **Suckling:** Savage; Norwich Wills; *NEHGR* 15 (1861):28. **Tidd:** Ferris; Wyman; Norwich Wills. **Towne:** W. G. Davis, *Ancestry of Amos Towne* (Portland ME: p.p., 1927); Hotten, *Persons of Quality*; Great Yarmouth Freemen's Rolls; Norwich Wills. **Tufts:** Pound, "Norwich Poor"; Norwich Wills. **Walker:** J. B. R. Walker, *Memorials of Walkers* (Northampton MA: p.p., 1861); Millican, *Register of Norwich Freemen*; Norwich Wills. **Ward:** Norwich Wills; Savage. **Warner:** Warner, *Descendants of Andrew Warner*; Essex Wills. **Whipple:** see Whipples in Source Notes to Table 9.

Table 22. Male Emigrants, Occupations Unknown

Agar: Savage; Essex Wills; *Great Migration Newsletter* 3 (1992):3. **Arnold:** *NEHGR* 52 (1898):374, 73 (1919):68; Waters, 2:882; Suffolk Wills; Norwich Wills. **Austin:** *NEHGR* 67 (1913):282–83; Roberts, 1st ser. 1:43; Suffolk Wills; M. B. Thompson, *Some New Hampshire Families* (p.p., 1977). **Bacon:** *NEHGR* 21 (1867); Wyman; Essex Wills. **Baker:** Wyman; Norwich Wills. **Barker:** Barker, *Barker Family*; Allen, *In English Ways*, 245; Sudbury Wills. **Barnard** (1): Savage; Essex Wills. **Barnard** (2): Waters, 2:1177; Essex Wills. **Bass:** *Bass Genealogy* (n.p., n.d.); *NEHGR* 107 (1953):218; Essex Wills. **Baxter:** F. Baxter, *Baxter Family* (New York: p.p., 1913); Norwich Wills. **Beale:** see his uncle John Beale in Source Notes to Table 14. **Beamsley:** Ferris; Savage. **Biggs:** *WMQ*, 44 (1987):317; *WP*, 3:108; Battis, *Saints and Sectaries*, App. I; Sudbury Wills; Suffolk Subsidy Rolls, 1522. **Blackwell:** Battis, *Saints and Sectaries*, App. I; Lincs Wills. **Blosse:** Everitt, "Marketing," *AgHE* 4:489; E. Kerridge, *Textile Manufactures* (Manchester: Manchester University Press, 1985), 214; Suffolk Wills. **Blott:** *Hale, House*; Wyman; Pope, *Pioneers*. **Boggis:** Suffolk Muster Roll, 1522; Pope, *Pioneers*; PCC; Waters, 2:1131; Sudbury Wills. **Boyden:** W. C. Boyden, *Thomas Boyden* (Boston: p.p., 1901); *NEHGR* 56 (1902):228, 93 (1939):279; Suffolk Wills. **Bright:** Allen, *In English Ways*, 145; *NEHGR* 13 (1859):98; D. H. Fischer, *Albion's Seed* (New York: Oxford University Press, 1989), 173; Sudbury Wills. **Brock:** *NEHGR* 47 (1893):278–79, 79 (1925):339, 144 (1990):124–37; Waters, 1:720; Suffolk Wills. **Brownes:** Rutman, *Winthrop's Boston*, 51, 53, 99–100, 111; *WP*, 3:66, 71–72, 83, 95; Wyman; Suffolk Wills. **Buffum:** W. G. Davis, *Ancestry of Sarah Johnson* (Portland ME:

p.p., 1960); Heyrman, *Commerce and Culture*, 183; *NEHGR* 35 (1881):68–69.
Bumpstead: *NEHGR* 57 (1903):332; Norwich Wills; Suffolk Wills. **Cable:** E. H.
Schenck, *History of Fairfield* (New York: p.p., 1889); Pope, *Pioneers*; Essex Wills.
Call: Hotten, *Persons of Quality*; Pound, "Norwich Poor"; Norfolk Records Office,
Hemsby Parish Registers, 1568; Great Yarmouth Freemen's Rolls. **Chadwicke:**
D. Arnando, *History of the Chadwick Family* (Alexandria VA: p.p., 1983); Essex
Wills. **Chandler:** *NEHGR* 135 (1981):94; Essex Wills. **Cheeseborough:** Savage;
Lincs Wills; M. Spurrell, *The Puritan Town of Boston* (Boston: Kay, 1972), 15;
Rutman, *Winthrop's Boston*, 63, 73, 74, 78, 210. **Childs:** Child, *Child Genealogy*;
WP, 2:136, 3:7, 142–44; Waters, 1:744; Allen, *In English Ways*, 145; Suffolk Wills.
Chubbock: *NEHGR* 15 (1861):25. **John Clarke** (1): Perzel, "Ipswich"; *WP*,
3:108, 177, 196; Northeast, "Boxford Churchwardens' Accounts"; Suffolk Wills.
John Clarke (2): *NEHGR* 54 (1900):138; Suffolk Wills. **John Clarke** (3): *NEHGR*
56 (1902):276; Waters, 1:546. **Jos. Clarke:** see John Clarke in Source Notes to Table
11. **Colbron:** *WP*, 2:69, 267; Rutman, *Winthrop's Boston*, 37, 54, 73, 79, 86; Essex
Wills. **Colby:** F. L. Weis, *Colby Family in Early America* (Concord MA: p.p., 1970);
Genealogical Descendants of Abraham Colby (Concord: p.p., 1895); *NEHGR* 49
(1895):104; Suffolk Wills. **Cole:** Suffolk Subsidy Rolls, 1522; "Boxford Church-
wardens' Accounts"; *WP*, 2:45; Sudbury Wills. **Collins:** see n. 21, Chapter 6.
Converse: Waters, 1:237; Essex Wills; see Edward Converse in Source Notes to
Table 14. **Coopers:** *NEHGR* 15 (1861):25, 26, 50 (1896):299; Allen, *In English
Ways*, 58; Norwich Wills. **Crabbe:** J. G. Bartlett, *Robert Coe, Puritan* (Boston: p.p.,
1911), 67; Sudbury Wills. **Crackbone:** Selement and Woolley, *Shepard Confessions*;
Essex Wills; David C. Dearborn, private communication. **Crafts:** J. M. and W. F.
Crafts, *Crafts Family* (Northampton MA: p.p., 1893); Savage. **Cram:** Savage.
Crane: Savage; Sudbury Wills. **Cutler:** A. Morse, *Cutler Genealogical Record* (Boston: p.p., 1867); Wyman; Norwich Wills. **Daniel:** *NEHGR* 83 (1929):183–92, 91
(1937):308. **Darrow:** Hotten, *Persons of Quality*; Savage. **Davies:** *NEHGR* 95
(1941):80; Sudbury Wills. **Dearborn:** Roberts, 2nd ser. 1:640–62; *NEHGR* 68
(1914):183, 111 (1957): 238; David C. Dearborn, private communication. **Devereux:** Ferris; *MHS Colls*, 3rd ser. 10:148; Venns; Cressy, *Coming Over*, 186. **Dix:**
J. E. Dix, *Five Yankee Families* (Decorah IA: p.p., 1982); Sudbury Wills. **Doggett:**
Doggett, *Doggett–Daggett Family*; Waters, 2:1310; Northeast, "Boxford Church-
wardens' Accounts"; Boxford Church ledger stones; Sudbury Wills. **Eddy:** n. 18.
Edmunds: Savage; Essex Wills. **Eldreds:** n. 23. **Elmer:** *NEHGR* 54 (1900):368.
Estow: Thompson, *Some New Hampshire Families*; *NEHGR* 142 (1988):258–60;
Millican, *Register of Norwich Freemen*; Norfolk Record Office, Hemsby Parish
Registers; my thanks to Barbara MacAllan for this reference. **Farrow:** *NEHGR* 15
(1861):25; Allen, *In English Ways*, 60; Norwich Wills. **Felton:** Felton, *Felton
Family*; see Benjamin Felton in Source Notes to Table 14. **Firman:** Roberts, 2nd
ser. 1:851; *WP*, 2:319, 3:142; Kerridge, *Textile Manufacturers*, 232; *NEHGR* 56
(1902):182; Sudbury Wills. **Fiskes:** *NEHGR* 86 (1932):406–35, 87 (1933):40–45,
141–46, 217–24, 367–74, 88 (1934):142–46, 265–73, 92 (1938):177–83; Cressy,
Coming Over, 48, 93, 125–26; *MHS Colls*, 3rd ser. 10:156–61, 4th ser. 6:397; *WP*,
3:394–95; J. R. Olorenshaw, *Notes on the History of Rattlesden* (p.p., 1905), App. I;
Suffolk Wills; Pope, "Fiske Diary," iii–xix. **Foote:** Ferris, 2:337; Waters, 2:1276;
Essex Wills. **Foster:** W. G. Davis, *Ancestry of Dudley Wildes* (Portland ME: p.p.,
1959); Waters, 1:41; Essex Wills. **Freeborne:** Savage; Suffolk Wills; Essex Wills. **J.
and W. French:** Waters, 1:674; Essex Wills; H. M. Kellogg, *Genealogy of the Bille-
rica French Family* (n.p., n.d.). **T. French:** Suffolk Muster Rolls, 1522; *NEHGR*
142 (1988):250–52; Waters, 2:954; *WP*, 3:108, 157; R. C. Fitch, *History of the
Fitch Family* (n.p., n.d.); Sudbury Wills. **Frost:** *NEHGR* 57 (1903):332; Suffolk

Wills. **J. and W. Fuller:** W. H. Fuller, *Genealogy of Fuller Descendants* (p.p., 1914); Waters, 1:465; Sudbury Wills. **M. Fuller:** Waters, 2:1406–7; Savage; Suffolk Wills. **Gates:** C. O. Gates, *Gates Family* (n.p., 1908); Ferris; Allen, *In English Ways*, 87, 136; Pound, "Norwich Poor"; Sachse, "Norwich Mayoralty Court," October 1630; *NEHGR* 92 (1938):257; Norwich Wills. **Godfrey:** Great Yarmouth Freemen's Rolls; John Demos, *Entertaining Satan* (New York: Oxford University Press, 1982), 327; Norwich Wills. **Goodwins:** Goodwin, *Goodwin Family*; *WP*, 3:273; *NEHGR* 45 (1891):171–73, 50 (1896):368–69, 55 (1901):24; *MHS Colls*, 4th ser. 1:94–95, 7, 44n.; PCC; Essex Wills. **Gosse:** *WP*, 2:276, 3:41; Suffolk Subsidy Rolls, 1522; *MHS Colls*, 5th ser. 1:198–99; Sudbury Wills; Norwich Wills. **Gould:** Waters, 2:1019; Sudbury Wills; Gould may have come from Tring, Herts. **Graves:** *NEHGR* 32 (1878):142; Waters, 2:896, 935; Essex Wills. **Griggs:** *NEHGR* 93 (1939):204; Sudbury Wills. **Guttridge:** *Hale, House*; *NEHGR* 96 (1942):383; Sudbury Wills. **Hadley:** W. D. Hadley, *Hadley Master Index* (p.p., 1986); Suffolk Wills. **Hale:** *Hale, House*; *NEHGR* 52 (1898):65; Essex Wills. **Hall:** J. Shepard, *John Hall* (New Britain CT: p.p., 1902); *NEHGR* 47 (1893):507–9, 62 (1908):168; *MHS Colls*, 2nd ser. 5:169–70; Essex Wills. **Hallock:** L. Hallock, *A Hallock Genealogy* (Orient NY: p.p., 1926). **Harrison:** Savage; Suffolk Wills. **Harte:** A. Andrews, *Descendants of Stephen Harte* (Hartford: p.p., 1875); Waters, 2:818–19; *NEHGR* 102 (1948):118; Essex Wills. **Hastings:** Savage; Allen, *In English Ways*, 145. **Hawkinses:** Wyman; Essex Wills; PCC. **Heaths:** *NEHGR* 32 (1878):142, 145; Essex Wills. **Heaton:** Savage; Rutman, *Winthrop's Boston*, 117, 140. **Hersey:** *NEHGR* 15 (1861):27; Savage. **Hills:** see William Hill in Source Notes to Table 19. **Hobarts:** see Peter Hobart in Source Notes to Table 7. **Holmes:** G. A. Gray, *Descendants of George Holmes* (Boston: p.p., 1908); *NEHGR* 58 (1904):21–22. **Hosier:** *WP*, 2:276; Essex Wills. **Howe:** *NEHGR* 62 (1908):285; *WJ*, 1:299, 2:47; Essex Wills. **Howes:** Savage; Sudbury Wills. **Hunting:** n. 19. **Hutchinson:** *NEHGR* 52 (1898):318–20; Roger Thompson, *Sex in Middlesex* (Amherst MA: University of Massachusetts Press, 1986), 117, 224; Norwich Wills. **Ireson:** Wyman; *Great Migration Newsletter*, 1st ser. 3 (1990):1, 19; *MHS Colls*, 5th ser. 5:340; it is possible that Ireson had been resident in Lincolnshire, as he had been a servant of Isaac Johnson. **Jacob:** *NEHGR* 15 (1861):25; Pound, "Norwich Poor"; Sachse, "Norwich Mayoralty Court," August and September 1630; Allen, *In English Ways*, 61; Norwich Wills. **Jeggleses:** *NEHGR* 52 (1898):242–44; Waters, 2:1408–10; Suffolk Wills. **Jennings:** Perzel, "Ipswich"; Nesta Evans, ed., "Wills of the Archdeaconry of Sudbury," *Suffolk Record Society* 29 (1987):304; *NEHGR* 57 (1903):197; *MHS Colls*, 3rd ser. 10:170; Suffolk Wills; Norwich Wills. **Jennison:** Ferris; Savage. **Kilbourn:** *Hale, House*. **Killam:** Hargrave, *Goodale–Goodell Forebears* (p.p., 1976); *NEHGR* 52 (1898):238–39, 56 (1902):344–45; Suffolk Wills. **King** (1): H. B. King, *King Genealogy* (Hartford: p.p., 1897); Waters, 2:1315; Essex Wills. **King** (2): Savage; Essex Wills. **Kingsburys:** Pope, *Pioneers*; *WP*, 3:2, 144, 188; K. Lockridge, *A New England Town* (New York: Norton, 1970), 13, 28, 31, 40; Sudbury Wills; Suffolk Subsidy Rolls, 1522; J. M. Kingsbury, private communication, gratefully acknowledged. **Knapps:** Suffolk Muster Rolls, 1522; *NEHGR* 92 (1938):380–83; *Watertown Records*; Cressy, *Coming Over*, 171; Thompson, *Sex in Middlesex*, 100–102, 177; Sudbury Wills; Essex Wills. **G. Knight:** *NEHGR* 15 (1861):28; Savage; Sudbury Wills. **R. Knight:** Pope, *Pioneers*; Waters, 1:703; **Lamb:** *WP*, 3:6; see Thomas Lamb in Source Notes to Table 14. **Lane:** *NEHGR* 47 (1893):414. **Large:** Allen, *In English Ways*, 254; Norwich Wills. **Lawson:** Battis, *Saints and Sectaries*, App. I; Lincs Wills. **Leavitt:** ibid.; Demos, *Entertaining Satan*, 500. **E. Lewis:** I. N. Lewis, *William Lewis* (Walpole MA: p.p., 1932); Suffolk Wills. **W. Lewis:** Lewis, *William Lewis*; Pope, *Pioneers*; Essex Wills. **Lincolns:**

Allen, *In English Ways*, 60; J. E. Morris, *Stephen Lincoln* (Hartford: p.p., 1895); see Thomas Lincoln in Source Notes to Table 16. **Livermore:** *NEHGR* 54 (1900):345–46; Waters, 1:563; F. G. Emmison, ed., *Early Essex Town Records* (London: Jenkins, 1971); Sudbury Wills. **Lockwoods:** H. W. Hodge, *Some Descendants of Edward Lockwood* (New York: p.p., 1978); *WP*, 2:276, 302; *NEHGR* 91 (1937):71, 98 (1944):78; Schenck, *History of Fairfield*, 392–93; Olorenshaw, *Rattlesden*, App. I; *New Haven Colony Records*, 3:77–89; Sudbury Wills. **Longley:** Wyman; *Great Migration Newsletter*, 1st ser. 3 (1990):21; Savage. **Loomis:** *NEHGR* 51 (1897):275; see Joseph Loomis in Source Notes to Table 9. **Ludkin:** Allen, *In English Ways*, 179, 255; see William Ludkin in Source Notes to Table 14. **Lumpkin:** Tyack, "Humbler Puritans," 254; Ferris; Essex Wills. **Lyman:** W. L. Holman, *Ancestry of Colonel J. H. Stevens* (Concord NH: p.p., 1948–52), 384; *NEHGR* 93 (1939):182; Demos, *Entertaining Satan*, 87; Essex Wills. **Marsh:** Pope, *Pioneers*; *NEHGR* 49 (1895): 370–71, 102 (1948):230; Waters, 2:1026; Essex Wills. **Mellowses:** Waters, 1:78, 113, 2:1289; Savage; Lincs Wills. **Metcalfe:** *WP*, 4:5; see Michael Metcalfe in n. 66, Chapter 4. **Minot:** *NEHGR* 2 (1847):171, 52 (1898):98–99; Tyack, App. I, xliv; Essex Wills. **Montague:** *NEHGR* 48 (1894):414, 57 (1903):378; Rutman, *Winthrop's Boston*, 78. **F. Moore:** *NEHGR* 39 (1885):299–301; Essex Wills. **J. Moore:** Waters 2:1236; Norwich Wills. **T. Moore:** n. 20. **Morrill:** see Abraham Morrill in Source Notes to Table 14. **Morris:** Wentworth, *Wentworth Genealogy*; Lincs Wills. **D. Morse, John Morse** (1), **and S. Morse:** *NEHGR* 84 (1930):70, 90 (1936):71, 92 (1938):385; P. McC. Morse, *Know Your Ancestors* (p.p., 1967); Sudbury Wills; Norwich Wills. **John Morse** (2) **and Jos. Morse** (1 and 2): Morse, *Know Your Ancestors*; Waters, 1:582, 2:1173, 1189; *NEHGR* 84 (1930):293, 92 (1938):385; G. R. Rendel, *History of Dedham* (Colchester: Grimston, 1938), 67; Essex Wills; Dedham Church wall memorials and ledger stones. **Moulton:** see n. 55, Chapter 5. **Moyse:** *NEHGR* 51 (1897):129–32; Essex Wills. **Munnings:** Pope, *Pioneers*; *NEHGR* 15 (1861):316, 38 (1884):378–79; Waters, 1:10; Essex Wills. George Munnings, cordwainer from Rattlesden, Suffolk, was not related. **Mygatt:** Tyack, App. B. **Nichols:** E. E. Hale, ed., *Notebook Kept by Thomas Lechford, 1638–41* (Cambridge MA: Wilson, 1885), 39–40; PCC; Essex Wills; a Walter Nicholls in Cambridge in 1635 was probably his brother. **Nutt:** *NEHGR* 141 (1987):56; Suffolk Wills. **Packer:** *NEHGR* 16 (1862):28; Norwich Wills; there may be elision of two emigrants here. **N. Palmer:** *NEHGR* 58 (1904):332; Sudbury Wills. **W. Palmer:** *NEHGR* 69 (1915):259, 70 (1916):342–43, 76 (1922):79–80, 158; *Great Migration Newsletter*, 1st ser. 1 (1990):6; Norfolk Record Office, Ranworth and Ormesby St. Margaret Parish Registers (I owe this reference to the kindness of Barbara MacAllan); Great Yarmouth Freemen's Rolls; Tyack, "Humbler Puritans," 183; Norwich Wills; Palmer was probably a husbandman. **Parke:** Waters, 1:146; Essex Wills. **Parkhurst:** Savage; Suffolk Wills. **Paysons:** *NEHGR* 15 (1861):304, 43 (1889):401, 95 (1941):81; W. H. Emerson, *Genealogy of the Descendants of John Eliot* (p.p., 1905); Essex Wills. **Peases:** P. J. Rice, *Pease Family* (Monticello KY: p.p., 1982); *WP*, 3:144; Pope, *Pioneers*; Essex Wills. **Pemberton:** *NEHGR* 47 (1893):393; see John Pemberton in Source Notes to Table 14. **Penniman:** G. W. Penniman, *Penniman Family* (Baltimore: Genealogical Publishing, 1981); *NEHGR* 29 (1875):145, 52 (1898):70, 107 (1953):19; Rutman, *Winthrop's Boston*, 36, 74. **Pepys:** *WP*, 4:218; Ely Wills; *Diary of Samuel Pepys*, 24 September 1660; Rutman, *Winthrop's Boston*, 141. **Pickram:** Savage; Pope, *Pioneers*; Sudbury Wills. **Pierce:** Rutman, *Winthrop's Boston*, 73–75; Lincs Wills. **Plimplin:** Waters, 1:145–46, 162; Sudbury Wills. **Pond:** Harris, *Daniel Pond* (Daniel may have been a son or brother of John, or son of Robert); Emerson, *Letters*, 63–65; see Robert Pond in Source Notes to Table 14. **Porter:** Andrews, *Descendants of John Porter*; *NEHGR*

50 (1896):23–24, 28–29, 48; Ferris, 2:568; Essex Wills. **J. Pratt:** *Pratt Directory* (n.p., n.d.); *Hale, House*; Ely Wills. **R. Pratt:** *NEHGR* 62 (1908):168; Savage; Essex Wills. **Prentice:** Savage; Essex Wills. **Quilter:** *NEHGR* 69 (1915):189–90; Perzel, "Ipswich"; Sudbury Wills; Norwich Wills. **Rayner:** *NEHGR* 57 (1903): 379, 67 (1913):164–67; Waters, 2:887; *Great Migration Newsletter*, 1st ser. 1 (1990): 6; Suffolk Wills. **Rice:** *Col. William Rice* (p.p., 1938); *NEHGR* 112 (1958):65–66; H. F. Porter, "Strutt–Biggs Relationships," *American Genealogist* 65 (1990):228– 29; Powell, *Puritan Village*, 25–50; Sudbury Wills; n. 8, Chapter 7. **Rishworth:** Savage; Lincs Wills. **Jas. Rogers:** Savage; Sudbury Wills. **John and T. Rogers:** *NEHGR* 67 (1913):324–25; Roberts, 2nd ser. 3:19–37; Essex Wills; see Ezekiel and Nathaniel Rogers in Source Notes to Table 7. **Rose:** C. Rose, *Descendants of Robert Rose* (San Jose CA: p.p., 1983); J. Coddington, "Birthplace of Robert Rose," *American Genealogist* 39 (1964):206; Sudbury Wills. **J. Ruggles** (1 and 2): P. J. Bowden, *The Wool Trade in Tudor and Stuart England* (London: Macmillan, 1961), 83; Suffolk Subsidy Returns, 1560; Waters, 2:1173–74; *WP*, 2:276, 316; Rutman, *Winthrop's Boston*, 36, 206; Sudbury Wills. **T. Ruggles:** see John Ruggles in Source Notes to Table 14. **Sandford:** G. M. Sanford, *Sanford Family* (Baltimore: Genealogical Publishing, 1975); D. L. Jacobus, *Families of Old Fairfield* (Hartford: p.p., 1927); Essex Wills. **Sanger:** Savage; *NEHGR* (1930):441. **Sayers:** Savage; Great Yarmouth Freemen's Rolls; Norwich Wills. **Scott:** Suffolk Subsidy Rolls, 1522; *NEHGR* 61 (1907): 168, 102 (1948):8–9; Rutman, *Winthrop's Boston*, 253; Savage; Sudbury Wills. **Scruggs:** n. 24. **Seaman:** Evans, "Wills of Sudbury," 627; Suffolk Wills. **Severance:** H. P. and H. S. Fieler, *Severance–Fieler Families* (p.p., n.d.); Savage; *WP* 3:310. **R. Sharp:** Pope, *Pioneers*; Waters, 2:894; Savage. **T. Sharp:** n. 25. **Sheffields:** *NEHGR* 75 (1921):83, 78 (1924):190–94; Sudbury Wills. **Shepard:** G. F. Shepard, *Shepard Families* (New Haven: p.p., 1973); *NEHGR* 135 (1981):90–91. **Shermans:** Waters, 2:1166–71, 1188; see Richard Sherman in Source Notes to Table 9, and Samuel Sherman in Source Notes to Table 16. **E. Skinner:** Cressy, *Coming Over*, 184; Ely Wills. **W. Skinner:** Starr, *Goodwin*, 240; Waters, 2:1205; Essex Wills. **Smart:** Waters, 2:1136; Norwich Wills; Smart may have been from Braintree, Essex, though it is also a Norfolk name. **H. Smith:** *NEHGR* 5 (1851):319–20, 51 (1897):125–32; Waters, 2:1121; Allen, *In English Ways*, 257; Wall, *Massachusetts Bay*, 94; Norwich Wills. ———— **Smith:** *WP*, 2: 319–20. **R. Smith:** Waters, 2:1357; Perzel, "Ipswich"; Barbara MacAllan, private communication; Norwich Wills. **Somerby:** see Anthony Somerby in Source Notes to Table 11. **Spring:** *WP*, 2:204, 3:294; Sudbury Wills. **Stearns:** *WP*, 2:276; *NEHGR* 41 (1887):272, 64 (1910):354, 69 (1915):195; Savage. **Stebbingses:** R. S. and R. L. Greenlee, *Stebbings Genealogy* (p.p., 1904); Luke Stebbins, *A Genealogy of Mr. Samuel Stebbins* (Hartford: p.p., 1771); Steven Innes, *Labor in a New Land* (Princeton: Princeton University Press, 1983), 206–7; Essex Wills; Suffolk Wills. **Steeles:** Starr, *Goodwin*; *Hale, House*; Fairstead Parish Register transcripts kindly communicated by the Honorable Guy Strutt; E. F. Steele, "Pedigree of Steele Family," NEHGS Library; *NEHGR* 106 (1952):167; *WP*, 4:36; Essex Wills. **Storre:** Savage, s.v. Storey; Lincs Wills. **Stowerses:** *NEHGR* 58 (1904):197, 64 (1910):278; Suffolk Wills; Wyman. **Symonds:** *NEHGR* 96 (1942):205; Great Yarmouth Freemen's Rolls; Savage; Norwich Wills. **Talcott:** *Hale, House*; Waters, 2:1125, 1130; *NEHGR* 51 (1897):134–38, 56 (1902):24, 57 (1903):275; *MHS Colls*, 4th ser. 1:94–95; Essex Wills. **Taylor:** Ferris: *WP*, 2:319–20; Sudbury Wills. **Tidd:** Wyman; see John Tidd in Source Notes to Table 14. **Tower:** *John Tower Tercentenary* (n.p., 1909); *NEHGR* 92 (1938):192, 102 (1948):307; Pound, "Norwich Poor," 29. **Towne:** L. S. Weissbach, "Townes of Massachusetts," *Essex Institute Historical Collections* 118 (1982):200–202; Pope, *Pioneers*; *NEHGR* 91

(1937):179. **Tucke:** Waters, 2:1400; Sachse, "Norwich Mayoralty Court," 35; Norwich Wills; Suffolk Wills. **Tuttles:** W. H. Tuttle, *John Tuttle* (Boston: p.p., 1868); Norwich Wills. **Wadsworth:** *Hale, House*; H. A. Wadsworth, *250 Years of the Wadsworth Family* (Lawrence MA: p.p., 1883); D. G. Allen, "Both Englands," in D. D. Hall and Allen, *Seventeenth-Century New England* (Boston: Colonial Society of Massachusetts, 1984), 68–69. **Waite:** D. P. Corey, *Waite Family* (Malden MA: p.p., 1913); Ferris; *NEHGR* 26 (1872):82, 31 (1877):160–62, 32 (1878):188–96, 47 (1893): 318–19; Essex Wills. **Wall:** Goodwin, *Goodwin Family*, 36; *NEHGR* 51 (1897): 139–41, 249–51; see James Wall in Source Notes to Table 14. **Ward:** Savage; Norwich Wills. **Ware:** E. F. Ware, *Ware Genealogy* (Boston: p.p., 1901); *NEHGR* 81 (1927):339; Suffolk Wills, s.v. Waior. **Warner:** Perzel, "Ipswich"; Ferris; Essex Wills. **Warrens:** A. B. Duty, *Warren Family* (p.p., 1985); *WP*, 2:276, 306, 3:6; *NEHGR* 65 (1911):354–55; Demos, *Entertaining Satan*, 112–13; Suffolk Wills; Sudbury Wills. **Waterburys:** *WP*, 2:276; *NEHGR* 65 (1911):135–36; Sudbury Wills. **Waters:** *WP*, 2:312; Sudbury Wills. **R. Webb:** Suffolk Subsidy Rolls, 1522; D. D. Hall, *Worlds of Wonder, Days of Judgment* (New York: Knopf, 1989), 50–51; Essex Wills; Dedham Church memorial tablets, brasses, and ledger stones. **W. Webb:** *NEHGR* 58 (1904):332; Sudbury Wills. **Welles:** Tyack, App. B; Essex Wills. **Jas. White:** Savage; Pope, *Pioneers*; Norwich Wills. **John White:** A. S. Kellogg, *Memorials of Elder John White* (p.p., 1860); *NEHGR* 25 (1871):25–26; *MHS Colls*, 4th ser. 1:95; J. G. Bartlett, in *Cambridge Historical Society Publications* 14 (1919):87; Essex Wills. **Whitman:** H. S. Whitman, *History of the Whitman Family* (Rutland VT: Tuttle, 1979); Norwich Wills. **Williams:** M. J. Weber, *A Williams Family Record* (n.p., n.d.); Great Yarmouth Freemen's Rolls; Colket; Norwich Wills. **Wincoll:** Pope, *Pioneers*, s.v. Thomas Wincoll; *WP*, 3:25, 234; Suffolk Subsidy Rolls, 1522; C. E. Wyncoll, *Wyncolls of Suffolk and Essex* (Colchester: Colchester Reference Library, 1910); *NEHGR* 94 (1940):235; PCC; Sudbury Wills; Waters, 1:77, 981; A. Sier, "Wincoll Family," *Essex Archaeological Society Transactions* 11 (1901):236–45; Thomas, *Diary of Sewall*, 1:322. **Windes:** Hawes, *Foster Records*; Pope, *Pioneers*; Suffolk Wills. **I. Wright:** Allen, *In English Ways*, 259; Norwich Wills. **N. Wright:** H. Whittemore, *Ancestral Lines of S. M. Whittemore* (p.p., n.d.); Savage. **S. and T. Wright:** D. L. Judd, *Ancestry of Siegel W. Judd* (p.p., 1980); W. H. Wright, *History of the Wright Family* (p.p., 1913); E. M. Barber, *Wright–Chamberlin Genealogy* (p.p., 1914); Essex Wills; Innes, *Labor*, 206. **Wyatt:** Perzel, "Ipswich"; Pope, *Pioneers*.

Table 24. Selected Women Emigrants

Note: References are additional to the Source Notes for husbands, which should also be consulted. For example, W. Holman, "Notes on the Appletons," cited in reference to Samuel Appleton (Table 5, n. 24, Chapter 3), contains important information about Judith Everard Appleton's dowry.

Ames: see n. 30, Chapter 6. **Appleton:** Essex Wills; Sudbury Wills; **Austin:** n. 47. **Bacon:** Essex Wills. **Baker:** Norwich Wills. **M. Barnard:** Essex Wills. **P. Barnard:** Waters, 2:1177; Essex Wills. **Bass:** *NEHGR* 107 (1953):218; Essex Wills. **Beale:** Norwich Wills; see Peter Hobart in Source Notes to Table 7. **Beecher:** Wyman; Essex Wills; the elder sister or aunt of James Barker (c1623–1702) of Harwich, whom she took to Charlestown in 1634, she had married, first, Thomas Copper of Harwich and Wapping and, second, Thomas Beecher, master of the *Talbot*, which sailed in the *Arbella* fleet in 1630. **Brackett:** Savage; Sudbury Wills. **Bradstreet:** see Thomas Dudley in Source Notes to Table 11. **Brown:** n. 30. **Buffum:** n. 49.

Buttolph: Harding, *Abraham Harding*; Essex Wills; see Robert Harding in Source Notes to Table 9. **Chaplin:** Sudbury Wills; Pope, *Pioneers*. **Chase:** Essex Wills. **Cheeseborough:** Savage; Lincs Wills. **Chickering** (1): see John Fiske in Source Notes to Table 7. **Chickering** (2): Roberts, 1st ser. 1:11; Suffolk Wills. **Chubbock:** *American Genealogist* 12 (1936):117. **Chute:** Essex Wills. **Clarke:** Savage. **Coddington:** Suffolk Wills. **Coe:** Sudbury Wills. **Cole:** Essex Wills. **Cotton:** Cressy, *Coming Over*, 180. **C. Coytmore:** see n. 28, Chapter 8. **M. Coytmore:** Waters, 1:160; *NEHGR* 106 (1952):15–17. **Cram:** Lincs Wills. **E. Curtis:** Essex Wills. **S. Curtis:** see John Eliot in Source Notes to Table 7. **Cushing:** Sachse, "Norwich Mayoralty Court," 6 January 1631; Norwich Wills. **Dane:** Essex Wills. **Daniel:** see Daniel Morse in Source Notes to Table 22. **Downing:** n. 54. **Dudley:** Savage. **Eddy:** see John Doggett in Source Notes to Table 22. **Farwell:** n. 50. **M. Felton:** see William Storey in Source Notes to Table 19. **E. Felton:** Great Yarmouth Freemen's Rolls; Waters, 2:1400–1402; Norwich Wills. **Fillingham:** *WP*, 3:484; see Benjamin Cooper in Source Notes to Table 16. **Firmage:** W. G. Davis, *The Ancestry of Sarah Johnson* (Portland ME: p.p., 1960); Great Yarmouth Freemen's Rolls. **Firmin:** see John Doggett in Source Notes to Table 22; Roberts, 2nd ser. 1:851. **Fisher:** *NEHGR* 102 (1948):309; see John Fiske in Source Notes to Table 7. **A. Fiske:** of Frenze Hall, near Diss; Savage; A. Campling, "East Anglian Pedigrees," *Norfolk Record Society* 13 (1940):73. **S. Fiske:** Savage; Suffolk Wills. **B. Fiske:** Suffolk Wills; Savage. **Folger:** see A. Fiske, above. **Foote:** Essex Wills. **Fosdick:** Essex Wills. **A. Foster:** Suffolk Wills; see Barnaby Windes in Source Notes to Table 22. **J. Foster:** Essex Wills. **Foulsham:** see Edward Gilman in Source Notes to Table 14. **E. French:** Essex Wills. **S. French:** Sudbury Wills; *NEHGR* 143 (1989):325–31; Essex Wills. **Gates:** Norwich Wills; Ferris. **Gilman:** Norwich Wills. **Goodale:** see Austin Killam in Source Notes to Table 22. **Goodwin:** Goodwin, *Goodwin Family*. **Greenleaf:** n. 42. **Gridley:** Sudbury Wills. **Guttridge:** Sudbury Wills. **Hale:** *NEHGR* 141 (1987):128–34; *WP*, 2:410; her husband, a Hertfordshire glover, is not to be confused with Thomas Hale of Great Maplestead, Essex, occupation unknown. **Hammond** (1): Sudbury Wills. **Hammond** (2): see Robert Payne in Source Notes to Table 9, and William Payne in Source Notes to Table 16. **Heard:** Sudbury Wills; see John Wyatt in Source Notes to Table 22. **Hill:** *NEHGR* 73 (1919):52; Lincs Wills. **M. Hobart:** Norwich Wills, s.v. Dewyng. **E. Hobart** (1): Sachse, "Norwich Mayoralty Court," 13 January 1631; Norwich Wills, s.v. Aylmer. **E. Hobart** (2): *NEHGR* 121 (1967):231; Allen, *In English Ways*, 257. **A. Hobart:** Pound, "Norwich Poor"; Norwich Wills. **Hough:** n. 37. **Howe:** see John Dane in Source Notes to Table 14. **Hubbard:** Suffolk Wills; PCC; Knapps were leading portmen of Ipswich. **Humphrey:** G. E. C., *Burke's Peerage* (London: Debrett, 1990), 3:342n.; see n. 15, Chapter 3. **Hunting:** Norwich Wills. **Huntington:** n. 44. **Hutchinson:** n. 46. **James:** Lincs Wills. **Johnson:** see Humphrey, above. **Kilbourn:** Sudbury Wills; Ely Wills; see John Moody in Source Notes to Table 5. **S. Kimball:** Essex Wills. **U. Kimball:** see Thomas Scott in Source Notes to Table 14. **Kingsbury:** Suffolk Wills. **Knight:** n. 31. **Lake:** Essex Wills; see Thomas Reade in Source Notes to Table 16. **Lane:** *NEHGR* 48 (1894):414. **Leager:** the widow of John Green of Hadleigh, who died in 1634. **Leverett:** Lincs Wills. **Lewis:** Essex Wills; see Daniel Morse in Source Notes to Table 22. **Lincoln:** F. J. Nicholson, "A Clue to the English Origins of Thomas Lincoln . . . and William Lane," *American Genealogist* 64 (1989):214–15, argues from entries in the Parish Registers that Lanes, like Lincoln the cooper, may have lived in Beaminster, Dorset; however, a Thomas Lane of Shipdham, Norfolk, husbandman, made a will there in 1592, and it was unusual for West Country people to settle in Hingham as late as 1635 or 1636; Norwich Wills. **Lockwood:** *NEHGR* 98 (1944):78. **Loomis:**

NEHGR 92 (1938):203. **Lord:** see John Waite in Source Notes to Table 22. **Loveran:** see P. Barnard, above. **Lumpkin:** Essex Wills; cf. Chute, above. **Lyman:** Essex Wills. **Mason:** Essex Wills. **Mellows:** nn. 30 and 37. **A. Merriall:** Suffolk Wills. **S. Merriall:** Merriall, *Joseph Merriall*. **Metcalfe:** Norwich Wills; Pound, "Norwich Poor"; Sachse, "Norwich Mayoralty Court," 6 February 1631. **Montague:** *NEHGR* 47 (1893):414. **Moody:** Sudbury Wills. **Moore:** see John Youngs in Source Notes to Table 7. **Morse:** Sudbury Wills. **Moulton:** *NEHGR* 142 (1988):260–63; Norwich Wills. **M. Munnings:** *NEHGR* 38 (1884): 378–79. **E. Munnings:** Sudbury Wills. **Nickerson:** see Nicholas Busby in Source Notes to Table 14. **Nutt:** Suffolk Wills. **Packer:** no Norwich Wills; the only Stream will I have discovered is from Northales, Suffolk, 1565. **Page:** *NEHGR* 141 (1987):141. **Palmer:** Norwich Wills. **Parke:** PCC. **R. Payne:** *NEHGR* 51 (1897): 127; see William Whiting in Source Notes to Table 9. **P. Payne:** see Robert Payne in Source Notes to Table 9. **Peck:** n. 39. **Penniman:** see John Eliot in Source Notes to Table 7. **Peter:** n. 41. **Philbrick:** see William Knapp in Source Notes to Table 22. **Phillip:** Norwich Wills. **Phillips:** Savage; *NEHGR* 110 (1956):276. **Pingry:** Essex Wills; Suffolk Wills. **Portmont:** see Richard Bellingham in Source Notes to Table 11. **Porter:** see Loomis, above. **Powell:** *NEHGR* 50 (1896):159; Suffolk Wills. **Proctor:** Sudbury Wills have Harpers in the Bury and Elveden areas. **Pynchon:** Essex Wills; see n. 18, Chapter 3. **Ray:** Sudbury Wills; *NEHGR* 105 (1951):164. **Read:** Suffolk Wills. **Rice:** see Edmund Frost in Source Notes to Table 14. **Ricroft:** Norwich Wills; cf. Cushing, above. **S. Rogers:** n. 38. **M. Rogers:** PCC; Essex Wills; she was the daughter of Robert Crane, gentleman of Coggeshall and Mary Sparhawk Crane. **Ruggles:** see John, Thomas, and William Curtis in Source Notes to Table 16. **Sawyer:** no Peaseley wills in Lincs Wills. **M. Scott:** Sudbury Wills; see Thomas Scott in Source Notes to Table 14. **K. Scott:** n. 48. **E. Scott:** Sudbury Wills. **Severance:** Essex Wills; see Henry Kimball in Source Notes to Table 14. **Shepard:** n. 40. **Sherman:** Essex Wills; she was the daughter of the wife of John Porter (the emigrant of unknown occupation from Messing, Essex) by a previous marriage. **Skelton:** no Travis wills in Lincs Wills, but she is "of Sempringham" in the Parish Register at her marriage in 1619. **Smead:** said to be the sister of Israel Stoughton, whose father had been rector of both Naughton, Suffolk (1586–94), and Coggeshall, Essex (1600–1606), but had been deprived for nonconformity; he was living in Great Totham, Essex, in 1610; members of the family subsequently settled in Somerset and London. **Smith:** see Anthony and Thomas Cooper in Source Notes to Table 22. **Snow:** Essex Wills. **Sparhawk:** Waters, 2:1187–89; see Edmund Angier in Source Notes to Table 9. **Stacey:** n. 34. **Stearns:** Sudbury Wills. **Stebbings:** Essex Wills. **M. Steele:** "of this parish" in Fairstead Parish Register, at her marriage in 1608. **R. Steele:** see John Talcott in Source Notes to Table 22. **Stone:** Essex Wills; Bartlett, *Stone Genealogy*. **Storre:** see William Hutchinson in Source Notes to Table 12. **R. Symonds:** Davis, *Ancestry of Dudley Wildes*; Norwich Wills. **D. Symonds:** see Roger Harlakenden in Source Notes to Table 5. **Talcott:** the cousin of Dr. Mark Mott, rector of Rayne, Essex, adjacent to Braintree; *Hale, House*; Sudbury Wills; Essex Wills; *WP*, October 1629. **Thompson:** n. 43. **Toppan:** Norwich Wills. **Towne:** see Firmage, above. **Townsend:** she may have been the sister of John Newdigate, merchant of Southwark, London; T. Rich, *Townsend Genealogy* (New Haven: p.p., 1985); Suffolk Wills. **Underwood:** see Chickering (1), above. **Vassall:** G. E. McCracken, "Vassalls of London and Jamaica," in L. L. Brook, ed., *Studies in Genealogy* (Salt Lake City: Association for Promoting Genealogy, 1990), 217–49; see Thomas King of Cold Norton in Source Notes to Table 22. **Wadsworth:** see R. Steele, above. **Ward:** there are four Edmunds wills at Great Hormead, Hertfordshire, 17 miles west-southwest of Haverhill. **Wardall:** Lincs

Wills. **Waterhouse:** n. 52. **E. Weld:** no Wises in Sudbury Wills. **M. Weld:** possibly a kinswoman of Hannah Dearsley Coe of Assington, Suffolk (see Coe, above); Sudbury Wills. **Welles:** see John Warner in Source Notes to Table 22. **Whipple:** Waters, 1:467; see Abraham Hawkins in Source Notes to Table 22. **Whiting:** n. 37. **Wilbore:** Essex Wills. **E. Williams:** Norwich Wills. **M. Williams:** n. 36. **Wilson:** *WP*, 2:254; she was the daughter of Sir John Mansfield, goldsmith and lord mayor of London, and the great-niece of Archbishop Grindal; her sister married the emigrant London merchant tailor, Robert Keayne; see Chapter 4, herein. **E. Winthrop** (1): n. 41. **E. Winthrop** (2): n. 35. **M. Winthrop:** n. 51. **Wright:** Essex Wills. **Wyeth:** see John Clarke in Source Notes to Table 11. **Young:** Great Yarmouth Freemen's Rolls; Norwich Wills. **J. Youngs:** Southwold Parish Register transcripts; Suffolk Wills. **M. Youngs:** *NEHGR* 51 (1897):244–46; Southwold Parish Register transcripts; Suffolk Wills.

Index

Wives' maiden names are given in brackets; a second surname is first husband's. Family members are entered under the same surname group. The following abbreviations are used: C = Cambridgeshire, E = Essex, H = Hertfordshire, K = Kent, L = Lincolnshire, N = Norfolk, S = Suffolk, SX = Sussex, Y = Yorkshire. Postal abbreviations, e.g., MA or CT, are used for the American colonies.